ENVIRONMENT
IN THE TRANSITION
TO A MARKET ECONOMY

Progress in Central and Eastern Europe
and the New Independent States

ORGANISATION FOR ECONOMIC CO-OPERATION AND DEVELOPMENT

ORGANISATION FOR ECONOMIC CO-OPERATION AND DEVELOPMENT

Pursuant to Article 1 of the Convention signed in Paris on 14th December 1960, and which came into force on 30th September 1961, the Organisation for Economic Co-operation and Development (OECD) shall promote policies designed:

- to achieve the highest sustainable economic growth and employment and a rising standard of living in Member countries, while maintaining financial stability, and thus to contribute to the development of the world economy;
- to contribute to sound economic expansion in Member as well as non-member countries in the process of economic development; and
- to contribute to the expansion of world trade on a multilateral, non-discriminatory basis in accordance with international obligations.

The original Member countries of the OECD are Austria, Belgium, Canada, Denmark, France, Germany, Greece, Iceland, Ireland, Italy, Luxembourg, the Netherlands, Norway, Portugal, Spain, Sweden, Switzerland, Turkey, the United Kingdom and the United States. The following countries became Members subsequently through accession at the dates indicated hereafter: Japan (28th April 1964), Finland (28th January 1969), Australia (7th June 1971), New Zealand (29th May 1973), Mexico (18th May 1994), the Czech Republic (21st December 1995), Hungary (7th May 1996), Poland (22nd November 1996) and Korea (12th December 1996). The Commission of the European Communities takes part in the work of the OECD (Article 13 of the OECD Convention).

OECD CENTRE FOR CO-OPERATION WITH NON-MEMBERS

The OECD Centre for Co-operation with Non-Members (CCNM) was established in January 1998 when the OECD's Centre for Co-operation with the Economies in Transition (CCET) was merged with the Liaison and Co-ordination Unit (LCU). The CCNM, in combining the functions of these two entities, serves as the focal point for the development and pursuit of co-operation between the OECD and non-member economies.

The CCNM manages thematic and country programmes. The thematic programmes, which are multi-country in focus, are linked to the core generic work areas of the Organisation (such as trade and investment, taxation, labour market and social policies, environment). The Emerging Market Economy Forum (EMEF) and the Transition Economy Programme (TEP) provide the framework for activities under the thematic programmes. The EMEF is a flexible forum in which non-members are invited to participate depending on the theme under discussion. The TEP is focused exclusively on transition economies. Regional/Country programmes, providing more focused dialogue and assistance, are now in place for the Baltic countries, Brazil, Bulgaria, China, Romania, Russia, the Slovak Republic (a candidate for accession to the OECD), and Slovenia.

Publié en français sous le titre :
LES ÉCONOMIES EN TRANSITION FACE A L'ENVIRONNEMENT
Progrès en Europe centrale et orientale et dans les nouveaux États indépendants

FOREWORD

This book examines environmental trends in Central and Eastern European countries (CEEC) and the New Independent States (NIS) of the former Soviet Union over the last eight to ten years. It is not a report on the state of the environment, but rather an analysis of the relationships between the transition to democratic, market-based societies and environmental conditions and policies.

The framework for the book is provided by the Environmental Action Programme for Central and Eastern Europe (EAP). The EAP was adopted by environment ministers at the second "Environment for Europe" Ministerial Conference in Lucerne, Switzerland, in April 1993. It aimed to integrate environment into the reform processes which were underway in the formerly centrally planned economies. At Lucerne, ministers also established a Task Force – the EAP Task Force – to facilitate implementation of the EAP. The book's main policy conclusions and recommendations reflect those of the fourth "Environment for Europe" Ministerial Conference, held in Aarhus, Denmark, in June 998. A key message is that while economic reforms have provided a crucial stimulus for environmental improvement leading to reductions in high pollution levels, many serious problems remain, and others have grown worse over the transition period. Continued efforts through partnerships between a wide range of actors will be essential to reinforce the environmental improvements achieved so far.

The book builds on the experience gained by EAP Task Force members; governments of CEEC, NIS, and OECD donor countries; international financial institutions and organisations; and partners from environmental NGOs, business and trade unions. The emphasis on partnership is reflected in the co-chairing of the Task Force, with one co-chair from the region and one from the European Commission. The leadership provided by Alan Gromov (Estonia), Leszek Banaszak (Poland) and Arcadie Capcelea (Moldova), as well as Tue Rohrsted, Tom Garvey and Jean-François Verstrynge (European Commission), is gratefully acknowledged.

The Non-Member Countries Branch of OECD's Environment Directorate, which has served as secretariat to the EAP Task Force, prepared the book. This activity was part of the programme of work of OECD's Centre for Co-operation with Non-Members. Tony Zamparutti was the primary author, with Brendan Gillespie serving as overall project manager. They have been supported by many people, notably Glen Anderson, Carla Bertuzzi, Laurie Manderino, Krzysztof Michalak, Aziza Nasirova, Dorte Pedersen, Grzegorz Peszko, Olga Savran and other members of the EAP Task Force secretariat. Magda Lovei and Gordon Hughes of the World Bank drafted Chapter 2, and many of their colleagues from the Bank have participated actively in the work, particularly Kristalina Georgieva. Magda Toth Nagy of the Regional Environment Center for Central and Eastern Europe (REC) and Olga Ponizova of Eco-Accord (Moscow) wrote background papers for Chapter 4, and Jernej Stritih, currently Executive Director of the REC, has contributed substantially in several roles. Graham Drucker of the European Centre for Nature Conservation (ECNC) and Agnieszka Koc, working for ECNC and the World Conservation Union (IUCN), provided background papers for Chapter 8. The book also builds on the work of the Project Preparation Committee and its secretariat at EBRD. Many others have provided information and valuable comments. Switzerland provided financial support for its preparation.

OECD 1999

Ultimately, the achievements on which this book reports depend on the dedication and commitment of people in CEE countries and the NIS, who have struggled to protect and enhance the environment, often in difficult circumstances. It is hoped that the book adequately reflects their efforts. The book is issued under my responsibility as OECD Secretary-General. However, it does not necessarily reflect the views of OECD, its Member countries or the representatives of the EAP Task Force.

Donald J. Johnston
Secretary-General of the OECD

TABLE OF CONTENTS

List of Abbreviations and Country Groups

Main Findings

Chapter 1
Introduction

Chapter 2
Economic Reform and the Environment

OECD 1999

Chapter 3
Reforming Government Institutions and Policies

Chapter 4
Public and NGO Participation

Chapter 5
Environmental Policy Instruments

Chapter 6
Environmental Financing

Chapter 7
Environmental Management in Enterprises

Chapter 8
Protecting Biodiversity

Chapter 9
International Co-operation

List of Boxes

List of Tables

List of Figures

Annexes

LIST OF ABBREVIATIONS AND COUNTRY GROUPS

CIS	Commonwealth of Independent States
EAP	Environmental Action Programme for Central and Eastern Europe
EBRD	European Bank for Reconstruction and Development
EC	European Commission
ECNC	European Centre for Nature Conservation
ECU	European Currency Unit. Replaced on 1 January 1999 by the euro.
EIA	Environmental Impact Assessment
EIB	European Investment Bank
EPE	Environment Programme for Europe
EU	European Union
GEF	Global Environmental Facility
IFI	International Financial Institution
ISO	International Standards Organisation
IUCN	World Conservation Union
LEAP	Local Environmental Action Programme
NEA	Nuclear Energy Agency
NEAP	National Environmental Action Programme
NEFCO	Nordic Environmental Finance Corporation
NIB	Nordic Investment Bank
NGO	Non-governmental Organisation
PPC	Project Preparation Committee
PPP	Purchasing Power Parities or Polluter Pays Principle
REAP	Regional Environmental Action Programme
REC	Regional Environmental Center for Central and Eastern Europe
TACIS	Technical Assistance to the CIS
UN	United Nations
UNDP	United Nations Development Programme
UN/ECE	United Nations Economic Commission for Europe
UNEP	United Nations Environment Programme
UNEP/GRID	UNEP Global Resource Information Database
UNIDO	United Nations Industrial Development Organisation
USAID	United States Agency for International Development
WWF	Worldwide Fund for Nature

OECD countries

The original Member countries of the OECD are Austria, Belgium, Canada, Denmark, France, Germany, Greece, Iceland, Ireland, Italy, Luxembourg, the Netherlands, Norway, Portugal, Spain, Sweden, Switzerland, Turkey, the United Kingdom and the United States. The following countries became Members subsequently through accession at the dates indicated hereafter: Japan (28th April 1964), Finland (28th January 1969), Australia (7th June 1971), New Zealand (29th May 1973), Mexico

(18th May 1994), the Czech Republic (21st December 1995), Hungary (7th May 1996), Poland (22nd November 1996) and the Republic of Korea (12th December 1996). The Commission of the European Communities takes part in the work of the OECD (Article 13 of the OECD Convention).

Central and Eastern European Countries (CEEC)

Albania, Bulgaria, Croatia, Czech Republic, Estonia, Hungary, Latvia, Lithuania, Former Yugoslav Republic of Macedonia (FYROM), Poland, Romania, Slovak Republic, Slovenia.

(Note: The book does not cover Bosnia and Herzegovina or Yugoslavia.)

The New Independent States of the former Soviet Union (NIS)

Armenia, Azerbaijan, Belarus, Georgia, Kazakhstan, Kyrgyz Republic, Moldova, Russian Federation, Tajikistan, Turkmenistan, Ukraine, Uzbekistan.

Visegrad Countries

Czech Republic, Hungary, Poland, Slovak Republic.

Baltic States

Estonia, Latvia, Lithuania.

Central Asian Republics

Kazakhstan, Kyrgyz Republic, Tajikistan, Turkmenistan, Uzbekistan.

Caucasus Republics

Armenia, Azerbaijan, Georgia.

CENTRAL EASTERN EUROPE
and
EUROPEAN NEW
INDEPENDENT STATES

0   500 km

Key indicators for CEE countries, 1997[a]

	Population (1000 inhab.)	Land area (1000 km²)	GDP per capita (US$)[b]
Albania	3 420	27	2 120
Bosnia Herzegovina	3 780	51	
Bulgaria	8 430	111	4 010
Croatia	4 500	56	4 780
Czech Republic	10 300	77	10 510
Estonia	1 460	42	5 240
FYROM	2 190	25	3 210
Hungary	10 170	92	7 200
Latvia	2 470	62	3 940
Lithuania	3 720	65	4 220
Poland	38 650	304	6 520
Romania	22 610	230	4 310
Slovak Republic	5 360	48	7 910
Slovenia	1 920	20	11 800

a) or latest available year
b) based on current purchasing power parities
Source: OECD, FAO, World Bank

Elaborated by UNEP/GRID-Warsaw.

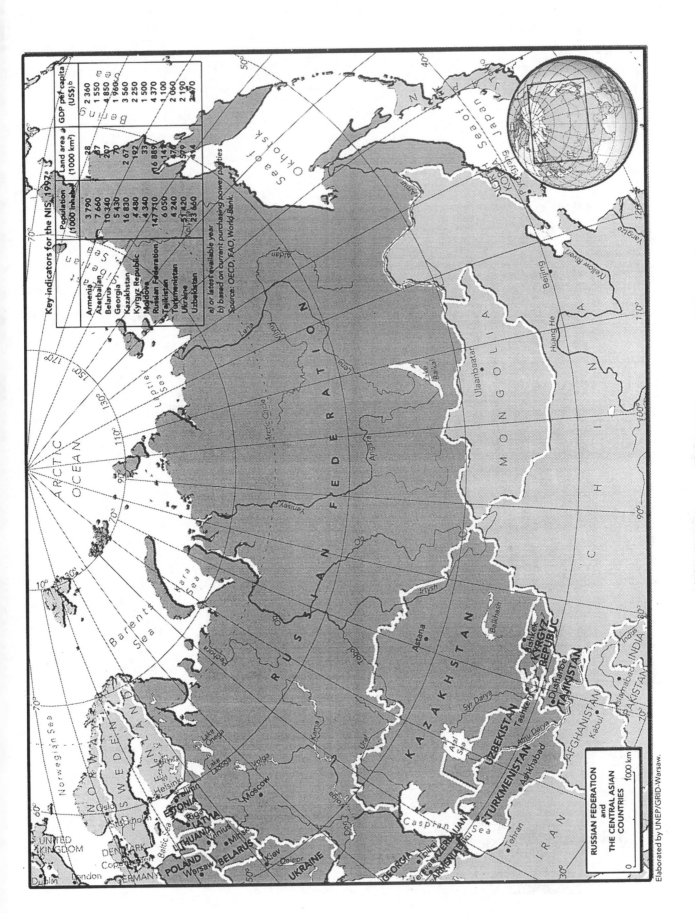

Elaborated by UNEP/GRID-Warsaw.

MAIN FINDINGS

The transition process has offered a unique window of opportunity to integrate environmental considerations into the emerging democratic, market-based societies of the central and eastern European countries (CEEC) and the New Independent States of the former Soviet Union (NIS). In 1993, the *Environmental Action Programme for Central and Eastern Europe* (EAP) provided a set of recommendations for how this could be done. Although the experience gained in implementing these recommendations has regionally specific features, many of the lessons learned are relevant for countries in other regions seeking to integrate environmental protection and economic development: The main recommendations of the EAP, and actions taken to implement them, are presented at the end of these Main Findings.

The EAP emphasised that economic reforms could generate efficiency gains that would reduce industrial pollution and other pressures on the environment. It also underlined that countries in the region needed to build on these gains by establishing effective environmental policies involving:

- priority-setting based on good analysis and public participation;
- an appropriate mix of policy, institutional and investment measures to tackle priority problems; and
- the allocation of scarce resources using cost-effectiveness as a guiding principle.

Experience gained over the last 10 years shows that economic, political and environmental reforms have been mutually supportive and reinforcing. Progress in economic and political reform has stimulated environmental improvements, and effective environmental policy measures have supported the broader reform process.

Economic and Environmental Reform

Economic reforms have helped generate resources for investment in cleaner, more efficient technologies; reduced the share of pollution-intensive heavy industries in economic activity; and helped curb pollution and waste generation as part of the shift towards more efficient production methods. Democratic reforms have unlocked demand for environmental improvement, which has translated into new, more effective environmental policies and institutions. These factors have led to a "decoupling" of pollution levels from economic output (in particular, reductions in emissions of key air pollutants have been greater than decreases in output); and as countries advanced in reform have returned to economic growth, this decoupling has continued. Consequently, serious pollution threats to human health have diminished.

In some of the countries where reform has been slower, the reverse is the case. The slow pace of economic reform and the ongoing economic crisis have impeded environmental improvement, and pollution levels and resource consumption have declined less than output. Lack of incentives for efficient operation of enterprises, as well as opportunities to profit from distortionary fiscal and monetary policies, have hindered implementation of "win-win" strategies such as energy efficiency and cleaner production. The absence of an appropriate incentive structure to reward efficiency compromises the achievement of environmental objectives. Since many environmental strategies, including the EAP, rely on "win-win" strategies, this has important implications for environmental policy at national, regional and global levels.

Even in the advanced reform countries, the pollution and resource intensities of their economies, and of most sectors, are still several times higher than in OECD countries. Depending on the pace of restructuring, it may take the countries acceding to the EU 20 years or more to meet all current EU environmental requirements; and this would still be far from a sustainable pattern of development. Prospects in the NIS are even more daunting. The life expectancy gap between Russia and Western Europe has continued to grow (exacerbated by socio-economic as well as environmental conditions); the adverse health impacts of contaminated drinking water, as well as extensive air pollution, are even more severe than in CEE countries; and the need for revenues has accelerated the exploitation of natural resources, often inefficiently and with negative environmental and social consequences. The overall economic costs of these impacts are substantial.

Governance and Environment

While economic reform appears to have been a necessary condition for environmental improvement, it has not been sufficient. The development of a new range of environmental policies and institutions, adapted to democratic, market-based societies, has also been essential to improve the environmental performance of transition economies. However, progress has been conditioned by the broader challenge of establishing effective systems of governance at national and sub-national levels. In a few countries, including several NIS, poorly functioning government institutions have become a major impediment to reform across all sectors and, in most countries of the region, the establishment of effective institutions has not kept pace with market liberalisation. Both the difficulty and importance of establishing effective institutions were underestimated at the beginning of the transition period.

In many countries, the development of the capacities of environmental institutions, the introduction of new policy instruments required for more effective environmental management, and the strengthening of biodiversity protection have been important achievements. However, some of the recommendations from 1993 on the need to streamline, make more realistic and better enforce policy instruments remain valid. A set of clear, predictable "rules of the game", equitably enforced, are needed to help shift transition economies towards more efficient, less environmentally damaging economic structures, not least by attracting foreign investment. There is also a need to reform management systems that involve excessive discretion and arbitrary decision-making by public officials, as they perpetuate "administered" economic relations and encourage corruption. These are challenges which environment shares with other policy sectors.

Politics, Civil Society and Environment

In the late 1980s, environmental issues played a central role in protests that ended communist regimes. A number of countries were able to take advantage of the window of opportunity early in the transition, make important environmental policy reforms, and start to integrate environment into the reform process. However, this window closed quickly. Faced with competing economic and social priorities, environment's place on the political agenda in most CEEC/NIS has fallen. Reflecting this change, environment today is only weakly established in party political systems and parliaments. Environment ministries have struggled to influence government policy but have suffered as much, if not more, than other sectors as government budgets have been tightened. Environment has appeared to be an expensive "add-on" and, as a result, has often been marginalised in countries where incentives for "win-win" policies are weak and budgetary resources are extremely limited.

Despite their weak position, environment ministries have nevertheless recorded important achievements. They were often among the first to reform policies and to attract external support. In the most advanced transition countries, a major part of environmental decision-making has been decentralised to the regional or local level. However, from a transition perspective, arguably their most significant contribution has been to support the emergence of civil society by promoting more open, participatory decision-making. One reflection of the importance of participatory decision-making is the adoption of the Convention on Access to Information, Public Participation in Decision-Making and Access to Justice in Environmental Matters at the Aarhus "Environment for Europe" Ministerial Conference in June 1998.

Environmental NGOs and the Regional Environment Center for Central and Eastern Europe have supported these developments, acting as catalysts for environmental and democratic reform. In some CEE countries and a few NIS, NGOs are constructively influencing environmental policy development; in other countries, the impact of environmentally oriented NGOs is limited. Until now many NGOs, particularly in the NIS, have relied on public or external financing of their work. To be effective in the longer term, they will need to build a stronger base of public support.

Environmental Financing

Macroeconomic imbalances and weak financial institutions have constrained the supply of affordable capital for investments by enterprises and public institutions throughout the region, though this is now changing in the advanced reform countries. Nonetheless, environmental investments in the advanced reform countries, as a percentage of GDP, compare favourably with those in OECD countries. Environmental funds (usually capitalised by pollution charges) and policy reforms that have prompted enterprise demand for environmental investments have been important factors in this respect. In slower reform countries, the economic context has been more difficult. In many NIS, output is at about half its pre-transition levels. Environmental policies rarely provide sufficient incentives for action, while environmental funds have been small compared to those in advanced reform countries. In a few NIS countries, environmental (as well as other) investments appear to be negligible. Throughout the region, policies and institutions require further strengthening in order to mobilise and channel domestic resources for priority investments.

The Enterprise Sector

Enterprises in advanced reform countries have invested both in less polluting production methods and in pollution control equipment. Some have started to implement environmental management systems such as the European Union's EMAS (Eco-Management and Auditing Scheme) or the International Standards Organisation for (ISO) 14 000 series. Still, enterprises in the region have made less progress than expected in integrating environmental objectives into overall management goals and methods. In many slower reform countries, weak incentives for environmental improvement, combined with the ongoing economic crisis, have provided little stimulus for environmental action by enterprises. In addition, foreign direct investment, which could introduce new technology and managerial know-how, has been concentrated in a few countries. In many of the slower reform countries, investors are deterred by high economic and political risks. Much more needs to be done in most CEEC/NIS to strengthen overall management capacities and establish a better basis for effective environmental management in enterprises. In particular, although a large share of industrial enterprises across the region have been privatised, in many countries effective structures for corporate governance have not yet emerged. As a result, their industrial enterprises have not focused on maximising profits and on more efficient resource use.

Preserving Biodiversity and Landscapes

The CEEC/NIS region has a remarkable wealth of biodiversity and landscapes. Under central planning, extraction of natural resources harmed large areas, although restrictions on movement and on independent economic activity helped keep some natural areas pristine. During the transition, many CEEC/NIS have expanded their networks of natural parks and other protected areas. However, slower reform countries have lacked the resources to manage such networks. International assistance has played a crucial role, but can only reinforce or catalyse domestic funding, not replace it. Moreover, protected areas are not sufficient to conserve biodiversity and landscapes: the key challenge for countries in the region is to integrate biodiversity management into sectoral policies and actions. A few advanced reform countries have taken initial steps to do so, in recent agriculture and forestry initiatives. Such efforts need to continue (indeed, OECD countries are also looking at ways to strengthen integration). In addition, many countries – in particular many NIS, which hold extensive oil, mineral and forestry resources – need to improve their management of natural resources with a view towards economically and environmentally sustainable development.

International Co-operation

Dialogue and co-operation between OECD donor and CEE countries have improved significantly since the early 1990s, in part through mechanisms such as the EAP Task Force and Project Preparation Committee. Important progress has also been made in co-operation with many of the NIS, although much remains to be done. Both donors and recipients have recognised that financing and technology, often a focus of attention in early co-operation efforts, are usually not by themselves the most effective means of addressing environmental problems. Those CEEC/NIS that have developed effective national policies and institutions have also been the most effective in attracting external support. Donors have learned that external support is most helpful when it is well co-ordinated, facilitates a country-"owned" process in which priorities are set by the host country, and fills gaps in local knowledge and capacity. Close relations and shared goals in a few regions, such as the Baltic Sea region, have also facilitated external support for transition economies.

After peaking in 1994, international flows of environmental assistance and finance have fallen slightly. To some extent, the decrease in environmental loans from International Financial Institutions (IFIs) has been offset by better integration of environmental considerations into their non-environmental projects. Most assistance and financing has gone to CEE countries, in absolute terms and even more on a per capita basis. Five countries received about half of all technical assistance and investment finance (the Czech Republic, Hungary, Poland, Romania and Russia). In countries with strong domestic financing, external assistance accounted for less than 10% of total environmental expenditures, although it has often played a catalytic role. Low-income countries, in contrast, received much smaller amounts but in many cases these provided crucial support for environmental projects. (Assistance and financing to CEE countries that are candidates for EU accession should increase drastically. In addition, greater aid should now flow to those countries affected by the Balkan conflict.)

The 1997 Kyoto Protocol to the Climate Change Convention represents a major new opportunity for international co-operation. In most CEEC/NIS, there is scope to reduce greenhouse gas emissions at lower cost than in market economies. The flexibility mechanisms in the Kyoto Protocol could exploit these differences and become an important source of financing for environmental projects in the region. However, important political and practical issues need to be resolved. Unless domestic policies to promote efficiency are put in place, projects implemented through these mechanisms are likely to have a limited catalytic or demonstration effect.

The Future

Compared to the early 1990s, the divergence in regard to environmental issues and economic conditions between CEE countries and the NIS has increased. Progress in 10 CEE countries has enabled them to begin the process of accession to the EU. Given the importance of environmental issues in the *acquis communautaire*, this will transform the approach to environmental issues in these countries. In addition, environmental pressures from sectors such as agriculture and transport may increase with accession. Substantial assistance will be provided to assist accession countries to comply with EU environmental directives, but this will fall far short of the Euro 120 billion in investments estimated to be required. Major policy reforms and institutional strengthening will be needed to ensure that targets are met at least cost, that EU assistance is used cost-effectively, and that environmental issues are well managed in the overall accession process.

There is no driver equivalent to EU accession for environmental improvement in the NIS. Lower levels of economic development, a slower pace of economic reform, weaker systems of governance and the tentative emergence of civil society have resulted in weaker demand for environmental improvement. A deepening and strengthening of co-operation with the NIS is now a pressing priority, including the transfer of relevant experience from CEE countries. Donor/IFI support is particularly needed to support policy reform and capacity building and to help finance pilot and demonstration investment projects.

The EAP recommendations have proved effective in countries that have actively pursued economic and political reform. Even though needs and priorities within the region have become more differentiated, there is scope to apply these recommendations more rigorously (Table 1). All countries would benefit from a deepening of economic reform, together with a strengthening of environmental policy frameworks and institutional capacities. Better priority-setting, more cost-effective use of resources, and more innovative approaches to mobilising and channelling financial resources for environmental investments are also common needs throughout the region. At the same time, there is heightened awareness that the EAP's primary

Table 1. **Implementation of the EAP's main recommendations**

Recommendation	Actions
1. *Establish environmental priorities, based on analysis of costs and benefits, to direct limited resources towards the most urgent problems.*	Some countries in the region have identified clear priorities in their environmental policies; others, in particular those which have been slower to reform, have continued to generate "wish lists". A few countries have used economic analysis to identify priorities and plan cost-effective actions to address them. In a number of cases, foreign assistance has helped overcome the lack of national capacities for economic and other types of analysis. Overall, much progress is needed in terms of building solid analytical bases for policy choices.
2. *Pursue "win-win" policies and projects that achieve both economic and environmental objectives: for example, removing energy and other subsidies, and promoting "good housekeeping" and less polluting technologies in industry.*	CEE countries have removed many direct subsidies to enterprises. In the NIS, low energy prices and distortions associated with macro-economic imbalances have limited "win-win" opportunities. A number of CEE countries have established programmes to encourage "win-win" actions, such as energy efficiency and cleaner production, but progress has been more difficult than originally expected.
3. *Where possible, use economic instruments for environmental management.*	Pollution charges have played an important role in many CEE countries and NIS. However, most countries would benefit from a further streamlining and targeting of economic and other policy instruments to improve the efficiency and effectiveness of their mix.
4. *Tackle local environmental problems first, in particular threats to human health.*	Some national policies have included protection of human health as one of their main criteria for priority-setting; often, these policies have focused on local environmental problems such as air pollution in "hot spots". Many regional and local governments have developed their own environmental action programmes.
5. *Donors should consider providing crucial support for projects that reduce transboundary pollution.*	Some donors have provided effective support for transboundary programmes, particularly regional sea programmes such as that for the Baltic Sea region. Some have established pilot joint implementation projects to tackle greenhouse gas emissions. There are cases, however, in which donor priorities have overridden local priorities.
6. *Governments in the region should clarify potential liabilities for past environmental damages at enterprises.*	A number of CEE countries have established mechanisms to clarify these potential liabilities in regard to newly privatised enterprises, thus addressing a key concern of potential foreign investors. A few NIS governments have considered such initiatives, although none has implemented them.
7. *Establish realistic, enforceable standards.*	Many CEE countries have reformed their ambient standards to more realistic levels; a few NIS have considered such reforms, but most continue to use unrealistically stringent standards.
8. *Involve local people in setting priorities.*	In all CEE/NIS countries, public participation has increased significantly. Some CEE countries have actively involved NGOs and other stakeholders in policy development; citizens have been involved in a number of local and regional environmental initiatives. Only a few NIS have strongly involved NGOs or others in policy development.
9. *Increase research, training, and exchange of information for priority setting.*	International forums, including the EAP Task Force and the Project Preparation Committee (PPC), have encouraged analysis, capacity building and information exchange for and among the countries of the region. In a few CEE countries, monitoring and research activities have been strengthened and more closely linked to decision-making. In some countries research capacity has been weakened.
10. *Build partnerships to address key problems.*	The quality of international environmental co-operation has improved. Some governments have worked with NGOs and the private sector in implementing programmes. However, the latter's potential to contribute to environmental improvements remains largely unexploited.

21

focus on pollution issues should be broadened to include sustainable management of natural resources; for example, management of the region's rich biodiversity (a positive legacy of central planning) needs to be better integrated with a range of sectoral policies. Progress towards sustainable development also requires better integration of social concerns with economic and environmental policies. A deepening of the solidarity and co-operation which have characterised the "Environment for Europe" process should continue to provide valuable and necessary support to the countries of the region.

Chapter 1

INTRODUCTION

1. The Challenge of Transition

1.1. *The environmental challenge*

The collapse of communism in Central and Eastern Europe, and the disintegration of the Soviet Union that followed, brought the region's serious environmental problems to the attention of the international community. Many of these problems had been obvious to those living in the region and were among the catalysts for change. Throughout the region governments had kept such data as existed on environmental conditions secret. The first international reports on these problems, published in the late 1980s and early 1990s, were dire. One sober assessment by a western institute concluded:

"The industrial regions of Central Europe are so choked by pollution that the health of children is impaired and the lives of adults shortened (WRI).

An independent survey of the environment in the former Soviet Union, based on official statistics, reported that central planning had left "an ecological nightmare" (Mnatsakanian).

The countries in this vast region are remarkably diverse – they range in population from Estonia, with 1.5 million inhabitants, to the Russian Federation, with over 148 million. Their land area, landscapes and level of economic development differ significantly. Nonetheless, economic central planning had created a common pattern of environmental problems:

- Most countries suffered high levels of industrial pollution. Not only did the economies of many countries centre around highly polluting industries such as chemicals and steel, but the production processes used were usually older and less efficient than those in OECD countries. Pollution prevention and control, as well as basic plant maintenance and repair, were often neglected.

- The air was highly polluted in industrial regions such as northern Bohemia in the Czech Republic, Upper Silesia in Poland and the Donetsk basin in Ukraine. In these and many other areas, smoke from coal and lignite used for industrial power and household heating added to the air pollution created by factory processes.

- Major rivers, such as the Vistula in Poland and the Donets in Russia and Ukraine, were heavily polluted by industrial and municipal waste water discharges (the Vistula and a number of other rivers were also heavily polluted by saline mine water discharges).

- The centrally planned economies used natural resources inefficiently – including timber, minerals, fuels, land and water. In the former Soviet Union, inefficient agricultural practices created widespread land degradation and related water policies brought severe environmental problems, including the drying up of the Aral Sea (Libert).

- Nuclear safety was neglected. This culminated in the 1986 Chernobyl disaster. After Chernobyl, there have been serious concerns about the safety of certain nuclear plants in the region. The improper disposal of nuclear wastes has also been an important problem, as well as the poor management of mine tailings at uranium mines in a range of countries from Bulgaria and the Czech Republic to many parts of the former Soviet Union.[1]

On the other hand, the region has a wealth of biodiversity and large areas of natural and near-natural habitats, far more extensive than those in Western Europe. The lower population density, particularly in the former Soviet Union, contributed to this natural wealth, but so did the practices of the former regimes, which restricted personal movement and the development of natural and forest areas. Moreover, a number of other environmental pressures were less severe in the centrally planned economies than in OECD countries, including levels of consumer wastes and of motor vehicle congestion.

Overall, the worst environmental problems were localised in specific "hot spots". Specific problems and issues, however, varied greatly across the region. Initial estimates of the cost of correcting environmental problems were high in nearly all CEEC/NIS.[2] In 1989, an official Polish estimate suggested that meeting the country's environmental goals would cost US$260 billion through the year 2020, over US$8 billion per year (Gillespie and Zamparutti). The size of these initial estimates led some observers to call for an "environmental Marshall Plan" for the region. However, there was no consensus on how to tackle the problems identified – either within the CEEC/NIS or among the donor governments and international organisations that wished to provide assistance and financing.

2. A Framework for Environmental Action

From the beginning of the transition, OECD countries and international organisations extended technical assistance to strengthen CEEC/NIS institutions and policies, together with financing to undertake investments in infrastructure and other areas.[3] Environment was one of the first areas for assistance and finance: donor countries and international organisations recognised the importance given to environmental issues in the public protests of the last years of the communist regimes and wished to help new governments tackle their severe environmental problems. Some observers also recognised that the reform process provided a unique opportunity to integrate environment into the region's economic and political development; indeed, some suggested that western technology and know-how would allow CEEC/NIS to "leapfrog" environmental problems found in OECD countries. Many CEEC/NIS environmental problems also had important transboundary and global effects. For example, coal-fired power plants and many heavy industrial plants emitted high levels of sulphur and nitrogen oxides to the atmosphere, contributing to acid precipitation across Europe. Some donor governments considered that pollution reduction efforts in the CEEC/NIS region could address these problems more cost-effectively than further actions in their own countries.

Both donor and recipient countries saw environmental protection as an element of international security and stability. At the 1992 summit of the Organisation for Security and Co-operation in Europe (OSCE), heads of state and of governments from almost all European countries (together with those of the United States and Canada) declared that "our comprehensive concept of security ... links economic and environmental solidarity and co-operation with peaceful state relations" (quoted in Price and Lester). Countries acknowledged that the severe local effects, as well as the transboundary dimension, of pollution had implications for regional security, as did cases of severe resource degradation, in particular those on an international scale such as the desiccation of the Aral Sea.

2.1. The "Environment for Europe" process

The initial years of environmental co-operation revealed a number of problems and difficulties in the relationship between donors and recipients. First, despite the calls for an "environmental Marshall Plan", donor and IFI financial contributions turned out to be lower than most recipients expected. Further, countries in the region felt that assistance was too often driven by the priorities of the donors and IFIs, and tied to the use of donor country consultants and the export of pollution control equipment. At times this assistance was inappropriate for local circumstances. CEE countries and the NIS felt that their own proposals for environmental investment projects were ignored (Connolly et al.). On the other hand, western donors and IFIs contended that recipient countries had not identified clear priorities for action among their environmental problems. They also found that CEEC and NIS lacked capacity to prepare and manage environmental projects in accordance with donor and IFI procedures. As a result, CEEC and NIS project proposals were often unrealistic and lacked the analysis necessary to make financing decisions. These difficulties slowed the preparation, approval and donor funding of investment projects in the region. The root causes of these problems lay on both sides.

The experience of environmental authorities under central planning had not prepared them for a dialogue with western donors and IFIs. Investment decisions under central planning were not made based on valuations of efficiency and effectiveness commonly used by IFIs. Policy-making was often a competition for investment resources among ministries. In addition, environmental authorities had had little success implementing laws and policies and scant influence over actions in the energy sector and other policy areas. Few environmental officials in the region appreciated the role of environmental institutions and policies in OECD countries, and few appreciated the value of donor and IFI "technical assistance" for institutional strengthening and policy reform. Instead, technology and finance were regarded as the main solutions to environmental problems.

In many OECD countries, members of the "development community" that provided assistance to developing countries were concerned that assistance to Central and Eastern Europe and the NIS would divert resources from their traditional clients. Developing countries also voiced their concern. Partly as a result, environment ministries often took the lead in providing environmental assistance to CEEC/NIS. Although some had long-standing contacts with CEEC/NIS environmental authorities, they had little experience providing technical assistance. Moreover, the collapse of centrally planned regimes and the transition to democracy and market-based economies were unprecedented: there was no clear model for the best form of assistance. Consequently, some bilateral donors, through environment ministries and other agencies, devoted greater efforts to encouraging investment projects in the region – often with export promotion as one of their goals – than to promoting policy reforms and institutional strengthening.[4]

These difficulties were compounded by the lack of a common strategy among donors, IFIs and countries in the region. Most donors and IFIs followed their own separate agendas, usually based on their own approaches to environmental issues and on their national or institutional interests (Connolly *et al.*). Early in the transition, the then 24 OECD countries had created a forum for co-operation on assistance to the region, the G-24, co-ordinated by the Commission of the European Communities. In the area of environmental co-operation, however, this mechanism had two key problems: first, it did not include CEEC or NIS in the discussions; and second, it brought donors and IFIs together to exchange information about their existing programmes, leading to a backward rather than a forward-looking orientation.

International co-operation was stronger in initiatives for the protection of common natural resources, such as the Baltic Sea Joint Comprehensive Action Programme. While these activities brought together donors, IFIs and recipient countries, each involved a limited number of participants (ongoing international initiatives, including the Baltic Sea Programme, are reviewed in Chapter 9).

In the early years of transition, environment ministers from the Western and former Eastern Europe had met in several different fora.[5] In 1991, Josef Vavrousek, head of the Federal Environment Commission of the then Czech and Slovak Federal Republic, saw the importance of the environment as a theme for building co-operation across the entire European region. He initiated a new process by inviting environment ministers from OECD countries and from the former Eastern Europe to the first "Environment for Europe" Conference, in June 1991 at Dobris Castle, near Prague. The conference called for "improved co-ordination and strengthening of national and international environmental programmes" (Dobris conclusions) and spurred the preparation of the *Environmental Action Programme for Central and Eastern Europe* (EAP), an initiative to tackle short-term environmental priorities in the region. The Dobris meeting also called for a long-term *Environmental Programme for Europe* to encourage convergence in environmental conditions and policies across Europe.

Although the Dobris conference did not adopt Vavrousek's proposal to create a permanent "council" of European environment ministers, it did start a process of regular ministerial conferences. The second "Environment for Europe" Conference was held in Lucerne, Switzerland, in April 1993; the third in Sofia, Bulgaria, in October 1995; and the fourth in Aarhus, Denmark, in June 1998 (the fifth is scheduled to take place in Kiev, Ukraine, in September 2002).

2.2. The Environmental Action Programme (EAP): an overview

The *Environmental Action Programme* (EAP) was prepared by an *ad hoc* working group of officials and experts from Central and Eastern Europe, the NIS, OECD countries and international financial institutions. It was based on studies of the region's environment – in particular, reviews of environment and health issues and of economic and environmental linkages – as well as the discussions, conclusions and recommendations of a series of international meetings on key environmental policy themes (Box 1.1). The European Commission chaired the *ad hoc* working group; the World Bank and OECD provided secretariat support, and the final document was drafted primarily by the World Bank (World Bank and OECD).

Box 1.1. International meetings that contributed to the EAP

The following meetings, many of which were organised by OECD and the World Bank, contributed to the development of the EAP. These meetings brought together officials and experts from the region, together with representatives of donor countries, IFIs and other international organisations.

- Meeting on Economic Instruments for Environmental Policies (Geneva, December 1991).*
- Workshop on Environmental Information Systems in Selected central and eastern European countries (Paris, December 1991).
- Conference on Privatisation, Foreign Direct Investment, and Environmental Liability in Central and Eastern Europe (Warsaw, May 1992).
- Conference on Energy and Environment in European Economies in Transition (Prague, June 1992).
- Environmental Policy and the Transition to a Market Economy in the New Independent States (Minsk, December 1992).
- Workshop on Taxation and Environment in European Economies in Transition (Paris, February 1993).
- Workshop on Economic Restructuring and the Environment (Budapest, March 1993).
- Municipal Waste water Treatment in Central and Eastern Europe: Present Situation and cost-effective Development Strategies (Laxenburg, Austria, March 1993).

---

* Organised jointly by OECD and UN/ECE.

At the Lucerne "Environment for Europe" Conference, environment ministers endorsed the EAP "... as a basis for action by national and local governments, the Commission of the European Communities, international organisations and financial institutions and private investors active in the region." The EAP presented practical recommendations for short-term actions (*i.e.* over approximately three to five years) that could be undertaken with existing resources. Key recommendations of the EAP are presented in Box 1.2.

The EAP broke new ground by analysing the region's environmental problems within the context of the ongoing economic and political transition. It emphasised that economic reforms, such as increases in the region's low energy prices, would, by themselves, lead to significant reductions in environmental problems. Environmental policies should build on and support economic reforms. The EAP recommended that governments and other actors in the region should, where possible, pursue "win-win" opportunities: policies and projects that lead to both economic returns and environmental improvement. The EAP also noted, however, that the transition to a market economy would lead to new pressures on the environment, such as those created by rising motor vehicle use.

The EAP emphasised that to achieve effective and lasting environmental improvement, CEEC and NIS governments and other actors needed to take a three-pronged approach, combining policy reforms, institutional strengthening and cost-effective investments – thus shifting the emphasis from a focus on investments alone. For example, for the protection of biodiversity, the EAP urged that CEEC and NIS,

---

Box 1.2.   **Principal recommendations of the EAP**

1. *Base environmental priorities on a careful comparison of costs and benefits.* The resources available for environmental improvements will be severely constrained in Central and Eastern Europe for the next five to ten years. It is essential that limited resources be applied to the most urgent problems first.

2. *Implement policies and invest in projects which provide both economic and environmental benefits.* "Win-win" policies include removing subsidies that encourage the excessive use of fossil fuels and water in industry, agriculture and households. "Win-win" investments include those in energy and water conservation, low-input and low-waste technologies, and expenditures on "good industrial housekeeping".

3. *Harness market forces for pollution control wherever possible.* Market-based instruments, such as pollution charges, fuel taxes, and deposit refund schemes, can help achieve desired levels of environmental quality at much lower costs than traditional regulatory approaches. Regulatory instruments will still be needed to control emissions of some micro-pollutants such as heavy metals – particularly lead – and toxic chemicals.

4. *Concentrate on local problems first.* Many people suffer health damage from exposure to lead in air and soil, airborne dust and sulphur dioxide, from nitrates in drinking water and from contaminants in water and food. Solving these problems will do the most to improve health and well-being. Measures to reduce emissions of pollutants in response to local concerns also should contribute to reducing transboundary and global emissions.

5. *Donor countries* should consider providing funding to accelerate measures to reduce emissions of transboundary and global emissions in countries of Central and Eastern Europe. Such funding would be particularly appropriate where the marginal costs of reducing emissions are lower in Central and Eastern Europe. Minimising the net cost of meeting international agreements is in the interests of individual countries and Europe as a whole. By lowering the net cost of reducing transboundary flows, countries could afford to act earlier or to adopt more stringent reduction targets.

6. *Clarify responsibility for past environmental damage.* Uncertainty about who will be responsible for past damage can discourage foreign and domestic investment and can impede the privatisation process. For practical reasons, governments will have to bear most of the costs of dealing with past emissions. Governments must define clearly the environmental standards that new owners must meet and the period of adjustment that will be permitted.

7. *Set standards that are realistic and enforceable.* Implement stricter standards over a ten to 20 year period, and ensure that industries comply with interim standards.

8. *Involve local people in setting priorities and in implementing solutions.* Neither governments nor donor institutions are equipped to judge how local inhabitants value their environment. A participatory approach is essential for the long-run sustainability of environmental improvements.

9. *More research, training, and exchange of information are needed to help decision-makers set sensible priorities.* Research should focus on the state of the environment in Central and Eastern Europe. Much more information is also needed on low-cost ways to reduce emissions of air and water pollutants from non-ferrous metal smelters, iron and steel plants, chemical plants, paper mills, and waste water treatment plants and on ways to conserve biodiversity.

10. *Finding, implementing, and financing solutions will require building partnerships.* Transferring know-how and clean technologies will require strong co-operation between East and West, between countries of Eastern and Central Europe, and within countries, between cities, institutions, and enterprises.

together with donors, combine policy measures (such as new legislation and national biodiversity strategies), including measures that integrate biodiversity concerns into agricultural and other policies; institutional strengthening for national and local authorities; and priority investments that integrate rural development with biodiversity and landscape protection.

Furthermore, the EAP recommended that CEE countries and NIS set their own environmental priorities through the development of National Environmental Action Programmes (NEAPs) and other environmental policy strategies. It suggested that they focus in particular on local problems, tackling first the most serious pollution threats to human health. An analysis carried out for the EAP confirmed that pollution was adversely affecting the health of children and adults in many "hot spots" in the region. The

EAP proposed two other main criteria for priority-setting: activities that entailed high economic costs, such as the destruction of valuable natural resources and pollution damage to buildings and equipment, should be halted, as should irreversible threats to biodiversity. Further, it emphasised that, as political, human and financial resources for environmental actions were likely to remain scarce, countries need to use effective, least-cost methods to tackle their priority problems. The EAP recommended that CEEC/NIS governments employ analytical methods, including health risk analysis and cost-effectiveness analysis, to identify priority issues and responses, and involve a broad range of interest groups and experts in the development and implementation of their policies.

Moreover, the EAP distilled environmental policy lessons from both OECD countries and CEEC/NIS. For example, it urged greater use of economic (or "market-based") instruments, such as pollution charges and emissions trading mechanisms, over more costly and less flexible regulatory methods (such as the "best-available-technology" approach widely used in OECD countries). It emphasised that countries in transition needed to benefit from these lessons, as they lacked resources to pursue more costly approaches.

2.3. International co-operation to implement the EAP

At the Lucerne Conference, the ministers created two international forums to assist the EAP's implementation: the EAP Task Force, to facilitate the implementation of the policy and institutional components and to promote the integration of environmental considerations into the process of economic reconstruction and institutional capacity building; and a Project Preparation Committee (PPC), to "... strengthen the linkage between donors, international financial institutions and central and eastern European countries, and facilitate the mobilisation of resources for the region..." (Lucerne Declaration).

The EAP Task Force was designed to bring together all countries involved in implementing the EAP – OECD countries, CEE countries and the NIS – together with IFIs and other international organisations. (In addition, representatives of industry and of environmental NGOs have participated as partners.) The ministers at Lucerne called for the Task Force to have two chairs: one a representative of the European Commission and a representative from the region, elected by CEEC/NIS delegations. The ministers invited OECD to host the Task Force's secretariat. (The work of the Task Force is described in Chapter 9.)

In contrast, membership in the PPC has been limited to the major bilateral donors providing financial assistance to the region and to the main IFIs providing environmental loans.[6] The Lucerne Conference asked the EBRD to host the PPC's secretariat; in addition, PPC officers have been based at both the EBRD and the World Bank. (The work of the PPC is described in Chapter 6.)

3. Reviewing Implementation of the EAP

The EAP emphasised that national and local actions in CEEC/NIS would be the key to its implementation. This book reviews such actions. Chapter 2 analyses the interaction between the economic transition and environmental conditions, a key theme of the EAP. Chapter 3 discusses the reform of government during the transition and describes the development of institutions and policies for environmental protection. Chapter 4 covers public information and participation, in particular the growth of NGOs and their involvement in policy development. Chapter 5 analyses the role of key environmental policy instruments, including standards and pollution charges, in environmental management. Chapter 6 reviews the development of financing for environmental investments. Chapter 7 looks at the enterprise sector, whose participation is necessary for implementing "win-win" approaches such as cleaner production. Chapter 8 discusses policies for biodiversity. Chapter 9 provides an overview of international co-operation efforts, which have played a crucial role in supporting environmental protection efforts in many CEEC/NIS (however, all chapters mention examples of international support).

The book uses the EAP as a framework for its analysis. However, the Environmental Action Programme was not a "blueprint" for countries to follow strictly. Rather, its impact on national actions and international co-operation efforts was often indirect. The EAP was intended as a "living document" whose conclusions and recommendations would be honed by implementation. A number of forums, and in particular the EAP Task Force, have discussed these policy issues regularly since the Lucerne Conference. One objective of this book is to capture the "state of the art" of this analysis and discussion.

NOTES

1. At both national and international levels, nuclear safety has largely been treated separately from other environmental issues. Nuclear issues are addressed in Annex XI.

2. Please note that the Environmental Action Programme for Central and Eastern Europe (EAP) used the term "Central and Eastern Europe" for both CEEC and NIS.

3. OECD's Development Assistance Committee defines technical assistance, also called technical co-operation, as including: 1) "education and training" for nationals of recipient countries; and 2) the provision of "consultants, advisers and similar personnel as well as teachers and administrators serving in recipient countries (including the cost of associated equipment)" (OECD).

4. This bias has been common in aid programmes. A recent World Bank review concluded: "Foreign aid has concentrated too much on the transfer of capital with (often) scant attention to the institutional and policy environment into which resources were flowing. This approach resulted from misunderstandings about development – overemphasising finance at the expense of policies and institutions – and from external and internal pressures on aid institutions" (World Bank).

5. These included the Bergen Ministerial Conference and the Dublin Ministerial Conference, both in 1990.

6. As of June 1998, the PPC's members included Austria, Belgium, Denmark, Finland, France, Germany, Luxembourg, the Netherlands, Norway, Sweden, Switzerland, the United Kingdom, the United States and the European Commission (EC). The Global Environment Facility (GEF), the European Bank for Reconstruction and Development (EBRD), the European Investment Bank (EIB), the Nordic Environmental Finance Corporation (NEFCO), the Nordic Investment Bank (NIB), and the World Bank and its International Finance Corporation (IFC). Italy, Japan, the EAP Task Force and the UN Development Programme (UNDP) were observers.

OECD 1999

REFERENCES

Conclusions of the Conference "Environment for Europe" (Dobris conclusions) (1991),
Dobris Castle, Czech and Slovak Federal Republic, 21-23 June.

Connolly, B., T. Gutner and H. Bedarff (1996),
Organizational Inertia and Environmental Assistance to Eastern Europe, in R.O. Koehane and M.A. Levy, eds. *Institutions for Environmental Aid: Pitfalls and Promise*, MIT Press, London.

Declaration by the Ministers of Environment of the Region of the United Nations Economic Commission for Europe (Lucerne Declaration) (1993),
Lucerne, Switzerland, 30 April.

Gillespie, B. and A. Zamparutti (1993/1994),
A Framework for the Environment in Eastern Europe, The OECD Observer No. 185, December 1993/January 1994.

Libert, B. (1995),
The Environmental Heritage of Soviet Agriculture, Cabi Publishing, Wallingford, United Kingdom.

Mnatsakanian, R.A. (1992),
Environmental Legacy of the Former Soviet Republics, centre for Human Ecology, University of Edinburgh.

OECD (undated),
Glossary from the report *Development Co-operation Report: Efforts and Policies of Members of the Development Assistance Committee*, [http://www.oecd.org/dac], Paris.

Price, T.L. and R.S. Lester (1998),
The OSCE's Economic Dimension on the Eve of the 21st Century, mimeograph, OSCE, Vienna.

World Bank (1998),
Assessing Aid: What Works, What Doesn't, and Why, Oxford University Press, Oxford.

World Bank and OECD (1993),
Environmental Action Programme for Central and Eastern Europe: Setting Priorities (Abridged version of the document endorsed by the Ministerial Conference at Lucerne, Switzerland, 28-30 April), Washington, DC.

World Resources Institute (WRI) (1992),
World Resources Report 1992-1993, Washington, DC.

Chapter 2

ECONOMIC REFORM AND THE ENVIRONMENT[1]

1. Environment in the Economic Transition

Transition to a market economy, for all its long-term rewards, has not been an easy process. In addition to the necessary but often difficult social, political and economic adjustments, the countries of Central and Eastern Europe and the New Independent States have had to cope with the environmental legacy of inefficient industries, obsolete and polluting technologies, and weak environmental policies.

In 1993, the EAP identified, among the region's many serious environmental problems, several that directly threatened human health and required immediate and urgent attention. These included:

- high levels of airborne particulates in urban and industrial "hot spots" from coal combustion by domestic users, small-scale enterprises, power and heating plants, and metallurgical plants;
- high levels of sulphur dioxide and other air pollutants in "hot spot" areas from the combustion high-sulphur coal and fuel oil by these and other sources;
- lead concentrations in air and soil linked to airborne emissions from industry and from the use of leaded gasoline; and
- contamination of drinking water, in particular by nitrates in rural well water.

A central principle of the EAP was that the process of economic reform and restructuring would eliminate the perverse incentives that underpinned many of the environmental problems of centrally planned economies (Box 2.1). It was recognised that economic reform alone was not a solution. Effective environmental policies, institutions and investments would be required to harness the positive forces of market reform and ensure that enterprises and other economic actors improved their environmental performance. This, in turn, would require economic stability and the prospect of sustained economic growth to encourage governments and industrial enterprises to take the steps needed to make more efficient use of energy and natural resources, mitigate pollution, and enhance the positive environmental effects generated by economic reform.

Many countries have made significant progress since the adoption of the EAP, introducing environmental initiatives at the local, regional and national levels. International co-operation has supported many of these efforts. On the other hand, economic transition has proved to be a much longer and more difficult process than most had anticipated. Progress has varied dramatically across countries. By 1998, several CEE countries had re-established sustained economic growth, but only two – Poland (which had embarked on economic and political reform before the rest of the region) and Slovenia – had surpassed their pre-transition level of real GDP. Several NIS have not progressed far in their economic reform programmes or achieved even a modicum of economic stability: their economies have fallen to one-half of pre-transition levels. In these countries, the fall in production has reduced the volumes of pollution generated, especially air and water pollution from large enterprises, but has had drastic human consequences. Moreover, without improvements in efficiency and environmental performance, short-term reductions of pollution may easily be reversed as and when production levels recover.

This chapter attempts to evaluate the combined effects of economic reform and other measures on environmental performance in the transition economies since 1989/1990. It focuses on the priorities identified in the EAP, examining several underlying factors – economic growth, industrial structure, energy intensity, and the composition of fuel use – that affect trends in volumes of pollution emissions, emission

---

Box 2.1. **Economic reform and environmental benefits**

The EAP emphasised that economic reform in several areas could bring significant environmental benefits:

– *Elimination of price controls and subsidies*, especially for fuels, would initially lead to increases in the costs of industrial production. Enterprises would adjust their production processes and seek energy and resource savings. Removing subsidies would also encourage industrial restructuring, including a shift towards less resource-incentive sectors.

– *Imposition of hard budget constraints*, coupled with changes in the incentive structure of enterprises, would encourage managers to improve the efficiency of their operations, reduce waste, and improve the overall management of resources.

– *Privatisation and favourable conditions for foreign investment* would improve enterprise governance, efficiency and profitability, as well as access to financing to renew outdated, inefficient and highly polluting apital stock.

– *Trade and market liberalisation* would increase the exposure of enterprises to international market requirements and management and environmental practices, as well as their access to cleaner production technologies.

---

intensities and ambient environmental quality. Its analysis compares advanced reform countries which have achieved improvements in environmental performance, in particular when measured in terms of pollution per unit of GDP, with those countries where economic and democratic reforms have proved slow and difficult. In general, these latter countries have not seen advances in environmental protection. (The advanced reform countries are identified in Table 2.1.) These countries started economic reforms early in the transition and pursued reform efforts fairly consistently. Annex V provides a series of indicators for the progress of economic reforms in CEEC/NIS as of mid-1998.

Many environmental problems remain to be addressed, even in the most successful reformers. This chapter compares current priorities for the air and water sectors, which appear to present the important threats to human health.[2] The overview covers all countries in the region including southern NIS countries, which were not included in the analysis for the EAP. The chapter does not cover key issues that have a less pervasive effect on human health in the region, including the management of biodiversity and of natural resources and the management of solid waste. More generally, this book does not attempt to review the state of the environment in the region. The European Environment Agency has recently published an overview that covers Western Europe, CEE countries and part of the NIS (Box 2.2).[3]

1.1. *Reform, economic growth, and restructuring*

The countries of the region began the economic transition with widely differing capabilities and have progressed at very different rates. The NIS that emerged following the break-up of the Soviet Union have had to cope with the disintegration of economic and political links, as well as the difficulties of establishing new monetary and fiscal systems. Many of them have faced high barriers in their efforts to develop markets outside the former Soviet Union, and have lacked the commercial traditions, human resources, and access to expatriate communities with capital that have eased the transition in some CEE countries.

In 1997, GDP per capita in the NIS was on average much lower than in CEE countries (Table 2.1). These figures, estimated using purchasing power parities (PPPs), indicate that living standards in the higher-income CEE countries such as the Czech Republic, Hungary and Slovenia are not far behind those in Portugal, the poorest European Union (EU) Member State.[4] In 1998, a continuing drop in oil and commodity prices, as well as the financial crisis in Russia and other NIS, further widened the gap between these countries and the advanced reform CEE countries. There are considerable uncertainties related to older GDP data for countries in the region, particularly NIS, due in part to differences in national accounting methods and economic uncertainties during the transition. (GDP data remain uncertain for some NIS.)[5]

Table 2.1. **GDP growth and GDP per capita**

	Real GDP as a percentage of 1989 value		GDP per capita, 1997 (US$)[a]
	1993	1997	
Central and Eastern Europe			
Albania	66	80	2 120
Bulgaria	76	67	4 010
Croatia	..	76	4 780
Czech Republic	79	90	10 510
Estonia	62	73	5 240
FYROM	..	..	3 210
Hungary	82	91	7 200
Latvia	49	54	3 940
Lithuania	68	70	4 220
Poland	88	112	6 520
Romania	76	82	4 310
Slovakia	75	95	7 910
Slovenia	89	104	11 800
New Independent States			
Armenia	37	46	2 360
Azerbaijan	44	33	1 550
Belarus	81	72	4 850
Georgia	25	27	1 960
Kazakhstan	70	57	3 560
Kyrgyz Republic	68	61	2 250
Moldova	56	36	1 500
Russian Federation	72	59	4 370
Tajikistan	55	..	1 100
Turkmenistan	82	..	2 060
Ukraine	79	49	2 190
Uzbekistan	88	90	2 470

.. Not available
Advanced reform countries are in bold.
a) Or latest available year. Converted using current purchasing power parity rates.
Sources: World Bank and OECD data.

Box 2.2. **Europe's Environment: The Second Assessment**

The European Environment Agency, an EU body, presented the first pan-European state of the environment report to the Sofia "Environment for Europe" Ministerial Conference. The Agency also presented a follow-up to the 1998 Aarhus Conference, called *Europe's Environment: The Second Assessment.* The report describes environmental issues in Europe as far east as the Urals, an area that includes many CEEC/NIS. It also describes environmental conditions and highlights policy actions over the previous five years, focusing on 12 issues: climate change; stratospheric ozone depletion; acidification; tropospheric ozone; chemicals; waste; biodiversity; inland waters; marine and coastal environments; soil degradation; urban environment; and technological and natural hazards.

For most of these issues, *Europe's Environment* concludes that there has been little progress in regard to environmental conditions. For seven of the 12, including waste, biodiversity, and the marine and coastal environments, it reports that conditions have grown worse. In contrast, there has been at least some progress in the development of policies to address many of these issues, though greater efforts are needed (for example, throughout Europe policies for the transport sector have failed to keep up with the growth of motor vehicle use and resulting congestion, air pollution and noise).

The pace of reform

Progress in implementing economic reform has been uneven among CEE/NIS countries. In advanced reform countries, state-owned enterprises have been privatised or at least subjected to much stricter budget constraints. Subsidies for energy and natural resources have been reduced (though rarely eliminated). Tax systems have been restructured, and efforts have been made to improve both the collection of taxes and the enforcement of regulations, including those relating to environmental performance. Overall, the cumulative impact of these reforms in CEE countries has been to bring them much closer to the market economies of Western Europe.

Russia – and many other NIS – have continued to shield their enterprises from market forces. As a result, industrial restructuring has proceeded slowly in these countries and privatisation – which has affected most enterprises in Russia but has barely started in some NIS – has not yielded the expected benefits. Few privatised enterprises have improved their economic performance, unlike their counterparts in advanced reform CEE countries, as ownership has often been transferred to former employees or managers without changes in economic incentives, management practices, traditional ties to government, or dependence on direct and indirect budget support (Box 2.3).

Throughout the region, there is growing recognition that the often rapid pace of liberalisation and privatisation has not been matched by the development of institutions necessary to support a well-functioning market economy. The advanced reform countries have made some progress. However, poorly working institutions in slower reform countries have resulted in serious distortions that vested interests have been able to exploit, often at significant social and environmental cost. High levels of poverty and inequality have fuelled disillusion with market reforms and further undermined the authority of governments to establish effective institutions.

Economic trends

All countries in the region experienced a more or less severe recession at the beginning of the transition, but there have been large differences between countries in terms of the depth of the recession and subsequent speed of recovery. Success in reinstating economic stability and growth has been strongly influenced by the progress in implementing market reforms (EBRD, 1997). Most countries had negative average growth rates during 1990-96. However, countries that were included in the former Soviet Union (including the Baltic States) experienced larger falls in real GDP than the CEE countries, other than those affected by war.[6] Despite occasional setbacks, advanced reform countries have succeeded in turning their economies around much sooner than slower reformers. By the mid-1990s, most had achieved a reasonable degree of macroeconomic stability, with nominal interest rates in the range of 10-20% per year, positive real interest rates creating genuine incentives for saving and investment, and a return to economic growth.

Although by 1998 only Poland had a level of real GDP significantly higher than that in 1989, most advanced reform countries could expect to achieve this goal within five years. Two other CEE countries, Bulgaria and Romania, have renewed economic reform efforts in recent years, which should bring sustained economic growth. Political instability in the Balkans, including the wars in the former Yugoslavia, has created some uncertainty for these countries and severe economic problems in others. By contrast, it is likely to take at least 10 years for the NIS countries to overtake the real GDP levels seen at the end of the 1980s.

Unemployment has risen sharply in many countries, partly as a result of the restructuring of industrial enterprises and partly because of the overall decline in economic activity. However, in some countries – particularly in the NIS – enterprises retained employees whom they could not afford to pay (in these countries, many workers are paid irregularly, often months late, and often in goods and by other in-kind methods rather than in money).[7] Thus, unemployment rose by about 10% in Poland between 1989 and 1997 but by only 2% in Ukraine; during that period, real GDP grew in Poland but fell by 58% in Ukraine. Overall, unemployment in the CEE countries peaked in 1994-95 but fell as economic growth resumed.[8] In the NIS, measured levels of unemployment are still rising and are likely to go much higher when disguised unemployment is transformed into open unemployment by the closure of bankrupt enterprises.

Box 2.3. **Russia's non-monetary economy**

By 1996, 70% of Russia's GDP was produced by the private sector. However, the privatisation of large enterprises lacked transparency, involved little competition and restrained access to foreign investors. In most cases, the government transferred assets cheaply to former enterprise managers and employees. The government made little effort to implement bankruptcy procedures for insolvent firms – a key condition for industrial restructuring in market-based economies.

Moreover, as the federal government cut its direct subsidies to enterprises (to under 2% of GDP by 1998), it (and other levels of government) increased indirect subsidies. They allowed enterprises to build up large tax and payment arrears and make payments via non-monetary mechanisms, and they provided various privileges and waivers on a case-by-case basis. Quasi-governmental institutions, such as extra-budgetary funds and utilities, also played a major role in this development. Enterprise tax and payment arrears ballooned by more than five times between 1995 and 1998.

At the same time, enterprises faced a severe liquidity crisis created by several factors, including tight federal monetary policy that restricted the creation of money; distortionary taxation that discouraged formal profits; high government borrowing that crowded out bank lending to enterprises; and a failure to establish a legal and institutional basis for financial markets, limiting this source of credit to enterprises.

The widespread accumulation of arrears, together with this liquidity crisis, helped fuel a "non-monetary" economy. By 1998, an estimated 50% of transactions among enterprises used non-monetary forms of payment. Moreover, enterprises made about 60% of their tax and other payments to the federal government in these non-monetary forms – and, in some cases, even higher proportions of their payments to regional and local governments and extra-budgetary funds. Four major types of non-monetary exchange have been used: barter (payments in kind), money surrogates (such as corporate promissory notes), offsets and debt swaps.

In this non-monetary economy, enterprises have had few incentives to improve the efficiency of their operations, including their use of natural and other resources, or to reduce wastes. As a result, there has been little industrial restructuring and efficiency improvement in Russia. Rather, in what Gaddy and Ickes call a "virtual economy", many enterprises are more interested in maintaining employment and production levels (at least to the degree possible), creating monopoly structures with their business partners, and maintaining good relationships with government officials than in producing profits. Therefore, their economic performance is extremely weak – often much weaker than official statistics indicate. Gaddy and Ickes suggest that the volume of real spending on plant and equipment in Russia's manufacturing sector in 1997 was about 5% of its 1990 level, and that investment in all productive sectors was about 17% of the 1990 level, far below officially reported figures. More generally, the extent of the non-monetary economy makes valuation difficult; indeed, nominal prices agreed between parties of non-monetary transactions (including nominal values of tax payments in goods, promissory notes and barter) often significantly diverge from market prices.

The lack of economic reform has severely limited improvements in environmental performance. Many firms have done little to improve their productivity or to invest in environmental protection. At the same time, environmental policy choices, such as waivers for pollution charges, or non-monetary transactions widely used by environmental funds, have become part of the system of soft budget constraints for enterprises.

Sources: Commander and Mumssen; Gaddy and Ickes; OECD, 1998*a*.

The liberalisation of prices, combined with weak monetary discipline, has led to severe episodes of inflation in almost all countries. By 1993, price levels had risen more than 10 times compared to the 1989 level in all of the CEE countries except the Czech Republic, Hungary and Slovakia. However, most advanced reform countries had started to bring inflation under control. In a majority, inflation had fallen under 40% by 1993 and under 20% by 1997 (Table 2.2). Some CEE countries, such as Bulgaria, experienced renewed macroeconomic instability and renewed high inflation in the late 1990s.

Most NIS have experienced some form of hyperinflation, with 1993 prices soaring to more than 200 times their 1989 levels. Many NIS established price stability after 1993: in eight of the 12 countries, 1997 inflation was under 30%. In some countries, inflation rates have varied greatly from year to year as a

Table 2.2. **Unemployment rates and inflation in CEEC and NIS**

Country[a]	Unemployment rates (per cent)		Inflation (per cent)	
	1993	1997	1993	1997
Central and Eastern Europe				
Albania	22	..	85	32
Bulgaria	16	14	73	1 100
Croatia	15	18	1 500	4
Czech Republic	3	4	21	9
Estonia	7	10	90	11
FYROM	28	36	340	1
Hungary	13	11	23	18
Latvia	5	7	110	8
Lithuania	4	6	410	9
Poland	15	12	35	15
Romania	9	7	260	150
Slovakia	13	13	23	6
Slovenia	14	14	33	8
New Independent States				
Armenia	5	11	3 500	14
Azerbaijan	16	19	1 100	4
Belarus	1	3	1 200	64
Georgia	7	5	3 100	7
Kazakhstan	1	4	1 700	17
Kyrgyz Republic	–	3	770	25
Moldova	1	2	790	12
Russian Federation	5	11	880	15
Tajikistan	1	3	2 200	88
Turkmenistan	..	..	3 100	84
Ukraine	–	2	4 700	16
Uzbekistan	–	–	530	72

.. Not available.
a) Advanced reform countries are in bold type.
Sources: EBRD, World Bank and OECD data.

result of erratic economic policies. Russia's 1998 financial crisis sparked inflation across the region. There are no mechanisms for monetary correction to protect savers and investors from the confiscatory effects of inflation.

Under these unstable conditions, there have been no incentives for enterprises in the NIS to invest time, labour and money in anything that will not produce an almost immediate return. Even simple measures to improve output and productivity, or to reduce the waste of energy or raw materials, have been of little significance in comparison with efforts to take advantage of the fiscal and monetary distortions created by rapid and fluctuating rates of inflation. In addition, high inflation and political, legal and other uncertainties have increased the risks and costs of long-term financing, further delaying investments in the replacement of outdated, highly polluting capital stock and other environmentally beneficial improvements. It is unrealistic to expect any substantial progress towards better environmental performance or, specifically, an increase in environmental investments until the core elements of macroeconomic stability are in place. The 1998 financial crisis has brought new uncertainty, even for those NIS that had made significant progress towards macroeconomic stability.

1.2. *Trends in industrial output and energy use*

The EAP predicted that structural changes generated by the process of economic reform during transition would be beneficial to the environment, promoting a shift from heavy industries towards less resource and pollution intensive sectors, improvements in the efficiency of resource use, and a switch from dirtier fossil fuels such as coal to cleaner fuels such as gas – trends that should reduce air pollution levels. This section reviews actual changes in these areas.

Industrial production

Figure 2.1 shows average trends for GDP and industrial output between 1989 and 1998 for the advanced reform economies and for slower reformers. While the transition process precipitated a collapse in GDP and industrial output in all countries, the advanced reformers stabilised and turned their economies around far earlier than the slower reformers, some of which have faced renewed economic instability and crisis in recent years.

Figure 2.1. **Trends in GDP and industrial output**
Index 1991 = 100

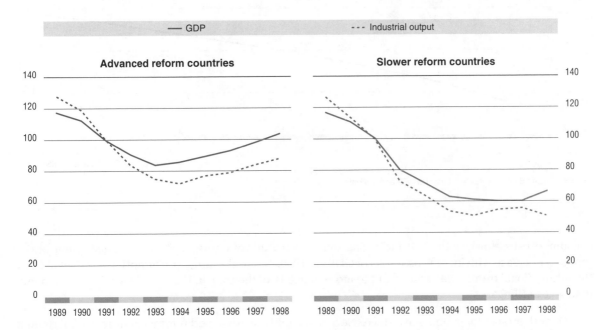

Unweighted averages of national trends.
Source: OECD.

Industrial output has fallen more sharply than GDP in both country groups, but the overall shift in the sectoral composition of GDP away from industry has been greater in the advanced reform economies. In the slower reformers, the industrial sector started to recover in 1995 although aggregate GDP was still falling, and in 1998 industrial output fell as GDP recovered slightly. Within the industrial sector, the initial decline in output from heavy industry, including chemicals and metallurgy, was particularly marked. These sectors have recovered somewhat since 1994, but account for a significantly smaller portion of industrial output than in the late 1980s.

Energy intensity

At the start of the transition, CEEC/NIS consumed high levels of energy per unit of GDP compared with market-based economies. Figure 2.2 shows energy consumption in four CEEC/NIS, compared with the trend for 22 OECD and developing market-based countries. (In market-based countries, energy

Figure 2.2. **Primary energy consumption and GDP, 1990**

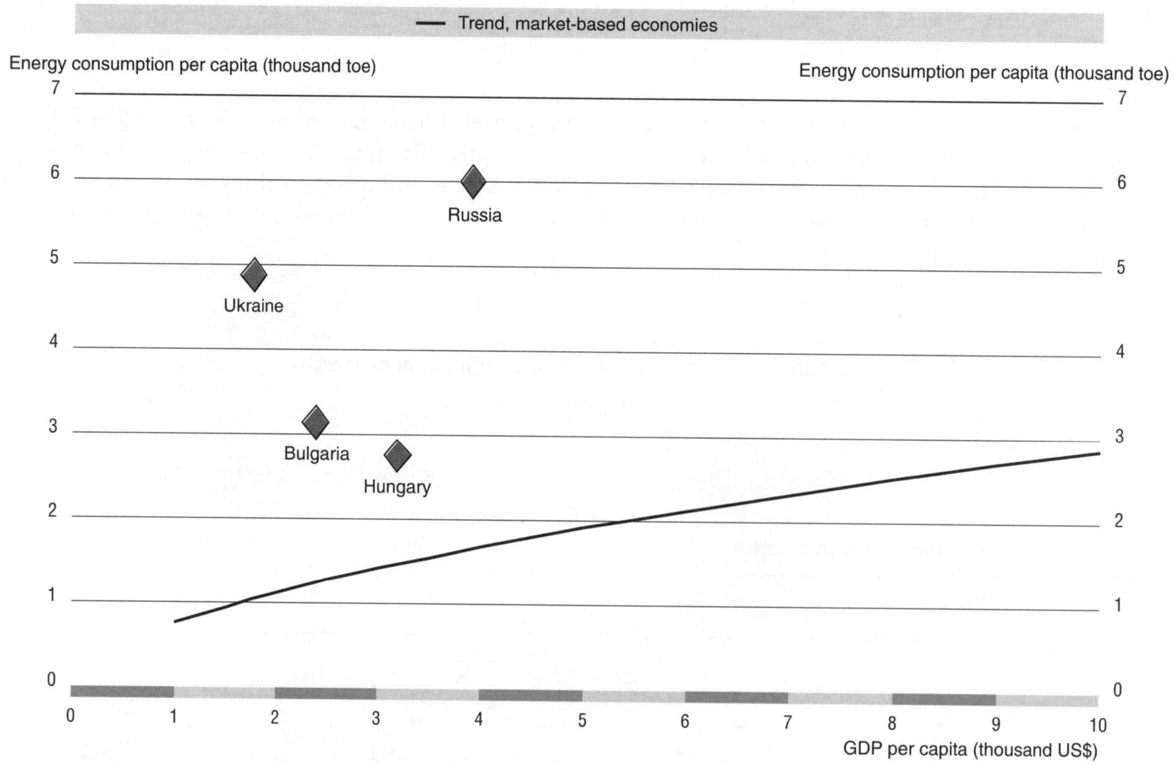

— Trend, market-based economies

Energy consumption per capita (thousand toe)

Energy consumption per capita (thousand toe)

GDP per capita (thousand US$)

Source: World Bank calculations, based on IEA and UN data.

consumed rises slowly with GDP, indicating that the amount of energy used to produce a unit of GDP tends to decrease with increasing levels of GDP.) In 1990, "excess" energy consumption – the level above the international trend – was equivalent to more than 80% of the total in Ukraine, 70% in Russia, and more than 40% in Hungary.[9]

Over the transition, energy use decreased measurably in advanced reform countries. It fell dramatically in slower reform countries, where 1996 energy use stood at half its 1989 level. However, the two groups of countries have followed different trends when energy use is compared to GDP, due to different policies for the transition. Most advanced reformers have increased energy prices to better reflect costs, while ensuring that most enterprises have regularly paid their energy bills. Industrial restructuring, including large-scale privatisation of industrial firms, has led to a decrease in the energy intensities of their economies. "Excess" energy consumption, compared to the international trend, declined in the advanced reform country group from 70% of total energy use in 1990 to 57% in 1995 (Figure 2.3). In particular, Poland, Hungary and the Czech Republic have made strong progress in converging with the international norm. More recent data indicate that these countries continued to converge in the late 1990s.

In contrast, many slower reform countries hesitated to embark on energy sector reforms, implemented them slowly or unevenly (as in Ukraine), or halted initial reforms (as in Belarus). In these countries, energy consumption remained nearly as "excessive" in 1995 as it was at the beginning of the transition. However, there were significant differences among individual countries. Energy intensities worsened and "excess" energy consumption increased in several countries (including Azerbaijan, Bulgaria and the Kyrgyz Republic), where no significant reform took place (Bulgaria and the Kyrgyz Republic subsequently began reform efforts). There were no significant changes in "excess" energy

38

Figure 2.3. **"Excess" energy consumption in advanced and slower reform countries, 1990 and 1995**

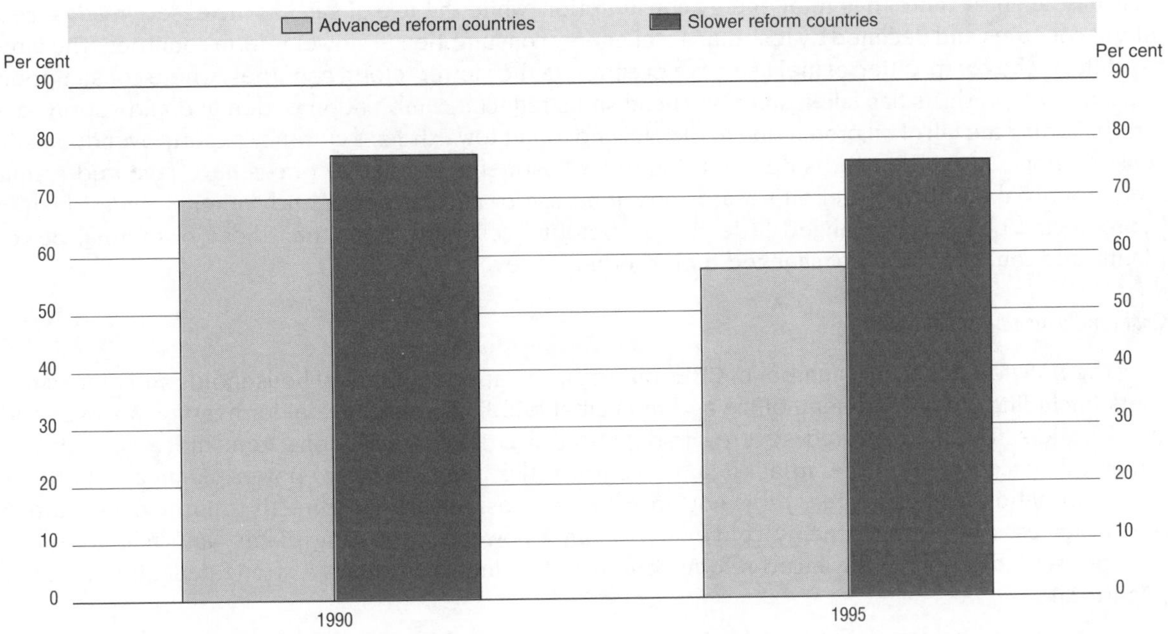

Source: World Bank calculations, based on IEA and UN data.

consumption in the Russia and Ukraine, while in some countries, including Kazakhstan and Romania, there was improvements. The fall in consumption in some countries, including Albania, Armenia and Georgia, was due to the impacts of war and severe restrictions on household energy consumption rather than structural changes and improvements in efficiency. Overall, slower reform countries had not started to narrow the efficiency gap between their economies and comparable market economies.

1.3. Changes in fuel use

The composition of total energy use has changed in many CEEC/NIS, but most significantly in the slower reform economies. Table 2.3 shows changes in the use of different categories of fuel between 1989 and 1996.

Table 2.3. **Trends in CEEC/NIS fuel use, 1989 to 1996**

	Advanced reform countries			Slower reform countries		
	1989 (TPES)	1996 (TPES)	Change (per cent)	1989 (TPES)	1996 (TPES)	Change (per cent)
Solid fuels	142.8	118.9	−17	344.3	223.5	−35
Petroleum fuels	52.1	48.7	−7	804.1	213.6	−73
Gas	31.5	39.1	+24	693.0	494.6	−29
Nuclear	15.6	14.9	−5	55.2	55.2	0
Other	1.5	1.8	+26	21.8	21.6	−1
TOTAL	243.4	223.4	−8	1 918.4	1 008.4	−47

TPES = total primary energy supply.
Source: IEA.

From an environmental perspective, any shift towards the use of gas, especially outside the power sector, is highly beneficial because of the resulting reductions in emissions of air pollutants such as particulates, and sulphur dioxide (SO_2). In both advanced and slower reform countries, the use of solid fuels has fallen by more than total energy consumption, while the use of gas has increased in advanced reform countries and declined by less than total energy consumption in slower reform countries. The largest shifts in the composition of fuel use have occurred in the slower reform countries, where consumption of petroleum products has fallen sharply. These shifts reflect a combination of demand and supply factors, including the fall of oil production in the NIS and a shift towards hard currency exports over domestic consumption. On the demand side, even limited adjustments in relative prices have favoured a shift away from coal and heavy fuel oil towards gas. (The use of nuclear power and "other" sources, mainly hydroelectric power, has changed little. Their operating costs are lower than those of thermal power plants, and countries have not changed their production levels.)

Coal combustion by small users

The EAP noted that, in a number of CEE countries, an important share of households and other small users (including older apartment, office and municipal buildings) burned coal for heating in stoves and small boilers. This had created severe air pollution in cities, as emissions from these "low stacks" remained concentrated in the urban area. (In contrast, the "high stacks" of power plants and factories spread pollution over wide areas.) It is not possible to measure such use directly, but the consumption of coal for uses other than energy conversion (mainly power and heating plants) and manufacturing provides an indication; in advanced reform countries, this indicator shows a strong decline in coal use (Figure 2.4).

In advanced reform countries, the trend away from small-user consumption of coal is likely to continue. Some advanced reform countries, including the Czech Republic, have only partly moved domestic coal prices to world market levels; further price increases should continue the shift towards gas.

Figure 2.4. **Final consumption of coal in advanced reform CEE countries, 1989 to 1995**
Index 1991 = 100

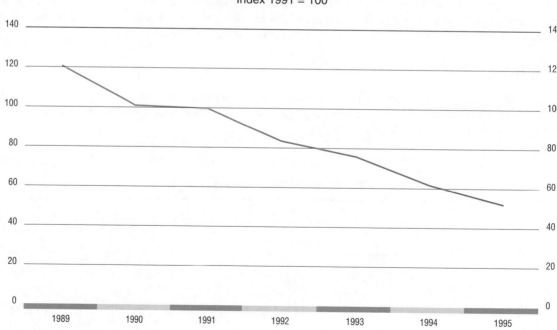

Excludes industrial consumption.
Source: World Bank calculations, based on IEA and UN data.

As these pricing distortions are gradually corrected, it is likely that the share of coal in energy consumption by households and other small users will continue to decline. As a result, coal would eventually become a fuel used almost entirely for power generation and by certain large industrial consumers, as is the pattern in Western Europe today.

Coal combustion by small users has been a problem in some parts of Kazakhstan, Ukraine and other NIS. There are indications that small users in some NIS have reduced their coal consumption. However, in many slower reform countries that produce coal, including Romania, Russia and Ukraine, prices are still implicitly subsidised, while average prices for natural gas and petroleum products have been increased (except in Russia, where gas prices have been controlled to subsidise both household and industrial consumers).

Motor vehicles and motor fuel consumption

In advanced reform countries, gasoline consumption – as well as the use of other petroleum products for transport – started to rise in 1993 (In a few countries such as Poland, this occured even earlier). By 1995, it had almost returned to its 1990 levels (Figure 2.5). The number of motor vehicles has been increasing rapidly (Table 2.4). In slower reform countries, gasoline consumption has more or less kept pace with the decline in GDP. However, in some slower reform countries, including Albania, Belarus, Russia and Ukraine, the increase in vehicle numbers has been larger than in most advanced reform countries, despite greater falls in GDP. Such growth may reflect the extent to which the ownership of motor vehicles was discouraged under the previous economic system. It also suggests that gasoline consumption will increase rapidly in slower reform countries as they return to economic growth.

Most of the increase in motorization has been concentrated in urban and metropolitan areas, which usually have higher incomes than rural areas. The average annual growth in passenger car numbers reached almost 7% in Warsaw and 5% in Budapest between 1985 and 1994, bringing greater traffic and con-

Figure 2.5. **Gasoline consumption in advanced and slower reform countries, 1990 to 1995**
Index 1991 = 100

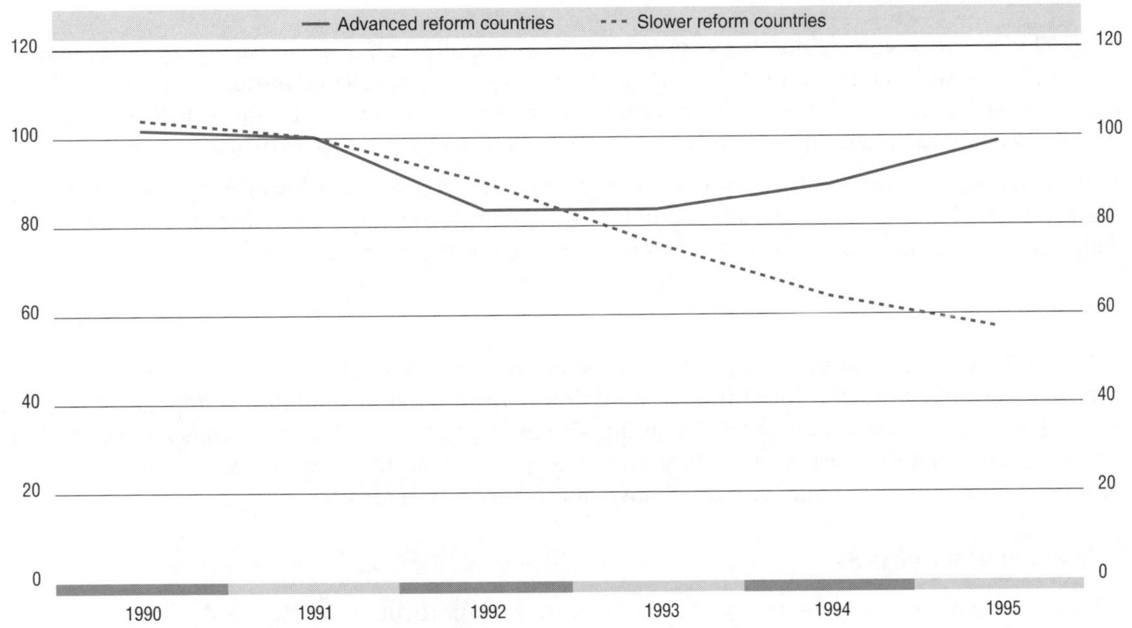

Source: World Bank calculations, based on IEA and UN data.

Table 2.4. **Motor vehicles in use in CEEC/NIS**

	Vehicles per 1 000 population (1996)	Percentage increase in number of vehicles, 1990-96
	CEE countries	
Albania	32	106
Bulgaria	225	33
Croatia	195	10
Czech Republic	350	39
Estonia	323	40
FYROM	142	15
Hungary	273	27
Latvia	188	30
Lithuania	238	49
Poland	249	50
Romania	125	69
Slovakia	220	9
Slovenia	385	26
	NIS countries	
Armenia	2	−65
Azerbaijan	49	−3
Belarus	102	69
Georgia	87	−19
Kazakhstan	81	−2
Kyrgyz Republic	32	−30
Moldova	54	1
Russian Federation	132	49
Tajikistan	2	−36
Turkmenistan	. .	. .
Ukraine	92	45
Uzbekistan	. .	. .

. . Not available.
Advanced reform countries in bold.
Source: World Bank estimates.

gestion. The growth in vehicle numbers appears to be especially high in some NIS cities. In Moscow, the fleet size almost tripled between 1985 and 1994 (TME). Even in some NIS countries where the total number of vehicles has declined or stagnated, urban traffic has increased considerably. In Almaty, Kazakhstan, the annual growth rate for the vehicle fleet was more than 15% between 1990 and 1996.

In advanced reform countries, new passenger cars have often had lower emissions levels than models produced earlier under central planning. However, in many large urban areas, in both advanced and slower reform countries motor vehicles have become the most important source of air pollution.

2. Air Pollution

The EAP predicted that the changes brought about by economic reform, reinforced by environmental policies and investments, would reduce emissions of the main air pollutants, improving urban air quality. This section reviews key trends, including the extent to which lower emissions have been translated into improvements in urban air quality, particularly in "hot spots". It also looks at reductions in lead emissions, an area in which many CEEC/NIS have made strong progress.

2.1. Trends in total emissions

Figure 2.6 shows the average trends in emissions of particulate matter (PM), SO_2 and NO_x in advanced and slower reform countries (as before, the trend in GDP is also included to show how pollution levels have changed in relation to developments taking place in the economy as a whole).

Figure 2.6. **Air pollution emissions and GDP, 1989 to 1996**

Index 1991 = 100

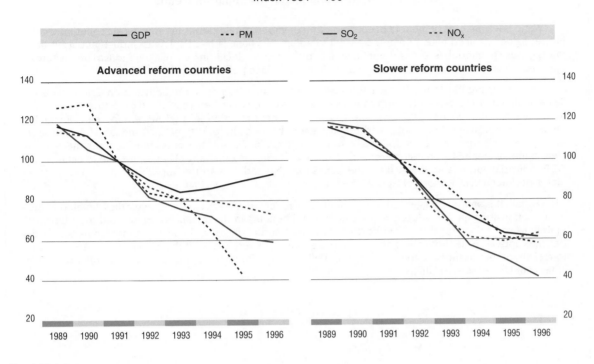

Unweighted averages.
Sources: OECD and national data.

In the advanced reform countries, emissions of all three pollutants fell faster than GDP and continued to fall, even as GDP levels started to grow. Particulates fell the most sharply. In these countries, economic restructuring and environmental actions appear to have played an important role in reducing air pollution (Box 2.4). In the slower reform countries, emissions of these pollutants have fallen approximately in line with GDP. Fall in output, rather than economic restructuring or environmental protection efforts, appears to have been the main factor (the sharper decline in SO_2 emissions may be due to the relative shift from fuel oil and coal towards other energy sources in these countries).

2.2. *Ambient air quality in urban areas*

Have reductions in air pollution emissions led to improvements in ambient air quality in urban areas and industrial "hot spots". The relationship between aggregate emissions and air quality is not a simple one, as ambient conditions arise from a complex set of factors including: local air pollution emissions; distant emissions; climate; geography; and the deposition rates of different pollutants. As the EAP noted, large stationary sources such as power plants and factories usually have "high stacks" that disperse their emissions over large areas, and thus can have a smaller relative impact on local air quality – and human health – than sources such as small coal-fired furnaces and motor vehicles.

A recent study for the EAP Task Force reviewed air pollution data in those countries analysed during preparations for the EAP (these included CEE countries as well as Belarus, Russia and Ukraine). It found that there had been improvements in air pollution in many cities, though often not as dramatic as the reductions in emissions (OECD, 1998*b*):

– Ambient levels of SO_2 *and particulates* had fallen in many cities. For SO_2, the public health problem can be said to have been reduced from widespread to localised in most, though not all, countries. On the other hand, most of the urban areas still had particulate levels of public health significance.

Box 2.4.   **Factors influencing air pollution trends**

World Bank analysis of the role of economic and environmental reforms in reducing air pollution levels in the region has used an econometric model to adjust for changes in GDP levels, industrial output and energy use. The model assesses the influence of other factors, including changes in industrial structures, improvements in production efficiencies, and efforts to reduce pollution levels.

Key results are illustrated in the figures below, which show trends in the adjusted emission levels of key air pollutants. In advanced reform countries, there has been a clear and sustained reduction in emission levels of particulate matter (PM), SO_2 and NO_x – pollutants identified in the EAP as important threats to human health in many "hot spots" and urban areas – beyond the effects of GDP, industrial output and energy use. This trend is clear in particular from 1992 to 1996. For the slower reform countries there is no clear trend: average SO_2 emissions remained constant, indicating that any changes are due to changes in GDP, industrial output and energy use – the factors that the model controlled for. While emissions of particulates declined slightly, those of NO_x increased.

Overall, this analysis suggests that economic reforms, environmental policies, and other developments over the transition have produced real environmental benefits in the advanced reform countries, beyond emissions reductions resulting from declines in output and energy use. In slower reform countries, such declines appear to be the main factors behind the emissions reductions. If these countries were to return to growth without further economic reforms and effective environmental policies, their air pollution emissions could increase accordingly.

Adjusted emissions intensities for advanced and slower reform countries

Index 1991 = 100

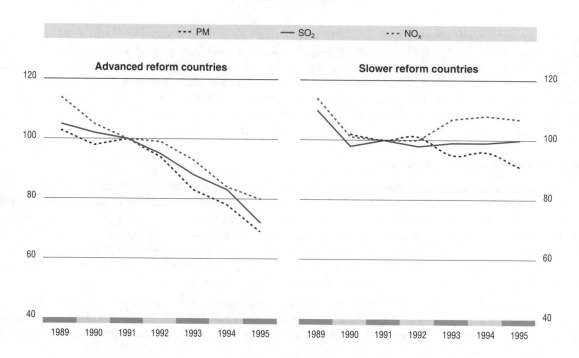

Indices of pollution levels adjusted for changes in GDP, industrial output, and energy use.
Source: World Bank calculations.

– Several countries – including the Czech Republic, Hungary and Poland – had made progress towards reducing ambient concentrations of *lead*. However, the data found were sporadic, suggesting that further monitoring of ambient levels and of human exposures (in particular, children's blood lead levels) is needed in many countries.

A World Bank survey of 30 urban areas in CEEC/NIS supported these conclusions: from 1989 to 1996, average levels of particulates and SO_2 in these cities fell (Table 2.5). These declines were most pronounced in cities in advanced reform CEE countries. In the cities in slower reform countries, NO_2 levels increased. This may be due to increasing traffic without improvements in motor vehicle emissions.

Table 2.5. **Urban air quality in selected CEEC/NIS cities, 1989 to 1996**

Average annual changes in per cent[a]

	Particulates	SO_2	NO_2
Advanced reform countries	–6.7	–6.3	–3.5
Slower reform countries	–4.8	–7.9	+4.9

a) Averaged over the cities surveyed.
Source: World Bank, based on WHO data.

Conditions in individual cities vary greatly. For example, the EAP Task Force study reviewed air quality data for Kazakhstan. In three cities out of the 20 which had data from 1989 to 1996, SO_2 levels were of concern (annual averages above 50 $\mu g/m^3$) and there was little evidence of improvement. The mix of air pollutants may be changing in cities where emissions from motor vehicles are increasing while those from other sources decline.[10]

2.3. Air pollution trends in "hot spots"

Air quality has improved in many of the highly polluted industrial "hot spots" in the region. In the Czech Republic, ambient concentrations of particulates and SO_2 decreased steadily over the 1990s in the Ostrava region and in north-west Bohemia (OECD, 1998*b*). In Bulgaria, metallurgy plants in cities including Plovdiv and Kurdjali improved their control for particulate emissions, reducing high emissions of heavy metals and high concentrations of airborne lead (OECD, 1996).

World Bank calculations for "hot spots" in Bulgaria, Poland and Russia show that air pollution emissions and ambient concentrations for both particulates and SO_2 have, in most cases, fallen steadily (Table 2.6). The Volga and Urals industrial areas in Russia are an exception – here, ambient particulates levels have increased. In Bulgaria's Maritsa Basin, ambient air quality improved faster than emissions levels. In this "hot spot", large power plants burning low-quality lignite are the main sources of emissions. As their pollution is dispersed over a wide area, it may contribute less to local air pollution (though it is an important source of transboundary pollution).

Table 2.6. **Air pollution trends in selected CEEC/NIS hot spots, 1990 to 1996**

Average annual change, in per cent

	Air pollution emissions		Ambient air quality	
	Particulates	SO_2	Particulates	SO_2
Upper Silesia, Poland	–15.9	–6.6	–6.9	–7.7
Maritsa Basin, Bulgaria	–2.7	–1.0	–6.9	–7.7
Industrial areas of the Volga and Urals regions, Russia	–9.6	–8.8	+2.8	–6.4

Source: World Bank calculations, based on Electrowatt (1998).

Box 2.5. **Industrial production and air quality trends in two "hot spots"**

Industrial "hot spots" in many countries show similarities because of common development paths. Upper Silesia in Poland and Kharkov-Donetsk in Ukraine's industrial belt are both centres of heavy industry with complex engineering infrastructure. Industrial production and, in particular, coal-based power and heat generation have been identified as the main source of air pollution in both regions. As a result, particulates are a major air pollution problem. Industrial output has declined in both regions, but in Upper Silesia the decline did not exceed 20% and, by 1997, industrial production had surpassed its 1990 level by 32 per cent. In Kharkov-Donetsk, industrial output in 1996 was less than 50% of the 1990 level.

Ambient concentrations of particulate matter (PM) increased temporarily in both areas during the early 1990s. However, the increase was reversed much sooner in Upper Silesia than in Kharkov-Donetsk. Whereas in Upper Silesia ambient concentrations have fallen steadily since 1991 despite increasing industrial production, in Kharkov-Donetsk the relative improvement has been smaller, as particulate emissions per unit of output have increased continuously. The underlying reasons for this phenomenon can be traced to differences in the economic reform measures and economic conditions of the two countries, as well as differences in environmental protection efforts.

In Upper Silesia, a switch to cleaner fuels, investment in new capital stock, and air pollution abatement measures all contributed to improving air quality. Environmental policy played an important role in encouraging these developments. Poland significantly increased its pollution charges early in the transition, and environmental funds used the revenues to finance pollution abatement investments. No improvement has taken place in Ukraine, where, because of serious macroeconomic difficulties, maintaining the production capabilities of existing capital stock and technologies received priority and planned investments in pollution abatement were delayed or abandoned. Of the 47 pollution abatement facilities scheduled to become operational in 1994, only 20 did so, and these met only 15% of the year's target for pollution reductions. Of facilities already in operation, over 20% were idle in 1994 due to growing shortages in funding for operations and maintenance, personnel and materials. Although many enterprises have cut production, their energy intensities have increased. The result has been an increase in emissions per unit of output, especially in power and heat generation. Deterioration in air pollution control has also been linked with inadequate environmental management practices in enterprises. Environmental regulations have often not been complied with, and often there has been no response by regulatory bodies.

Particulate concentrations and industrial output indices in Upper Silesia and Kharkov/Donetsk, 1990 to 1997

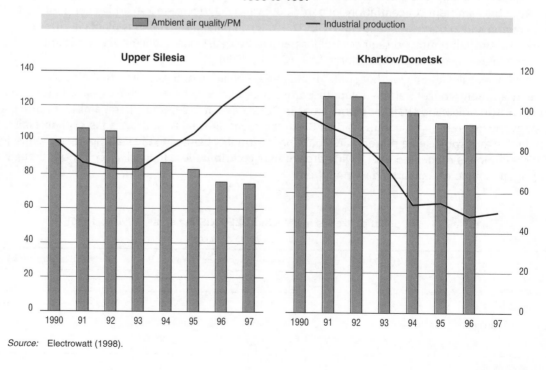

Source: Electrowatt (1998).

There are important differences between trends in advanced reform countries, where air pollution reductions appear in part to reflect economic reforms, and those in slower reform countries, particularly the NIS, where they appear mainly to be the result of falling production levels. A comparison between two "hot spots" – Upper Silesia in Poland and the Kharkhov-Donetsk region in Ukraine – illustrates the interaction between economic trends, environmental policy and air quality (Box 2.5). Air quality has improved in Upper Silesia as industrial production has increased. Little air quality improvement has been seen in the Kharkov-Donetsk region, even though industrial production has declined.

Overall, these results suggest that progress towards improving environmental quality in the most polluted regions has been relatively slow in the slower reform countries, especially in the NIS. They highlight the difficulty of achieving sustained improvements in environmental performance in the absence of effective economic reform. "Hot spots", by their very nature, contain large concentrations of inefficient and polluting heavy industrial plants. Progress in the privatisation and restructuring of large heavy industries has been slower than in other sectors of the economy throughout the region, even in advanced reform countries. Without budgetary discipline and measures to enforce better management, these plants tend to continue inefficient practices, though at a lower level of output, so that there is little or no improvement in environmental performance in terms of pollution intensity. Sustained improvements will require painful decisions to restructure or close plants.

2.4. *Reducing lead emissions*

Many countries in the region have dramatically reduced their emissions of airborne lead, a key threat to human health, in particular child cognitive development (Table 2.7). In most of these countries, industrial emissions of lead have decreased. Several large industrial plants in CEE countries have made pollution control investments to cut their lead emissions. As a result, their industrial lead emissions have decreased, often despite increases in output (Lovei and Levy). Less progress has been made in pollution abatement in NIS countries, where declining industrial emissions have been primarily linked with reduced production.

Table 2.7. **Total lead emissions in selected CEEC/NIS, 1990 and 1996**

Metric tonnes

	1990	1996	Reduction
Belarus	748.0	24.5	–97%
Bulgaria	432.6	251.9	–42%
Croatia	468.0	286.7	–39%
Estonia	183.9	51.9	–72%
Kazakhstan	1 770.0	1 509.0	–15%
Lithuania	46.3	17.4	–62%
Poland	1 395.8	1 025.6	–27%
Slovakia	166.7	91.7	–45%
Ukraine	3 655.4	897.9	–75%
Uzbekistan	626.8	312.5	–50%

Source: DEPA.

Advanced reform CEE countries have made significant progress in phasing out leaded gasoline (Figure 2.7). Maximum allowed lead concentrations were gradually reduced from levels as high as 0.7-0.8 grams per litre (g/l) of gasoline to 0.15 g/l during the late 1980s and early 1990s. In most of these countries, unleaded gasoline has been promoted by differentiated taxation (making it less expensive for end users) and by measures to encourage the use of vehicle emission control devices. Slovakia phased out leaded gasoline completely in 1995, and Hungary is scheduled to do so in 1999. Other advanced reform countries are planning to complete the phase-out of leaded gasoline by 2000 (Box 2.6). Less progress has been made by in slower reform CEE countries, such as Bulgaria and Romania, where leaded gasoline continues to dominate domestic consumption.

Figure 2.7. **Market share of unleaded gasoline in selected countries, 1997**

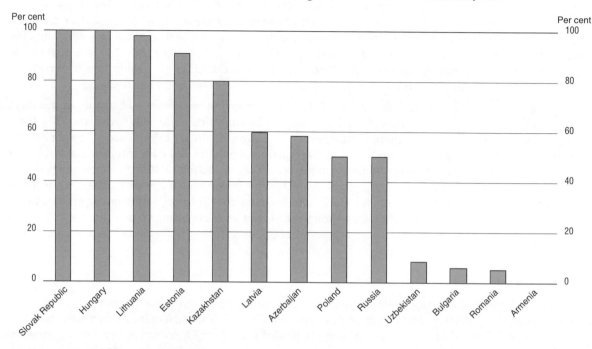

Azerbaijan, 1996 data; Hungary, 1999 projections.
Source: World Bank estimates.

Although a reduction in the lead added to gasoline has been observed throughout the NIS, an intentional effort to remove lead was not the cause. Rather, the low octane requirements of the old vehicle fleet and the availability of excess refining capacity allowed the production of gasoline without addition of lead (Lovei). Without policies to support lead phase-out, the recent reductions in vehicular lead emissions in NIS may be reversed as their vehicle fleets increase and become more modern and excess refining capacity diminishes.

Box 2.6. **Pan-European strategy to phase out leaded gasoline**

At the Third "Environment for Europe" Conference in Sofia, Bulgaria, in October 1995, ministers supported the phase-out of leaded gasoline. As a follow-up, at the initiative of the government of Denmark and the United Nations Economic Commission for Europe (UN/ECE), a *Task Force on the Phase-Out of Lead in Gasoline* was established with the aim of preparing a pan-European Lead Phase-out Strategy. The strategy, adopted by the Aarhus "Environment for Europe" Conference in June 1998, set out the following objectives:

– By 1 January, 2005, leaded gasoline will not be marketed in European countries;
– As intermediate targets, countries undertake to:
  • reach an 80% market share of unleaded gasoline by 1 January, 2002, at the latest; and
  • set a maximum limit for the lead content of regular gasoline (0.15 g/l) and "unleaded" gasoline (0.014 g/l), to be achieved by 1 January, 2000.

(Five CEEC/NIS indicated that they would meet these targets by 2008 rather than 2005.)

Source: DEPA.

3. Water Pollution and Access to Safe Drinking Water

The EAP noted that most urban inhabitants in CEE countries and in Belarus, Russia and Ukraine had access to reasonably safe drinking water. It identified only one major water pollution threat to human health: nitrate contamination of rural drinking water wells. At the same time, the EAP noted that severe water pollution in a number of countries harmed river ecosystems.

The EAP predicted that economic reforms would not have a strong influence on water pollution. Although restructuring should reduce industrial discharges, and a reduction in agricultural subsidies should reduce the use of agricultural chemicals and thus their runoff into rivers and streams, in most countries households and other municipal sources generate the largest share of water pollution, and their discharges would not be directly affected by economic changes. This section looks at water pollution trends and also at access to safe drinking water, a growing concern in many NIS. (In addition, development policies and engineering projects under central planning severely disrupted water ecosystems, most notably the Aral Sea in Kazakhstan and Uzbekistan.)

3.1. Water pollution

Aggregate trends

There is little aggregate data on water pollution in the region. However, several indirect indicators suggest that pollution levels have decreased in both advanced and slower reform countries (Table 2.8). For example, industrial water use, total waste water discharges (by volume), and fertiliser and pesticide use have all decreased. Many advanced reform countries have made significant investments in municipal waste water treatment plants, which should further reduce water pollution loads.

Table 2.8. **Indirect indicators of water pollution discharges, 1990 to 1996**

Average annual change, in per cent

	Advanced reform countries	Slower reform countries
Industrial water abstractions	−13.8	−9.6
Effluent discharges[a]	..	−12.1
Consumption of mineral fertilisers	−13.1	−24.5
Consumption of pesticides	−19.4	−8.7

.. Not available.
a) Discharges from industry and municipal sources, in total volume of water.
Source: World Bank estimates.

Identifying overall water quality trends can be difficult, as these are often linked to local factors. The EEA has compiled data from stations monitoring water quality across 13 CEEC/NIS. For four key types of water pollutants, the number of stations reporting the highest levels of pollution had decreased (Figure 2.8). However, for three of these four types, the number of stations reporting very low levels – equivalent to those commonly found in unpolluted rivers – had fallen only slightly (EEA, 1998). While these results need to be interpreted carefully, they suggest that water quality in many CEEC/NIS rivers is improving.

Trends in advanced reform countries

Reports suggest that there have been important improvements in advanced reform countries. In the Czech Republic, for example, discharges of BOD_5 (a parameter for biological oxygen demand, a measure of the organic pollution of water bodies) from point sources such as industrial plants and municipal

Figure 2.8. **River water quality in CEE countries and selected NIS**[a]

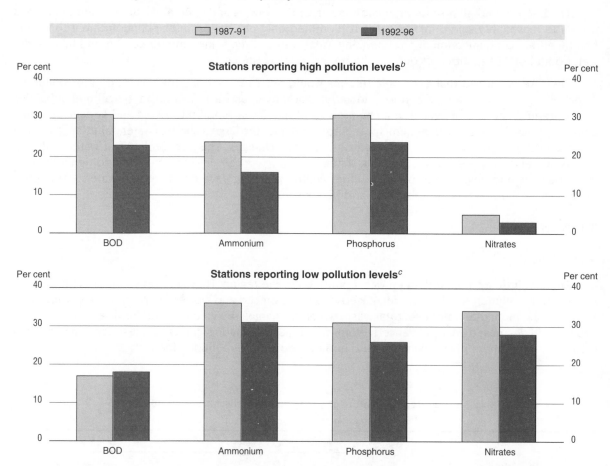

a) Data from Belarus, Bulgaria, Czech Republic, Estonia, Hungary, Latvia, Lithuania, Moldova, Poland, Romania, western Russia, Slovak Republic and Ukraine. Numbers of stations reporting varies by date and parameter (between 91 and 247).
b) High pollution levels: BOD, > 5 mg O2/l; ammonium, > 3.1 mg N-NH4/l; dissolved phosphorus, > 0.13 mg P/l; Nitrate, > 2.5 N-NO3/l.
c) Low pollution levels: BOD, < 2 mg O2/l; ammonium, < 0.4 mg N-NH4/l; dissolved phosphorus, < 0.03 mg P/l; Nitrate, < 0.3 N-NO3/l.
Source: EEA (1999).

sewage systems declined by almost two-thirds between 1990 and 1996 (Figure 2.9). Over the transition period the Czech Republic has financed the construction of new waste water treatment plants, reducing discharges from the most important point sources, municipal sewage systems. In addition, demand for increasingly expensive fertilisers and pesticides, another key source of water pollution, decreased substantially over this period. As a result, water quality in several key rivers improved (OECD, 1999).

In the Baltic States, too, water pollution discharges from point sources have fallen significantly (Figure 2.10), together with agricultural runoff from fertiliser and pesticide use. However, aggregate data from these three countries show that the decline in discharges has not led directly to an improvement in river water quality. This may be due to an accumulation of nutrients in the environment.

Trends in slower reform countries: evidence from "hot spots"

Water pollution trends in three industrial "hot spots" suggest that slower reform countries have not achieved similar improvements. In both Upper Silesia, Poland, and the Volga-Urals region of Russia, BOD discharges have fallen steadily. In Poland, however, this has taken place amidst rising industrial production, while declines in the Volga-Urals region correspond to falling industrial production. Moreover,

Figure 2.9. **Czech Republic: waste water discharges from point sources, 1990 to 1996**

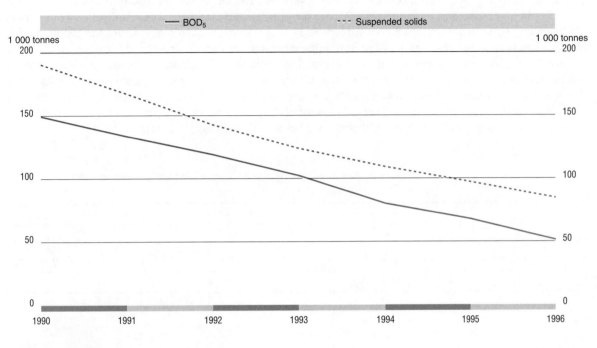

Source: OECD, 1999.

Figure 2.10. **Water pollution in Baltic States, 1992 to 1996**

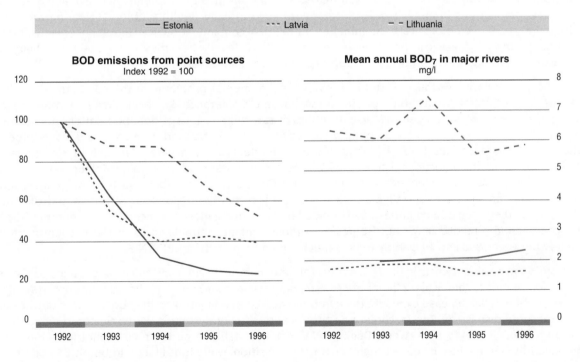

Source: Baltic Environmental Forum (1998).

there have been only minor overall reductions in Ukraine's Kharkov-Donetsk region. Trends in surface water quality in these three "hot spots" follow a similar pattern (Table 2.9). In addition, the EAP noted that discharges of saline waters from coal mines was a serious problem in several countries, in particular the Czech Republic, Poland and Ukraine. While Poland has constructed plants to remove saline from mine water discharges to the Odra River (though not yet for the Vistula), the problem remains serious in Ukraine. A further concern is that, in the Volga-Urals region, data show that concentrations of metals have increased in several rivers. A review of water pollution problems in Sverdlovsk Oblast, part of this region, shows that the lack of maintenance and repair for water pollution treatment equipment presents a serious threat (Box 2.7). This may be an important problem in other "hot spots" in slower reform countries, particularly in the NIS. As slower reform countries have made few investments in municipal or industrial waste water treatment, pollution discharges could increase significantly with a revival of economic growth.

Table 2.9. **Trends in water pollution in selected hot spots: BOD levels, 1990 to 1996**

Average annual change, in per cent

	Level of pollution discharges	Surface water quality
Upper Silesia, Poland	−14.6	−4.0
Volga-Urals, Russia	−7.6	−6.8
Kharkov-Donetsk, Ukraine	−0.6	+0.3

Source: World Bank estimates, based on Electrowatt (1998).

3.2. Access to safe drinking water

The EAP identified nitrate pollution of rural drinking water wells as a priority water pollution problem for human health in many countries (Box 2.8). While this problem may remain serious in many rural locations, it appears to be overshadowed by other drinking water issues, particularly in the NIS. In southern NIS, limited access to piped water creates significant health problems. Across many of these countries, breakdowns in municipal water treatment have brought health problems. Health problems arise mainly from microbiological contamination, rather than contamination from industrial or agricultural pollution – though these can have severe effects at local level when they enter the food chain or unprotected (and poorly treated) water supplies, as in Sverdklovsk oblast.

The preparations for the EAP did not review environmental problems in the southern NIS – the Caucasus and Central Asian republics. Since the Lucerne Conference, however, these countries have joined the EAP process. The Central Asian republics in particular have large rural populations not served by drinking water systems; in a few urban areas, water must be obtained from communal standpipes. These countries have high levels of infant and child mortality and, in particular, high levels of infant deaths from intestinal infectious diseases, which are commonly spread from poor drinking water. Infant mortality from intestinal infections in Caucasus and Central Asian republics such as Azerbaijan and Turkmenistan has been several times higher than levels in northern NIS, such as Russia and Ukraine (Table 2.10). (Levels in CEE countries have been even lower. In the most advanced reform countries, they are comparable to those in Western Europe.) Although infant mortality rates in these countries fell slightly between 1990 and 1995, they remain much higher than in other CEEC/NIS.

Amid the economic crisis in the NIS, municipal water companies in many cities have found it difficult to pay for treatment chemicals or finance necessary maintenance and repair of their distribution systems. These problems can increase exposure to microbiological contaminants, and may be linked to outbreaks of waterborne disease. In Russia, cholera outbreaks and cases of dysentery were registered in Moscow and other large cities in 1995 (World Bank, 1998). Infant mortality in northern NIS countries – Belarus, Russia and Ukraine – has increased slightly over the transition, while it has fallen in both CEE countries and southern NIS (Caucasus and Central Asian Republics).

Box 2.7.   Sverdlovsk: declining industrial production, but no improvement in water quality

Sverdlovsk *oblast* (region) is one of the major centres of heavy industry in the Russia, with a strong concentration of ferrous and non-ferrous metallurgy, machinery, and electric power generation plants. Its most pressing environmental problem is the contamination of water bodies with heavy metals and toxic chemicals. For the past 10 years, drinking water has been polluted and an estimated 90% of the population has been using substandard, often hazardous, drinking water. The problem is further aggravated by inadequate drinking water treatment and poor water supply facilities.

The rivers in the *oblast* are among the most polluted in the Urals region, with practically all water bodies classified by environmental authorities as "very dirty" or "exceptionally dirty". Despite a 30% decline in industrial production from 1990 to 1994 and related decreases in waste water discharges, water quality failed to improve and in some cases further deteriorated. The Neyva River, for example, had to be re-classified from "dirty" to "very dirty". Although the water quality standards used in Russia are often more stringent than those in Western European countries, concentrations of pollutants in the *oblast*'s rivers often exceeded the maximum limits for fishing by several hundred times.

Most pollution discharges originate from industrial plants and municipal waste water treatment plants. Common pollutants include oil products, ammonium salts, and various heavy metals. Among the complex factors affecting pollution and water quality, two stand out:

- the presence of already accumulated pollutants, which diminishes the effects of relatively short-term decreases in discharges; and
- the negative effects of declining capital stock, deferred operations and maintenance measures, and lack of pollution abatement as a result of the general economic crisis and weak environmental management and regulatory efforts.

Pollutants from past discharges accumulated in bottom sediments of water bodies represent a major source of continuous contamination. Additional pollution comes from contaminated soils, which are washed into adjacent water bodies, and from contaminated biota. Unless accompanied by lasting pollution abatement measures, revival of economic activity in the *oblast* will produce a further build-up of contaminants.

Due to the economic crisis during transition, scheduled investments in industrial pre-treatment and sewage treatment facilities have fallen substantially behind schedule. There has been a serious decline in spending on the operation, maintenance and repair of existing equipement. As a result, most water treatment installations are outdated and overloaded. For more than half, their conditions are considered to be at "emergency" levels. These problems create serious risks that discharges and accidental releases of water pollution will increase.

Source: Electrowatt (1998).

---

4.   The Health Impacts of Environmental Problems

Among the EAP's main criteria for setting priorities, reducing environmental impacts on health was one of the most important. The previous sections suggest that economic reforms and environmental policies have brought permanent reductions in air pollution emissions in many advanced reform CEE countries, resulting in at least some improvements in the air quality problems that threatened human health. In particular, many countries across the region have reduced airborne lead levels, a key health risk. At the same time, access to safe water is a major problem in many NIS. This section reviews health trends in the region and looks briefly at a broad comparison of the air pollution and water problems across the CEEC/NIS region.

4.1. *Health trends in* CEEC/NIS

There has been a disturbing divergence in life expectancy between CEEC/NIS and Western European countries. This divergence started in the 1960s, as life expectancies stagnated (and sometimes fell) in CEEC/NIS. It widened sharply after 1989, especially among males and particularly in the NIS. In

---

Box 2.8.   Nitrate contamination of rural well water

The EAP identified six countries where high nitrate levels had been measured in rural drinking water at levels that could cause methemoglobinemia in children: Hungary, Slovakia, Romania, Bulgaria, Lithuania and Belarus. The decline in use of agricultural chemicals, a key source of nitrates, should have reduced this threat, though it is also linked to contamination from human waste water. A recent review of environmental health issues in CEEC/NIS found systematic data on water quality in rural drinking water wells in only two CEE countries and one NIS (this suggests that few countries have undertaken systematic monitoring).

– Data from Romania show that nitrate contamination of well water continued to be an important problem in some rural areas, and related infant health problems remained unacceptably high.

– In Estonia, where the problem had not been identified previously, monitoring of several thousand rural wells between 1993 and 1996 showed that less than 5% had high levels of nitrate contamination. This low level, together with systematic monitoring, suggests that the problem has been well managed.

– In Kazakhstan, a country not covered in the analysis for the EAP, reports suggest that nitrate contamination of rural wells is a major problem.

Source: OECD, 1998*b*.

Table 2.10.   **Infant mortality rates in CEEC/NIS**[a]

	Total infant deaths per 1 000 live births		Infant deaths from infectious diseases, 1994 (per 1 000 live births)
	1990	1995	
CEE countries[b]	18	16	0.2
Northern NIS[c]	16	17	0.6
Southern NIS[d]	32	31	5.1

a)   Unweighted averages.
b)   Does not include Albania, Bosnia and Herzegovina, and FYROM.
c)   Includes Belarus, Moldova, Russia and Ukraine.
d)   Includes Armenia, Azerbaijan, Georgia, Kazakhstan, Kyrgyz Republic, Tajikistan, Turkmenistan and Uzbekistan.
Sources: World Bank and WHO data.

Russia, for example, the average life expectancy for males fell from 63.8 years in 1990 to 57.3 in 1994; death rates for adult males in particular increased sharply. Similar trends have been observed in other NIS. Deteriorating socio-economic conditions have been the main reason for declining health and life expectancy in the region (Box 2.9), although declining health care systems have also contributed.

Overall, pollution has been a much less important health factor than socio-economic conditions. At the same time, overall health levels can exacerbate risks from pollution. For example, studies in the early years of the transition indicated that high blood levels of lead had stronger neurobehavioural effects in children in Hungary and Poland than in Western countries, possibly due to poorer nutrition and other types of socio-economic deprivation (OECD, 1998*b*). On a much wider scale, the estimates in the following section suggest that the impact of air pollution on health in the NIS has grown, due to the decline in overall health levels, even though air quality has improved in some cities.

4.2. The impact of air and water problems

Recent World Bank research has tried to compare the impact of air and water pollution problems across the region. The study has had to cope with two major difficulties. First, much key data have been

---

Box 2.9. Social problems during the transition

In many NIS, the transition's economic crisis has had severe social effects. Declining GDP, hyperinflation, unemployment and unpaid wages had, by the mid-1990s, brought large sectors of the population below the poverty level: about 40% of Russians and Ukrainians and an even higher share of the population in some Central Asian countries (based on UNDP calculations, using US$4 per day per person at purchasing power parity rates as the threshold for poverty). In many CEE countries, poverty has been less widespread; nonetheless, over 30% of the population in Bulgaria and 40% in Lithuania fell below the poverty level.

There are indications that poverty levels (as well as mortality rates) have decreased in some CEE countries as they have returned to economic growth. In contrast, the 1998 economic and financial crisis in Russia and other NIS will likely deepen poverty in these countries and could aggravate health problems and mortality.

_____

Source: EBRD, 1997.

---

of uncertain reliability or unavailable. Country and regional estimates of air pollution were based on a sample of 77 cities. These include many of the largest cities in the region, they represent only a fraction of total populations. Air pollution levels are used to estimate health impacts, although these depend on actual exposures to contaminants – these depend on a variety of factors. A second problem arises in comparing the effects of air and water pollution, as they can have different impacts. Air pollution in the CEEC/NIS region is almost entirely an urban problem, whereas rural populations bear most of the costs of

Figure 2.11. **Total burden of mortality and illness in CEEC/NIS associated with environmental factors, 1995**

Thousands of DALYs

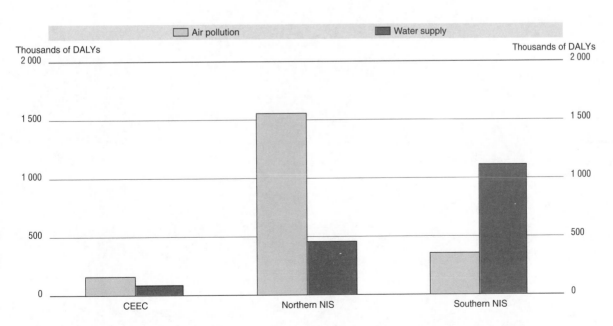

Northern NIS include Belarus, Moldova, Russia and Ukraine; southern NIS include Armenia, Azerbaijan, Georgia, Kazakhstan, the Kyrgyz Republic, Tajikistan, Turkmenistan and Uzbekistan.
Source: World Bank calculations.

contaminated water. Most of those who die or fall ill as a result of air pollution are over 40 years old, while deaths and illnesses resulting from dirty water are concentrated among children, especially infants and children under age five. While there are no universally accepted ways of comparing these impacts, the results presented here use a measure called disability-adjusted life years (DALYs).[11]

The study suggests that the health impacts of air pollution and water supply problems cause an estimated 3.9 million DALYs lost per year across the whole region (a more detailed discussion of estimated health impacts can be found in Annex II). The most serious environmental problems are found in the NIS. Air pollution in northern NIS countries causes 1.6 million DALYs per year lost, and the lack of safe water in the southern NIS countries results in 1.1 million DALYs per year lost (Figure 2.11).[12] When measured on a per capita basis, however, the water problems in the southern NIS countries are by far the most serious, causing an estimated 17 DALYs lost per 1 000 population each year. Air pollution in the northern NIS causes about 7 DALYs lost per 1 000 population each year. In contrast, CEE countries account for a small share of health impacts, whether measured in total DALYs lost or on a per capita basis, suggesting that reductions in air pollution since 1990 have greatly reduced related health threats in this region. While further research is needed, these results provide an important perspective for identifying region-wide priorities for environmental action based on human health considerations.

NOTES

1. This chapter is based largely on research for a World Bank technical paper *Economic Reform and Environmental Performance* by Magda Lovei and Gordon Hughes (1999, forthcoming).

2. Nuclear risks are not considered here.

3. In addition, nearly all countries in the region have published national state of the environment reports. UNEP/GRID (Arendal) has compiled information from many of these at its web site (www.grida.no). OECD and UN/ECE have conducted environmental performance reviews of several CEEC/NIS, analysing their environmental conditions and policies.

4. GDP per capita, calculated using purchasing power parities (PPPs), was approximately US$14 000 in Portugal in 1997 (compared to US$22 000 in Germany, a higher-income EU Member country). Purchasing power parities are based on the domestic prices of goods. For many CEEC/NIS, PPPs yield higher GDP per capita than market exchange rates. For example, GDP per capita in Russia at market exchange rates was about US$2 200 in 1997.

5. GDP per capita is increasingly recognised as a flawed measure of human welfare, though alternatives developed thus far also involve considerable uncertainties.

6. Estimates of GDP for the countries that were part of the former Soviet Union before the transition were probably substantially overstated, as a result of distorted prices and the inclusion of a significant fraction of output that was effectively of negligible value.

7. Countries differ in how they measure unemployment, making comparisons difficult.

8. It should be noted that many older workers have left the labour force as a result of early retirement policies or discouragement, so that levels of total employment are still well below those in the late 1980s.

9. The trend was calculated based on the energy consumption per capita of 22 market economies with similar climates, using the logarithm of their GDP per capita figures as the explanatory variable (Argentina, Austria, Belgium, Chile, Denmark, Finland, Ireland, France, Germany, Japan, the Netherlands, New Zealand, Portugal, South Africa, South Korea, Spain, Sweden, Switzerland, Turkey, the United Kingdom, the United States and Uruguay).

10. Neither study tracked levels of tropospheric ozone, a key component of photochemical smog generated from components of motor vehicle emissions. It is common in Western European and North American cities whose major emissions come from motor vehicles.

11. DALYs (disability-adjusted life years) are a measure of the burden of disease, combining life years lost due to premature death and fractions of years of healthy life lost as a result of illness or disability. The years of life lost at each age are valued to reflect the different social weights usually given to illness and premature mortality. Years lost are also discounted. Thus, the death of a baby girl represents a loss of 32.5 DALYs, and the death of a woman at age 60 represents 12 lost DALYs (values are slightly lower for males, who have lower life expectancies).

12. The estimated impacts of water problems presented here aggregate two issues: lack of access to safe drinking water, the most important problem in all parts of the region; and urban households without adequate connections to sewage systems. Their impacts are presented separately in the Annex II.

REFERENCES

Baltic Environmental Forum (1998),
    Baltic State of the Environment Report, Riga.

Commander, S. and C. Mumssen (1998),
    Understanding Barter in Russia, European Bank for Reconstruction and Development (EBRD) Working Paper No. 37, London, December.

DEPA (Danish Environmental Protection Agency) (1998),
    Country Assessment Report to the UN/ECE Task Force to Phase Out Leaded Petrol in Europe, Copenhagen.

Electrowatt (1998),
    Trends in Exposure to Air Pollution and Contamination of Drinking Water – Five Case Studies, Draft report prepared for the World Bank.

European Bank for Reconstruction and Development (EBRD) (1996),
    Transition Report, London.

European Bank for Reconstruction and Development (EBRD) (1997),
    Transition Report, London.

European Bank for Reconstruction and Development (EBRD) (1998),
    Transition Report Update, London.

European Environment Agency (EEA) (1998),
    Europe's Environment: The Second Assessment, Elsevier Science Ltd., Oxford.

Gaddy, C.G. and B.W. Ickes (1998),
    Russia's Virtual Economy, Foreign Affairs, September-October.

International Energy Agency (IEA) (1997),
    Energy Efficiency Initiative, OECD, Paris.

Lovei, M. and B. Levy (1997),
    Lead Exposure and Health in Central and Eastern Europe, in M. Lovei, ed., *Phasing out Lead from Gasoline in Central and Eastern Europe. Health Issues, Feasibility, and Policies* World Bank, Washington, DC.

Lovei, M. (1997) ed.,
    Phasing Out Lead from Gasoline in Central and Eastern Europe. Health Issues, Feasibility and Policies. World Bank, Washington, DC.

Murray, C.J. and A.D. Lopez (1996) eds.,
    The Global Burden of Disease, The Global Burden of Disease and Injury Series, 1. Harvard School of Public Health, Harvard University Press, Cambridge, Massachusetts.

OECD (1996),
    Environmental Performance Reviews: Bulgaria, Paris.

OECD (1997),
    Environmental Data Compendium 1997, Paris.

OECD (1998a),
    Economic Survey: Russia, Paris.

OECD (1998b),
    Public Exposure to Priority Pollutants Identified in the Environmental Action Programme for Central and Eastern Europe: Five Years On, Paris.

OECD (1999),
    Environmental Performance Reviews: Czech Republic, Paris.

TME (Institute for Applied Environmental Economics) (1995),
    Urban Transport and Air Pollution: Trends and Policy Options, draft paper prepared for the World Bank, The Hague.

WHO (World Health Organization) (various years),
    World Health Statistics Annual, Vienna.

World Bank (1992),
   World Development Report 1992: Development and the Environment, Oxford University Press, New York.

World Bank (1997a),
   World Development Indicators 1997, Washington, DC.

World Bank (1997b),
   World Development Report 1997: *The State in a Changing World*, New York, Oxford University Press.

World Bank (1998),
   World Development Indicators 1998 on CD-ROM, Washington, DC.

Chapter 3

REFORMING GOVERNMENT INSTITUTIONS AND POLICIES

1. Introduction

By the late 1980s, most central and eastern European countries had created central environmental authorities, as had the former Soviet Union. However, these authorities were limited to a co-ordinating role, as many responsibilities for environmental protection remained dispersed among sectoral agencies; as a result, they generally had low institutional capacities, budgets and influence. Nonetheless, the skills and commitment of environmental officials, and the information which they had compiled, helped to establish initial frameworks for environmental policy in many countries.

Early in the transition, some countries in the region took important steps to strengthen their environmental institutions and policies; however, in many countries there was a perception that external financing for investment projects was the main solution to their serious environmental problems. The EAP, distilling key policy and institutional lessons from OECD countries and from the region itself, focused attention instead on the need to link new investment with policy and institutional reforms (Chapter 1).

This chapter reviews CEEC and NIS actions and achievements in the areas of institutional strengthening and policy reform. The EAP acted as a catalyst that supported and accelerated many of these actions and achievements. Moreover, international assistance programmes provided crucial support for institutional strengthening and policy reform in many CEEC/NIS (some cases are mentioned in this chapter; Chapter 9 presents an overview of international assistance and finance in the region).

Many reforms would have been made without the EAP or external support. Early in their transition, Poland and a few other countries undertook reforms later recommended by the EAP to the region as a whole. Overall, domestic conditions have been the main factors behind progress on the environment. Over the course of the transition, countries that have made the most progress in economic, democratic and institutional reform have been the most successful in addressing their environmental problems.

2. Strengthening Institutions

This section reviews the development of institutional capacity to formulate and implement effective environmental policies. First, however, it reviews the progress of overall government reform and the development of *good governance*: these are vital in terms of establishing the conditions for well-functioning markets, promoting the quality of life of citizens, and strengthening democracy and civil society (OECD, 1998). Building effective environmental institutions has been both supported and constrained by the overall reform of public institutions during the transition.

2.1. *Reforming government*

The transition to democratic societies and market-based economies has required reform of the state: the role, methods and goals of public institutions have had to change to support these goals. For example, governments have had to learn to "steer" rather than "row" national economies (World Bank, 1997). As a result, many government institutions have no longer been needed, while others, such as those for environmental protection, have had to be strengthened. Countries in transition have had to improve governance, reform existing institutional arrangements and develop new capacities (Box 3.1).

Box 3.1.   **Key elements of good governance**

While there are many ways of defining good governance, several key elements are necessary. These include:

Technical and managerial competence: in all governments, civil servants need ongoing training to ensure that their skills keep pace with new changes and requirements.

Organisational competence is required in order for government institutions to make good use of staff skills. Many governments need to strengthen basic management.

Reliability, predictability and the "rule of law": decisions taken by governments must be founded in laws that protect individuals and enterprises from arbitrary actions. A reliable, predictable rule of law is essential for individuals and firms to make good decisions. This requires governance that: is free from distortionary incentives, such as corruption, nepotism, patronage, or the "capture" of state institutions by narrow private interests; guarantees individual and property rights; and achieves some level of social stability. While good governance requires written laws, regulations and procedures as the basis for government actions, excessive specificity can lead to rigidities or the risk that these written provisions will be applied selectively.

Accountability is both an end in itself – as a basic democratic value – and a means of developing more efficient and effective state institutions. Accountability is a key way to ensure that politicians and public servants use their powers appropriately, in accordance with the public interest. Governments need, first, to clarify who is accountable for what and, second, to ensure that institutions and civil servants are held accountable for their decisions and performance. Formal reporting requirements as well as mechanisms for external scrutiny (such as independent audit offices and ombudsmen) can strengthen accountability. In democratic systems, politicians should be accountable for their decisions and performance: ministers to parliament, and the parliament to voters.

Transparency requires openness and the availability of good information, so that higher levels of administration, external reviewers and the general public can verify the performance and compliance with the law of government institutions and civil servants. Transparency is necessary to ensure the rule of law and to ensure accountability.

Participation gives government institutions access to important information about the needs and priorities of individuals, communities and private businesses, in order to make good decisions that enjoy public support. Participation is a basic element of democracy, and in many OECD countries – as in many CEEC/NIS – citizens have called for greater opportunities to participate in government decision-making.

The development of good governance is an ongoing process. Many OECD countries have undertaken reforms in recent years to improve the efficiency and effectiveness of regulatory systems (and remove unnecessary regulations that hinder market pressures); to improve the efficiency and effectiveness of government services; and to increase transparency, accountability and public participation.

Source: Based on OECD, 1998.

Institutional reform has proved to be a slow and difficult process, requiring not only restructuring but also changing the "culture" of public institutions (Margulis and Vetleseter). The culture of government under central planning did not support good governance, as it lacked in particular accountability, transparency, participation and the rule of law. Some key actors in the early years of the transition, including national leaders and international organisations, have recently acknowledged that not enough attention was devoted to the institutional aspects of transition (Kolodko; Stiglitz). The EBRD's 1998 *Transition Report* judged that the "rapid pace of liberalisation and privatisation has not been matched by concomitant progress in the development of institutions necessary to support a well-functioning market economy" (EBRD, 1998). Across the region, countries have differed greatly in terms of the pace of government reform; economic crisis and political instability have been obstacles to reform in some countries, including many NIS.

Reform in CEE countries

Some CEE countries – in particular Visegrad countries and the Baltic States – have made important progress in restructuring and reforming the state. In particular, several countries, including Poland, have passed laws for a professional civil service. These provide public officials with career guarantees, helping to shield them from arbitrary political decisions. Civil service systems can help governments retain officials with important technical and managerial skills and, more generally, can encourage officials to act with greater respect for the law.

At the same time, new conditions over the transition have made it difficult for some governments to develop and maintain capacity in key areas: in many countries, the fast-growing private sector can offer skilled professionals such as economists and lawyers salaries several times higher than those in government. As a result, some state institutions have not been able to build adequate capacities in these crucial areas; in many cases skilled staff have left, both for higher salaries and where poorly managed state institutions have not made good use of their skills.

In many CEE countries, the "culture" of government has changed only slowly, and key elements of good governance – such as the rule of law, accountability, transparency and participation – have remained weak. In some countries, legislation has continued to prescribe strong bureaucratic intervention in economic activities. Many public officials have held significant discretionary powers without proper guidelines or checks. In some cases, interest groups have been able to gain undue influence in some government agencies. Arbitrary bureaucratic interference in economic activities has remained common. These factors have increased opportunities for corruption. While the depth of the problem has varied greatly from country to country, even the most advanced CEE countries need to take further steps to establish good governance and strengthen government institutions: indeed, this will be a key task for countries seeking EU accession (Box 3.2). In a few CEE countries where reforms have lagged, such as Bulgaria and Romania, recent governments have tried to accelerate the pace of reform (EAP Task Force). In other countries, such as Albania and Bosnia and Herzegovina, governments have faced serious obstacles as they tried to rebuild public institutions after periods of political instability and conflict.

Box 3.2.   Strengthening government institutions for EU accession

Although most CEE countries have made important progress in reforming government, countries seeking accession to the EU will need to take further steps for institutional strengthening and reform. The European Commission has stated that government capacity to implement EU legislation will be one of the key criteria that accession countries will have to meet, and it has identified a number of key institutional problems that most accession countries need to address. These include:

- poorly functioning judicial systems – in many CEEC, courts are overloaded and judges lack experience and training in new legislation. An effective judiciary is necessary to establish a strong rule of law;
- lack of local government financial autonomy and institutional capacity;
- lack of civil service laws;
- corruption, which is reported in many countries.

Overall, the EC has indicated that CEEC need to increase their institutional reform efforts, particularly in these areas, to be able to implement EU legislation in the medium term.

Source: Fournier.

Reform in the NIS

In the NIS, government institutions have faced severe problems. Ongoing economic difficulties have slowed reform and drained the capacity of government institutions; some countries have also experienced political instability. In some NIS, state institutions have been "captured" by economic interests that have then worked with them to oppose further reforms. In this context, efforts to reform and restructure government have proceeded slowly at best.

Starting conditions have varied greatly. Russia inherited most of the Soviet Union's central public administration. Other NIS have built their national administrations using the republican institutions set up under the USSR. In general, however, these were not prepared to govern newly independent countries. The Caucasus and Central Asian republics in particular inherited weak public institutions. These countries have thus faced the dual challenge of reforming the methods of government and building new public institutions.

Some NIS have taken important steps to restructure and reform government and a few have strengthened their environmental institutions. Nonetheless, the slow pace of reform has created problems in some countries In Ukraine, for example, many highly skilled people entered government after independence but left in subsequent years; only recently has Ukraine passed a civil service law that could have retained some of these skilled staff (Demydenko). Many NIS have been slow to restructure government agencies, even in the face of declining budgets. As a result, some agencies have remained overstaffed in certain areas and understaffed in others. Governments have paid their officials poorly and late.

Poor governance has been a crucial problem for the transition in the NIS. A World Bank report has noted that "low state capability in the former Soviet republics is a serious and mounting obstacle for further progress in most areas of economic and social policy" (World Bank, 1997). The direct economic effects have been severe. The EBRD's Chief Economist has written that "the current crisis in Russia arose largely from a failure of the state – its inability to collect taxes, to enforce laws, to manage its employees and to pay them..." (Stern). The ineffectiveness of many NIS governments, together with widespread reports of corruption, have severely harmed public confidence and trust: in turn, the low level of state authority has undermined efforts to build more effective institutions (EBRD). In this context, it is not surprising that only a few NIS have been able to strengthen their environmental institutions.

2.2. Strengthening national environmental institutions

Across the region, the progress of overall government restructuring and reform has established the framework for the development of environmental institutions.

Competence and capacity of environmental institutions

Some CEE countries have devoted serious efforts to strengthening the administrative and technical capacities of their national environmental institutions. In these countries:

- overall ministry responsibilities and staff have grown (Box 3.3);
- ministries have strengthened environmental monitoring and information systems as well as inspectorates (Chapter 5);
- ministries have established central policy units to bring together staff with policy analysis and preparation skills; and
- in some countries, environmental funds have adopted more effective procedures (Chapter 6).

In many cases, technical assistance efforts have supported institutional strengthening. For many CEE environment ministries, however, the pace has slowed in recent years as the environment has been eclipsed by other political priorities (Chapter 4).

Many CEE environment ministries have had difficulty attracting expertise in key areas, including economic analysis and legal support, due to high salaries available in the private sector. In some CEE countries, environment ministries have faced greater budget restrictions than other ministries and have not been able to match salaries available elsewhere in government (these differences can occur when governments lack a proper civil service system). At the same time, in many CEE countries environmental expertise has grown considerably in universities and consulting companies. Environment ministries that have developed the capacity to manage outside consultants have been able to use such expertise effectively.

Box 3.3. **The growth of Slovenia's environmental institutions**

In Slovenia, the Ministry of Environment and Physical Planning grew from 300 staff members in 1991 to 1 200 in 1995. This total includes the Nature Protection Authority, created in 1993, which implements many of the Ministry's environmental and biodiversity protection programmes, as well as the National Inspectorate. Over the same period, the Ministry's tasks have steadily expanded, from a focus on water management to other areas of pollution control, as well as physical planning and biodiversity protection. The Ministry has acquired a fairly high level of technical equipment. One problem, however, is attracting highly skilled professionals such as computer engineers, economists and lawyers, as salaries are higher in the private sector. In addition, the Ministry has lacked inspectors to adequately monitor pollution from enterprises. Local administrations have also strengthened their environmental capacities, though this remains a key area for work.

Sources: UN/ECE (1997); Slovenian reports to the EAP Task Force.

In nearly all CEEC/NIS, budget deficits have created pressures to reduce the size of the public sector. Environmental authorities, particularly in the NIS, have faced severe difficulties, as they have continued to lack capacity in basic areas such as policy formulation and economic and financial analysis. In some NIS, in particular the Caucasus and Central Asian republics, environmental monitoring and information systems have largely collapsed due to lack of funding. In other NIS, environmental institutions have not been restructured and have continued to employ excess staff in certain areas while lacking resources in others that are crucial; this has been the case with Russia's environmental monitoring and information systems (Chapter 5). Moreover, in many NIS and a number of CEEC poor management practices have continued, including strong hierarchies that have demoralised staff, as well as a poor circulation of information that has inhibited co-operation between different offices within environmental authorities.

Overall, only a few NIS environmental authorities have been able to strengthen their capacities in recent years (Box 3.4). In these countries, high-level political support for reform as well as dedicated officials to carry it out have played a key role – in contrast, public support for improved environmental protection has not been strong and has not been a driving force in the NIS (Chapter 4). In most NIS (as well as CEE countries such as Albania and FYR of Macedonia), institutional capacity remains a key challenge in regard to developing and implementing environmental policies.

Accountability, transparency and the rule of law

In many CEEC/NIS, environment ministries have taken the lead within governments in establishing mechanisms for public access to information and public participation in decision-making. In some CEE countries, these mechanisms correspond to approaches in Western Europe; in many NIS, in contrast, legal rights giving public access to environmental information and to participation in environmental decisions are often not applied effectively. Across the region, the recently signed Aarhus Convention should strengthen access to environmental information and to participation (Chapter 4).

Despite this progress on transparency and participation, in many countries environmental officials have continued to enjoy wide discretionary powers without proper oversight or transparency. Excessive discretion has been a danger, in particular, in regard to inspection activities and enforcement of pollution regulations, where there are risks of corruption. Discretionary application of environmental requirements can slow the development of a predictable, reliable framework of rules, in turn undermining incentives for polluters to comply. Discretion has often been greatest in the NIS, where governments have moved slowly to establish accountability, transparency or the rule of law; in many NIS, public pressures for environmental protection have also been weaker (Chapter 4). An example of discretion is the pollution charge "waivers" in Russia. Polluters can request to receive credit for their pollution control investments, to be

---

Box 3.4.   **National environmental institutions in the NIS**

Russia inherited the Soviet Union's central environmental institutions. However, the main national environmental authority, designated a ministry in 1992, was downgraded to a State Committee in 1996 and lost its responsibilities for natural resources management. Over this period, staff has been cut severely and the State Committee's influence within government has declined markedly. Separately, a 1995 World Bank loan created a quasi-government agency, the Committee for the Preparation and Implementation of International Projects (CPPI), to assist environmental policy development and institutional strengthening, together with a National Pollution Abatement Fund (NPAF) to finance projects. CPPI has attracted skilled environmental experts and officials, including many from the State Committee. In addition, with decentralisation, regional and local environmental authorities have assumed increased powers while the State Committee's capacities have decreased (Box 3.5).

In Ukraine and Belarus, Soviet-era environment committees formed the core of environment ministries created after independence. The Ukrainian ministry has had great difficulty retaining highly skilled staff such as economists, financial experts and lawyers: other ministries have been able to offer salaries up to twice as high, while those in the private sector have been even higher.

Other NIS had weak environmental institutions before independence. In the Caucasus republics, environment committee or ministry budgets have fallen significantly over the transition period: in Azerbaijan, environment committee spending fell by over 50% in dollar terms between 1993 and 1997. (In these countries, where there have been fewer employment alternatives, environmental authorities have had less of a problem with staff turnover.)

A few NIS have strengthened their environmental authorities. In the Kyrgyz Republic, the environment committee was upgraded to a ministry after independence. From 1989 to 1997, its staff increased from about 350 to almost 600 employees and its position within the government became stronger. Kazakhstan's Environment Ministry recently was given greater responsibility for natural resources management. Moldova's environment department became a ministry in 1998, and its funding has grown, resolving some of its most acute budget difficulties (in the mid-1990s, some offices of the environmental inspectorate lacked both modern monitoring equipment and motor vehicles for inspectors to visit sites).

Sources: EAP Task Force, 1998; country reports to the EAP Task Force; UN/ECE, 1998.

---

applied against pollution charges. Environmental authorities grant these waivers on a regular basis, but they have few written procedures to guide them; moreover, there has been little transparency that would allow the public to review how decisions were made (Chapter 5). Such problems are not confined to the environmental sector. The EBRD's 1998 *Transition Report* stated that the "complexity and uncertainty of the legal framework [in the NIS] allows far too much discretion to public servants – a major factor contributing to the high level of corruption in the region" (EBRD).

In some cases, foreign experts and technical assistance programmes have encouraged CEEC/NIS environmental authorities to retain such discretionary powers. Often this advice has inappropriately applied experience from the United States and some Western European countries, where environmental authorities have in recent years sought ways to increase the *flexibility* of rigid environmental regulations. In the Netherlands, for example, authorities have long used discretion when applying environmental laws, often through direct negotiations with polluters. Strong government institutions, together with a tradition of transparency and strong public participation, have enabled this approach to be effective. In the CEEC/NIS, however, discretionary powers without accountability or transparency can slow the development of the rule of law, diminish public confidence in environmental institutions, and reduce the effectiveness of policy instruments.

The political authority of environmental institutions

In nearly all countries in the region – particularly in many NIS – environmental authorities have faced a difficult political barrier as environmental concerns have declined in importance on public and political agendas over the course of the transition. At the start of the transition, environmental movements were strong in many countries (Chapter 4); in a few CEE countries, environmental leaders used this window of opportunity to strengthen ministries and introduce innovative policies. Throughout the region, this window has largely closed. While some environment ministries have worked with their counterparts in sectors such as energy and transport, often this co-operation has been based on environmental reforms undertaken early in the transition. In other countries, especially in many NIS, sectoral ministries have paid little attention to environmental issues (section 4). Moreover, in recent years few mainstream political parties in the CEEC/NIS have supported innovative approaches to environmental policy; as a result, few recent environment ministers have undertaken strong reforms.

The process of EU accession has started to renew political attention to environmental issues in the 10 CEE candidate countries. Environment is an important area within EU legislation (the so-called *"acquis"*); to implement the EU's environmental directives effectively, candidate countries will have to strengthen their environment ministries and environmental investments (Annex III).

In a few cases, NIS environmental leaders and officials, with the crucial support of international assistance and finance, have been able to build momentum for reform (Box 3.9 on Kazakhstan describes one such case). In most NIS, however, there is little domestic or international pressure to strengthen environmental institutions and policies.

2.3. *Decentralising environmental management*

Under central planning, national institutions formulated environmental policy; local and regional offices and governments mainly followed and implemented these decisions, using resources transferred from the centre. During the transition, patterns of decentralisation have varied significantly across CEEC/NIS, although nearly all countries have established democratically elected local governments and most have elected regional governments. Decentralisation could strengthen environmental management by bringing it closer to the public and to local concerns, thus enabling greater accountability, transparency and participation. However, where public participation is not strong and there are few mechanisms for accountability or transparency, local economic interests could weaken environmental protection.

Across the region, national governments have devolved certain rights and responsibilities for environmental management to the local and regional levels. Many local and regional governments have established or strengthened environment offices that have played an important role in managing local and regional issues. In many countries, local governments now control local infrastructure such as district heating networks and waste water treatment plants. In addition, many national environmental authorities have established or strengthened their own regional offices. One important problem in countries throughout the region is that national governments have decentralised many powers and responsibilities without the equivalent right to raise revenues, leaving local and regional governments dependent on central government budget transfers and severely restricting their capacity to act on environmental (and other) issues.

The development of local and regional environmental capacity has varied greatly. In Visegrad and Baltic countries, in particular, many regional and local governments have established relatively effective environmental offices. This process has taken place more slowly in other CEE countries and in the NIS. Many local and regional governments in countries with low GDP per capita – including many in the Balkans, the Caucasus and Central Asia – have not been able to develop institutional capacities for environmental management. In some NIS, national governments have continued to restrict local and regional autonomy (HIID and IRG). In contrast, decentralisation has been chaotic in Russia, and the division of responsibility between federal and regional environmental institutions has remained unclear. Nonetheless, a few local and regional governments in Russia have been in the forefront of environmental protection (Box 3.5).

Despite these difficulties, a few local and regional governments, particularly in CEE countries, have developed their own environmental policies to tackle priority issues within their territories. These include Local and Regional Environmental Action Programmes (LEAPs/REAPs) and Local Agenda 21

Box 3.5. Decentralising environmental management in Russia

The Russian Federation has experienced a great shift of power from Moscow to the regional govern-ments. However, Russia's new constitution gives little guidance on the division of responsibilities between Moscow and the regions. A patchwork of bilateral agreements have been used to try to define these issues. Some wealthy regions, including those rich in oil and other natural resources, have acquired broad powers, while discussions and struggles over power-sharing and fiscal relations have continued, creating great uncertainty across all policy areas.

In environmental management, the federal role has diminished significantly in recent years. One rea-son is that the State Committee for Environmental Protection in Moscow has had difficulty funding its regional committees as well as federal environment programmes. Some wealthier regions, in particular those leading on economic reforms, have covered this funding gap, developed their own environmental programmes (some have even increased their environmental funding over the transition), and made inno-vations in their environmental institutions and policies.

Their actions can provide models for other regions and for national authorities. For example, the regional administration in Tomsk region has created an environmental prosecutor's office to strengthen enforcement, and it has improved integration by establishing an Environmental Co-ordinating Council bringing together key regional agencies whose responsibilities affect environmental protection. Nizhniy Novgorod region has established an environmental council that includes representatives of NGOs, industry and other stakeholders. Many donors have preferred to work with those regions pursuing environmental reform, rather than with the federal authorities.

In some regions, however, governments have given even lower priority to environmental protection than at the national level, as local economic interests have had strong political weight: here, decentralisa-tion appears to have weakened environmental protection. Poorer regions have relied mainly on diminish-ing federal allocations, together with resources from their local and regional environmental funds, to keep environmental institutions functioning.

As the role of Russia's federal environmental institutions has diminished, and as regional approaches have followed different paths, there has been a growing concern that Russia is losing a federal framework to address trans-regional issues (including the management of extensive river systems, such as the Volga, and the environmental issues associated with inter-regional trade).

Sources: OECD, 1999; Kotov and Nikitina; Zamparutti and Kozeltsev.

---

initiatives (Box 3.6 describes the experience of two Bulgarian cities). There have been a wide variety of approaches, due to the great differences in the scope of problems and the capacities of institutions. Donors have helped to support many of these initiatives.

Local and Regional Action Programmes, in particular, have been effective means of implementing the EAP. In CEE countries, these initiatives – as well as broader, long-term Local Agenda 21 projects – have increasingly been self-sustaining, financed by local resources and developed by local experts. In contrast, national and donor support will continue to be crucial for initiatives in the NIS. In a few NIS, national environmental policies have been closely tied to regional and local initiatives. In Kazakhstan, for example, the new environmental and sustainable development policy was based on environmental priorities identified at the regional level (Box 3.9). In other countries, including Moldova and Ukraine, national policies have promoted the development of REAPs and LEAPs. A number of donors and inter-national organisations have supported these efforts: in Moldova, for example, UNDP has started to assist LEAPs. Donors have supported local and regional environmental institutions in other areas as well. The EC TACIS Programme has sponsored "twinning" between CEEC/NIS cities and cities in Western Europe. A number of donors have provided technical assistance directly to reform-oriented local and regional governments in the NIS.

Box 3.6.   **Local Environmental Action Programmes in Bulgaria**

The city of Stara Zagora started to work on its LEAP in 1993, and the city of Kurdzhali began the following year. Both based their programmes on Bulgaria's 1992 Environmental Strategy Study and its 1994 Update (Box 3.10). In Stara Zagora, the city government asked an NGO, *Ecoglasnost-Stara Zagora*, to co-ordinate preparation. In Kurdzhali, the city directly oversaw preparation of the LEAP. The US government, working through an NGO, the Institute for Sustainable Communities, assisted both efforts.

These cities used priority-setting methods to identify key problems, together with participatory methods to discuss and decide on actions. In both cities, air pollution from motor vehicles, household and district heating, and industrial plants were major problems, as was solid waste generation and management. Their LEAPs identified policy measures and low-cost investments to address these issues, including: better traffic management; energy efficiency initiatives; low-cost loans to encourage conversion from coal to natural gas heating; and higher waste fees to help finance better solid waste collection and disposal. In both cities, industrial enterprises undertook some measures to reduce air pollution.

Sources: EAP Task Force, OECD, 1996*a*.

In many CEE countries, the role of local and regional governments is likely to increase, particularly as the EC has noted that local governments in candidate countries need to build institutional capacities and financial resources for implementing environmental policy (EC, 1998*a*). Many NIS cover huge land areas, and local and especially regional institutions can play a key role in environmental management; however, the slow pace of economic and political reform will likely hinder progress in many countries.

3.   Reforming Environmental Policy[1]

The environmental policies developed before transition had several fundamental defects, including:
- overly ambitious planning goals, based on unrealistic standards;
- centralised decision-making and regulated allocation of resources;
- a focus on technological solutions;
- severely restricted public access to information and participation; and
- poor implementation.

Environmental plans often presented long "wish lists" of investment projects, while priorities effectively were set in closed discussions about state budget and resource allocations. Little attention was given to monitoring and evaluating the results of such plans.

The EAP urged that countries in the region take a new approach to policy development and implementation. It emphasised that "the most urgent problems will only be solved if clear goals are established at the outset and the most efficient way to achieve each goal is identified." Nearly all countries in the region have developed new national environmental policies in the transition period (Annex VI lists the main policies that CEEC and NIS prepared through mid-1998). The scope and objectives of these new policies have varied significantly (Box 3.7). After the 1993 Lucerne Conference that endorsed the EAP, countries have used the EAP's recommendations as reference points for policy development; moreover, many countries developed *National Environmental Action Programmes* (NEAPs) that were directly inspired by the EAP.

Sustained, high-level political support has been one of the crucial factors for policy success. In addition, donors and international organisations have assisted many CEEC/NIS to develop their environmental policies. However, external assistance has been most effective when it has supported ongoing reforms rather than imposing policy directions. In addition, the EAP Task Force has played an important role in promoting an exchange of experience among CEEC/NIS officials who have co-ordinated the development of NEAPs and other policies (Box 3.8).

Box 3.7. Main types of CEEC/NIS environmental policies

– *Broad strategies*. Many CEEC and a few NIS – including Poland and the Baltic States – developed comprehensive environmental strategies early in their transition. These identified major national environmental problems, presented basic, internationally recognised principles for environmental management, and proposed key areas for new legislation. In CEEC, in particular, these strategies represented a clear break from environmental programmes under central planning.

– *Action-oriented policies*. Many countries, including the three Baltic States, prepared detailed, short-term programmes as a follow-up to their broad strategies. These usually identified priorities and clear objectives, and often were called NEAPs. A number of countries combined this approach directly with their broad strategies. Many CEEC and NIS – including Bulgaria, Moldova and Kazakhstan – used their first policy documents of the transition both to establish principles and institutions for environmental management and to identify short-term actions.

– *Incremental strategies*. In a few NIS such as Belarus, Russia and Ukraine, new policies built on existing approaches. These documents suffered the weaknesses of their predecessors: they identified many long-term goals without setting priorities among them or developing strategies to achieve them.

– In addition, all countries have developed *sectoral strategies* for specific fields such as biodiversity, air pollution management and water management. These have often followed broader national strategies.

While CEEC/NIS have adopted different types of environmental policies, several trends and lessons regarding policy development have emerged. Most importantly, the development of successful policies has incorporated four key elements:

– *priority-setting*, within and across environmental media, based on transparent criteria and analysis as well as necessary political considerations;

– *broad participation* of major stakeholders to build political and public support for action;

– cost-effective and financially feasible *implementation plans* that establish realistic objectives and quantitative targets and involve an appropriate mix of policy, institutional and investment actions; and

– *monitoring* to track the impact of policy implementation on environmental quality, to guide periodic *policy reviews and updates*.

A number of countries have used all these elements in the development of their national environmental policies; others have introduced specific ones, depending on the context. In all cases, the policy *process* has been as important as the eventual policy *document* – indeed, the process of policy development has played a strong role in strengthening environmental institutions and policy integration and in setting the stage for policy implementation.

Box 3.8. The NEAP Co-ordinators Network

The EAP Task Force has supported the development of national policies in the region by organising a network of CEEC and NIS officials responsible for co-ordinating policy development. There were six full meetings of the "NEAP Co-ordinators Network" from 1994 to 1998, as well as three meetings of NIS co-ordinators to focus on specific problems in their countries. Overall, the Task Force has played an important role in several areas:

– accelerating the dissemination of key principles and best practices for environmental management;

– supporting a process of "learning by doing" and information exchange among policy co-ordinators;

– encouraging the engagement of NGOs in the process; and

– providing a framework to increase dialogue and co-operation between countries in the region on the one hand and donors, IFIs and international organisations on the other.

3.1. *Priority-setting*

The identification of realistic priorities has been one of the most important factors in successful policies. In the best cases, priority-setting exercises have brought together a wide range of stakeholders, which have helped gather and examine environmental information and have participated in the priority-setting exercises. Priority-setting also requires strong analysis of policy issues, based on objective and transparent criteria. Combining these elements has been difficult, although many CEEC and NIS have made strong progress: for example, in Kazakhstan regional working groups applied priority-setting methods developed by national and international experts (Box 3.9). In contrast, some NIS have not yet introduced priority-setting, and their policies have continued to present long lists of proposed actions and objectives.

Box 3.9. **Kazakhstan's NEAP for Sustainable Development**

Kazakhstan's National Environmental Action Programme for Sustainable Development benefited from high-level political support, strong external assistance, a dedicated "core team" of national officials and experts, and a fairly broad participatory process to identify national priorities.

In 1996, The President of Kazakhstan asked the government to prepare a national development strategy, including environmental and sustainable development strategies. The Ministry of Environment formed a team to prepare a National Environmental Action Programme for Sustainable Development (NEAP/SD), drawing on both the EAP and *Agenda* 21 as well as the Environment Programme for Europe. Kazakhstan's national and regional governments funded the NEAP/SD; a number of external sources assisted, including the World Bank, UNDP, the EC TACIS Programme and the German government. This assistance proved quite effective: donors recognised that the NEAP/SD office could be a strong counterpart; in turn, foreign experts played an important supporting role by introducing new policy methods and analysis, but they remained advisors, not leaders, within the overall process, which was co-ordinated by the NEAP/SD office.

The NEAP/SD office organised regional consultations to identify and set priorities among major environmental problems, using the methodologies developed through external assistance. These meetings were followed by national summary seminars to formulate overall policy decisions and actions. All these meetings brought together regional and local officials, representatives of other ministries, NGO leaders, and national and external experts. Through this open process, the first attempted in the country, the participants reached an overall consensus on policy actions, resisting pressures from special interests.

Seven priority issues were identified, grouped according to geographical area:
  – shortage of water resources (southern Kazakhstan);
  – degradation of pastures and arable lands (southern Kazakhstan);
  – air pollution in urban areas (eastern Kazakhstan);
  – solid industrial and consumer waste (eastern Kazakhstan);
  – water pollution by waste waters (eastern Kazakhstan);
  – water pollution from oil extraction (Caspian Sea area); and
  – lack of forests needed to protect biodiversity.

Kazakhstan's government adopted the NEAP/SD in late 1997, as part of the President's "Strategy 2030". At the same time, the Ministry of Environment was merged with the Ministry of Natural Resources, strengthening its capacity to implement the programme. The new policy did not, however, include a clear financing strategy. The Ministry has proposed establishing a national environmentai fund to help finance the actions identified, but indicated that donor and IFI financing will be needed for many of the projects.

Source: Kazakhstan reports to the EAP Task Force.

Many countries have made serious efforts to apply the priority-setting criteria proposed by the EAP: protecting human health; halting actions that result in high economic costs, such as the destruction of valuable natural resources and pollution damage to buildings and equipment; and stopping irreversible threats to biodiversity. In addition, the EAP also underlined the importance of identifying cost-effective solutions. In many countries, these EAP criteria have provided a starting point for the development of more detailed national criteria (for example, some countries have included social and economic issues among their criteria).

Environmental authorities in the region have faced several obstacles in making in-depth analyses of environmental problems and potential solutions. First, in many countries environmental information systems did not provide crucial data on environmental conditions and pressures in forms that policy makers could use. As a result, in a number of CEEC and NIS environmental authorities have had to seek additional data; often this has ultimately improved these information systems. On the other hand, the continuing decline of information systems in some NIS has presented an ongoing hurdle for policy development (Chapter 5). Second, communication between different departments within environment ministries has usually been poor. In developing new national policies, many ministries have set up central policy departments to bridge these distances and to lead an overall analysis of environmental problems; in addition, representatives of different departments have participated actively in the policy process.

A third problem has been the weak capacity of environmental authorities to conduct and utilise economic and other types of analysis. In some countries, national experts in universities and consulting companies have been able to undertake these types of analysis for policy-makers. In others, external assistance has played a key role in providing experts for this analysis. In either case, environmental authorities have had to learn how to manage national and foreign consultants: where this has not occurred, they have not been able to use expert advice properly, or have not established sufficient "ownership" of the results. Despite these difficulties, a growing number of countries have used methods such as risk assessment, the valuation of environmental damages, and cost estimates of mitigation measures to identify cost-effective actions. Moreover, these have proved valuable tools for convincing economic ministries and others to assign a higher priority to environmental policy. At the same time, further skills development is needed in many countries, particularly in the NIS.

3.2. Broad participation

The development of participatory approaches has been a learning process. At the start of the transition, environmental officials in many countries were reluctant to encourage participation or share decision-making, even within their ministries. In a few countries, policies were developed by a small group of officials without strong consultation within environment ministries. Progress has been slow, particularly in the NIS. However, officials have learned that participation can broaden support for new policies, and environmental authorities have frequently improved their mechanisms for participation. In particular, many authorities have expanded their co-operation with NGOs; through this process, many NGOs have developed their skills for policy analysis and dialogue (Chapter 4).

3.3. Effective implementation plans

The most effective policies have established clear sequences of priority actions. Some early policy documents, such as Poland's 1991 National Environmental Policy, identified short, medium and long-term issues for action. In other countries, such as the Baltic States, broad strategies identified short-term priorities that were addressed in subsequent action-oriented programmes such as NEAPs.

Nearly all environmental policies in the region have lacked adequate financing strategies – a key problem, in particular for implementation, and a common one across all sectors of public policy in the region.[2] Some CEEC/NIS environmental policies have included cost estimates of investment and other actions to be undertaken; a few have identified potential revenue sources. However, few efforts have been made to systematically review potential costs and revenues and to balance the two. In addition, although most environmental policies cite the Polluter Pays Principle, many countries need to take further steps to implement it. At the same time, the severe economic crisis in the NIS has posed a significant obstacle to increased public and private spending on the environment. A pilot financing strategy prepared in Lithuania could provide a model for other countries to consider. (Chapter 6 discusses several key issues related to financing.)

3.4. *Evaluating and revising policies*

Provisions for evaluating and revising policies can help keep a focus on their results and maintain their momentum. In some countries, environmental authorities must report regularly on the progress of policy implementation. The Czech Ministry of Environment has had to present a yearly report to Parliament on the progress of the 1995 State Environment Policy; Moldova's Environment Ministry has set up an office to monitor NEAP implementation and make regular reports.

As yet, only a few countries have formally revised their national policies. Bulgaria revised its 1992 Environmental Strategy Study after two years (Box 3.10). (More recently, Bulgaria's government has updated its environmental policy goals in a cross-sectoral National Development Plan for 2000 through 2006.) Other countries plan to review environmental policy progress regularly: for example, Estonia's NEAP includes plans for revisions every three years. In some cases, environmental authorities have reviewed their progress towards national policy goals in the development of later sectoral policies.

Box 3.10.   **Bulgaria's environmental strategies**

Bulgaria's 1992 Environmental Strategy Study was developed with strong support from the World Bank and the US government – both provided experts to assist, in particular, with analysis and priority-setting. This support helped build the Environment Ministry's capacities for policy development, and Bulgarian officials and experts played a much more central role in co-ordinating and preparing a 1994 update of the Strategy, although World Bank and US support continued. Moreover, participation of Bulgarian experts and stakeholders outside government, limited for the 1992 strategy, was stronger in preparing the later one. The 1994 revision was undertaken because the 1992 version had assumed that Bulgaria's government was about to start rapid economic reforms; this did not happen, and the 1994 strategy identified additional approaches, such as low-cost pollution prevention actions, in the context of slow reform.

Both the 1992 and 1994 strategies brought important advances in environmental programmes and contributed to reductions in pollution. Both policies identified air pollution as a priority:

- The 1992 strategy proposed revising Bulgaria's stringent and unenforced ambient air standards; in 1994, the Ministries of Environment and Health jointly agreed to revise standards for eight key pollutants, including particulates, sulphur dioxide and lead.

- The 1994 strategy identified high air emissions of lead and other heavy metals from non-ferrous metallurgy plants as a health risk deserving immediate action. After pressure from environmental authorities (as well as ongoing public protests), the lead and zinc smelters in Plovdiv and Kurdjali installed improved particulate control equipment to reduce these emissions.

Overall, however, implementation was hindered by unexpected changes in government that occurred just after each strategy was prepared. As a result, only the Environment Ministry – not the full government – approved each of them.

Source: OECD, 1996*a*.

3.5. *Strengthening environmental policies*

In 1998, the EAP Task Force reviewed the development of NEAPs and related policy initiatives in the region. Its report, presented to the June 1998 Aarhus Ministerial Conference, included a series of recommendations for strengthening policy development (Box 3.11).

Box 3.11.   **EAP Task Force recommendations on NEAP development**

1. The main principles in the EAP remain valid and should be applied more rigorously. This would help countries acceding to the EU to devise cost-effective accession strategies, and the NIS to move more decisively from the development to the implementation of NEAPs.

2. All countries should strengthen the "demand" for environmental improvement. While this will be shaped, in part, by the level of economic development, demand can be stimulated by:
   - implementing market reforms which promote more efficient use of resources;
   - establishing a clear environmental policy framework which builds on these reforms; and
   - building a constituency involving parliamentarians, NGOs and other stakeholders in order to strengthen public and political support for environmental improvement.

3. Environmental policies, including NEAPs, will be most effective when they are based on:
   - priority-setting, within and across environmental media, based on political considerations and transparent criteria and analysis;
   - participation of major stakeholders to build political and public support for agreed actions;
   - cost-effective and financially feasible implementation plans which establish realistic objectives and quantitative targets and involve an appropriate mix of policy, institutional and investment actions; and
   - active monitoring to track the relations between policy implementation and changes in environmental quality for periodic policy reviews and updates.

4. Short-term, results-oriented programmes should be developed as part of longer-term strategies; ultimately, strategies for sustainable development. Initially, priority should be given to establishing an appropriate policy and institutional framework; amongst other things, this will facilitate the elaboration of effective investment programmes at a later stage. Achieving targets and registering success are the best ways to promote self-sustaining programmes.

5. Environment ministries should build the following capacities to drive the development and implementation of NEAPs:
   - consolidated responsibility for the elaboration of an integrated environmental policy;
   - mechanisms to engage a wide range of experts, as well as all relevant stakeholders;
   - an information system to support decision-making and the dissemination of information to the public; and
   - staff who can manage, support and facilitate the analytical, policy and consultative processes.

6. The capacity of environment ministries to promote the integration of environmental considerations into decision-making in other sectors should also be strengthened. In particular, greater use of economic analysis would help demonstrate more effectively the benefits of environmental policies; while the development of financial plans as part of NEAPs would facilitate their implementation. Priority should be given initially to integration in areas where "win-win" opportunities are greatest; eventually more difficult trade-offs will also need to be addressed.

7. Further decentralisation of environmental management responsibilities and the development of environmental action programmes and initiatives at the regional and local level should be encouraged, and the results of successful initiatives disseminated more widely. However, decentralisation should be accompanied by the means for implementation and avoid excessive fragmentation of capacities, resources and responsibilities.

8. External support should facilitate a country-owned process in which priorities are set by the host country, and fill in gaps in local knowledge and capacity. Its goal should be to support the establishment of a self-sustaining process of environmental policy development and implementation. External finance should complement domestic resources in CEEC; while in the NIS it could have an important catalytic effect during the transition period in helping to create domestic financing mechanisms to facilitate NEAP implementation.

9. As priorities become more differentiated, the EAP Task Force should continue to provide a flexible framework in which CEEC and NIS support each other and exchange experience on effective environmental policies. It should also help to further strengthen co-operation with various stakeholders, including western partners. As the transition develops, more concrete actions are needed to engage the private sector in a constructive dialogue on improving environmental conditions.

Source: EAP Task Force, 1998.

4. Policy Integration

Policy integration refers to the process of improving linkages between the environment and the economy. Integration is vital for environmental protection and for progress towards sustainable development (Box 3.12). The EAP emphasised that key CEEC/NIS sectors such as energy, industry, transport and agriculture have profound effects on the environment, and it urged governments in the region to strengthen policy integration. The transition provided a window of opportunity for introducing "win-win" approaches into sectoral policies, such as programmes to encourage cleaner production in industry.

Box 3.12.   Policy integration

Policy integration is the process of improving linkages between the environment and the economy – as such, it should contribute directly to the goal of sustainable development. It includes:

– recognising and defining the key elements of environment-economy interdependence;

– exploiting opportunities for achieving environmental and economic objectives together ("win-win" policies and actions); and

– evaluating trade-offs among competing objectives when "win-win" paths are not available.

To undertake these tasks, governments should take environmental costs and benefits into account in their economic policy decisions. Co-ordination between government policies for the environment and those for the economy can be undertaken through: improved institutional co-ordination between ministries; the inclusion of economic objectives in environmental policies (environmental policy choices should, *inter alia*, take account of economic costs and benefits) and of environmental objectives in sectoral strategies, such as those for energy, industry and transport; and the use of government instruments and actions to implement such goals.

Integration also requires government policies and private initiatives that encourage individual economic actors to factor environmental concerns into their decisions – this is emphasised by the Polluter Pays Principle (for pollution) and the User Pays Principle (for natural resource use).

Source: OECD, 1996c.

Over the course of the transition, countries that have pursued economic reform have indeed seen reductions in some environmental pressures, particularly in industrial air pollution (Chapter 2). However, in some countries with wide fiscal and monetary distortions, perverse incentives have promoted rent-seeking rather than efficiency; as a result, there have been few "win-win" opportunities. Even in the countries most advanced in economic reform, much remains to be done to improve the coherence between their economic and sectoral policies and their environmental goals.

4.1. Institutional aspects

Under central planning, most CEEC and NIS governments had rigid vertical structures with little working level communication between sectors. In most countries, officials in economics, industry and other ministries paid little attention to environmental issues, and public and political pressure was often needed in the early years of transition to encourage sectoral authorities to consider environmental issues (Chapter 4).

As a result of these pressures – and also in recognition of the cross-cutting effects of environmental policies – environmental and sectoral ministries in some countries have started to work together more closely. Many governments have established inter-ministerial committees to promote co-operation on

75

environmental issues. In some cases, particularly in Central and Eastern Europe, environmental and sectoral ministries have co-operated on joint programmes: for example, in Poland the environment and industry ministries have worked together to encourage cleaner production in industry. In addition, environment ministries in many CEE countries and some NIS have involved their counterparts in the preparation of environmental policies.

In a number of CEE countries, sectoral ministries and agencies have established their own environmental offices to address environmental issues influencing their sector. These have included environmental impact assessments, which have been required for most large energy and transport projects in CEE countries. Several international environmental agreements have had important sectoral implications, in particular for energy and industry, which contribute large shares of the pollutants regulated under the Geneva Convention on Long-Range Transboundary Air Pollution as well as the greenhouse gases regulated by the Framework Convention on Climate Change. The EU accession process will introduce further environmental requirements that will affect many sectors (Annex III).

4.2. Sectoral policies and "win-win" actions

Sectoral policy strategies in a number of countries have referred to environmental objectives. However, few such strategies have specified actions to achieve environmental objectives.

In a few cases, environmental and sectoral authorities have agreed on "win-win" policy actions that pursue objectives in both spheres. Environmental and privatisation officials in the Czech Republic, Poland, Romania and other CEE countries have put in place mechanisms to address environmental issues in privatisation. These mechanisms have led to clean-up of environmental damage and have removed a potential obstacle to investment in newly privatised enterprises. In Hungary, environment and agriculture ministries have jointly developed and implemented programmes to monitor the degradation of agricultural land and to protect biodiversity in farming areas. In these cases, sectoral and environment ministries have agreed on "win-win" policies where mutual opportunities and benefits were clear.

On the other hand, policy integration has been limited where sectoral and environmental policies need to make trade-offs. Reconciling transport and environment in CEEC/NIS, for example, requires difficult trade-offs as well as a search for new solutions. Indeed, OECD countries are only starting to search for solutions to environmental problems related to transport; during the transition, most CEE countries have converged with existing transport policies and conditions in OECD countries rather than considering alternate paths (Box 3.13).

There have been fewer examples of effective policy integration in the NIS. Institutional problems have been one reason: for example, NIS governments have retained a vertical structure of government and have made little reform of ministries; environmental authorities have continued to have a low standing in government; and public pressure on sectoral ministries to address environmental issues has not been strong. As a result, officials in many sectoral ministries have little incentive to pay attention to environmental goals.

The slow pace of economic reform has severely limited "win-win" opportunities. In Russia, indirect government subsidies to enterprises, weak bankruptcy provisions and confiscatory tax regimes have helped perpetuate a "virtual economy" relying heavily on barter trade (Chapter 2). Russia has only slowly reformed energy prices, and collection rates for fuel and electricity payments have been poor. In these circumstances, Russian enterprises have few incentives to pursue energy efficiency or cleaner production programmes even when these could reduce their production costs. Further economic reform will be needed in many NIS before "win-win" opportunities become apparent.

In evaluating the progress of policy integration in CEEC/NIS, it must be recognised that progress in OECD countries has been slow. A 1996 report to OECD environment ministers noted that "Environmental aspects often receive little attention at the strategic level, and consideration only at later planning stages of projects, while the environmental implications of new sectoral policies are not always recognised" (OECD, 1996b).

Box 3.13.   **Transport and environmental policy: difficult integration**

In most CEE countries and many parts of the NIS, motor vehicle numbers and use, both for passenger and freight transport, are growing rapidly. As a result, motor vehicles are an increasingly important source of urban air pollution and other environmental problems (Chapter 2). Concurrently, urban and national public transport systems in the region, once extensive and strongly subsidised, have faced severe financial problems and declining service and ridership. Motor vehicle traffic in the region is expected to continue growing rapidly. A study of 14 CEEC/NIS predicted that, if current policies continue, by 2010 passenger car use will have doubled compared to 1994 levels; by 2030, it will have increased a further 150%. Road freight traffic is expected to increase even more rapidly.

To tackle motor vehicle air pollution, a number of CEEC governments have adopted stringent environmental standards for motor vehicle fuels – for example, reducing the maximum level of sulphur in diesel for transport fuels – and for emissions from new automobiles. These new standards are based on those in the EU. In addition, many CEEC/NIS have reduced the lead content of gasoline and have pledged to phase out leaded gasoline by 2005 (Chapter 2). However, some air pollution emissions – in particular those of NO_x – may continue to rise despite these measures, due to the increase in motor vehicle numbers and use. Motor vehicle emissions of CO_2, a greenhouse gas, are expected to increase rapidly.

Despite these trends, CEEC/NIS transport policies have integrated environmental goals. A few recent policies have referred to such goals. Hungary's 1996 framework transportation policy identified the protection of human life and the environment as one of its four strategic "directions", but it proposed large investments in road infrastructure, which could further increase motor vehicle traffic (Hungary's policy cites integration with EU economies as a major reason for its emphasis on new road infrastructure). Similarly, an independent review of transportation policy in Poland estimated that, up to 2010, the government will spend over 10 times as much on road investments as rail investments. There are only a few cases where transport and environment ministries have worked closely together: in Lithuania, for example, these ministries co-operated on the country's 1992 Transport and Environment Programme and on subsequent transport documents.

At the local level, many CEEC cities have entered a vicious circle of "more cars, more traffic, worsening public transport" – ironically, at the same time that Western European cities are trying to reverse these trends and reduce transport-related environmental problems. These problems are estimated to represent as much as 3 to 4% of national GDP in OECD countries. A 1995 ECMT/OECD Workshop urged CEEC cities to learn from western experiences, and to develop integrated urban transport strategies focusing on two areas of action: managing traffic growth and restructuring public transport systems. The integration of transport and environmental objectives in international assistance and finance to the region has also been difficult. For example, IFI financing appears to have strongly favoured highway projects over those for public transport. International initiatives may provide some impetus for greater policy integration. OECD has developed sustainable transport guidelines for Member countries. In 1997, transport and environment ministers from the UN/ECE region met in Vienna to discuss common issues; in 1998, high-level transport and environment officials from G-8 countries met in the United Kingdom and concluded that further policy integration was necessary, in particular with regard to infrastructure choices.

Sources: ECMT; ECMT/OECD; ISD; RIIA; Trafico Verkehrsplanung.

4.3. *Strengthening policy integration*

Recently the EU has devoted greater political attention to integration: for example, at their June 1998 Cardiff summit, EU heads of government called for greater attention to environmental issues in EU agriculture, energy and transport policies. This could encourage CEE candidate countries to undertake similar efforts.

The process of EU accession will likely prompt candidate countries to devote greater attention to policy integration at the working level. For example, CEE governments will have to ensure stronger interministerial co-operation to address EU requirements in areas such as chemicals management. Greater, stronger policy integration could reduce the high costs of approximation with the EU's environmental legislation (EC, 1998a).

Recent global and regional initiatives could encourage policy integration in both CEE countries and the NIS. In particular, under the Kyoto Protocol on climate change several countries have pledged to cut or limit their greenhouse gas emissions (compared to 1990 levels); this may encourage integration with the energy sector, a key source of emissions. The Protocol launched several mechanisms that could produce new assistance and finance for climate change projects in countries across the region and also provide incentives for integration (Annex IV).

NOTES

1. This section is based largely on the EAP Task Force's report to the 1998 Aarhus Conference, *Evaluation of Progress in Developing and Implementing National Environmental Action Programmes* (NEAPs) *in* CEEC/NIS (EAP Task Force, 1998).

2. This stems from the legacy of central planning. CEE governments have also overlooked financial and even budgetary analysis in other sectors, as well as in preparing their national programmes for EU accession. In its first review of accession efforts, the European Commission noted that "none of the candidate countries undertook a comprehensive needs assessment involving realistic costing and budgetary forecasting" (EC, 1998*b*).

REFERENCES

Demydenko, A. (1998),
  personal communication, UNDP, Tashkent, Uzbekistan, December.

EAP Task Force (1998),
  Evaluation of Progress in Developing and Implementing National Environmental Action Programmes (NEAPs) in CEEC/NIS, OECD, Paris.

European Bank for Reconstruction and Development (EBRD) (1998),
  Transition Report 1998, London.

European Commission (EC) (1998a),
  Accession Strategies for Environment: Meeting the Challenge of Enlargement with the Candidate Countries in Central and Eastern Europe, Communication from the Commission to the Council, the European Parliament, the Economic and Social Committee, the Committee of the Regions and the Candidate Countries in Central and Eastern Europe, Brussels.

European Commission (EC) (1998b),
  Reports on Progress Towards Accession by Each of the Candidate Countries: Composite Paper, [http://europa.eu.int/comm/dg1a/enlarge], Brussels].

European Conference of Ministers of Transport and OECD (ECMT/OECD) (1996),
  Sustainable Transport in Central and Eastern European Cities, Paris.

European Conference of Ministers of Transport (ECMT) (1997),
  Issues in Sustainable Transport: The Case of Hungary, Paris, February.

Fournier, J. (1998),
  Administrative Reform in the Commission Opinions Concerning the Accession of the Central and Eastern European Countries to the European Union, in OECD/SIGMA, *Preparing Public Administrations for the European Administrative Space*, Sigma paper No. 23, OECD.

Georgieva, K. and J. Moore (1997),
  Bulgaria, in J. Klarer and B. Moldan, eds., *The Environmental Challenge for Central and Eastern European Economies in Transition*, John Wiley & Sons, Chichester, UK.

Harvard Institute for International Development and Environmental Policy and Institutional Resources Group (HIID and IRG) (1998),
  Measuring the Environmental Transition in Eastern Europe and the Newly Independent States, prepared for US AID, Washington, DC, May.

Institute for Sustainable Development (ISD) (1998),
  Options for the Development of the Transportation System in Poland, Warsaw, February.

Jehlicka, P. and M. Branis (1998),
  Environmental Protection and Capacity Building in the Czech Republic, in KPMG, *Environmental Policy and the Role of Foreign Assistance in Central and Eastern Europe*, report to the Danish Environmental Protection Agency, Copenhagen.

Kolodko, G.W. (1997),
  The Economics and Politics of Transition: Observations of a Policymaker, presentation to the OECD Development Centre Workshop on the Economics and Politics of Transition to an Open Market Economy, Paris, December.

Kotov, V. and E. Nikitina (1998),
  Environmental Protection and Capacity Building in Russia, in KPMG, *Environmental Policy and the Role of Foreign Assistance in Central and Eastern Europe*, report to the Danish Environmental Protection Agency, Copenhagen.

Lovei, M. and C. Weiss (1997),
  Environmental Management and Institutions in OECD Countries: Lessons from Experience, Environment Department Paper No. 46, World Bank, Washington, DC, March.

Margulis, S. and T. Vetleseter (1998),
  Environmental Capacity Building: A Portfolio Review, in *Environment Matters at the World Bank*, World Bank, Washington, DC.

OECD (1995),
> Donor Assistance to Capacity Development in Environment, Paris.

OECD (1996a),
> Environmental Performance Reviews: Bulgaria, Paris.

OECD (1996b),
> Environmental Performance in OECD Countries: Progress in the 1990s, Paris.

OECD (1996c),
> Integrating Environment and Economy: Progress in the 1990s, Paris.

OECD (1998),
> Public Management in Support of Social and Economic Objectives: Issues for Discussion, background paper for the Emerging Market Economy Forum Workshop on Public Management, Paris, December.

OECD (1999),
> Environmental Performance Reviews: Russia, Paris (forthcoming).

Ponizova, O. (1998),
> Public Participation in the NIS, background paper for the EAP Task Force secretariat, Eco-Accord, Moscow, April.

Royal Institute of International Affairs/Chatham House (RIIA) (1998),
> G-8 Environment and Transport Futures Forum, London.

Stern, N. (1998),
> Foreword to Transition Report 1998, EBRD, London.

Stiglitz, J. (1998),
> Whither Reform? Ten years of the Transition, speech to the World Bank Conference on Development Economics, April.

Trafico Verkehrsplanung (1997),
> Pilot project – Environmentally Sustainable Transportation in the CEI Countries in Transition in Europe – Case Study – Executive summary, report prepared for UNEP, OECD and the Austrian Federal Ministry for the Environment, Youth and Family Affairs, Vienna, October.

United Nations Economic Commission for Europe (UN/ECE) (1997),
> Environmental Performance Reviews: Slovenia, United Nations, Geneva.

United Nations Economic Commission for Europe (UN/ECE) (1998),
> Environmental Performance Reviews: Republic of Moldova, United Nations, Geneva.

World Bank (1996),
> World Development Report 1996: From Plan to Market, Oxford University Press, Oxford.

World Bank (1997),
> World Development Report 1997: The State in a Changing World, Oxford University Press, Oxford.

World Bank (1998),
> Assessing Aid: What Works, What Doesn't, and Why, Oxford University Press, Oxford.

Zamparutti, A. and M. Kozeltsev (1998),
> Environmental Issues in Tomsk Oblast, in A Regional Approach to Industrial Restructuring in the Tomsk Region, Russian Federation, OECD, Paris.

Chapter 4

PUBLIC AND NGO PARTICIPATION[1]

1. Introduction

The EAP emphasised that public awareness of environmental problems, public pressure to solve them, and public participation in decision-making were essential for the development and implementation of effective environmental policies. These had been driving forces for environmental protection in OECD countries, but had been suppressed in centrally planned economies. The EAP urged the new democratic governments in the region to improve their provision of environmental information, in order to strengthen public awareness and develop mechanisms for public participation in environmental policy discussions and decisions. Moreover, the EAP stressed that environmental NGOs that bring together concerned citizens can contribute to the policy process – in OECD countries these groups have played a key role in translating public awareness of environmental issues into political pressure for action. Environmental NGOs are part of the region's growing "civil society" of independent associations and networks, which is filling the once-empty space between governments and the public; as such, their presence and work can also strengthen democracy in the region (Box 4.1). For these reasons, the EAP urged CEEC/NIS environmental authorities to strengthen their co-operation with NGOs.

This chapter reviews the development of public participation in environmental policy. It first considers public interest in and concern for the environment, using public opinion surveys as rough indicators. Two key actors are discussed: the media, which in most countries have been the public's main source of information on the environment, and environmental NGOs.

The chapter then reviews the progress of CEEC/NIS governments in establishing legal rights and administrative mechanisms for public access to government information, decision-making processes and the courts. These sections highlight public and NGO actions that have made use of these rights and mechanisms.

2. Public Opinion and the Environment

Throughout the region, environmental issues were prominent in the political, economic and social changes of the late 1980s. The environment was the first "open" issue for political activity in many countries. The 1986 Chernobyl disaster catalysed environmental movements as well as wider opposition to communist regimes (Stec). Environmental movements played an important role in the protests that brought down a number of regimes and, in some countries, green parties were prominent in the first non-communist governments (Box 4.2). In the early 1990s, public concern and political attention to environmental issues decreased as the economic problems of transition worsened. Many anti-communist leaders active in environmental movements moved to mainstream political formations after the fall of the communist regimes, and green parties lost votes and power.

Opinion surveys provide some information on the general public's concern for the environment. Their results need to be interpreted carefully, however. Although surveys are now common – they are frequently used in CEE countries to gauge public opinion – these are new tools for the region. Their results are not always reliable, particularly in the NIS, as many people are wary of unsolicited questions about their opinions.

Box 4.1. **The development of democracy and civil society**

The development of democratic institutions and societies has been one of the main challenges of transition. Democracy involves several formal elements. One recent study defined these as: inclusive citizenship; the rule of law; separation of powers; elected power-holders; free and fair elections; freedom of expression and alternative sources of information; associational autonomy; and civil control over the security forces (Kaldor and Vejvoda). Just as important for working democratic systems are the attitudes of citizens towards democratic institutions (Weingast) and the presence of a civil society that contributes to the interplay between citizens and decision-makers. Key elements of civil society include "a free and independent media, political parties representing diverse opinions and positions, trade unions and employers' associations, and educational establishments that open intellectual horizons," as well as NGOs such as formal and informal citizens' groups (Cohen).

Democracy and civil society have prospered most in transition countries in Central Europe, such as the Czech Republic, Hungary and Poland. Proximity to Western European democracies may have encouraged this progress. The process of EU accession is expected to strengthen democratic development in these and other candidate countries. The EU has indicated that the development of democratic systems will be a key criterion for accession (Annex III). Progress has been difficult in other countries. In many NIS the ongoing economic crisis, together with the difficulties that new democratic institutions have faced in formulating and carrying out policies during the transition, have reduced public support for all reforms. (Some NIS, such as Belarus, have moved awFay from both democratic and market-oriented reforms.)

Despite these difficulties, many countries across the region have made important efforts to establish more democratic systems. Many of them have seen strong growth in the number of NGOs active in areas ranging from cultural activities to social assistance to environmental protection. By the mid-1990s, according to one estimate, there were about 3 000 NGOs in Georgia, 12 000 in Hungary, 10 000 in Slovakia, and 50 000 in Russia.

Sources: Cohen; Kaldor and Vejvoda; Weingast.

Recent surveys have indicated that, at least in a few CEE countries, the public has continued to view environmental issues as important. In a 1997 survey in Poland, respondents listed damage to the environment as the second most important threat to the country after crime (in the early 1990s, environmental issues were ranked first in importance); in most other CEE countries, surveys have ranked damage to the

Box 4.2. **Environmental movements in late 1980s**

In Central and Eastern Europe, environmental movements such as the Danube Circle in Hungary, Eco-glasnost in Bulgaria, the Lithuanian Green Movement, and the Polish Ecology Club played an important role in protests against communist regimes in the late 1980s. Their opposition halted potentially dangerous projects started under central planning, such as the Zarnowiec nuclear power plant in Poland and the Gabcikovo Dam in Hungary. In several countries environmentalists, through green parties and other political movements, became part of the first democratic governing coalitions. The Slovenian Green Party, for example, controlled four ministries, including those responsible for environment and energy.

In the USSR, many environmental groups formed in the late 1980s organised public protests against potentially dangerous projects. In 1989, NGOs campaigned against a project to reverse the flow of Siberia's "northern rivers": more then 500 000 people in 100 cities took part in demonstrations, and 1 million signed petitions. In a few republics, groups such as Moldova's Ecological Movement were prominent supporters of political reform. A number of green parties formed as the USSR began to break up. In Ukraine, they were influential in Parliament in the early 1990s.

environment lower. Respondents to a 1996 poll in Hungary identified it as the sixth most important threat to society after, for example, crime, poverty and unemployment. A 1994 poll in Estonia identified the environment as the fifth most important issue (Nagy).

In the NIS, some surveys suggest that the public has a strong concern for the environment. In 1998, over 50 per cent of respondents in Ukraine, about 60 per cent of those in Kazakhstan, and almost 70 per cent of those in Russia said that environmental protection should come before economic growth (USIA). It is likely, however, that in people's daily lives they focus on more immediate problems. In a 1994 poll conducted in four regions of western Russia, only 12 per cent of respondents listed environmental issues as one of their main concerns in everyday life; almost 60 per cent mentioned the "chaos and instability of life" and slightly more mentioned financial problems (Zhdanovich). Disparities in survey results support observations that most citizens in the NIS see environmental issues as an important issue for government action, but – amid their present problems – not a priority for their own action or participation.

Public attention to environmental issues has fallen at the national level in both CEE countries and the NIS, although some issues such as construction of waste disposal sites and nuclear power plants continue to arouse concern at the local level.[2]

3. The Media and the Environment

Throughout the region, newspapers, television and radio have been among the main sources of information about environmental issues for much of the public. While economic and social problems have moved environmental issues off the front page in most countries, some newspapers and television programmes in CEE countries and (to a much more limited extent) in the NIS have established regular reporting on the environment. Overall, the public has probably become much better informed about the environment than it was at the beginning of the transition. However, the media have often focused on disasters, reported in sensationalistic terms. Journalists writing about the environment have sometimes lacked a strong understanding of the issues.

3.1. The media in CEE countries

In a few CEEC countries, such as the Czech Republic, Hungary and Poland, national TV channels have broadcast regular environment programmes. A number of radio programmes have also been devoted to the environment. In Hungary, a programme called "Oxygen" has provided in-depth coverage of environmental policy. Many national newspapers and weekly news magazines have included regular environment pages. Almost all CEE countries have national environmental magazines, most of which focus on nature and nature protection.

Most national newspapers, news magazines and radio and television news organisations have had environmental journalists on their staff. In several countries, including Hungary, Poland and Romania, these journalists have established their own associations. There has been a lack of well-trained environmental journalists, in particular at the local level. A number of organisations, including the REC and some journalists' associations, have provided training.

3.2. The media in the NIS

Overall, the media in the NIS have paid less attention to the environment than has been the case in CEE countries. NIS journalists and editors have shown little interest in the topic. In a 1996 survey conducted by Eco-Accord, only about 10 per cent of them expressed a desire to cover environmental issues regularly. A few prominent NIS newspapers, such as *Moskovski Komsomolets* and *Segodnya* in Russia, have had regular environment pages – but most newspapers and other media have covered the environment only occasionally and have usually focused on accidents and controversies. There have been a few radio and TV environmental programmes, but these have not reached wide audiences. A number of magazines and other publications on environmental issues started in the late 1980s and early 1990s, often with external support such as grants from western foundations. Most had small circulations and few turned out to be financially viable. The large environmental publications that have survived have been supported by state subsidies. These include ECOS magazine (with a circulation of about 21 000) and the newspaper *Green World* (40 000), both published in Russia and supported by the State Committee for Environmental Protection.

One key obstacle for journalists has been a lack of information. In the 1996 Eco-Accord survey, 77 per cent of respondents said they did not receive interesting, timely information on environmental issues. NIS environmental authorities have not given co-operation with the media a high priority. However, there are a few examples of good practice. In Georgia, the Environment Ministry has organised regular press conferences and established good relations with national newspapers and radio and television organisations. In Kazakhstan, the Ministry's NEAP/SD office has worked actively to inform journalists about its activities. Few NGOs in the NIS have established close contacts with the media.

As in CEE countries, many journalists covering environmental issues in the NIS have lacked knowledge and training. A few training programmes for environmental journalists have been organised, for example by a TACIS project on environmental awareness, (Box 4.3) and by some Russian NGOs, including Eco-Accord, the Centre for Wild Nature Conservation and Ecoline. Professional associations for environmental journalists have only recently been organised in the NIS. By mid-1998, they had been created in Moldova and Ukraine.

Box 4.3.   **The TACIS project on environmental awareness in the NIS**

In 1997 and 1998, the EC TACIS Programme undertook a project to promote environmental awareness in the NIS. The project informed parliamentarians about environmental issues; strengthened NGOs' capacities to work with the media; and encouraged environmental journalism, providing training seminars and supporting environmental programmes on radio and television. The project initiated over 50 TV programmes on the environment across the NIS, a weekly environmental radio magazine in Russia, and a daily radio soap opera, also in Russia, focusing on environmental themes (one episode featured a cameo appearance by British Prime Minister Tony Blair).

―――――――
Source: TACIS.

---

4.   Environmental NGOs

Throughout the region, the number of NGOs grew rapidly in the late 1980s and early 1990s. NGOs have tried to act as catalysts for environmental improvement. They have provided environmental information to the public, undertaken environmental protection projects (especially for biodiversity protection) and participated in government decision-making. In a few countries, particularly in Central Europe and the Baltic States, NGOs have played an important and constructive role in environmental policy development and implementation. In other CEE countries and in many NIS, however, the NGO movement so far has had only a limited impact. The NGO movement throughout the region continues to face serious difficulties. Most NGOs have been small and poorly funded; many, particularly in the NIS, have relied mainly on grants from foreign donors and foundations for their work. Few NGOs have developed a broad base of public support.

4.1. *The growth of NGOs in the region*

A 1996 Regional Environmental Centre (REC) census counted around 3 000 environmental NGOs in CEE countries (Table 4.1). Almost two-thirds were located in just countries: the Czech Republic, Hungary and Poland. On a per capita basis, the three countries with the largest number of NGOs were the

Czech Republic, Hungary and Slovenia. Through the first half of the 1990s, NGO growth was very dynamic. About 200 new groups were formed each year in CEE countries. Their growth seems to have stagnated in recent years. The census showed that most NGOs were small. The majority had under 25 members, and over 70 per cent operated only on a local or regional basis. Most did not have paid staff.[3]

Table 4.1. **Environmental NGOs in Central and Eastern Europe**

	Number of NGOs	NGOs per 1 million population
Albania	45	14.1
Bosnia and Herzegovina	38	10.9
Bulgaria	100	11.8
Croatia	187	39.0
Czech Republic	520	49.5
Estonia	35	21.9
FYROM	73	36.0
Hungary	726	69.1
Latvia	60	22.2
Lithuania	81	21.3
Poland	600	15.5
Romania	210	9.0
Slovakia	141	26.1
Slovenia	114	57.0
Total	2 930	

Source: REC, 1997.

The NGO movement has been weaker in the NIS. Here, too, the late 1980s and early 1990s was a period of strong growth (Figure 4.1). In Moldova and Russia, growth slowed after 1991. Reports suggest that after 1995 NGO growth slowed further in these two countries and in other NIS. It is difficult to estimate the total number of NGOs operating in the NIS. One problem is that many groups have operated (sometimes very actively) without being registered.[4] The best estimates indicate that there are 1 000 to 1 500 environmental NGOs in Russia, as many as 500 in Georgia, over 200 in Ukraine, about 200 in Kazakhstan and over 70 in Moldova. (There are fewer groups per capita in Russia and Ukraine than in any CEE country; Moldova, Georgia and Kazakhstan fall into the same range as CEE countries.)

Most NGOs in Russia and Ukraine are small – in 1995, about half had fewer than 25 members. Over one-third of NGOs in Russia and Ukraine operate at the local level (that is, in a single city or town) and many others operate at the regional level; only 10 per cent of Ukrainian and 3 per cent of Russian NGOs operate at national level. In Moldova, a much smaller country, 50 per cent of NGOs focus on national issues (REC, 1995).

4.2. *Financial support for NGOs*

Most NGOs in the region have small budgets. In CEE countries, almost one-half were operating on budgets under US$1000 per year (Figure 4.2), according to the REC's census. Three-quarters reported their financial situation to be either unstable or very poor.

NGOs in Central and Eastern Europe have received financing mainly from foreign donor governments, foreign private foundations and domestic governments. In the early years of transition, foreign public and private sources provided the majority of funding for these NGOs. The REC, the Environmental Partnership for Central and Eastern Europe, the Soros Foundation, the EC PHARE Programme, the Worldwide Fund for Nature (WWF) and Milieukontakt Oost-Europa have been among the most important external funding sources. The REC in particular has played a crucial role in supporting the region's NGOs (Box 4.4). External financing has gone mainly to NGOs that focus on national or international issues, even though these account for only one-quarter of all NGOs in the region. Few external resources have reached local groups.

85

Figure 4.1. **NGOs in Moldova, Russia, and Ukraine, by year of creation (as of 1995)**

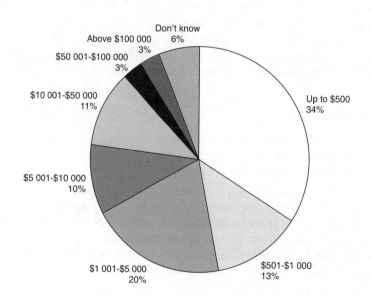

Time of NGOs creation: ☐ Before 1987   ☐ 1987-1991   ■ 1991-1995

Source: REC, 1995.

Figure 4.2. **Annual budgets of CEE NGOs**

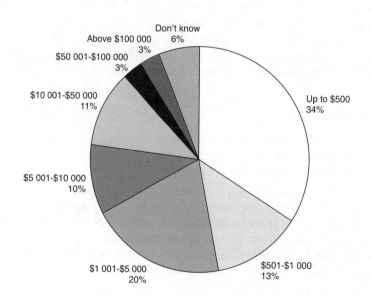

Source: REC, 1997.

Box 4.4.   The REC and NGOs in Central and Eastern Europe

The Regional Environmental Center for Central and Eastern Europe (REC) is a non-advocacy, not-for-profit organisation that assists in solving environmental problems in Central and Eastern Europe. It is based in Szentendre, Hungary, and has offices in most CEE countries. The Center encourages co-operation among NGOs, governments, businesses and other environmental stakeholders, supports free exchange of information, and promotes public participation in environmental decision-making. The EC, the US, Hungary and other countries have helped fund the its activities.

Since 1990, the REC has provided grants, training, information and fellowships to NGOs in CEE countries. It has been a crucial source of NGO funding. In its survey, over 20 per cent of all CEEC NGOs reported that the Center's grants covered one-quarter or more of their budgets. This support has been especially important in southern CEE countries, where the economic situation has remained difficult and funding from other sources has been limited. The REC's local offices have provided training in areas such as fundraising and institutional building. One recent REC project developed manuals, organised workshops and provided grants to build NGO capacity for public participation. The project also organised roundtable discussions between NGOs and government officials on the Aarhus Convention. The REC has developed training materials on public participation methods for environmental NGOs and other actors in southern CEE countries. These materials were produced in English and local languages (Albanian, Bulgarian, Hungarian and Romanian).

Source: REC, 1997.

Between 1995 and 1998, external assistance to CEE NGOs declined by over 20 per cent, but an increase in domestic government sources more than made up for this shortfall (Figure 4.3). Trends have varied significantly between countries. In Poland, Hungary and the Czech Republic, domestic funding rose dramatically over this period. By 1998, it exceeded foreign assistance in all three countries. This trend was most dramatic in Poland, where external assistance fell to only 5 per cent of total NGO funding in 1998. External assistance has continued to make up the lion's share of funding for NGOs in southern CEE countries such as Albania, Bulgaria and Macedonia. In some of these countries, including Bulgaria and Macedonia, both external assistance and total NGO funding fell sharply in 1998 (REC and Milieukontakt Oost-Europa).

Government grants, mainly from environment ministries and environmental funds, have been the main source of domestic financing for CEE NGOs. Few NGOs have developed autonomous sources. Only one in six received the majority of its funding from national private donations and membership dues (REC, 1997). In 1997, Hungary adopted a law allowing citizens to designate 1 per cent of their income tax to support civil groups. This provision could increase private support for environmental NGOs. However, CEE countries lack a tradition of donation-funded organisations, making it difficult for NGOs to raise money. This is particularly true in countries with low per capita incomes, where individuals have little disposable income. Few national NGOs have sought to develop wide memberships or seek alternative funding sources, in part because many have so far been able to obtain sufficient funding from external sources and national government bodies.

In the NIS, too, assistance from OECD countries has played a crucial role in strengthening NGOs and funding their activities. Many NGOs, especially those operating at the national level, have received most of their funding from external sources. Groups such as ISAR – the Initiative for Social Action and Renewal, which is supported by the US government and private US foundations – and Milieukontakt Oost-Europa of the Netherlands have provided training and financial support to NIS NGOs. From 1993 to 1997, ISAR distributed over US$2.5 million in grants to NGOs in the NIS for projects ranging from public awareness to pollution monitoring, and an additional US$2 million for partnerships between NIS and US organisations (US AID). Western groups have also provided computers and modems to NIS NGOs, greatly expanding their communication capacities. Domestic government and private sources have provided few resources.

Figure 4.3. **Funding for NGOs in Central and Eastern Europe**

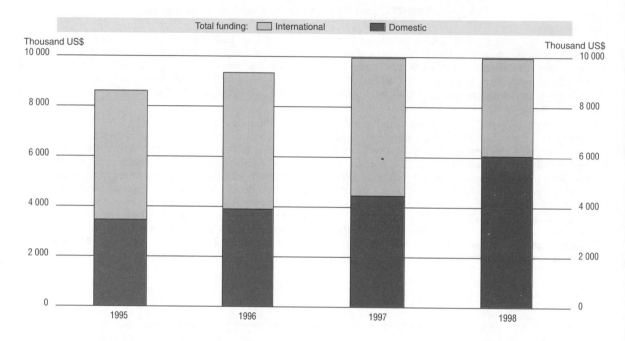

Does not include private domestic donations, such as membership dues. In most cases these have provided only a small share of total funding.
Source: REC and Milieukontakt Ost-Europa.

A planned network of new RECs in the NIS may provide further support for NGOs. The 1995 Sofia Conference called for the creation of these new centres. As yet, their development has been slow. Establishment of the first two, in Georgia and Moldova, was only announced at the 1998 Aarhus Conference. Others are to be established in Russia, Ukraine and Central Asia.

4.3. NGO *activities and impacts*

NGOs in the region are diverse and have worked on a wide variety of issues and activities. In many countries, a few main types of NGOs can be identified (Francis). E*xpert groups* bring together professionals who work on environmental issues, such as university researchers. Most expert groups focus on national or international issues. *"Lifestyle" groups* push for radical environmental and lifestyle changes. In many countries these NGOs were prominent in the first years of transition, but their role in the overall NGO movement has since declined. Until recently, few expert or "lifestyle" groups sought to develop broad public membership or support. Most focused their outreach on winning external and domestic grants for their projects. This tendency has been strong in the NIS, where the most active elements of the environmental movement have been "professional NGOs" located in capitals and large cities with paid staff members. They have been largely funded by foreign sources – a fact that has sometimes given them a negative public image.

Nature/landscape protection groups have had greater interest and success in developing a broad membership. Some of these groups existed on an official basis under communist regimes; others were established during the transition. A number of nature protection groups, such as the Biodiversity Conservation Centre in Moscow, have undertaken extensive projects and campaigns, often with international financial support (Box 4.5). Many *local issue groups* have also sprung up to address local problems and protect local natural resources. Eco-Initiative, in Tomsk, Russia, has campaigned against proposals to build new nuclear reactors in neighbouring Seviersk, a formerly "closed" nuclear research and production centre (Zamparutti and Kozeltsev). Most of these groups have lacked expertise and financing, but many have developed close contacts with their local communities.

Box 4.5.   **The Biodiversity Conservation Centre (BCC)**

The BCC, based in Moscow, has undertaken a number of biodiversity and nature protection campaigns. One of these opposed timber cutting in Karelia's old-growth forests, on Russia's border with Finland. National and regional authorities, environmental groups and consumer unions in Russia, Finland and other European countries participated. One Finnish timber company, Ensso, agreed to stop cutting in these forests and several German firms agreed not to buy wood which had come from them. The Kostomuksha regional administration in Republic of Karelia also prohibited all timber cutting in several old-growth areas. Since 1995, the BCC has organised a yearly "March for Parks" to attract public attention to the plight of protected areas in the NIS, The rallies, events and seminars usually attract over 100 000 people across the NIS. The BCC has also lobbied the Russian Duma (Parliament) to support these areas. In 1996, it obtained an additional 38 billion roubles for Russia's *zapovedniks* (natural reserves). The Centre has also trained national park staff and specialists in Russia. It has received international support for its activities from a variety of sources, including the MacArthur Foundation, the UK know-how Fund, the Soros Foundation and the Global Environmental Facility.

Source: Ponizova.

While these four categories indicate some of the main types of NGOs, groups in the region have evolved over the transition. Thus, some NGOs that could be classified as "expert" groups have come to provide key "services", such as legal advice and assistance, for national environmental movements. Other national NGOs have taken important roles in the policy process by organising referenda, participating in government and parliamentary discussions on environmental policy, working with local communities, and helping implement environmental projects. Some national NGOs, particularly in CEE countries, have focused on specific issues such as transport and environment and have built national and international NGO networks to push for policy changes.

A few CEE NGOs have worked actively with the media, providing information on their activities and on environmental issues. This has been less common in the NIS, although there have been some important examples. The NIS-wide Socio-Ecological Union Centre for Information and Co-ordination, as well as Green Woman in Kazakhstan, have prepared regular press releases on NGO environmental activities. The NIS offices of the international NGO Greenpeace have worked closely with the media. Greenpeace-Russia reported that it initiated 137 TV news reports on the environment in the second half of 1997.

Still, many NGOs in the region, especially those working at the national level, lack strong links with the public at large. Only a few have a wide membership or a prominent public image. Developing such links could give NGOs greater weight in policy debates, and also encourage broader public awareness and participation.

4.4. NGO *networks*

Co-operation among NGOs can enhance their impact. In almost all CEE countries, NGOs have developed national networks that hold regular meetings and share skills and expertise. Such networks have been strongest in the Visegrad and Baltic countries. (In a few CEE countries, however, co-operation has been hindered by serious splits within the NGO movement.) National NGO networks have been rare in the NIS, although individual NGOs have often co-operated on an informal basis. NGOs in Moscow have had limited ties with those in the rest of Russia.

At the international level, NGOs in the region have established their strongest ties with Western European and North American NGOs, which have often provided financing and training. A few NGOs have participated in pan-European forums, including the NGO meetings parallel to the Sofia and Aarhus "Environment for Europe" Conferences. Overall, co-operation among NGOs in the region has not been as strong, although a few have worked together on cross-border projects. Recently, several CEE NGOs have formed coalitions on common issues including energy, transport, nature conservation, biodiversity and international financing; 15 groups from nine countries have participated in the Bankwatch Network, which has monitored IFI policies and activities in the region. In the NIS, about 40 NGOs have created a common network to co-operate on NEAPs (Box 4.10). Co-operation between NGOs in CEE countries and those in the NIS has been rare, although a few projects supported by the REC and other groups have encouraged such co-operation.

5.   Public Access to Environmental Information

Nearly all CEE countries and NIS have laws that, at least in principle, guarantee the right of public access to environmental information held by the government. In practice, access to information has varied significantly across the region. Most CEE governments have made good progress over the past five years in providing information. Some of the approaches developed have matched or surpassed those in Western European countries. In the NIS, most governments have been reluctant to provide information and often have not fully implemented existing legal provisions.

5.1. *Access to information in* CEE *countries*

In nearly all CEE countries, laws have established a "passive" obligation for governments to provide environmental information (*i.e.* environmental authorities must respond to citizen and NGO information requests.) These requirements are mainly found in framework environment laws. A few countries such as Hungary and Lithuania have also passed laws establishing principles and procedures for public access to all areas of government information. The EU accession process has encouraged the development of specific laws on access to environmental information. Several governments have recently adopted laws based on the EU's directive on environmental information.[5]

In most countries, citizens have been able to obtain information from environment ministries without great difficulty. Many environment ministries have established offices responsible for providing environmental information, although their capacities and the scope of their work have varied significantly. The new OECD countries (the Czech Republic, Hungary and Poland) have set in place the most advanced systems for providing information (Box 4.6). The Baltic countries also have well-functioning systems. Environmental authorities in most CEE countries have developed procedures for providing information that go beyond the legal requirements. Nonetheless, many governments still apply broad exemptions to the types of information that can be released to the public. Commercial secrecy has been a common justification for denying environmental information. Adoption of the Aarhus Convention should lead governments to reduce such exemptions (Box 4.7).

Environmental authorities in nearly all CEE countries have provided some information on a routine basis. Nearly all have published annual state of the environment reports. Environmental ministries and other government bodies in several countries have set up web pages on environmental conditions and policies.[6] A few countries have provided ambient air pollution information directly to the public. In many large cities the media have disseminated daily information on air pollution levels; in a few, including Budapest and Krakow, authorities have set up electronic billboards in central districts to indicate pollution levels.

5.2. *Environmental information in the* NIS

In most NIS, governments have been reluctant to respond to requests for environmental information; in most of them, laws refer to public access to information but do not specify government procedures for providing it. Often, only good personal relations with key officials have resulted in the release of information. Few NIS citizens have been aware of their rights to obtain environmental information, so pressures to establish more open procedures have been weak.

Another problem is that government agencies have occasionally requested payment for environmental information. Sometimes the charges have reflected administrative costs; in other cases officials have tried to use them for revenue raising; and, in a few instances, high charges have represented

---

Box 4.6. Access to information and participation in Hungary

Hungary's Environment Ministry opened a Public Information Office in July 1997 to respond to requests for environmental information from the public as well as NGOs, enterprises, and local and regional governments. In the same year, it concluded an agreement with 18 national and local NGOs (selected through a competitive tender) to assist in operating 16 local information centres in co-operation with regional and local environmental authorities. The Ministry has disseminated draft and final policy documents and other information via the "Green Spider", an electronic network used by NGOs. In 1997, it also created a GRID office, in co-operation with UNEP, that has provided environmental information, including a "popular" version of the national state of the environment report destined for the general public and for schools. The government has established an Ombudsman for Data Protection, who recently ruled that environmental authorities should disclose information on enterprise emissions to the public, overruling arguments that this would harm commercial confidentiality.

Hungary's 1995 framework environment law specifies the public's right to participate in environmental policy decisions (Hungary and Poland are the only countries in the region whose laws specify this right). Under this law, the Environment Ministry has developed procedures to inform NGOs about the development of environmental laws, regulations and policies and to solicit their comments on drafts of these at an early stage through discussions and written submissions. Ironically, the introduction of these formal procedures coincided with a change in government and a decline in informal co-operation between the Ministry and NGOs.

Source: Denisov; REC, 1998*a*.

---

attempts to restrict access to information. In 1997, when the local newspaper in Leninogorsk, Kazakhstan, stopped publishing official data on air and water quality, an NGO, Biosphere, applied to the city environmental laboratory for the data but was asked to pay a high price. As in CEE countries, information related to enterprise activities has also often been denied on the basis of "commercial confidentiality". In Russia, information related to nuclear waste management and related issues has on occasion been declared a state secret. In a few cases, the government has sought to prosecute NGO members and environmental journalists who released such information.

In some NIS, the large number of government institutions responsible for collecting and disseminating environmental information has created problems for citizens and NGOs, who sometimes have not been able to identify which agency held what data. Other problems stem from the deterioration of environmental monitoring systems in the NIS, which in some countries has been so severe that key data often are not collected.

The provisions of the Aarhus Convention could significantly improve the legal basis and operating methods for obtaining information in the NIS. A separate initiative could also provide a step in this direction: in December 1997, the CIS Parliamentary Assembly, which brings together NIS parliamentarians to discuss common issues, proposed a draft law on environmental information as a model for consideration by national parliaments. (This law had been drafted by a Moldavian NGO, Biotica, and submitted to that country's parliament.)

A growing number of NIS governments actively provide information to the public, for example in the form of national state of the environment reports as well as reports on specific environmental problems. In Russia, the SoE report is distributed as a supplement to the government-sponsored *Green World* newspaper. In a number of NIS, however, SoE reports have not been disseminated widely or actively outside the government (in Belarus only 500 copies are printed). The public has the right to apply to receive a copy, but often few groups or citizens are aware of the existence of such reports. In a few cases, national and local environmental authorities have provided environmental monitoring data on a regular basis to the public. Since Chernobyl, the governments of Ukraine and Belarus have provided information on radioactivity levels.

Box 4.7. **The Aarhus Convention**

The "Environment for Europe" process has promoted public participation. At the 1995 Sofia Conference (see Chapter 1), environment ministers endorsed the "Sofia Guidelines", which encouraged the development of national laws and procedures on access to information, participation and justice. The Guidelines were an important stepping stone for the negotiation of the Aarhus Convention signed by 35 countries, including 11 CEE countries and five NIS, during the June 1998 "Environment for Europe" Conference. (The Convention must now be ratified by at least 16 countries to enter into force, a process that will probably take a few years.) Nearly all UN/ECE countries participated in negotiations on the Aarhus Convention (its formal title is the Convention on Access to Information, Public Participation in Decision-Making and Access to Justice in Environmental Matters). These countries invited NGOs to participate in most phases of negotiation. This strong NGO involvement went beyond that allowed in previous international negotiations and may set a precedent for future international environmental negotiations. The Convention provides clear definitions and specifies minimum procedures for exercising basic rights, including:

Access to Information. Key provisions of the Aarhus Convention include:

– environmental information held by public authorities should be accessible to the public through clear and transparent procedures. Exemptions should be limited and clearly defined. These can include the protection of intellectual property rights, confidentiality of personal data, and national security;

– grounds for refusal should be narrowly interpreted. Public authorities should balance the protection of specific interests against the public interest in environmental protection, and emissions information should almost always be disclosed;

– public authorities must reply to requests within a specific period and justify refusals to provide information;

– public authorities can make reasonable charges for information and must publish the scale of charges;

– public authorities must collect, update and disseminate environmental information;

– public authorities should actively disseminate to the public documents on environmental legislation, policies and programmes as well as international conventions and other significant documents.

Access to Participation. The Aarhus Convention specifies key elements for public access to decision-making:

– public authorities must give notice that a decision will be made, in sufficient time for the public to prepare and participate in the process;

– members of the public should have the opportunity to submit comments, information and analyses;

– decisions should be in writing, and should specify the reasons they were taken;

– public input should be considered in the final decision.

Access to Justice. The Convention states that the public should have access to judicial or administrative review if procedural rights to access to information or participation are infringed, and also to seek the enforcement of environmental laws. Under the Convention, the public should have access to an independent and impartial review body that can provide adequate and effective remedies, including injunctive relief, and whose decisions are binding on the public authority. The process should be timely and inexpensive, with procedures established in law and final decisions in writing and publicly accessible.

The Convention's provisions will help strengthen these rights in CEE countries and the NIS (as well as many Western European countries). They include a clear and broad definition of environmental information. As yet, this is defined in few CEEC/NIS laws, and government offices and courts have often used restricted definitions. The Convention's broader definition may prompt non-environment ministries to provide better environmental information – addressing a common problem throughout the region (as well as in Western Europe). At the same time, the Convention has a number of weaknesses. For example, its strongest provisions on public participation refer to government decisions on specific issues, while provisions concerning public participation in the development of environmental legislation and programmes are only presented as recommendations to governments. The Convention's provisions for monitoring government compliance have been criticised by NGOs as too weak, reducing the incentives for full implementation (Wates).

A number of NIS environmental authorities have web pages.[7] However, use of the internet in these countries has remained limited. Few NIS environmental authorities have prepared "popular" forms of their SoE or other reports for non-specialised audiences. This has been a vital gap, as the public, the media and even NGOs often lack basic knowledge and understanding of environmental issues. The development of national environmental information agencies could provide a stronger institutional basis for public information and environmental education. Russia has created such an agency, although it has mainly provided information to other government bodies rather than to the public (UN/ECE).

6. Public Access to Participation in Decision-making

Nearly all CEE governments have made significant progress in developing mechanisms for public participation, in particular since the 1995 Sofia "Environment for Europe" Conference. While some CEE practices have matched or exceeded those in Western Europe and have satisfied many provisions of the Aarhus Convention, in the NIS the public and NGOs have often found it difficult to gain access to decision-making.

6.1. *Participation in CEE countries*

Due to the expanded opportunities for access, NGOs in most CEE countries have played an important role in parliamentary and government discussions on draft laws and programmes. However, NGO participation has largely depended on *ad hoc* mechanisms rather than established procedures. For the public at large, referenda and legislative initiatives have created some opportunities for participation; so far, neither mechanism has had a major impact on national environmental policies (Box 4.8).

Box 4.8. **Referenda and legislative initiatives in Central and Eastern Europe**

As yet, there has been only one attempt to call a national referendum on an environmental issue. In 1995, several NGOs in Slovenia gathered signatures for a referendum to close the Krsko nuclear power plant but failed to obtain the legal minimum required. Referenda have become more common at the local and regional levels. In a few CEE countries – including the Czech Republic, Hungary, Poland and Slovakia – citizens have the right to call local referenda. Experience with those on environmental issues has been mixed. In Poland, all local referenda so far have failed because of low voter turnout (at least 30 per cent participation is required for the results to be valid). In southern Hungary, several towns held a referendum in 1997 on construction of a low-radiation waste storage facility. Bélaapátfalva, where the facility was to be built, voted in favour of the proposal, but nearby towns voted against it. As of late 1998, this question had not been resolved.

There has also been only one example of a legislative initiative. In 1994, environmental NGOs in Poland collected signatures to submit amendments to the draft constitution being prepared in the Sejm, the national parliament. Although they failed to obtain the necessary number of signatures, the Sejm's Constitutional Commission adopted many of their proposals to include environmental rights in the Constitution.

Source: REC, 1998a.

Co-operation between NGOs *and parliaments*

In a number of CEE countries – particularly the new OECD countries (the Czech Republic, Hungary and Poland) and the Baltic States – members of parliament and environmental NGOs have established co-operative links. Most parliaments in these countries have set up offices and procedures to provide public access to information on their activities: an important first step towards participation. The parliaments of the Czech Republic, Hungary, Lithuania and Poland have information centres where the public can obtain draft and final documents as well as speeches and other materials. Some parliaments provide similar information via the internet. Those in Hungary and Poland have established "lobby lists" by means of which NGOs and other groups can sign up to receive information on specific issues and invitations to committee hearings. Often, NGOs have worked closely with parliamentary environment committees – attending committee meetings and preparing position papers and recommendations on policy issues as well as draft legislation. Even in these cases, co-operation has mainly been based on political affinities and personal contacts rather than established procedures. Some NGOs have tried to influence parliamentary debates through petitions and proposals. In Hungary a national NGO, the Air Action Group, has presented yearly alternative "green budgets".

In other countries, NGO co-operation with parliaments has remained difficult. NGOs and citizens have often had difficulty obtaining access to information on parliamentary work. However, there have been recent signs of change. In 1997, the environment committee of Bulgaria's National Assembly invited NGOs to discuss amendments to the national Environmental Protection Act (this was the first such invitation; and NGO proposals were not incorporated into the amendments). Overall, parliaments in the region could play a stronger role in developing and overseeing the implementation of national environmental policies, in particular by increasing opportunities for participation and promoting stronger public support (Box 4.9).

NGO *participation in government policy-making*

In a number of CEE countries, NGOs have used opportunities for participation to make an impact on national environmental policies. The Estonian Environment Ministry has invited NGOs to participate in discussions on the drafting of environmental laws, including those on EIAs and nature protection. In 1996, when Estonian NGOs criticised a proposed national forestry policy, the government invited an NGO representative to take part in the commission developing the policy. In many countries, NGOs have actively assisted in the preparation of NEAPs and other environmental initiatives. NGO representatives have also participated in sustainable development commissions and in the development of nature and biodiversity policies. The Albanian Society for the Protection of Birds and Mammals initiated and drafted the country's nature protection law. This group and other NGOs also helped prepare Albania's National Strategy for Nature Conservation and Biodiversity.

NGOs have participated in government committees and boards, such as government environmental advisory councils. Hungary's National Council for Environmental Protection was established in 1996 with seven NGO members, as well as seven representatives of the scientific community and seven business and industry representatives. The Council has expressed its opinion on draft laws concerning nuclear energy, nature conservation and other topics, and on Hungary's NEAP and NEHAP. In a few countries, NGO representatives have sat on the boards of national and regional environmental funds. Thus they have shared decision-making powers rather than just submitting comments and proposals. In Poland the supervisory board of each regional fund, as well as the board of the National Fund for Environmental Protection and Water Management, has included one NGO representative. In Bulgaria, both the Ecofund National Trust and the National Environmental Protection Fund have had an NGO member on their boards.

A number of CEE environment ministries have explored ways to strengthen co-operation with NGOs. In late 1997, Slovenian NGOs initiated discussions with the Ministry of Environment on procedures for access to information and participation in drafting environmental laws, regulations, strategy and policy documents. In Romania and Bulgaria, recent governments have increased co-operation with environmental NGOs.

One continuing problem across CEE countries is that sectoral ministries whose decisions have major environmental implications – such as industry, finance, transport and agriculture – have shown little interest in co-operating with environmental NGOs. Ratification and implementation of the Aarhus Convention should lead to greater public participation in the decisions of these ministries.

Box 4.9. **Involving parliaments in environmental policy**

In 1997, CEEC/NIS NEAP co-ordinators, other environmental policy officials, and parliamentarians participated in an EAP Task Force workshop in Stockholm on the involvement of parliaments in the development and implementation of national environmental policies. Participants agreed that more effective co-operation on environmental policy between CEEC/NIS environment ministries and parliaments required a firm and sustained commitment by the two groups. Participants underlined several benefits and potential approaches:

- Parliaments can play an important role in mobilising public support for environmental issues and introducing public views into political debates. They are well-placed to promote and assure active involvement of the public and other stakeholders in environmental decision-making. Good working relations among members of parliament , government officials and various interest groups, such as local governments, environmental citizens' organisations, consumers' organisations, business and industry, could generate commitments and voluntary actions, help avoid conflicts, and link environmental issues into the overall process of reform.

- Parliaments and governments in many CEEC/NIS needed to build more effective working relationships. As a first step, closer co-operation between green MPs and environment ministry officials should be cultivated, for the development of short-term environmental policy initiatives and longer-term sustainable development strategies.

- Building broader support for environmental issues among MPs is an important element in the development of an "environmental (sustainable development) constituency" in parliaments.

- The development and maintenance of formal and informal communication channels is essential for an effective parliamentary-governmental dialogue, which can help develop a shared vision for environmental protection and sustainable development. Governments should provide MPs with regular, concise and relevant information (such as indicators and projections concerning the state of the environment, budget implications, analyses of environmental damage, and costs and benefits of environmental policies and programmes). Parliaments could also play an important role in improving media coverage of NEAPs and environmental issues.

- Early involvement of MPs in the development of methodologies and the design of NEAPs and other government programmes could ensure consensus and smooth implementation.

- The examination of proposed legislation prepared by the government is an important democratic safeguard, and a basic responsibility exercised by parliaments on behalf of society. Parliaments could organise public hearings, commission research reports, and receive independent expert evidence.

- The effectiveness of environmental policies and legislation can be increased if their elaboration is linked to parliamentary debate on national budgets. Parliaments can play a key role by ensuring that adequate financing and other resources are available for implementation.

- The oversight function of parliaments in CEEC/NIS needs to be further developed to allow MPs to monitor and evaluate objectively how government policies and programmes are being implemented.

- In countries seeking EU membership, an open exchange of information between parliaments and ministries could help resolve issues arising from the approximation process. Accession countries should balance the pressure for rapid adoption of EU legislation with a review of domestic policy objectives and priorities.

Source: EAP Task Force.

Participation in EIAs, land-use planning and permitting

Nearly all CEE countries have laws requiring environmental impact assessments of major infrastructure, industrial and other projects (Chapter 5). These laws call for public hearings as part of the decision-making process. In practice, a number of obstacles have limited the extent and value of public participation. Hearings in most countries have taken place at a late stage; public authorities often have not provided wide notice of hearings; NGOs and the public have had difficulty reviewing the often complex assessment documents; and there have been few provisions to monitor implementation of EIA decisions. (It should be noted that many of these problems also exist in Western European and other OECD countries.)

A few CEE governments and NGOs have proposed or put in place innovative mechanisms to tackle these problems. A number of countries have considered provisions to involve the public early in the EIA process. To provide additional opportunities for participation, NGOs in the Czech Republic have organised parallel public hearings to supplement official ones. In Poland, EIA commissions have assisted the public by providing information on complex technical issues. Romania's new EIA legislation will require a review of projects' environmental impacts after five years.

Most CEE countries have established provisions for public participation in decisions on local and regional land-use plans. Usually these provisions only require public hearings on final drafts. Public authorities in a few countries must also inform the public when they start to prepare land-use plans. In Poland, for example, citizens can comment on the terms of reference proposed. Public participation has been rare in decisions on pollution permits for industrial plants. In most countries, only parties that can prove they are directly affected can participate in the relevant negotiations; in the Czech Republic, Hungary and Poland, however, any recognised environmental NGO is allowed to participate (REC, 1998a).

Participation at local and regional levels

Often, elected officials and NGOs have stronger relations at the local than at the national level. Informal and *ad hoc* mechanisms rather than compliance with formal legal procedures have generally been the basis for participation. In some cities and towns NGO activists have been elected or chosen as members of councils, committees and advisory groups. In a number of cases, NGOs and local authorities have co-operated on environmental issues. For example, in the Czech Republic local authorities and a local NGO, South Bohemian Mothers, were involved in court cases related to construction of the Temelin nuclear power plant. Several municipalities formed an association which, in 1997, successfully won a court case reversing a government decision to withhold information about the plant. Separately, the NGO launched a court action contending that EIA procedures had not been properly followed (as of early 1999, this case had not yet been decided).

Local NGOs have also participated in the development of local environmental programmes such as LEAPs. In many cases, participation by the general public as well as by non-environmental groups such as labour unions and church organisations has not been strong.

6.2. Public participation in the NIS

NIS environmental authorities have been more reluctant then those in CEE countries to involve either NGOs or the general public in decision-making. National laws in several NIS give citizens the right to take part in discussions of government environmental programmes, but environmental authorities have rarely provided public information on draft laws or policies or organised fora or other procedures for public comment. Nonetheless, since the early 1990s these authorities have increasingly sought NGO participation although such participation has often been limited to experts from "professional" NGOs, chosen on the basis of personal contacts.

Participation at the national level

Environmental authorities in a few NIS have involved NGOs in the preparation of national environmental policies and laws, such as National Environmental Action Programmes (Box 4.10), and the development of National Agenda 21 documents and sectoral environmental programmes. In Russia, NGO representatives participated in expert group discussions on the national Environmental Education Programme (as of early 1999, this programme had not yet received government approval). In Georgia, NGOs were involved in the preparation of the country's 1996 Nature Protection Act. NIS parliaments have occasionally invited NGOs to comment on draft environmental laws. Overall, however, parliamentarians in the NIS, as in CEE countries, could make additional efforts to support environmental policy and promote public and NGO participation (Box 4.9).

A number of NIS environmental authorities, including those in Ukraine and Russia, have created national advisory environmental councils whose members (usually chosen by the minister) have included NGO representatives. Although many NGOs have criticised these councils for providing only a

Box 4.10. **Participation of NIS NGOs in NEAP development**

In recent years most NIS have developed new national environmental policies including NEAPs. Policy preparation has often been a catalyst for improving NGO participation. Environmental authorities in some NIS have tried to involve NGOs and the public from the start of NEAP preparation. In Kazakhstan, for example, the NEAP/SD office widely disseminated information to NGOs and the media. NGO participation in the process was strong. In Georgia, the Ministry of Environment has organised weekly meetings with NGOs informing them about its programmes and projects. It also asked NGOs to prepare background papers for some NEAP working groups. The NGOs themselves, with the support of Western European NGOs, organised a workshop for a wider public in August 1997. As a result of this meeting, NGOs and the Georgian government agreed to set up an NGO NEAP Information Centre.

In other NIS, environmental authorities have broadened opportunities for NGO participation over the course of NEAP development and implementation. In Moldova, the government had invited NGOs only for the final discussion of the draft NEAP. Later, environmental authorities invited them to take part in NEAP implementation activities. Separately, both the government and Parliament have organised temporary "commissions" bringing together experts and NGO representatives to discuss environmental programmes. In Russia, NGOs were not invited to participate in the preparation of the first NEAP (elaborated between 1994 and 1996); in response, 49 of them prepared an alternative NEAP. The State Committee for Environmental Protection later invited two NGO representatives to participate in the Inter-Ministerial Council preparing Russia's second NEAP. With NGO support, the State Committee also organised public hearings and developed a NEAP Communication Strategy.

Experience with NGO participation has highlighted the importance of several lessons:

– Public information and participation are most effective if planned from the beginning of the policy process.

– NIS government officials need training in public participation methods and procedures.

– Governments should prepare and disseminate timely and readable public documents on policy developments.

– NGOs need strengthening to improve their contribution to policy development.

– Co-operation with international NGOs has helped NIS groups contribute to policy discussions and disseminate public information on policy developments.

Recently a network of NIS NGOs interested in NEAPs has been created, uniting over 40 groups in seven countries. This should help strengthen NGO participation in NEAP development.

_____

Source: Ponizova.

very limited opening for participation, their work may lead to opportunities for greater participation and better government-NGO co-operation. Similar councils have been organised at the regional level in Ukraine and in a few regions of Russia.

Participation at local and regional levels

NIS NGOs and citizens have promoted a few local and regional referenda on the environment. In Kostroma *oblast* in Russia, NGOs organised a referendum that blocked construction of a nuclear power plant (Box 4.11). Local and regional governments have in few cases worked closely with NGOs. In 1995, the Environmental Protection Committee of Russia's Krasnodar region supported an NGO newspaper, *Environmental Boomerang*, which disseminated environmental information, NGOs in the Russian city of Lipetsk proposed a local energy conservation programme in 1996 and convinced authorities to adopt it. However, many NIS regional and local authorities have been reluctant to allow increased public and NGO participation, and local and regional NGOs have been too weak to establish a greater opening.

> ### Box 4.11. The nuclear power plant referendum in Kostroma *oblast*
>
> Starting in the early 1990s, NGOs in Kostroma *oblast*, Russia, organised a campaign against a federal government proposal to build a nuclear power plant. With the support of national and international groups including Greenpeace, Kostroma NGOs collected signatures in favour of a referendum from over 6 per cent of voters (the minimum required was 1 per cent). Non-environmental associations in the region also participated strongly in the campaign, which led to the first popular referendum on the environment in Russia, whose Constitution mentions the right to popular referendums and whose 1991 framework environment law specifically allows referenda on environmental issues. The referendum was held in December 1996. Almost 60 per cent of the regional electorate took part, and 87 per cent of voters rejected the proposal.
>
> ─────────
> *Source*: Kozeltsev.

Participation in environmental assessments

Active public or NGO participation in environmental assessments has been rare in the NIS. In most NIS, a large number of project proposals have undergone an environmental assessment but there have been few provisions for participation. Although proponents are required to publish information on the environmental consequences of their projects, and in principle the public has the right to make comments, these procedures are not always followed. Public hearings have not been required and have been rare. A recent analysis of assessments of investment projects proposed to Russia's National Pollution Abatement Fund for financing found that, in over 80 per cent of cases, there was little or no provision for public participation (Ponizova). In most NIS, the public has the right to carry out a parallel independent environmental review with open hearings. In practice, public participation has been poor even where this has taken place – probably because, for most NIS citizens, environmental problems have continued to have a relatively low priority. The NIS do not have a tradition of active public participation in decision-making.

Public information and participation have also been rare in the development of local and regional land-use plans. Moldova is one exception. Its 1996 Law on Construction and Territorial Planning requires consultations with the public. Citizens' groups invoked this requirement, soon after the law was passed, to block construction of a US fast-food restaurant in a park in the capital (REC, 1998*b*).

7. Access to Justice

Access to justice, particularly to the courts, is a basic guarantee of rights. In most CEE countries and NIS, citizens have, at least in principle, the right to challenge government actions that deny environmental information or restrict participation in environmental decisions, as well as the right to seek enforcement of environmental laws. In practice, public access to the courts is a new and undeveloped area. The Aarhus Convention explicitly sets out these rights, and its eventual ratification should help improve citizen and NGO access to justice.

7.1. *Access to justice in CEE countries*

In nearly all CEE countries, citizens and NGOs have the right to initiate court procedures to challenge government decisions. In many of those countries, laws have specifically established this right for claims that access to environmental information or participation has been unfairly limited. It can be more difficult to take polluters that violate environmental laws to court. In many countries, citizens and NGOs can bring such cases only if they are directly affected by the violation. In the Czech Republic, Slovenia and Romania, however, NGOs can seek court actions to stop any violation of environmental laws, either by authorities or by polluters.

Citizens and NGOs have experienced several difficulties in obtaining access to the courts, including high legal costs and court fees. Court procedures have often been extremely slow, and only in a few countries do courts have the power to grant "injunctive relief", stopping a potentially harmful activity during lengthy proceedings. Nonetheless, in a growing number of cases citizens and NGOs have sought rulings to implement and enforce environmental requirements. In the Czech Republic, a project to build a highway through Prague was halted on the grounds that it had not undergone an environmental impact assessment (REC, 1998a). In many CEE countries, national NGOs such as the Centre for Public Advocacy in Slovakia and the Polish Environmental Law Association have established legal services that assist citizens, other NGOs and local communities to undertake environmental court cases. In other countries, especially in the Balkan region, appeals to the courts have been rare and few NGOs as yet provide legal services.

A few countries, such as Hungary, have established "ombudsmen", official citizen's representatives who can investigate citizen's challenges of government actions. Appeals to ombudsmen have been relatively inexpensive compared to court proceedings. In Hungary, an ombudsman's ruling increased public access to corporate environmental information (Box 4.6).

7.2. *Access to justice in the* NIS

In all the NIS, citizens have the right of access to the courts, at least in principle. There have been several obstacles in practice. Court costs have been high relative to average household incomes; there have been few environmental lawyers to assist them in environmental cases; and there is little tradition of seeking redress for environmental or other problems through the courts. Indeed, few citizens are aware of their right of access to the courts. Courts in many NIS face more serious capacity problems than those in CEE countries and an independent judiciary is, at least in practice, a new idea.

Despite these obstacles, NGOs and other groups have initiated several court cases. These have often arisen out of environmental assessments. A few NIS NGOs – such as Ecojuris and Environment and Human Rights Protection in Russia, and Eco-Pravo in Ukraine – have provided legal support. The most important cases have had mixed results (Box 4.12).

Box 4.12.   **Environmental court cases in the NIS**

Several important court cases in the NIS have challenged inadequate procedures used to assess the environmental impacts of projects. In June 1997, a coalition of Russian NGOs, including Ecojuris, the All-Russia Society for Nature Protection and the Socio-Ecological Union, together with the chair of the Duma's environment committee, asked Russia's Constitutional Court to overturn a decision of the President and government in favour of a project to build a high-speed railway from Moscow to St. Petersburg on the grounds that a proper environmental assessment had not been made. In particular, such an assessment was needed to review the impact on a protected natural area through which proponents planned to run the line. Their petition was rejected, but a group of Duma deputies submitted a new one. As of late 1998, this case had not yet been decided. Partly due to the controversy generated, the government pledged not to start construction before 2000.

In Ukraine, an NGO, Zelenyi Svit, and a local company went to court in 1995 to stop construction of a fertiliser terminal in the town of Mykolaiv (the local company contended that pollution from the proposed terminal would harm the health of its workers nearby). Ecopravo-Lviv, an environmental law NGO, represented the two plaintiffs, arguing that the environmental impact documents had not been made public, that construction had started before the assessment procedure ended and that public opinion had not been considered (100 000 local residents had signed a petition against the terminal). A lower court ruled that construction should stop. However, the Ministry of Environment (a defendant along with the terminal proponents) appealed and the ruling was overturned.

Sources: Kozeltsev; Ponizova; REC (1998b).

NOTES

1. This chapter is based on two background papers: the first, on CEE countries, is by Magda Toth Nagy of the Regional Environmental Center for Central and Eastern Europe (REC) in Szentendre, Hungary, and the second, on the NIS, is by Olga Ponizova of Eco-Accord, an NGO based in Moscow. It also draws strongly on two of the four volumes published by the REC under the title *Doors to Democracy*. These review trends and practices in public participation in CEE countries and the NIS (all four volumes were published in June 1998; the third volume covers Western Europe and the fourth presents a pan-European overview).

2. In some cases, the basis of local protests appears similar to the "not in my back yard" (NIMBY) syndrome common in OECD countries.

3. The census was based on REC local office mailing lists. The study defined an NGO as "an officially or otherwise clearly identifiable group of citizens or other public association that:
   – does not act as an official government body;
   – is a not-for-profit organization;
   – functions at a local, regional, national and/or international level;
   – pursues environmental work as one of its major statutory activities.
   In the study, trade unions, political organizations, businesses and academic institutions were excluded from the target population" (REC, 1997).
   Recent reports indicate that the number of NGOs has continued to grow. Over 150 were reported active in Bulgaria in early 1999.

4. Many NGOs that focus on other issues (*e.g.* women's rights, human rights, trade unions, enterprises) have worked on environmental protection. These are not included in this analysis.

5. Directive 90/313/EEC on the Freedom of Access to Information on the Environment.

6. For example, the Czech Ministry of Environment's web page can be found at www.env.cz; that of the Latvian ministry is at www.varam.gov.lv. A site maintained by UNEP/GRID (Arendal) provides links to the web pages of many CEEC/NIS environmental authorities (see www.grida.no).

7. For example, the Kazakh Centre for the National Environmental Action Programme for Sustainable Development has set up its web page at www.neapsd.kz. UNEP/GRID (Arendal) at www.grida.no provides links to many of the NIS web pages.

REFERENCES

Brady, K. (1998),
New Convention on Access to Information and Public Participation in Environmental Matters, Environmental Policy and Law, 28/2, 1998.

Cohen, J. (1998),
Civil Society under Construction: a Challenge for Europe, in OSCE – A Need for Co-operation: Toward the OSCE's Common and Comprehensive Security Model for Europe for the Twenty-first Century, Copenhagen [http://www.una.dk/osce/essays/].

Denisov, N.B. (1999),
personal communication, UNEP/Grid (Arendal), Arendal, Norway, April.

EAP Task Force (1998),
Evaluation of Progress in Developing and Implementing National Environmental Action Programmes (NEAPs) in CEEC/NIS, OECD, Paris.

Francis, P. (1998),
personal communication, EAP Task Force secretariat, Paris, September.

Institute for Sustainable Development (ISD) (1997),
Frustrated Hopes: Independent Overview of Implementation of Agenda 21 in Poland, Institute for Sustainable Development, Warsaw, September.

Kaldor, M.I. and Vejvoda (1998),
Democratization in East and Central European Countries, International Affairs, 73:1 (1997), pp. 59-82, cited in J. Cohen (1998).

Kozeltsev, M. (1998),
personal communication, Moscow, July.

Lovei, M. and C. Weiss Jr. (1997),
Environmental Management and Institutions in OECD Countries: Lessons from Experience, Environment Dept. Paper No. 46, World Bank, Washington, DC, March.

Nagy, M.T. (1998),
Background Paper for the EAP Task Force Secretariat on Public Participation in Central and Eastern Europe, Regional Environmental Center for Central and Eastern Europe (REC), Szentendre, Hungary, April.

Ponizova, O. (1998),
Background Paper for the EAP Task Force Secretariat on Public Participation in the NIS, Eco-Accord, Moscow, April.

Regional Environmental Center for Central and Eastern Europe (REC) (1995),
New Regional Environmental Centers. A Feasibility Study on Establishing New Regional Environmental Centers for Countries beyond the Mandate of the Regional Environmental Center for Central and Eastern Europe, REC, Szentendre, Hungary.

Regional Environmental Center for Central and Eastern Europe (REC) (1997),
Problems, Progress and Possibilities: A Needs Assessment of Environmental NGOs in Central and Eastern Europe, REC, Szentendre, Hungary, April.

Regional Environmental Center for Central and Eastern Europe (REC) (1998a),
Doors to Democracy: Current Trends and Practices in Public Participation in Environmental Decision-making in Central and Eastern Europe, REC, Szentendre, Hungary, June.

Regional Environmental Center for Central and Eastern Europe (REC) (1998b),
Doors to Democracy: Current Trends and Practices in Public Participation in Environmental Decision-making in the Newly Independent States, REC, Szentendre, Hungary, June.

Regional Environmental Center for Central and Eastern Europe (REC) and Milieukontakt Oost-Europa (1998),
Trends in Funding: An Overview of Domestic and International Funds Available for Central and Eastern European Environmental NGOs, Milieukontakt Oost-Europa, Amsterdam, June.

101

Saladin, C. and B. Van Dyke (1998),
> *Implementing the Principles of the Public Participation Convention in International Organizations*, Center for International Environmental Law, background document for the NGO session of the "Environment for Europe" Conference, Aarhus, Denmark, June, Friends of the Earth/Europe, Belgium.

Stec, S. (1998),
> *Environment, Democracy and Wealth: Environmental Law Reform in Eastern Europe*, unpublished paper, Utrecht University Institute for Constitutional and Administrative, Utrecht, the Netherlands, April.

TACIS (1998),
> *Environmental Awareness Throughout the NIS*, information note, European Commission, Brussels.

UN-ECE Committee on Environmental Policy (1998),
> *Progress in the Implementation of the ECE Guidelines on Public Participation in Environmental Decision-making*, document submitted to the "Environment for Europe" Conference, Aarhus, Denmark, June.

US Information Agency (USIA) (1998),
> *Majorities in Former USSR Want Cleanup of Environment First – then Economic Growth* (M-67-98), USIA, Washington, DC, 4 May.

Wates, J. (1998),
> *The Public Participation Convention – An NGO Perspective*, presentation to the GLOBE Conference "Our common garden, Aarhus, Denmark, 21-22 June 1998.

Weingast, B.R. (undated),
> *The Political Foundations of Democracy and the Rule of Law*, summary of IRIS Working Paper No. 54, Center for Institutional Reform and the Informal Sector (IRIS), University of Maryland, College Park, Maryland, USA [http://www.inforM.umd.edu/IRIS/weiwp54.html].

Zamparutti, A. and M. Kozeltsev (1998),
> *Environmental Issues in Tomsk Oblast*, in OECD/CCNM *A Regional Approach to Industrial Restructuring in the Tomsk Region*, Russian Federation, OECD, Paris.

Zhdanovich, O. (1998),
> *Environmental Public Opinion Polls in the Russian Federation*, background pager for the EAP Task Force secretariat, July.

Chapter 5

ENVIRONMENTAL POLICY INSTRUMENTS

Introduction

Countries in the region have used a "mix" of policy instruments for pollution management, in which ambient standards, facility environmental permits and pollution charges have all played prominent roles. Many countries introduced these instruments under central planning. In the early years of the transition, new democratic governments strengthened existing instruments and added new ones.

The EAP reviewed progress in the early 1990s and urged countries in the region to improve the effectiveness of their policy instruments. It encouraged them to reform their pollution charges and strengthen the use of these and other "economic instruments" for pollution management. Moreover, the EAP also urged countries to improve the institutions and systems that support pollution management, including those for environmental monitoring and information and for ensuring polluter compliance.

This chapter looks at the effectiveness of environmental policy instruments in CEEC/NIS, using several criteria:[1]

- *Environmental effectiveness*: the extent to which policy instruments yield improvements in environmental conditions – in particular, those improvements identified as priority objectives under national environmental policies. For pollution control mechanisms such as pollution charges, this requires that the instrument establish at least basic incentives for compliance.

- *Economic efficiency*: the extent to which policy instruments promote cost-effective approaches to pollution reduction. Mechanisms that allow industrial plants flexibility in terms of the methods and time frame for pollution reduction can greatly increase overall cost-effectiveness. With a longer time frame for compliance, plants can invest in less polluting production methods rather than "end-of-pipe" pollution abatement equipment.

- *Administrative and compliance costs*: these include the costs for environmental authorities to administer the instrument, including costs of measurement, monitoring and revenue collection – particularly in relation to the resources these institutions have available. When environmental authorities lack minimum resources to implement and enforce an environmental requirement, compliance will likely be poor. The administrative and managerial costs for polluting enterprises are also important. Instruments that create high costs have less chance of being accepted by polluters.

Other issues related to the effectiveness of policy instruments include:

- *"Dynamic" effects*: while some instruments are static, others can create ongoing incentives for pollution reduction, encouraging industrial innovation.

- *Support of the public and acceptability to polluters* are key elements for implementation in democratic, market-based economies. Public and community participation can be an important driving force for pollution reduction and can encourage polluters to accept environmental requirements. Such acceptance in turn encourages polluter compliance efforts.

- *Wider economic effects*: pollution management instruments can affect the competitiveness of polluting industries; they can also have distributional and employment implications.

- *Establishing good governance* is a key issue for transition countries. The implementation of policy instruments should help – and, at the very least, not harm – the development of governance, including accountability, transparency and the rule of law. In effective pollution management, governments need to establish clear, predictable environmental "rules" for polluters to follow.

– *Use of revenues*: several economic instruments, including pollution charges, raise revenues. In many CEEC/NIS, environmental funds channel these revenues to pollution control investments and other environmental expenditures. The effectiveness of this spending is a key element in their overall policy effectiveness.

This chapter looks at policy instruments used in CEEC/NIS for pollution management, and discusses several trends and issues. However, many important factors, starting with the administrative capacities of environmental authorities, vary greatly from country to country; more in-depth reviews of effectiveness would require a country-by-country analysis – and possibly examination of specific "hot spots" or industries. The OECD and UN/ECE reviews of countries' environmental performance have contributed to this type of analysis.[2] To improve the effectiveness of their policy instruments, countries in the region will need to carry out their own regular, in-depth evaluations.

1. Ambient Environmental Standards

Ambient standards set maximum concentrations of a pollutant in a specific medium, such as air, water or soil, to protect human health and ecosystems. Such standards can indicate targets for policy measures. Before the transition, nearly all countries in the region had developed ambient standards for air and water, as had most OECD countries; however, air and water standards in CEE countries and the former Soviet Union were often much more stringent than those in OECD countries or than guidelines recommended by the World Health Organisation (WHO). For example, many air quality standards in Moldova – based on Soviet standards – have been significantly more stringent than WHO guidelines (Table 5.1). Many countries in the region had set standards for hundreds or even thousands of different pollutants. Overall, the CEEC/NIS ambient standards reflected "ideals" for human health protection, but in practice were not used to move towards this goal.

The CEEC/NIS ambient standards were part of an overall system of pollution management that had little effect in reducing pollution levels. Although ambient standards and ambient conditions were used in principle to calculate emissions limits for individual polluters, negotiations between authorities and polluters often "adjusted" these emissions requirements (see below). As a result, air pollution in many seriously polluted "hot spots" continued to exceed standards several times over. At the same time, these stringent standards gave an impression that environmental conditions in less polluted areas were worse than they actually were (Box 5.1), which has made it difficult for the public, authorities or bilateral donors to identify priorities for action. Some standards for individual pollutants were, in certain areas, even more stringent than naturally occurring background concentrations.

Ambient standards also exceeded CEEC/NIS administrative capacities to monitor them. In effect, although countries set a great many standards, they could measure pollution levels for only a few. In the early 1990s, Hungary had standards for about 380 air pollutants but monitoring stations measured at

Table 5.1. **Selected ambient air quality standards in Moldova compared with WHO guideline values**

Pollutant	Moldova standards	WHO guideline value
Carbon monoxide (CO)	5.0 mg/m^3, 20 minutes	100 mg/m^3, 15 minutes
	. .	60 mg/m^3, 30 minutes
	. .	30 mg/m^3, 1 hour
	3.0 mg/m^3, 24 hours	10 mg/m^3, 8 hours
Ozone (O$_3$)	0.16 mg/m^3, 20 minutes	. .
	0.03 mg/m^3, 24 hours	0.12 mg/m^3, 8 hours
Sulphur dioxide (SO$_2$)	0.50 mg/m^3, 20 minutes	0.5 mg/m^3, 10 minutes
	0.05 mg/m^3, 24 hours	0.125 mg/m^3, 24 hours
	. .	0.05 mg/m^3, 1 year

. . Not available.
Source: UN/ECE.

Box 5.1. **Water quality in Lithuania**

The stringent ambient standards developed under central planning made it difficult to identify the most urgent environmental problems in CEEC/NIS. Many observers concluded from initial reports of standards being exceeded over extensive areas that environmental quality was poor across the entire region. For 80% of the courses of Lithuania's rivers, levels of BOD_5 were above ambient standards in the mid-1990s – and for one-quarter of these "polluted" river courses, concentrations exceeded twice the maximum level. However, for most stretches, river water quality in Lithuania was acceptable by EU standards, whose maximum allowable BOD_5 limits were three times as high as the Soviet standards used in Lithuania.

_____

Source: Semeniene *et al.*

---

most 10. Belarus has used Soviet standards, which refer to over 1 700 air pollutants (OECD, 1997*a*). For many pollutants, monitoring equipment was not sensitive enough to measure concentrations at the low levels they specified.

The EAP recommended that countries in the region adopt simpler, more realistic standards that could be monitored more easily, and that they look at EU standards and WHO guidelines in making such reforms.

1.1. *Reforming ambient standards*

Since the EAP was endorsed, several CEE countries have followed its recommendations and revised their ambient standards, in particular for those pollutants identified as the most serious threats to human health – such as concentrations of particulates, SO_x and NO_x in the atmosphere. (In many countries, this has required close co-operation between environmental and health authorities, as the latter have traditionally set ambient standards.) Most CEE countries have used the values adopted in EU legislation or those recommended by WHO guidelines as a basis. Furthermore, many countries have tied the new standards more closely to pollution control actions. In Bulgaria, the Ministries of Environment and Health agreed in 1994 to revise air quality standards for eight pollutants, including SO_2 and particulates. The new standards have been linked to smog alert programmes in large cities: when standards are exceeded, cities should adopt temporary measures to reduce traffic and industrial activity and cut pollution levels. Concurrently, Bulgaria's regional inspectorates improved their monitoring equipment to track these priority pollutants more accurately (bilateral donors aided these monitoring improvements). Many other CEE countries have improved air pollution monitoring, and several have developed smog alert programmes for large cities.

In several NIS, environmental and health officials have considered the reform of ambient standards. Environmental authorities in Ukraine have proposed less stringent ambient air quality standards for a set of priority pollutants; Moldova has considered similar reforms. As of late 1998, however, such reforms had not yet been adopted. In some cases, there has been opposition to the "weakening" of pollution standards.

Countries in the region will need to continue their development of ambient standards. For example, a number of countries in Western Europe have introduced new types of standards for ecosystems, such as those identifying critical ecosystem loads for acid deposition. The Second Sulphur Protocol of the Convention on Long-Range Transboundary Air Pollution has encouraged this approach. A number of countries in the region have used risk assessment methods to supplement ambient standards, particularly to link ambient conditions to the identification of priorities for action (Box 5.2). In addition, research has shown that the smallest airborne particulates – those under 10 microns (mm) in diameter (also known

_____

Box 5.2. **Using risk assessment and management to identify environmental priorities**

In several cases, CEEC/NIS policy-makers have used risk assessment methods to identify the most important pollution threats and set priorities for clean-up measures. These methods estimate the probabilities of harm to human health (or the environment) from specific sources of pollution or other hazards.

The Czech Republic has used risk assessment and management techniques to make decisions on the sequence and extent of clean-up of contaminated soil at industrial sites. In the early 1990s, foreign investors and CEE governments used very stringent soil standards – including those developed in OECD countries such as the Netherlands – to determine the extent of clean-up necessary at contaminated industrial sites (while CEEC/NIS had extensive lists of air and water quality standards, few had soil standards). The resulting clean-ups were extremely expensive, even for sites that presented only minor risks to human health. As an alternative, the Czech Environment Ministry introduced risk analysis and risk management guidelines in 1996. These described procedures to identify the most cost-effective approaches to protect human health, taking into account future site use. This approach is increasingly used in Western Europe. In the Netherlands, soil standards are now used as "trigger values" for risk analysis rather than as clean-up objectives. Similarly, risk analysis was used for clean-up decisions in Germany's eastern *Lander*, where the number and extent of contaminated sites made it too costly to use uniform soil standards.

In Russia, a US-funded project used risk analysis to identify cost-effective air pollution measures in six cities. In Volgograd, the study identified the emissions that presented the greatest health threats to the city's population. Researchers then used this information, together with data on pollution reduction costs, to identify the most cost-effective pollution reduction actions (the most effective investments cost as little as US$100 per death avoided).

Risk assessment and management can require new forms of technical expertise not available in all countries of the region. In these cases, donor technical assistance can play an important role. In Volgograd, Russian and foreign experts worked together closely on risk assessment; in the Czech Republic, the government employed domestic consulting companies to develop and implement the new methods.

Sources: Goldenman; Larson *et al.*; Strukova.

---

as PMIOs) – create the greatest risks for human health.[3] A few CEE countries, such as Poland, have introduced ambient standards for these particulates. The EU has started to review its ambient air standards in light of new health information; this process may lead to the proposal of new, stricter requirements. Candidate countries seeking to join the EU would have to follow such revisions.

1.2. *Ambient standards, permits and emissions limits*

In nearly all countries, industrial plants and other large, stationary pollution sources must have facility environmental permits. These set air and water emissions limits that, in principle, are based on ambient standards and conditions.[4] Most CEEC/NIS environmental authorities have set separate emissions requirements for each point source at a facility and for each pollutant emitted. (A few countries, however, have used facility-wide standards, "netting" emissions across different point sources.)

Pollution charges and non-compliance fees are in turn tied to emissions. Polluters pay charges on their air pollution emissions and water pollution discharges up to their permit limits; they pay non-compliance fees, usually at rates several times higher, for pollution levels above these limits. There have been several variations on this scheme. Russia and a number of other NIS have used a three-tier system for air pollution charges (Box 5.3); other countries, such as Hungary and Bulgaria, have only used non-compliance fees for air and water pollution. Some CEEC/NIS have established other types of permit and charge requirements, such as for solid and hazardous waste generation.

Box 5.3. Emissions limits in Russia

In Russia and some other NIS, environmental authorities have used a "three-tier" system. Permits set "maximum" emissions limits, based on air pollution models, as well as "temporary" limits that are negotiated directly with polluters. Polluters pay one charge rate on emissions below the "maximum" limits; a second, higher rate on emissions between these and the higher "temporary" limits; and a third, even higher rate on emissions above the "temporary" limits (the second and third rates could be considered non-compliance fees).

In many cases, polluters have found the "maximum" limits too strict to be attainable with their current resources. In a few cases, these limits have been impractical. Standards for waste water discharges in Nizhniy Novgorod, Russia, have been more stringent for some parameters than the standards for drinking water. At the same time, environmental authorities have had wide discretionary powers and few guidelines for negotiating the "temporary" limits. In many cases, these have been set at values close to actual pollution levels, yielding little incentive for pollution reduction.

Sources: APWG; Garanin.

Discretionary powers of environmental authorities

In many CEEC/NIS, environmental authorities have had wide discretionary powers to adjust pollution limits and charges in negotiations with polluters (Vincent and Farrow). "Temporary" limits have been set in Russia and some other NIS, mainly through negotiation (Box 5.3). In some countries, environmental authorities have had wide discretion to issue charge "waivers" (Box 5.4).

Box 5.4. Pollution charge waivers

Environmental authorities in many CEEC/NIS have allowed enterprises to reduce their required charge or fine payments by the amount of their pollution abatement and control investments. In Russia, the total amount of pollution charge "waivers" has become far larger than the revenues actually collected from polluters. This widespread use of waivers reflects the economic system that has taken root during Russia's transition. Government soft credits for enterprises, via tolerance of tax arrears and other indirect mechanisms, have fuelled a barter economy and discouraged enterprise restructuring and reform. In the case of the charge waivers, environmental authorities appear to have exercised little oversight of the investments claimed (or the basis for their valuation). As a result, waivers appear to have little effect in reducing pollution.

Several CEE countries have also used charge waivers, though environmental authorities have exercised greater supervision in granting them. In Latvia, authorities have developed procedures for enterprises to request waivers, as well as monitoring and compliance measures to ensure that they undertake the investments promised. Some countries have limited the magnitude of waivers. In the Czech Republic, an enterprise can request to waive a maximum of 40 per cent of the charges it is assessed.

The use of waivers presents several dangers. Most importantly in transition economies, it increases the risk of corruption common to other discretionary uses of authority. Waivers granted indiscriminately can also undermine the basic logic of pollution charges, which should provide incentives for pollution reduction. When polluters retain these sums, they substitute their own priorities for social preferences regarding use of the funds. However, in some countries the waiver system appears to have been an important mechanism for gaining polluter acceptance of the charge system.

Sources: Golub; OECD, 1999.

These discretionary powers – in particular when accountability and transparency are poor – may not result in environmental improvements and may increase risks of corruption. They can endanger the development of a clear, consistent rule of law establishing basic environmental requirements for polluters and undermine any incentives for compliance. This situation is completely different to that in many OECD countries, where experience with implementing regulatory systems is leading to experimentation with more flexible policy approaches involving more administrative discretion.

2. Economic Instruments[5]

The EAP urged countries in the region to use economic instruments where possible to reduce pollution cost-effectively (Box 5.5). At the time the EAP was written, most CEE countries and NIS had established pollution charge and non-compliance fee systems. The EAP noted that pollution charge systems in the region were often complex and difficult to administer. It recommended that countries simplify them, to improve environmental effectiveness, and introduce other economic instruments. This section looks at CEEC/NIS efforts towards these goals. It focuses on pollution charges and non-compliance fees – particularly those for air pollution and waste water discharges, which have been the most prominent in terms of pollution management. However, countries in the region have used many other types of economic instruments, including natural resource charges and deposit-refund systems (Annex VII provides an overview of economic instruments used in CEE countries). Under central planning,

---

Box 5.5. Economic and other instruments for pollution management

Economic instruments mainly use financial incentives and disincentives to influence behaviour affecting the environment. They are often contrasted with "command-and-control" regulatory approaches, such as technology standards that specify production or pollution control equipment that plants must use.

In principle, the use of economic instruments such as the pollution charges adopted by most CEEC/NIS can: 1) reduce economic costs compared to technology standards, as they give polluters greater flexibility to choose how to make pollution reductions; 2) provide an ongoing incentive to reduce pollution; and, in some cases; 3) create a revenue raising mechanism for the state. These considerations suggest that economic instruments such as pollution charges should be more cost-effective than "command-and-control" approaches and, by creating ongoing incentives for pollution reduction, have a "dynamic" effect. The extensive use of pollution charges in the CEEC/NIS region is thus of interest to many OECD countries, as well as others interested in developing more cost-effective approaches to pollution management.

In practice, there is not a simple dichotomy between economic instruments and regulatory approaches. Only economic instruments such as pollution charges use *prices* to influence polluters. In theory, this approach provides the greatest flexibility for polluters to choose how to reduce their pollution levels. In some cases, such as controlling particularly hazardous substances, regulatory approaches are clearly more effective than economic instruments.

Both economic instruments and regulatory approaches can specify pollution *quantities*. This is the case for uniform emissions standards that set maximum facility pollution levels for an entire class of polluters, and also for economic instruments such as tradeable permit systems that set maximum pollution levels across a geographic area (Box 5.7). Many OECD countries have relied extensively on technology standards to regulate pollution from large stationary sources, such as power plants and manufacturing plants. This approach gives the least flexibility to polluters (perhaps because the instrument itself is inflexible, environmental authorities in many OECD countries undertake extensive case-by-case negotiations with polluters when developing facility permits based on technology standards). In practice, most countries have used combinations of different instruments. For example, most CEEC/NIS have combined pollution charges with emissions limits specified in permits. Some countries use *information provision and public participation* to encourage pollution reduction.

Sources: OECD, 1997c; OECD, 1997f.

many CEEC/NIS neglected waste management, though some countries have recently strengthened their policy instruments in this area. Environmental liability requirements, although not always classified as an economic instrument, can provide an ongoing incentive for enterprises to reduce pollution levels.

2.1. *Pollution charges and non-compliance fees*

National environmental policies state several objectives for pollution charges and non-compliance fees, including: raising revenues for environmental investments; creating incentives for pollution control and reduction; enforcing permit requirements; and implementing the Polluter Pays Principle. In practice, revenue raising has been the most important goal and the main function of these charges (Bluffstone). Revenues have gone to environmental funds that then allocate them for environmental projects. In several CEE countries, charge systems have raised large sums – over US$500 million in Poland in 1996, for example. In most other countries, including many NIS, charge revenues have been much lower (Chapter 6 describes the role of environmental funds and Annex VIII provides data on selected funds). However, the effectiveness of pollution charge and non-compliance fee systems has been mixed when considering other criteria, such as their administrative costs or their direct incentives to reduce pollution levels.

Administrative costs

The complexity of the permit and charge systems entails significant administrative costs. For both air emissions and waste water discharges, environmental authorities have had to calculate and then monitor emissions limits for dozens of pollutants at hundreds of point sources. There is little information on the costs involved, either in theory or practice. However, environmental authorities across the region have lacked the capacity to monitor emissions of all these pollutants properly. In a few countries, budget shortfalls and capacity problems have reduced emissions monitoring to a minimum.

Incentive effects

Pollution charges and non-compliance fees have not created strong incentives for pollution abatement or reduction. Even in the countries with the highest charges, like Poland, rates have been several times below the cost of pollution control equipment, suggesting that polluters find it cheaper to pay the charges (OECD, 1994). In other CEEC/NIS, rates have been much lower (Table 5.2). In some countries, including Russia, inflation has severely eroded the real value of charge rates (Figure 5.1). The few Western European countries that have used pollution charges have set them much higher (Table 5.2).

Other factors have limited the potential incentive effect of charges in CEEC/NIS. For example, Russia and some other countries have used a system by which an enterprise's total charges are capped when its profits are low. In the ongoing economic crisis, many polluters have not paid the charges assessed (just as many have not paid other taxes). In Nizhniy Novgorod in Russia, only one-quarter of waste water charges were paid in 1996. Of those enterprises that paid, many did so in barter rather than money (Garanin). A number of other countries, particularly the NIS, have experienced similar payment problems.

Despite these problems, pollution charges in at least a few CEE countries have created incentives for low-cost pollution reductions. A survey of enterprises in Lithuania found that many were undertaking low-cost measures to reduce their air pollution levels, and thus their charge payments (Bluffstone). Pollution charges have created incentives for some pollution reduction measures in Poland (Anderson and Fiedor).

Non-compliance fees, which apply when an enterprise exceeds its permitted level of pollution, are set at rates several times higher than the charges and should create stronger incentives to meet the emissions limits specified in the permits (Bluffstone). However, monitoring and enforcement limitations have blunted their incentive effect. The design and application of non-compliance fees have varied from country to country. In a few, such as Hungary, they have been low and environmental authorities have had little power to stop continuing emissions above permit levels. Some enterprises have therefore emitted pollution above their permit limits for long periods of time. In some countries, with more stringent non-compliance fee systems, collection rates have been low. Polluters in Lithuania paid only 50 to 60 per cent of non-compliance fees levied for air and water pollution, but almost 100% of the pollution charges levied (Klarer and McNicholas).

Table 5.2. **Indicative pollution charge rates in selected CEEC/NIS, 1997**

	Air pollution: SO$_x$ (US\$/tonne[a])	Water pollution: BOD (US\$/tonne[a])
CEE countries		
Lithuania	104	220
Poland	176	1 000-4 000[b]
Romania	..	11
NIS		
Russia	4[c]	..
OECD countries		
France[d]	..	54 000[e]
Sweden[d]	4 100[f]	..

.. Not available.
a) Converted from local currencies to US\$ using PPPs.
b) Varies according to industry.
c) Rate for emissions within maximum permittable emission limits.
d) France and Sweden: rates are for 1995.
e) For the Seine-Normandie Water Agency.
f) For NO$_x$ emissions; Sweden uses a product charge (30 SKR/kg) on the sulphur content of coal, oil and peat.
Sources: Klarer and McNicholas; OECD, *Environmental Performance Reviews: France* (1997); OECD, *Environmental Performance Reviews: Sweden* (1996).

Figure 5.1. **Decline in the real value of Russia's pollution charges (1990 = 100)**

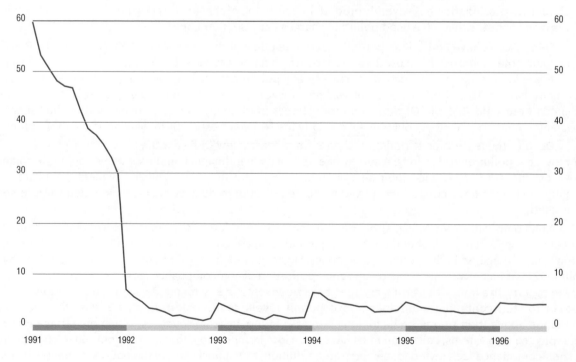

Source: Golub.

In many NIS, the slow pace of economic reform has severely limited any potential incentives. Weak bankruptcy provisions and indirect government subsidies have undermined the market forces that could encourage enterprises to maximise profits, including by reducing their pollution charge payments.

Despite these shortcomings, in at least a few countries a system of permits, charges, fines and environmental fund allocations has reduced pollution. In both the Czech Republic and Poland, pollution charge revenues have fallen since 1996, suggesting that these environmental policy instruments, together with economic restructuring and reform, have contributed to pollution reduction (Klarer).

Strengthening pollution charges

A few CEEC/NIS have taken (and others have considered) steps to strengthen pollution charge and non-compliance fee systems, and pollution management more generally. However, from the start of the transition, environmental authorities in many CEEC/NIS have concentrated on maintaining existing charge rates in the face of inflation and opposition from polluters. Lithuania has simplified its system for air pollution charges, reducing the number of different rates and pollutants covered. In Ukraine, a proposal was made to cut the number of pollutants subject to charges from hundreds to 25 air and 10 water pollutants. In Russia, foreign and domestic experts have outlined key steps to strengthen air pollution management: in particular, they have suggested developing a simplified system for small and medium-sized polluters (Box 5.6). These recommendations could be useful in other CEEC/NIS, where the number of small and medium-sized enterprises has grown rapidly.

Box 5.6. **Reforming air pollution instruments in Russia**

The Harvard Institute for International Development (HIID) worked with Russian environmental economists and policy specialists to develop practical recommendations for reforming air pollution management. These were based in part on the results of studies carried out in six Russian cities, in co-operation with the State Committee for Environmental Protection and with regional and local committees. Recommendations regarding emissions limits and pollution charges include:
- Develop a simplified system of charges for small and medium-sized polluters. This would allow environmental authorities to focus compliance efforts on the few large polluters that, in many cities and industrial areas, generate a large share of air pollution.
- For these large polluters, raise the multipliers for non-compliance fees (*i.e.* the rates for emissions above the "maximum" and "temporary" limits).
- Develop ambient standards and related emissions limits for total particulates (Russia has ambient standards for several types of particulates, but not for total particulate concentrations, which are a major factor in health risks).
- Develop a formal, consistent and transparent approach to granting pollution charge "waivers".
- Require large polluters to report their annual emissions to the public.

These recommendations could provide an important first step towards strengthening the current system of emissions limits and charges.

The study, supported by US technical assistance, also recommended that local environmental authorities use risk assessment and risk management to identify and analyse key health threats from air pollution, as well as cost-effective options for reducing the most dangerous emissions. A related HIID project had demonstrated these techniques in the six cities studied.

Source: APWG.

A variety of new economic instruments have been applied. Hungary has used a *product charge* on motor fuels to raise revenues for its environmental fund. Hungary and Latvia have introduced several product charges – on packaging and other products – to encourage recycling (the effectiveness of these charges is not yet clear). *Charges on pollutant content* of fuels and other raw materials offer a further opportunity to reduce pollution. In 1997 Slovenia introduced a tax on the carbon content of fuels.[6] (In Western Europe, Sweden has implemented a charge on the sulphur in coal, diesel and domestic heating oil, and peat.[7]) Kazakhstan has established a *tradeable permit system* to reduce air pollution in Almaty (Box 5.7). Tradeable permit systems could provide cost-effective mechanisms for pollution control and reduction. CEEC/NIS (like most OECD countries) have rarely considered this tool, which needs to meet a number of important prerequisites to function well, including effective government oversight.

Box 5.7. Tradeable permit schemes

Under a tradeable permit system, a polluter that emits less that the permitted level of a specific pollutant can sell the unused portion (the "allowance") to another polluter, which can then emit the equivalent amount above its permitted level. Thus, while total emissions remain capped, polluters can trade to determine the most cost-effective allocation of the limit. A polluter will sell an allowance if it can reduce its pollution at a cost lower than the price another polluter is willing to pay. This system has been used mainly in the US. In many urban areas with high levels of air pollution, total emissions from stationary sources are capped and new enterprises that need to emit air pollutants must "buy" allowances from existing ones. On a national basis, tradeable permits have been used to reduce total emissions of specific pollutants such SO_x generated by power plants and other large sources.

In the only trading system implemented in the region, Kazakhstan set up a pilot scheme in 1996 in the capital, Almaty, under which about 1 200 enterprises have traded emissions allowances for three air pollutants. Environmental authorities have used the trading scheme to steadily cut pollution levels in the city, reducing the total emissions limit for these pollutants by 7% a year. There has been one small-scale "trading" experiment in Central and Eastern Europe. In a pilot project in the city of Chorzów in Poland, a power plant and a steel mill were allowed to comply jointly with their permitted emissions requirements, significantly reducing their combined pollution control costs and hastening compliance with standards. A study carried out jointly by Czech and US experts estimated that trading of SO_x allowances among polluters in the district of Sokolov in the Czech Republic could yield at least a 15% cost savings for pollution reduction efforts.

As strong monitoring and enforcement is necessary (emissions levels have to be measured accurately), emissions trading works best when the number of pollutants and the number of facilities involved are relatively limited. Trading among facilities in highly polluted areas could reduce emissions of key pollutants cost-effectively, as in Almaty and Chorzów. Systems for nation-wide trading could play a role in meeting national environmental goals, such as air pollution requirements for NO_x, SO_x or CO_2 generated by power plants and other large facilities. Trading could work in a similar fashion for key waste water pollutants discharged into a river basin.

Many CEEC/NIS environmental officials continue to be hesitant about this mechanism. Countries seeking EU accession are concerned that its legislation does not allow emissions trading. The Kyoto Protocol has proposed international trading mechanisms for CO_2 emissions (Annex IV). This could encourage tradeable permit schemes in many countries, including some CEEC/NIS.

Sources: Stavins and Zylicz; Vincent and Farrow.

Countries should also seek to integrate their charge systems (and other economic instruments) more closely with fiscal policy objectives. This would help strengthen environmental protection, and could alleviate the fiscal burden on enterprises. OECD countries have discussed options for "greening" their tax systems, such as reducing labour taxes and increasing environmental ones (OECD, 1997*b*). A few CEEC/NIS have also considered such options. Slovenia's carbon tax represents an important step in this direction, as its revenues are not earmarked for environmental purposes but go to the central government budget (Klarer and McNicholas).

Those CEE countries seeking EU accession now face the challenge of integrating their current mechanisms with those in its environmental legislation. Although the EU has called for greater flexibility in pollution management and greater use of economic instruments, its legislation at present makes little use of either (Annex III).

2.2. Economic and other instruments for waste management

Under central planning, CEEC and NIS had few standards or other requirements aimed at controlling industrial and hazardous wastes. Disposal methods were often poor. There was little investment in landfills or other waste management methods. Enterprises accumulated large amounts of waste on site, and household wastes were often not separated from potentially more hazardous industrial wastes but were buried in common landfills along with municipal wastes.

Over the transition, many CEE countries have introduced new *standards* to define hazardous wastes, along with more stringent requirements for their disposal. Many CEEC and some NIS have also improved their transboundary controls of hazardous wastes in accordance with the Basel Convention. The Czech Republic, Hungary and Poland have taken a lead in this area; as part of their accession to the OECD, they implemented the Basel Convention along with related OECD Decisions on hazardous waste movements and on chemicals management.

Many CEEC/NIS have used solid and hazardous *waste charges*; often these were in place before the transition. In many countries, enterprises must pay waste generation charges (which usually go to environmental funds) as well as separate disposal fees. However, both have been low and compliance has often been poor. A few countries have started to increase disposal fees, both for enterprises and households, in order to finance new waste facilities and strengthen enforcement. The Czech Republic's 1998 Waste Management Act strengthened charges for municipal and other inert solid waste and for hazardous waste. These will rise steadily between 1999 and 2003. The revenues will go mainly to municipalities to help meet costs related to waste management. A portion of the charges on hazardous wastes will go to the State Environmental Fund. Czech environmental authorities have closed many landfills and hazardous waste incinerators that lacked sufficient environmental safeguards (OECD, 1999).

A few CEEC have introduced *product charges* on items that generate consumer waste. Hungary and Latvia have introduced charges on packaging materials, used batteries, used tyres and other items. Estonia and Poland have also introduced charges on packaging materials. The effectiveness of these instruments has not been clear. Hungary's charge on packaging materials, for example, has to be collected from hundreds of retailers. Enforcement has been difficult and administrative costs high. The debate over the introduction of this charge did prompt some enterprises producing packaging materials to establish recycling programmes (Lehoczki).

2.3. Environmental liability

In some OECD countries, strong legal provisions for environmental liability have been vital in encouraging enterprises to reduce their pollution and other environmental damages, and thus have helped to implement the Polluter Pays Principle (OECD, 1998). Liability means that polluters should remediate or provide compensation for environmental problems they create, and correct or provide compensation for damages caused to third parties. (In many countries, liability provisions are strongest for accidental releases of pollution and may not apply to actions allowed under the polluters' permits, such as emissions within limit values.) Strong liability laws make it easier for citizens affected by pollution or other environmental problems to seek damages via the courts. They have catalysed market pressures for environmental performance, and they have created a strong incentive for enterprises to adopt environmental management and cleaner production programmes to avoid potentially costly damage payments. In some countries, financial institutions such as banks, as well as financial markets, have started to scrutinise enterprises for their environmental performance and potential environmental liabilities (Holtzmann).

113

In some CEEC/NIS, civil laws have provided a basis for environmental liability and NGOs have sought damages against major polluters in a number of court cases (Chapter 4). Environmental liability has also been a concern for potential foreign investors, in particular large corporations, which have closely investigated environmental problems such as soil contamination and other past damage at the site of CEE enterprises before making investments.[8] These issues prompted some CEE countries to develop programmes to address liability issues, including clarification of responsibilities for past environmental damage at enterprises undergoing privatisation (Goldenman).

A few CEE countries have passed laws to strengthen environmental liability requirements for current and future pollution. Estonia's new framework environmental law, for example, makes enterprises strictly liable for environmental damage to third parties – even if these enterprises were operating within the requirements of their permits (Gornaja, et al.).

Liability provisions have not had a major influence in encouraging CEEC/NIS enterprises to reduce pollution. One reason is that liability laws require an effective judicial system to be meaningful. In many CEE countries and NIS, the court systems have remained poorly funded and inefficient. The region has also had few lawyers capable of preparing and arguing cases against polluters. Nonetheless, over the long term environmental liability requirements can provide a strong incentive for pollution reduction. EU legislation does not cover environmental liability, but some EU countries such as Germany have established strong liability provisions. With this trend in mind, CEE countries seeking to join the EU should consider strengthening their liability legislation.

3. Environmental Impact Assessments

Environmental impact assessments (EIAs) review the ecosystem and human health effects of proposed projects, such as those for large industrial plants, major roads and other infrastructure. In both OECD countries and many CEEC/NIS, project proponents must prepare an environmental impact statement (EIS) for review by designated experts. These experts often sit on a state commission dedicated to reviewing EIAs. Most EIA laws include "screening lists" that identify the types of projects subject to EIA requirements.

EIA procedures are intended to have *environmental benefits*. In most countries, EIA decisions can block projects whose impacts will be unacceptable; require project modifications; or specify environmental requirements to be met. Under some EIA laws, the process can evaluate project design alternatives to identify the option with the lowest environmental impacts. In principle, EIA requirements should induce proponents to consider environmental issues and impacts in project design, ensuring cost-effective environmental protection. Moreover, EIAs usually can have provisions for public participation and thus contribute to the development of democracy. When not properly designed and implemented, EIA procedures can result in high administrative and compliance costs without significant results.

3.1. *Environmental assessments in* CEE[9]

Since 1989, nearly all CEE countries have adopted EIA procedures. In some countries, the EU's 1985 EIA legislation, as well as the 1991 Espoo Convention on EIA in a Transboundary Context, have encouraged development of these procedures. Bilateral donors have also supported the development and implementation of EIA procedures in several CEE countries (Box 5.8). EIA legislation in most CEE countries requires proponents to make their impact study publicly available, and provides for a notice and comment period, often including a public hearing. The number of EIAs varies significantly among countries. Hungary has had a relatively stringent screening procedure, including high thresholds for the minimum size of projects (20 EIAs were performed in 1996). In Poland, with similar screening rules, 25 were carried out in that year; in Bulgaria, which has had a less strict selection process, there were about 1 000 EIAs.

Impact assessments have blocked some project proposals. About 10% of 500 projects considered in the Czech Republic between 1992 and 1997 were stopped or withdrawn (OECD, 1999). In most cases, EIAs in CEE countries have ensured that projects met national and local environmental requirements. Some EIAs have approved a project but asked proponents to strengthen environmental protection in project construction and operation.

Box 5.8.   Donor and IFI support for EIAs

Bilateral donors – in particular the Netherlands, the UK, the US, and the EC PHARE Programme – have played a major role in assisting the development of EIA laws and regulations in CEE countries. A number of donors have also organised workshops on impact assessment methods. IFIs, such as the EBRD and the World Bank, have carried out EIAs for many of their projects in the region. In some cases, lessons and experience from these EIAs have helped strengthen national EIA procedures. IFIs have involved some CEE experts in the preparation of EIAs for their projects in the region, allowing a direct transfer of experience. In addition to this external assistance, after the 1995 Sofia "Environment for Europe" Conference CEE countries established a "Sofia Initiative" on EIAs, providing a forum to discuss common issues and exchange experience. Croatia chairs this forum, and the Regional Environmental Center provides its secretariat.

Sources: Dusik; Kennedy.

In several countries, environmental authorities have faced capacity problems in trying to implement EIA procedures. This has been a particular problem in CEE countries that have carried out large numbers of assessments without strong institutional capacities. It has been difficult for them to ensure quality assessments. In these countries, authorities should consider applying stricter screening procedures to make certain that limited resources are used to review the most important projects (Bulgaria undertook such a reform in 1997, reducing the number of EIA reviews carried out annually.) A further problem is that many CEE officials who work on EIAs – in particular at the local level – could use additional training and standardised manuals on technical issues related to EIA procedures, as well as training in managing public participation and conducting public hearings. In addition, environmental impact statements have often not been of high quality. Several CEE countries, including the Czech Republic, Croatia and Poland, have addressed this issue by establishing accreditation systems for consultants who prepare these documents. A few countries have introduced a formal "scoping" process to specify elements and approaches for each impact statement. This process should help focus analysis on key project impacts. In Estonia and Hungary, scoping regulations provide for public participation at this early stage.

In the EU accession process, candidate countries will need to strengthen their EIA procedures. Although most CEE countries have developed legislation compatible with the EU's 1985 EIA Directive, these laws will have to be revised to implement the EU's more stringent 1997 Directive, which includes more detailed screening requirements, further specifications for the preparation of environmental impact statements, and provisions for transboundary EIAs.

A number of CEE countries have also established *strategic environmental impact assessments* to review sectoral policies and land-use plans (so far, only a few Western European countries, such as the Netherlands and Switzerland, have used this mechanism). CEE experience with these methods has only started. As of mid-1998, the most active country, Slovakia, had undertaken three strategic EIAs; Estonia had undertaken two. The Czech Republic started a strategic EIA of its energy policy in 1998. Strategic EIAs could play an important role in the integration of environmental issues into sectoral policies. This has been an important issue for discussion and analysis among CEE countries participating in the Sofia Initiative on Environmental Impact Assessment.

3.2. *Environmental assessments in the* NIS[10]

In the NIS, environmental assessments have been based on the Soviet system of state environmental reviews introduced in the late 1980s. Under this system, expert committees review the environmental impacts of nearly all new industrial projects, as well as many modifications to existing activities. The committees can make binding decisions to block or modify the projects. There were few provisions for public information or participation, and in most NIS these have remained underdeveloped.

Several NIS have carried out minor reforms to the Soviet review system. These countries have continued to require reviews of nearly all new projects; several thousand state environmental reviews have been carried out each year in Belarus, Ukraine and Uzbekistan, and up to 100 000 in Russia. This has greatly strained administrative resources, limiting the attention that environmental authorities and expert committees can devote to each project proposal. In most NIS, regulations state that impact studies should be released to the public. Most of them have also introduced provisions for public participation through a parallel review process, the public environmental review. In practice, opportunities for public participation have remained rare. In Russia, only about a dozen public reviews have been conducted since the early 1990s.

A few NIS, such as Armenia and Moldova, have undertaken more extensive reforms of the earlier procedures, adopting screening lists to focus assessments on the most important projects, requirements for preparing environmental impact statements, and further procedures for public hearings. Such reforms could strengthen review systems in other NIS. In Armenia and Moldova, lack of training and institutional capacity has slowed the implementation of these reforms; for example, few officials have had experience in organising public hearings.

Across the NIS, informal estimates suggest that expert reviews have rejected between 10 and 20% of all project proposals. While many proposals were probably modified and then resubmitted, these reviews appear to have reduced environmental risks from at least some potentially dangerous projects. In addition, most NIS have provisions for environmental review of sectoral plans and strategies, though in practice these have rarely been used.

The NIS can take several steps to strengthen environmental reviews. The reforms in Armenia and Moldova provide models for other countries. In these two countries and others, officials and experts working on environmental reviews need training, guidance manuals and other support. So far, there have been few mechanisms for capacity building, or fora in which officials from different NIS could exchange experience. The Central European University in Budapest has held yearly training courses for experts, NGO representatives and government officials. In Russia, environmental NGOs have tried to promote the use of public review procedures. The Ecoline Public Environmental Review Centre in Moscow has produced guidelines for public participation and has provided support and training for groups wishing to participate in assessments, and similar centres have been created in eight Russian regions. Private foundations in the US and Western Europe have supported these and related NGO efforts in the NIS. A few bilateral donors, including US AID and the Netherlands, have also provided assistance. The US has assisted the development of environmental assessments in Ukraine.

4. Environmental Information Systems

Effective environmental information systems are vital for environmental management, including the design and implementation of policy measures. These systems comprise the staff, equipment and procedures for collecting and organising environmental data and synthesising it for policy makers and the public (Rump). At the start of the transition, most CEEC and NIS collected a large volume of environmental data, but the different agencies involved rarely shared data. When they did, there were doubts about compatibility. Data quality was often uncertain, data collected were often incomplete, little work was done to analyse or synthesise data for policy development, and environmental information was rarely released to the public (OECD, 1993; 1996). The EAP urged countries to improve monitoring of ambient conditions and verification of emissions levels, particularly in "hot spot" areas; to set up integrated national information systems to ensure co-ordination among different agencies; and to base their policies on clear information that should be made available to the public.

Over the transition, many CEE countries have greatly improved the quality of their environmental monitoring data. Foreign technical assistance programmes have strongly reinforced national efforts, providing both equipment and training. Most CEE countries have devoted national resources to improving monitoring equipment and institutions. An important share of CEE and external resources has been used to improve monitoring in "hot spots", such as Katowice and Krakow Provinces in Poland, as well as in large cities.

Most CEE countries have also created national institutions and networks to bring together data from different monitoring networks and to share, analyse and disseminate it. In some countries, monitoring institutions have received important autonomy to help ensure the independence and accuracy of their data. Estonia created an Environmental Information Centre under the Ministry of Environment and set up a new national monitoring programme. Bulgaria has established a National System for Environmental Monitoring (Box 5.9). In most CEE countries, inter-agency co-operation has improved – though in Bulgaria and elsewhere important problems remain. In addition, CEE countries (as well as NIS) have improved the integration of national information systems with international networks, including those co-ordinated by the European Environmental Agency (EEA) and UNEP. This international co-operation has made possible exchange of experience among countries; assisted efforts to improve data quality and international compatibility; and helped strengthen national reporting for international conventions and other commitments (Annex X).

Box 5.9.   **The development of Bulgaria's Environmental Monitoring System**

In Bulgaria, both domestic initiatives and external assistance have increased the quality of environmental information. The Bulgarian government established a National System for Environmental Monitoring in 1994, co-ordinated by the National Centre for Environment and Sustainable Development. The PHARE Programme and other donors provided new monitoring and computer equipment. Data quality has greatly improved, and regional inspectorates have been able to send data to the Centre on a daily basis. Environmental authorities have provided information to the public. Radio stations in Sofia and several other cities have used local monitoring data to provide daily reports on urban air pollution levels.

A number of problems have remained. Some government agencies responsible for collecting data have not provided the data on a regular basis. Bulgaria has had difficulties using and integrating all the equipment and methods provided by technical assistance from different donors. In some years the state budget and the national environmental fund, which have funded the operational costs of monitoring, have not provided sufficient resources to cover the higher costs of new equipment, so that monitoring offices had to curtail some activities. Another problem is that authorities have started to charge for the release of some types of data, potentially restricting public access.

Sources: Georgieva and Moore; Milushev.

Most CEE countries have greatly increased the amount of environmental data and information provided to the public. Most of them now produce annual state of the environment reports that present data from main sources. An increasing number provide this information through the Internet and other electronic networks. Many countries have used environmental indicators to present data more clearly to policy-makers and the public (often these have been based on OECD's "core set" of environmental indicators). The three Baltic States, working with the Baltic Environmental Forum in Riga, developed a common set of indicators and use these to produce a common state of the environment report. In a few CEE countries, recent laws have strengthened the public's right of access to environmental information. A few environmental authorities have established central and regional offices to respond to public requests for information.

Despite this progress, some important weaknesses remain. In all CEE countries (as in all NIS), emissions monitoring has not fulfilled the needs of complex pollution charge systems. In some CEE countries, including Bulgaria, funding for monitoring and information systems has remained tight. Governments could also make further efforts to provide information to the public in clear and simple formats that could increase public awareness of environmental issues and policy goals.

In most NIS, environmental information systems have faced even more severe problems, including drastic cutbacks of their budgets. In Russia and Belarus, environmental funds have played a vital role by financing environmental monitoring in the face of budget cuts. Funds in Belarus provided over US$1 million for monitoring activities and equipment in 1995; in the city of Gomel, the local environmental fund financed new monitoring equipment and paid the salaries of most staff involved in pollution monitoring (OECD, 1997a). Some NIS – including Russia – have been slow to implement reforms, such as addressing areas of overstaffing and overlapping of responsibilities among agencies. As a result, limited resources have been used ineffectively, reducing even further the performance of their information systems. In Russia, at least 16 national agencies gathered or treated environmental information in the mid-1990s. The State Water Committee alone employed 10 000 people for monitoring. To reform the system, Russia's national government approved a Unified State System of Environmental Monitoring. However, implementation of these reforms has remained slow (OECD, 1996).

While the northern NIS had relatively extensive monitoring systems at the start of transition, other countries, particularly in Central Asia and the Caucasus, had relatively weak systems that were subsequently pushed close to collapse by budget cutbacks (World Bank, 1998). National efforts, supported by international assistance, have recently started to rebuild these systems. In Central Asia, several assistance programmes have played an important role: the EC TACIS Programme has helped to develop information on regional water use under the Aral Sea Programme; Switzerland has provided monitoring equipment to a number of countries; the Netherlands has helped to develop information systems for land-use planning; and UNEP has worked with countries to prepare a regional state of the environment report.

5. Improving Compliance

Under central planning, government institutions and mechanisms to enforce environmental requirements were weak and had little influence on the main polluters, large state-owned enterprises. Over the transition, most CEE countries have strengthened their legal basis and institutions for enforcement, creating or strengthening national environmental inspectorates and introducing new tools for enforcement (Box 5.10). The EAP underlined the importance of these efforts and the need for consistent, effective enforcement of environmental legislation.

In Poland, one of the government's first environmental reforms was to strengthen the powers of the national inspectorate, PIOS, to monitor industrial emissions and to impose sanctions. Inspectors were given the right to make unannounced visits to industrial plants to check compliance, as well as the power to close down a production line or even an entire enterprise in cases of serious violations. Poland also increased the inspectorate's budget; this financing, together with external assistance, greatly expanded the PIOS's ability to monitor pollution levels. Efforts in Poland and other CEEC to strengthen enforcement benefited from strong public support for environmental action, at least early in the transition.

5.1. Obstacles to stronger enforcement

Many CEE countries and nearly all NIS have faced continuing institutional capacity problems that have weakened enforcement. One problem is that, while the CEEC/NIS systems of ambient standards and permitted emissions limits have had a strong theoretical base, their effective implementation has been extremely difficult if not impossible. Under the approach used in nearly all CEEC/NIS, enterprises must report their air and water pollution emissions to environmental inspectorates (enterprises' self-reporting has often been based on estimates of production levels rather than actual measurements). Inspectorates have the right to check emissions levels. Even in countries where inspectorates have

---

Box 5.10. **Enforcement tools**

Environmental enforcement refers to actions and mechanisms to ensure that polluters comply with environmental requirements and do not endanger the environment or human health. Enforcement actions can include: inspections of polluting facilities; sanctions and other actions to compel compliance; and negotiations with polluters to address compliance problems.

Countries in the region have used several main enforcement tools. *Environmental permits* have been the basis for enforcement actions. These legal documents, negotiated with major polluters, specify limits for pollution levels and state other operating requirements. Permit requirements have provided the basis for *pollution limits, charges and fees*. Most CEEC and NIS have also developed *environmental assessment* procedures. In some countries, the results of these assessments have been linked to later permit negotiations for approved projects.

In many CEEC and NIS, environmental inspectorates can also *close* either entire plants or specific production lines to enforce compliance. In Romania, environmental authorities closed a highly polluting lead smelter in Baia Maria. A few countries use closures extensively; Moldova's authorities issued 60 temporary closure orders in 1997. However, this may be due in part to the weakness of other enforcement tools. In most CEEC/NIS, closures are used relatively rarely.

Many CEEC/NIS inspectorates undertake *negotiations* with polluters to set permit levels and other requirements. Although negotiations between inspectorates and polluters play an important role in some Western European countries, these usually have strong inspectorates as well as systems to ensure their accountability – factors missing in many CEEC/NIS.

At the same time, CEEC/NIS inspectorates have often lacked formal procedures to deal with enterprises that do not meet permit requirements. Drastic measures, such as plant closures, can create political opposition, while financial sanctions have remained relatively weak, even in some countries that have strengthened their inspectorates such as the Czech Republic. To address this problem, Poland's inspectorate has started to use negotiated *compliance schedules*, under which polluters agree to a timetable for compliance actions, together with strict sanctions if deadlines are not met. Under this mechanism (similar to the pollution charge waivers used in other countries), enterprises can retain a portion of the pollution charges and non-compliance fees they are assessed and invest it in pollution control actions. The Czech Republic has also used compliance schedules on a pilot basis.

Sources: Farmer; INECE; OECD, 1997e; 1997f; 1999; UN/ECE.

greatly improved their staff and monitoring equipment, such as Poland, these bodies have lacked the resources to check monitoring data effectively for all polluting enterprises and all pollutants. In many other CEEC/NIS, inspectors have had little adequate equipment or resources to measure emissions. The number of environmental inspectors in Moldova fell by about one-half from 1990 to 1995; many offices of the environmental inspectorate lacked modern monitoring equipment and even motor vehicles for inspectors to use to visit enterprises in 1995, though funding has since grown (UN/ECE). Many CEEC/NIS have had only low penalties for enterprises that report inaccurate emissions data. These enterprises have had a strong incentive to report less than their actual emissions, as these levels are used to calculate pollution charges and non-compliance fees (Anderson and Fiedor).

The complexity of current permit, emissions limit and charge systems – which cover dozens if not hundreds of pollutants, in particular for air pollution – has contributed to these problems. (In contrast, many enterprises across the region discharge their waste water to municipal systems. Although this has created problems for waste water treatment plants, there have been fewer point sources for inspectorates to monitor.) Monitoring problems – for air pollution as well as hazardous and solid wastes – have grown as the number of small and medium-sized enterprises has increased significantly.

5.2. *Responses*

A few CEEC/NIS have tried to respond to these problems. Faced with many pollutants and a growing number of enterprises to track, inspectorates in a few countries have focused their efforts on the most important polluters. Early in the transition, Poland's national environmental authorities identified the country's 80 worst polluters (and regional inspectorates identified an additional 800 polluters). Each enterprise had to develop and implement an environmental programme; authorities focused inspections on these companies. Lithuania's inspection system, adopted in 1994, has divided polluters into four classes, based on size, and inspectorates have controlled the largest polluters more frequently. In Russia, the HIID recommendations for air pollution management have suggested that environmental authorities focus their limited resources on the largest polluters (Box 5.6).

A few countries have tackled funding problems by developing earmarked financing mechanisms to ensure funding for inspectorates. Under Romania's new system, polluting enterprises must pay regular permit fees whose revenues cover monitoring and enforcement actions. A few countries have also improved the transparency and accountability of their inspectorates. In Poland and a few other CEE countries, NGOs can participate in permit negotiations.

5.3. *Environmental enforcement and transition in the* NIS

Despite these efforts, in many NIS, in particular, the slow pace of economic reform together with the low political standing of environmental issues have made enforcement extremely difficult. For example, inspectorates have had great difficulty inducing industrial enterprises that operate at a fraction of their capacity to comply with or even consider environmental requirements. Many NIS enterprises have remained state-owned or have retained strong ties to governments; in some cases, such enterprises have had political support to delay compliance with environmental requirements. NIS environmental authorities have sometimes had difficulty persuading highly polluting enterprises with strong export revenues to address their pollution problems (see, the case study of Norilsk Nickel in Chapter 7). Overall, enforcement will likely remain poor without further economic and institutional reform and strengthened political and public support for environmental protection.

5.4. *Co-operation and evaluation*

Two steps can help CEEC/NIS identify opportunities to tackle their often severe enforcement problems. First, inspectorate officials and high-level policy-makers in the region can exchange experience on enforcement problems and approaches – this has so far largely been missing. Two international initiatives have recently created forums for such exchanges (Box 5.11).

Box 5.11.   **International co-operation to strengthen enforcement**

Two recent international initiatives have brought together enforcement agencies in the region. The International Network for Environmental Compliance and Enforcement (INECE) grew out of multilateral discussions among OECD countries in the 1980s. INECE has extended these discussions to a global level. The network, co-ordinated by the Netherlands and US governments, has organised regular conferences on compliance and enforcement and has produced training materials for national inspectorates. INECE has started a work programme for the region. Its first workshop for CEE and NIS officials was held in Vilnius, Lithuania, in May 1998. Separately, the EU's informal Network for the Implementation and Enforcement of Environmental Law (IMPEL) has organised a network for accession countries, through which current EU members and accession countries will be able to discuss key issues and exchange information on enforcement of the EU's environmental legislation.

Sources: EC; INECE.

Second, countries in the region can strengthen enforcement – and, more generally, the effectiveness of pollution management – by undertaking regular evaluations of their pollution control instruments and compliance mechanisms. Most ambient standards, economic instruments and other instruments used in CEEC/NIS were developed without analysis of their environmental effectiveness, economic impacts, administrative costs or other effects. Environmental authorities in the region should consider making regular evaluations of the impacts and effectiveness of their policy instruments (OECD, 1997c). This will require the use of economic analysis as well as other methodologies. Some CEEC/NIS have gained experience with these types of analysis in developing their recent environmental policy strategies.

6. The Role of Information and Participation in Pollution Management

The EAP noted that the public's awareness of and concern for the environment, together with NGO and political pressures, can be a driving force for environmental protection. These concerns and pressures can also work together in regard to the implementation and enforcement of pollution requirements. Recent World Bank studies of pollution control efforts in different regions of the world have indicated that:

"… even in industrial countries, environmental legislation is just an initial step in the long and complex process of *creating a social consensus* – backed by legal instruments – on what is acceptable environmental behaviour" (Hanrahan *et al.*; emphasis added).

In some CEEC/NIS, public information and participation has played an important role in encouraging pollution reduction. The public attention given to enterprises on Poland's lists of "worst polluters" (mentioned above) helped – along with enforcement efforts – to prompt these enterprises to reduce their environmental damage. In Bulgaria, public protests against severe, health-threatening air pollution emissions from ferrous and non-ferrous metal smelters – together with temporary closures enforced by environmental authorities – encouraged the plants to install better dust control equipment (OECD, 1997a). Co-operative approaches have also led to action. Several regional and local governments have undertaken environmental action programmes (REAPs and LEAPs) with the participation of NGOs and industry. In Ostrava, in the Czech Republic, an action programme set up working groups to bring these different interests together and used risk assessment methods to identify the most serious pollution threats to human health; local industry subsequently installed improved dust control equipment and took other steps to reduce severe air pollution.

Over the course of the transition, most CEEC/NIS governments have increased public access to environmental information, as well as opportunities for public participation in decision-making. These measures have helped to improve public knowledge and awareness of environmental issues. In a number of CEEC/NIS, NGOs, industry and other interests have participated in the formulation of new environmental policies. This has helped develop consensus for environmental goals as well as the actions to achieve them. In a few CEE countries, enterprises have taken voluntary measures for environmental protection such as adopting cleaner production and environmental management programmes.

A few countries plan to introduce new instruments that will promote public awareness such as Pollutant Release and Transfer Registers (Box 5.12). Their use in the region will need to take account of data quality problems related to self-reported emissions data. In addition, environmental management systems can encourage enterprises to undertake voluntary environmental management efforts and to disclose their emissions levels and enterprise goals to the public. CEE countries seeking to join the EU can promote this approach by adopting the EMAS (Eco-Management and Audit Scheme) Directive on a priority basis.

As yet, few environmental authorities in the region have considered the full potential of public awareness and participation in regard to enforcement activities. For many CEE countries, greater public access to information and participation – together with closer co-operation between government, environmental NGOs, and business and industry – can provide new pillars for strengthening pollution management, as well as for environmental policy in general, particularly at the regional and local levels.

Box 5.12. **Pollutant release and transfer registers**

Several OECD countries have established Pollutant Release and Transfer Registers (PRTRs). These databases aggregate information on potentially harmful releases to the environment, as reported by enterprises. Their data should be easily retrievable – either by pollutant, media (air, water or solid waste) or source (plant or enterprise). PRTRs help environmental authorities bring together and manage data on pollution, and thus help policy-makers identify more clearly which polluters are releasing key pollutants, what is being released, and where. In addition, this information should be available, either in whole or in part, to the public via regular reports (in some countries, data are available on the Internet). In some countries, PRTRs have been voluntary; in others, including the US, enterprises are required to report pollution data for the national PRTR, called the Toxics Release Inventory. In nearly all cases, countries that have established effective PRTRs have developed these with the participation of key stakeholders, including business and industry representatives as well as environmental NGOs. PRTRs have shown several benefits:

- Governments have used them to monitor progress towards pollution objectives and to identify pollution reduction priorities.

- In addition, PRTRs, by bringing together data on releases to different media, have helped environmental authorities increase communication between specialists separately on air and water pollution and solid and hazardous waste generation.

- Enterprises have found that collecting data for PRTRs can identify opportunities to reduce resource waste and improve their efficiency. In some cases, authorities have used PRTRs to identify those enterprises with high pollution releases and have assisted them in introducing cleaner production and other approaches for pollution reduction.

- For the public, PRTRs have provided basic information for participation in environmental decision-making. Public access to the data has often been a crucial element. In some OECD countries, public access to pollution information has led top enterprise managers to focus on environmental issues and to develop and support internal enterprise goals for pollution reduction.

In a few cases, PRTRs can provide a direct tool for pollution reduction efforts. For example, the US EPA used PRTR data to identify 600 companies that were the main sources of emissions of 17 toxic chemicals and urged them to reduce their emissions by 33% by 1992 and 50% by 1995. Although there were no incentives or sanctions to ensure compliance, these goals were met.

A few CEE countries have started to introduce PRTRs. In Poland, amendments in 1997 to the country's framework environment law set up a national public register of pollution releases together with public registers providing data on enterprises' non-compliance fees, other fines and permit requirements. In the Czech Republic, the Environment Ministry undertook a pilot PRTR project in co-operation with an NGO and the Chemical-Technological University. Environmental authorities in both Hungary and Slovenia have studied the introduction of PRTR systems.

International co-operation has encouraged the development of PRTRs. In 1996, OECD recommended that Member countries establish PRTRs. An OECD *Guidance Manual for Governments* on developing PRTRs was prepared. OECD, in co-operation with UNITAR and the Swiss government, has also held informal workshops on PRTRs in different regions of the world to encourage non-member countries to adopt PRTRs; one workshop (held near Prague in 1997) was held for CEEC/NIS. In a few cases, bilateral donors and international organisations have assisted PRTR development in individual countries. The US government and UNITAR have assisted Slovakian environmental authorities to develop a PRTR proposal. The EU Directive on Integrated Pollution Prevention and Control will require member and candidate countries to set up PRTRs. The Aarhus Convention calls on countries to "progressively establish" such mechanisms (and there have been proposals to develop a protocol on PRTRs within the Convention).

Sources: Fénérol; OECD, 1997d; OECD, 1997f; REC.

NOTES

1. These criteria are based in particular on OECD (1997*c*), as well as OECD (1995).

2. As of 1999, OECD has undertaken reviews of Belarus, Bulgaria, the Czech Republic, Hungary, Poland and Russia (all but the Czech and Hungarian reviews were undertaken in co-operation with UN/ECE); UN/ECE has undertaken reviews of Estonia, Lithuania, Moldova, Slovenia and Ukraine.

3. Some OECD countries have gone further and developed standards for particles under 2.5 microns in diameter.

4. Many CEEC/NIS use dispersion models for air pollution emissions, together with data on ambient air pollution levels in relation to ambient standards, to set emissions limits for each facility.

5. This section draws on several sources, particularly Klarer and McNicholas.

6. This is called a *tax* because its revenues go to the general government budget. The revenues from pollution *charges* are "earmarked" for environmental expenditures.

7. The charge has been SKr 30 per kilogram of sulphur content in coal and peat, and SKr 27 per 0.1 per cent sulphur content (by weight) per cubic metre of fuel oil. This charge has had a strong incentive effect, significantly reducing SO_x emissions and therefore collecting far less revenues than expected (OECD, 1997*c*).

8. As yet, foreign investors have paid less attention to environmental liability issues in the NIS, possibly because they have faced greater risks and obstacles making direct investments here than in CEE countries.

9. The discussion of EIAs in CEE countries draws in particular on the report on the *Sofia Initiative on Environmental Impact Assessments* presented at the Aarhus Ministerial Conference.

10. The discussion of environmental assessments in the NIS is based largely on Cherp (1998*a* and 1998*b*).

REFERENCES

Afseh, S., *et al.*,
> *Controlling Industrial Pollution: A New Paradigm*, Policy Research Working Paper No. 1672, World Bank, Washington, DC.

Anderson, G. and B. Fiedor (1997),
> *Environmental Charges in Poland*, in R.A. Bluffstone and B.A. Larson, eds., *Controlling Pollution in Transition Economies: Theories and Methods*, Edward Elgar, Cheltenham, UK.

Antal, I., *et al.* (1998),
> *Health and Environmental Co-operation on the Regional Level in Hungary*, in Assessing *Environmental Health Problems in Central and Eastern Europe and the* NIS: *The Role of Data and Indicators*, OECD, Paris.

Air Pollution Working Group (APWG) (1997),
> *Practical Recommendations for Improving Air Pollution Policy in Russia*, Environment Discussion Paper No. 37, Harvard Institute for International Development, Cambridge, Massachusetts, January.

Bluffstone, R.A. (1997),
> *The Use of Economic Instruments in European Transition Economies: Past Trends and Prospects for the Future*, paper presented at the UN/ECE-OECD Workshop on the Role of Economic Instruments in Integrating Environmental Policy with Sectoral Policies, Pruhonice, Czech Republic, October.

Cherp, O. (1998*a*),
> *Environmental Assessment in the* NIS, background paper for OECD, April.

Cherp, O. (1998*b*),
> personal communication, Central European University, Budapest, June.

Demydenko, A. (1998),
> personal communication, UNDP, Tashkent, Uzbekistan, December.

Dusik, J. (1998),
> personal communication, Regional Environmental Center (REC), Szentendre, Hungary, March.

European Commission (EC) (1998),
> *Accession Strategies for Environment: Meeting the Challenge of Enlargement with the Candidate Countries in Central and Eastern Europe*, communication from the Commission to the Council, the European Parliament, the Economic and Social Committee, the Committee of the Regions and the Candidate Countries in Central and Eastern Europe.

Farmer, A.M. (1998),
> A *Draft Survey of the Enforcement Institutions of the* ECE-INECE *Countries and Activities Relating to Permitting, Non-compliance Response, Enforcement Tools and Transboundary Issues*, presented at the first Europe and Central Asia Conference of the INECE, Vilnius, May.

Fénérol, C. (1998),
> personal communication, OECD, Paris, October.

Fournier, J. (1998),
> *Administrative Reform in the Commission Opinions Concerning the Accession of the Central and Eastern European Countries to the European Union*, in OECD/SIGMA *Preparing Public Administrations for the European Administrative Space*, Sigma paper No. 23, Paris.

Garanin, Y.A. (1998),
> *Financing Water Supply and Waste Water Treatment Systems: A Case Study of Nizhniy Novgorod City*, in *Environmental Financing in the Russian Federation*, OECD, Paris.

Georgieva, K. and J. Moore (1997),
> *Bulgaria*, in J. Klarer and B. Moldan, eds., *The Environmental Challenge for Central and Eastern European Economies in Transition*, John Wiley & Sons, Ltd., Chichester, UK.

Goldenman, G. (1997),
> *Privatisation and Environmental Liability in CEEC and the NIS: Reviewing Progress Since the 1992 Warsaw Conference*, presented to the Eighth EAP Task Force meeting, Paris, November.

Golub, A. (1998),
   Environmental Financing in the Russian Federation, in *Environmental Financing in the Russian Federation*, OECD, Paris.

Gornaja, *et al.* (1997),
   Estonia's Mixed System of Pollution Permits, Standards, and Charges, in R.A. Bluffstone and B.A. Larson, eds., *Controlling Pollution in Transition Economies: Theories and Methods*, Edward Elgar, Cheltenham, UK.

Hanrahan, D., *et al.* (1998),
   Developing Partnerships for Effective Pollution Management, in *Environment Matters at the World Bank: Annual Review*, World Bank, Washington, DC.

Harvard Institute for International Development and Environmental Policy and Institutional Resources Group (HIID and IRG) (1998),
   Measuring the Environmental Transition in Eastern Europe and the Newly Independent States, prepared for US AID, Washington, DC, May.

Holzmann, U. (1998),
   Environmental Liability in Europe: Concerning the Need for a European Directive on Environmental Responsibility, European Environmental Bureau, Brussels, January.

International Network for Environmental Compliance and Enforcement (INECE) (1998),
   Principles of Environmental Compliance and Enforcement, (http://www.inece.org).

Jehlicka, P. and M. Branis (1998),
   Environmental Protection and Capacity Building in the Czech Republic, in *Environmental Policy and the Role of Foreign Assistance in Central and Eastern Europe*, commissioned by the Danish Environmental Protection Agency, KPMG, Copenhagen.

Kennedy, W. (1999),
   EIA and Multilateral Financial Institutions, in *Handbook of Environmental Assessment*, Blackwell Science Ltd, Oxford (forthcoming).

Klarer, J. (1999),
   personal communication, Regional Environmental Center for Central and Eastern Europe (REC), Szentendre, Hungary, April.

Klarer, J. and J. McNicholas (1999), eds.,
   Sourcebook on Economic Instruments – Central and Eastern Europe, Regional Environmental Center for Central and Eastern Europe (REC), Szentendre, Hungary.

Kozeltsev, M. and A. Markandya (1997),
   Pollution Charges in Russia: The Experience of 1990-1995, Environment Discussion Paper No. 15, Harvard Institute for International Development, Cambridge, Massachusetts, January.

Larson, B.A., *et al.* (1999),
   The Economics of Air Pollution Health Risks in Russia: A Case Study of Volgograd, in World Development, Elsevier.

Lehoczki, Z. (1998),
   personal communication, Budapest University of Economics, June.

Lovei, M. and C. Weiss, Jr. (1997),
   Environmental Management and Institutions in OECD Countries: Lessons from Experience, Environment Dept. Paper No. 46, World Bank, Washington, DC, March.

Milushev, M. (1998),
   personal communication, Sofia.

OECD (1993),
   Environmental Information Systems and Indicators: A Review of Selected Central and Eastern European Countries, Paris.

OECD (1994),
   Environmental Performance Reviews: Poland, Paris.

OECD (1995),
   The St. Petersburg Guidelines on Environmental Funds in the Transition to a Market Economy, Paris.

OECD (1996),
   Environmental Information Systems in the Russian Federation: An OECD Assessment, Paris.

OECD (1997a),
   Environmental Performance Reviews: Belarus, Paris.

OECD (1997b),
   Environmental Taxes and Green Tax Reform, Paris.

OECD (1997c),
   Evaluating Economic Instruments for Environmental Policy, Paris.

125

OECD (1997*d*),

Pollutant Release and Transfer Registers (PRTRs): A Tool for Environmental Management and Sustainable Development, paper presented at the PRTR Workshop for the Americas, San Juan del Rio, Mexico, 29-31 July.

OECD (1997*e*),

Project on Environmental Permitting of Industrial Facilities: Status and Future Endeavours, Paris, November.

OECD (1997*f*),

Reforming Environmental Regulation in OECD Countries, Paris.

OECD (1998),

Eco-efficiency, Paris.

OECD (1999),

Environmental Performance Reviews: Czech Republic, Paris.

Regional Environmental Center for Central and Eastern Europe (REC) (1998),

Doors to Democracy: Current Trends and Practices in Public Participation in Environmental Decision-making in the Newly Independent States, REC, Szentendre, Hungary, June.

Rump, P. (1998),

The Development of Environmental/Health Information Systems in Countries with Economies in Transition, in Assessing Environmental Health Problems in Central and Eastern Europe and the NIS: The Role of Data and Indicators, OECD, Paris.

Semeniene, D., et al. (1997),

The Lithuanian Pollution Charge System: Evaluation and Prospects for the Future, in R.A. Bluffstone and B.A. Larson, eds., Controlling Pollution in Transition Economies: Theories and Methods, Edward Elgar, Cheltenham, UK.

Semichaevsky, A. (1998),

Reforming Environmental Standards and Environmental Monitoring Systems in Selected Countries of Central and Eastern Europe, background paper for OECD, February.

Sofia Initiative on Environmental Impact Assessment (1998),

report to the "Environment for Europe" Conference, Aarhus, Denmark, June 1998, Regional Environmental Center for Central and Eastern Europe (REC), Szentendre, Hungary.

Stavins, R. and T. Zylicz (1995),

Environmental Policy in a Transition Economy: Designing Tradeable Permits for Poland, HIID Environment Discussion Paper No. 9, Harvard Institute for International Development, Cambridge, Massachusetts.

Strukova, E. (1998),

Cost-effectiveness Analysis of Health Risk Reduction: Volgograd Case Study, in Assessing Environmental Health Problems in Central and Eastern Europe and the NIS: the Role of Data and Indicators, OECD, Paris.

United Nations Economic Commission for Europe (UN/ECE) (1998),

Environmental Performance Reviews: Republic of Moldova, United Nations, Geneva.

Vincent, J. and S. Farrow (1997),

A Survey of Pollution Charge Systems and Key Issues in Policy Design, in R.A. Bluffstone and B.A. Larson, eds., Controlling Pollution in Transition Economies: Theories and Methods, Edward Elgar, Cheltenham, UK.

World Bank (1996),

World Development Report 1996: From Plan to Market, Oxford University Press, Oxford.

World Bank (1997),

World Development Report 1997: The State in a Changing World, Oxford University Press, Oxford.

World Bank (1998),

Transition Toward an Healthier Environment: Environmental Issues and Challenges in the Newly Independent States, Washington, DC.

World Bank and OECD (1993),

Environmental Action Programme for Central and Eastern Europe: Setting Priorities – Abridged version of the document endorsed by the Ministerial Conference at Lucerne, Switzerland (28-30 April), Washington, DC.

Chapter 6

ENVIRONMENTAL FINANCING

1. Introduction

Strong environmental institutions and policies, broad public support for environmental protection, and effective, well-enforced pollution control instruments all provide strong incentives for economic actors to undertake environmental protection initiatives, including investments that bring about reductions of pollution and other pressures. Meeting the demand for the means to finance such investments is the focus of environmental financing.

Financing has been one of the most important issues considered in international fora, including the "Environment for Europe" process (Box 6.1). This chapter provides an overview of environmental financing from the perspective of both demand and supply. It then presents information on levels of domestic environmental financing, as well as international assistance and financing. Key mechanisms for environmental financing are described, from capital markets to environmental funds. In regard to municipal infrastructure, such as waste water treatment plants, government policies play a major role in determining both the demand for, and supply of, financing. The last section of this chapter reviews municipal infrastructure. Several financing issues related to the enterprise sector are covered in Chapter 7. Chapter 8 discusses financing for biodiversity and landscape preservation.

Box 6.1. **The evolution of environmental financing discussions in the "Environment for Europe" process**

The EAP emphasised that the bulk of financing for environmental investments in the CEEC/NIS would have to come from domestic sources. It highlighted the importance of priority-setting in project selection, strengthening domestic environmental financial institutions to ensure the most cost-effective use of resources, and using external financing in a catalytic and strategic way.

After the EAP was endorsed in 1993, environmental financing continued to be an important issue in the "Environment for Europe" process. At the 1995 Conference in Sofia, there was recognition that "the obstacle to increased financing is not so much a lack of foreign capital as the high cost of commercial capital, the limited flexibility of financing mechanisms, and problems in linking priority needs with the available financing" (Sofia Declaration). It was acknowledged that demand for environmental financing was still low throughout the region. However, most discussions focused on the supply of financing, in particular the development of innovative financial mechanisms and the role of "soft" financing.

Since Sofia, the growing divergence in contexts and priorities between advanced transition countries and others, particularly the NIS, has become more evident. These developments have shown that environmental financing needs to be analysed more systematically as the interaction between demand and supply. An EAP Task Force report to the Aarhus Conference follows such a perspective, emphasising linkages between policies and instruments (to create demand and raise revenues), institutions (to channel scarce resources most cost-effectively) and investments (originating from various economic sectors), and the interaction between domestic and external financing.

Sources: OECD and PPC (1995); OECD (1998a).

1.1. *Demand for environmental financing*

In general terms, the demand for environmental financing reflects the willingness of polluters, and users of environmental resources, to pay for investments intended to address environmental problems. It is shaped by the level of countries' economic development and the stringency with which environmental standards are set and enforced. Demand also reflects the perceived and actual severity of environmental problems.

Two sectors undertake most environmental projects and create the demand for environmental financing: enterprises and municipalities. Enterprises (which may be state or privately owned) primarily invest in projects directed towards pollution prevention, treatment and control at their own plants. Municipalities, which also make pollution-related investments, primarily invest in infrastructure for municipal services such as water supply, waste water treatment, solid and hazardous waste disposal, and district heating. Many users benefit from the resulting infrastructure and services. In both sectors, decisions about environmental investments result from an interaction between demand and supply. However, differences in their ability to raise revenue, and the means available to them, result in different types of financing for enterprises and municipalities.

In profit-seeking enterprises, investments are generally evaluated on their financial merits, that is, the risk-adjusted future rate of return relative to the amount of the initial investment. While enterprises' environmental investments can produce "returns" in the form of reducing negative externalities[1] (such as pollution), most enterprises are interested above all in their own potential cost savings, for example through reduced raw material or resource use, reduced waste treatment and disposal costs, and avoidance of pollution charges, fees and fines or non-compliance sanctions.[2] Environmental policy instruments should provide incentives for enterprise investments, although, as Chapter 5 has shown, these instruments remain weak in many of the CEEC/NIS. According to the Polluter Pays Principle (PPP), enterprises should use their own resources – and raise their own financing – for investments to meet environmental policy requirements (Box 6.2). Implementing the PPP has been an important policy goal for many countries in the region but has proved difficult, in particular where enterprises face economic crisis and unstable macroeconomic conditions. In response, many CEEC/NIS governments have tried to strengthen the supply side of environmental financing by using environmental funds and other instruments. Their environmental financing programmes are directed towards providing greater financial incentives and structuring credit terms to suit the specific characteristics of environmental investments.

For municipalities, the decision to undertake environmental investments is driven by national as well as local and regional environmental policy goals, by social and health policy goals (particularly provision of safe drinking water), and by the application of instruments such as pollution fees and fines, which in most CEEC/NIS are levied on discharges by municipal waste water treatment companies. Government environmental financing programmes as well as user charges have been crucial in helping finance municipal infrastructure and services in OECD countries and some CEEC/NIS.

In many CEE countries, particularly advanced reform countries, there has been a recent increase in demand for environmental investments. In most countries economic growth has resumed, generating resources for investment; macroeconomic stabilisation has helped reduce interest rates and inflation; the reduction of subsidies on energy, water and other resources has created incentives for greater efficiency; new trade relations have required exporters to pay more attention to environmental issues; new policies and programmes, including NEAPs, and economic instruments have promoted better implementation of the Polluter Pays Principle; decentralisation is creating demand for better environmental services at the local level; public awareness and, in some cases, willingness-to-pay for environmental improvements are increasing; and obligations under regional and global environmental conventions are leading to investments, often with international assistance.

Accession to the EU will transform the demand for environmental investments in the countries concerned. Some early estimates suggested that the total investment cost for the 10 accession countries to comply with EU legislation on air quality, urban and industrial waste water, and solid and hazardous waste management are on the order of ECU 120 billion (EDC). Assuming a relatively short compliance period, these figures far exceed current levels of expenditure and the resources which might be made

---

Box 6.2. **The Polluter Pays Principle**

The Polluter Pays Principle (PPP) provides the framework for environmental financing in market economies. According to the PPP, polluters use their own resources to finance measures required to comply with environmental standards. The government's role in combatting pollution is to establish the policy and institutional framework from which demand for financing will emerge. On the supply side, the PPP provides for exceptions in transition periods to the "no subsidy" philosophy. Subsidies or soft financing may be justified for projects where significant externalities such as human health effects are involved, or where there is potential for damage to natural capital or for irreversible environmental impacts. More specifically, subsidies should:

- not introduce significant distortions in international trade and investments;
- be limited to sectors which would otherwise have great difficulty complying with environmental requirements; and
- be limited to a well-defined transition period and adapted to the specific social and economic problems associated with the implementation of a country's environmental policy.

In many OECD countries, government subsidies have financed one-half or more of water and waste water infrastructure investments. Municipalities in the CEE countries and NIS are even more constrained than their counterparts in OECD countries, particularly in their ability to raise revenue from households either through user fees or local taxes. Since many of the problems faced by enterprises in transition economies result from past practices of the state, the state may be expected to bear some of the costs of reducing pollution. Given that a large share of domestic subsidies is derived from pollution fees paid by polluters, it has been argued that well-targeted subsidies during the transition are consistent with the Polluter Pays Principle (Peszko and Zylicz).

The PPP is an established policy principle in most CEE countries, but it requires further implementation. In a number of NIS, it is not strongly established. Its implementation requires a clearer separation of the roles the state plays as a source and regulator of economic activity. In most NIS, the PPP is interpreted theoretically to mean that the polluter should pay the costs of damage caused by its pollution (Adeishvili and Waughray). Because such a principle is difficult to operationalise, it often reduces to the idea that polluters should pay some pollution charges as a source of revenue for environmental authorities.

---

available for some countries by the EU. Determining a realistic compliance period, and designing cost-effective strategies which strike a realistic balance between the demand for and supply of financing, will be a massive challenge.

No equivalent demand exists in the NIS. Several are classified as developing countries; in the others, generally low personal and corporate wealth levels are reflected in the weak demand for environmental investments. Macroeconomic and fiscal policy failures contribute to high inflation and stringent lending conditions that discourage most types of investment. In addition, enterprises and local governments are still heavily subsidised; NEAPs are still under development and have yet to be implemented; there is little public demand for environmental improvements; and the "implementation gap" in regard to achieving the objectives set out in regional and global environmental conventions is greater than in the CEE countries. Weak demand for environmental improvements has made it difficult to secure allocations from state budgets and to establish new domestic financing mechanisms.

2. Trends in Environmental Financing

This section describes domestic environmental expenditure in six countries between 1990 and 1996. It then provides an overview of international assistance and financing. Although international sources have played a key role throughout the region, overall the data indicate that, for most countries, domestic sources finance the majority of environmental expenditure. In such cases, external financing generally has a catalytic role or is used to support projects of international significance. In low income countries, external support can constitute a significant proportion of environmental investments and may be crucial to support investments in basic environmental services.

129

2.1. *Domestic expenditures*

A Danish-supported EAP Task Force study assessed trends in pollution abatement and control (PAC)[3] expenditure in six countries selected to represent a range of economic and environmental characteristics: Georgia, Hungary, Lithuania, Poland, Russia and Slovenia (OECD, 1998c). While the results suggest region-wide trends, they also show that during the complex and difficult transition to a market economy the overall levels, sources and types of expenditure can vary greatly from country to country. Although the data collected provide indicators of national efforts to protect the environment, the EAP emphasised that important environmental improvements will also result from investments in renewing industrial capital, as they introduce modern, less-polluting, more efficient industrial production methods. Such investments, discussed further in Chapter 7, are generally not measured by these indicators.

The main findings of the study include the following:

– In most of the countries, domestic pollution abatement and control investments increased overall between 1990 and 1996 but peaked in 1994 (Figure 6.1). Poland is an important exception to this trend.

– In the most advanced transition countries (Poland, Hungary, Slovenia), PAC investments as a percentage of GDP match or exceed those in several high-income OECD countries such as Germany. Per capita (calculated using purchasing power parities), they match or exceed levels in OECD countries at comparable income levels such as Portugal (Table 6.1).

– In Russia, these investments are comparable with those in low-income OECD countries as a percentage of GDP.[4]

– In Georgia, which has faced civil war and ongoing political instability during the transition, these investments appear to be virtually non-existent.

Figure 6.1. **Trends in domestic pollution abatement and control investments, 1990 to 1996**
Index using constant domestic prices, with 1993 = 100

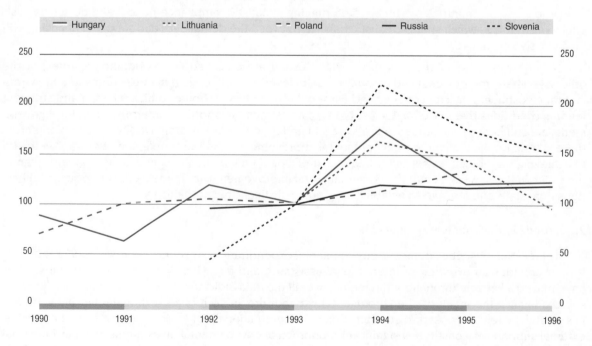

Source: OECD, based on national statistics.

Table 6.1. **National pollution abatement and control investment per capita and as a share of GDP, 1996**[a]

	Per capita (US$)[b]	% of GDP
	Case study countries	
Georgia	..	..
Hungary	57	0.6
Lithuania	33	0.6
Poland	72	1.1
Russia	24	0.4
Slovenia	48	0.4
	Selected western European countries	
Germany[c]	111	0.5
Portugal	50	0.4

.. Not available
a) Data for Poland and Germany refer to 1995, data for Portugal to 1994.
b) Calculated using purchasing power parities.
c) Western Germany only.
Source: OECD, based on national statistics.

- Overall, there is a positive correlation between PAC investments and level of economic development, as measured by GDP per capita. Expenditures in some countries are significantly above the average trend. This may be a reflection of strong environmental policies (Figure 6.2).

- The public sector share of investments in Hungary, Lithuania and Poland has increased in the 1990s. Where it is possible to break down public sector investments, the share from local governments' budgets can be seen to have increased.

Figure 6.2. **PAC investments and GDP, 1995**[1]

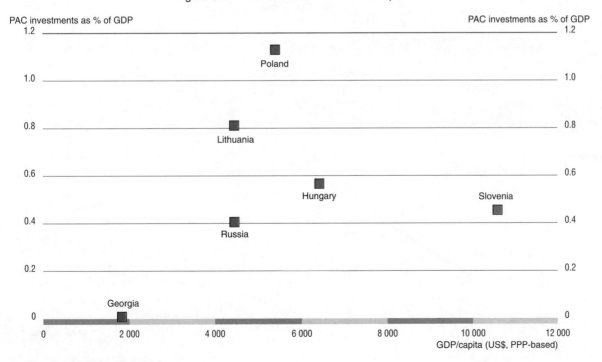

1. Based on the abater principale.
Source: OECD, based on national statistics.

OECD 1999

– Air and water protection account for the overwhelming share of investments. Air quality is most important in Poland and Slovenia, and water quality in the others. Waste represents an insignificant share in all countries except Hungary.

Domestic sources of financing

Public sector environmental expenditures in transition countries have relied on three major domestic sources of financing: local government revenues, transfers from central government budgets, and grants or soft loans from environmental funds. The relative importance of each source varies from country to country. In 1994, local government in Hungary provided 79% of PAC investments, compared with 21% from the central government. In 1996, local government in Poland provided 84%, compared with 16% from the central government. In Lithuania, however, local government provided only 3% of PAC investments in 1996 and the central government 97%.[5]

Budget transfers, which historically had financed infrastructure investments, have largely dried up in the NIS during the transition and the associated economic downswing, with local governments turning to other sources such as environmental funds or, increasingly, postponing investments. In the CEE countries, budget transfers for environmental purposes have declined in importance while loans and polluters' own resources have increased in importance during this period. In the Czech Republic, budget resources dropped from 44% of total resources in 1992 to 14% in 1997 (Ministry of Environment letter). In the Baltic States, substantial budget resources have been channelled through Public Investment Programmes (PIPs), primarily to support environmental infrastructure investments.

In the CEE countries, environmental funds have played an important role in financing environmental expenditures. In Poland, they financed about 32% of environmental investments in 1996 (down from their earlier level of more than 40%) and in Hungary, Lithuania and Slovenia about 20% (Figure 6.3). They covered only about 5% of investments in Russia.[6] Despite recent efforts to strengthen them, environmental

Figure 6.3. **PAC investments: share of domestic financing from environmental funds, 1990 to 1996**

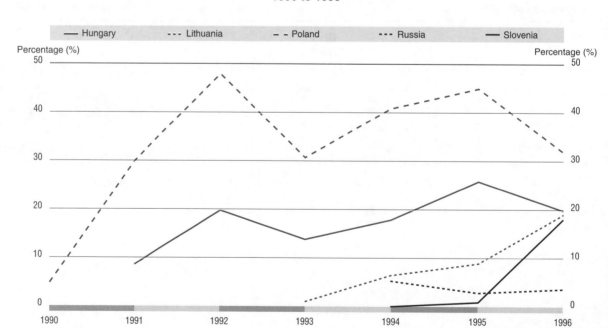

Slovenia – estimate.
Source: OECD, 1998.

funds in Russia and other NIS face a number of difficulties in the present economic situation, including pressure to consolidate their revenues into national or regional budgets; low collection and charge rates for pollution fees; increased use of money surrogates; and the need for institutional strengthening of fund management units (OECD, 1998*c*).

Enterprises' own financial resources, combined with grants and soft loans provided by environmental funds, represent their major sources of domestic financing for environmental investments. Since enterprises pay environmental charges and fines and these revenues are often used to capitalise environmental funds, the contribution of their own resources is actually larger than it appears.

Except in the advanced transition countries, such as the Czech Republic and Poland, domestic commercial loans have not played a role in either private or municipal environmental financing. In the NIS, commercial lending is not developed and even when loans are available, the terms are not attractive to borrowers.

2.2. *International assistance and financing*

Throughout the transition, donor countries and IFIs have provided technical assistance (for training, policy reform and similar activities) and financing (usually for investment projects) in a number of areas. Almost US$1 billion per year in official assistance and financing was specifically targeted for environmental protection in the CEEC/NIS. This represented close to 10% of their total official assistance and financing in the region. These figures are based on an EAP Task Force survey of donor countries and IFIs (Annex I).

Overview of trends

Donor countries have mainly provided assistance in the form of grants. Between 1994 and 1997 their commitments fell slightly (Figure 6.4), from over ECU 450 million (US$550 million) to under

Figure 6.4. **Trends in environmental assistance and financing to CEEC and to NIS**

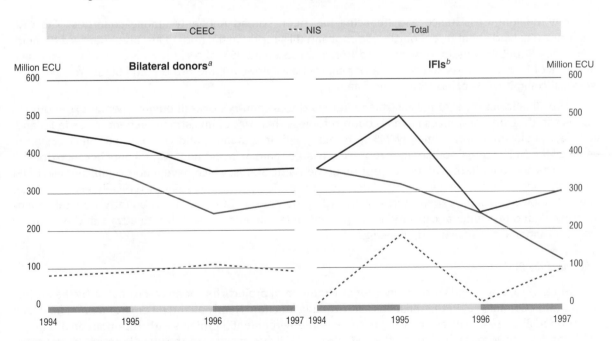

a) Includes EC. 1997 data incomplete.
b) Environmental projects only.
Source: OECD, based on donor and IFI data.

ECU 400 million (US$450 million). This reflected the steady fall in all OECD country assistance to developing and transition economies. A few donors have supported environmental protection through other mechanisms, including debt-for-nature swaps and export credits (Box 6.3)

Box 6.3. Export credit financing

Government export credits from OECD countries have helped finance enterprise investments in the CEEC/NIS region, particularly by financing the export of capital equipment, including for pollution abatement. A few export credit agencies have now made environmental due diligence reviews a regular part of their financing decisions. OECD countries have also discussed the possible development of common environmental guidelines for export credit agencies. These guidelines could have an important effect by improving the environmental sustainability of their lending. Although export credits have sometimes played an important role in financing investments, they have relatively short terms. Net flows of official export credits to the CEEC/NIS, which reached US$1.6 billion in 1992, have been neutral in recent years. In 1996, there was a net flow of US$12 million back to creditor countries.

Source: OECD, 1999b.

IFI financing for environmental projects in the region fell between 1994 and 1997, from ECU 350 million (US$400 million) to just over ECU 300 million (US$340 million). IFI financing typically involves loans for large projects; levels of financing to the NIS fluctuated significantly from year to year. While loans to CEE countries fell steadily, this decrease was offset to some extent by increased integration of environmental components in non-environmental projects, and by IFI loans for projects with significant environmental benefits.

Environmental assistance and financing has been spread unevenly among countries. The CEE countries received about three-fourths of donor and IFI support in the mid-1990s. Five countries (Poland, the Czech Republic, Russia, Hungary, and Romania) received 45% of technical co-operation assistance and 56% of investment assistance. On a per capita basis, however, the three Baltic States received the greatest commitments of assistance and financing.

The significance of external assistance in regard to a country's overall environmental expenditures varies widely. External sources have accounted for less than 10% of investment expenditures in Poland, Russia and Slovenia, approximately 25% in Hungary, 80% in Lithuania, and virtually 100% in Georgia.[7] In many of the NIS, external sources may represent a large share of investment capital only because domestic sources are so limited. With the exception of the Baltic States, which have made significant use of IFI loans for public sector environmental infrastructure projects, external sources typically account for at most 25% of investment expenditures in the CEE countries (OECD, 1998c). A country's overall policy framework and institutional capacity are important determinants of its ability to attract and effectively use international assistance and financing.

The role of the PPC

Since 1993, donor and IFI assistance for environmental projects has been co-ordinated by the Project Preparation Committee (PPC), which has a networking function. Nearly all the IFI environmental financing mentioned above – as well as financing of some non-environmental projects with important environmental benefits – have passed through the PPC (Box 6.4). It has facilitated the development of potential investment projects by matching donor technical assistance for feasibility studies with IFI project goals. It has also helped with project implementation by putting together financing packages. These packages,

---

Box 6.4. PPC projects

Lucerne to Sofia. In the PPC's first two years, IFI boards and funding agencies approved 26 of its projects, with total costs of ECU 1.2 billion (about US$1.5 billion). Bilateral donors provided ECU 80 million (about US$80 million) in support of these projects.

Sofia to Aarhus. IFI boards and funding agencies approved 33 new PPC projects between the 1995 Sofia Conference and the 1998 Aarhus Conference. These projects had total investment costs of ECU 2.3 billion (about US$2.6 billion). IFI financing committed ECU 1.2 billion (about US$1.4 billion); bilateral donors matched this with ECU 245 million (US$285 million) in assistance (recipient countries providing most of the remaining share). The PPC matched 55 further projects, with investment costs of ECU 2.6 billion (almost US$3.0 billion). At the time of the Aarhus Conference, these awaited final approval.

Value added. The PPC reported to the Aarhus Conference that, in terms of the value added of its work:

- the PPC had been an effective mechanism for matching donor financing with projects already in the IFIs' pipelines;

- PPC officers had assisted IFIs in developing priority environmental projects;

- the PPC had contributed to strengthening CEEC/NIS capacities to identify, prepare and finance environmental projects; and

- the PPC had substantially improved understanding between donors and IFIs.

Source: PPC.

---

combining IFI loans and donor grants, have lowered borrowing costs for countries in the region. In addition, the PPC has helped strengthen recipient country capacities for project preparation and increased communication between bilateral donors and IFIs. The PPC has largely focused on public environmental infrastructure projects. By and large, PPC projects have not involved industrial enterprises. In a few cases, the PPC has supported private sector investments in municipal waste water treatment projects.

2.3. *New international sources of financing*

Support for accession from EU institutions

The 10 CEE countries seeking to join the EU will need to mobilise significant domestic resources to finance investments to meet its environmental requirements (Annex III). The EU is establishing several new financing mechanisms to support such investments. Although they will fall short of total requirements, the amounts will be significant in relation to the total annual environmental expenditures of the accession countries. The new mechanisms are intended to leverage additional funds from CEE governments, environmental funds and IFIs. The European Commission is working closely with the REC to support the applicant countries in devising accession strategies and identifying potential projects. Environmental funds could serve as intermediaries during the accession process, matching project proposals with domestic and external financing, although many of them would need to strengthen their institutional capacities for such a task. In the future, the EC plans to increase its efforts to leverage private sector financing.

The EU's overall investment support will focus on four critical aspects of enlargement: direct promotion of compliance with EU norms; integrated regional development programmes; support for the banking sector to better meet the needs of small and medium enterprises; and support for large scale infrastructure projects. In the last area, the EC launched a centrally managed Large Scale Infrastructure Facility, with Euro 150 million for 1998 and 1999, to co-finance environment and transport projects with the IFIs.

135|

In the period 2000 to 2006, the EC plans to significantly expand its support for accession countries. An Instrument for Structural Policies for pre-Accession (ISPA) will provide Euro 1 billion per year to finance accession-related investments in environment and transport. (A separate agricultural facility of Euro 500 million per year will assist the applicant countries to integrate their agricultural policies with those of the EU.) The PHARE Programme, with a yearly budget of Euro 1.5 billion, will continue to provide support for accession over a wide range of areas, including environment. However, 70% of PHARE funds will be targeted for investment support (reversing its previous focus on technical assistance). PHARE support for environmental investments will be limited mainly to strengthening so-called "regulatory infrastructure" needed to ensure compliance with EU environmental legislation (European Commission).

The European Investment Bank, the EU's long-term financing institution, will also expand its efforts to support the accession process. It has committed Euro 3.5 billion, to be lent through 2000 using a special "pre-accession facility", to help the accession countries comply with the requirements in the *acquis communautaire* and strengthen the physical infrastructure linking them with the EU. As environmental improvements have been identified as a priority for the accession countries in meeting the requirements of EU legislation, it is expected that EIB lending for environmental investments will be substantial. Other IFIs also expect to help finance accession-related investments in the accession countries.

Accession-related resources will transform environmental financing in the applicant countries. Substantial resources must be spent over short periods of time. While financing may be available on favourable terms, identifying appropriate projects and establishing a policy and institutional framework to ensure that resources are used cost-effectively represent major challenges. If these challenges are not met, there is a risk that accession-related financing will "crowd out" other sources of financing and inhibit rather than support the development of market-based environmental financing mechanisms such as municipal bonds (described below). A further risk is that environmental concerns will not be strongly integrated into financing for other sectors such as transport or agriculture. If this were the case, new financing could exacerbate environmental pressures caused by these sectors even as it reduced other environmental problems.

Climate change mechanisms

The three Kyoto mechanisms (Box 6.5) established under the Kyoto Protocol of the UN Framework Convention on Climate Change present unique opportunities for the CEEC/NIS to finance environmental improvement projects. These mechanisms will not be operational until at least the year 2000, but there is substantial interest in them in many countries. (Climate change issues are discussed further in Annex IV.)

2.4. The growing role of private capital flows

Private capital flows, including international loans and equity investments, to developing and transition countries have expanded rapidly over the past decade. Foreign direct investment (FDI), a key form of international equity investment, has grown rapidly in the CEEC/NIS in recent years, reaching US$17 billion in 1997, about 50% higher than all official assistance and finance. FDI flows show a similar pattern to those in other regions, *i.e.* high concentrations in a few countries. Further efforts are needed in other countries to reduce political and regulatory risks for investors. Private capital flows are expected to grow further, raising questions about their environmental effects as well as their role *vis-à-vis* that of foreign aid.

In principle, policies that favour open trade and investment policies could contribute to a country's development by improving the efficiency of environmental resource use, reducing existing distortions which may already be damaging the environment, and promoting the development, transfer and adoption of more "environmentally friendly" technologies. (The following section reviews the role that international commercial banks can play in support of the environment.) However, research and debate on the environmental impacts of trade and private capital flows continue. (Chapter 7 reviews trends and evidence concerning potential impacts related to FDI in the region.) Harnessing FDI and other private flows more effectively for environmental purposes is a key challenge for countries in the region.

Box 6.5.   **Kyoto climate change mechanisms**

Joint Implementation (JI): Annex I* countries would be eligible to participate in this mechanism. Under a JI programme, individual governments or private sector entities could invest in emissions reduction (and possibly carbon sequestration) projects. These projects would earn credit that could be applied towards attainment of the country's targeted emissions limit under the Kyoto Protocol. CEEC/NIS that are part of the Annex I group could serve as host countries for JI as a means to obtain financing for environmental projects. Bilateral donors have already supported projects in the region under a pilot mechanism, Activities Implemented Jointly (AIJ). This experience will have an important bearing in defining JI programme specifications and determining future opportunities and limitations of this mechanism for CEEC/NIS.

Emissions Trading (ET): This mechanism would allow trading of greenhouse gas (GHG) allowances or credits among Annex I countries. Countries will be able to sell part of their assigned emissions amount under the Kyoto Protocol on an international market. This revenue could provide a potential source of financing for environmental investments in CEE/NIS Annex I countries. A significant question for countries in the region with substantial forest cover is whether credit will be received for enhancement of sinks in addition to emissions reductions. It has not been determined when such a trading programme would begin, but verification and monitoring are likely to be key programme design issues.

Clean Development Mechanism (CDM): Under this mechanism, Annex I country governments or private entities could receive credit towards the country's targeted Kyoto Protocol emissions target by investing in emissions reduction (or possibly carbon sequestration) projects in non-Annex I countries. This provides a potential financing opportunity for NIS countries which are not in the Annex I group.

---

*   Annex I countries are those which have committed themselves to specific reduction targets for greenhouse gas emissions by the period 2008-2012. In the CEEC/NIS region, this includes Bulgaria, Croatia, the Czech Republic, Estonia, Hungary, Latvia, Lithuania, Poland, Romania, Russia, Slovakia, Slovenia and Ukraine.

OECD's Development Assistance Committee (DAC), whose members include most OECD country development agencies, has discussed the importance of private capital flows and made recommendations on how to integrate them with development financing and assistance (Box 6.6). Donor countries, IFIs and the CEEC/NIS should consider these recommendations as they discuss the future role of international assistance and financing for environmental protection in the region.

3.   Environmental Financing Mechanisms

In advanced reform countries, policies supporting economic reform and macroeconomic stabilisation have encouraged the development of working domestic capital markets that can supply financing to both enterprises and municipalities. In slower reform countries, capital markets and institutions have often remained weak and have had little incentive to finance these sectors. Governments in the CEEC/NIS region as well as IFIs and donors have supported mechanisms that supply financing specifically for environmental projects. This section reviews the development of financial markets and the role of commercial banks in the region. It then discusses several types of environmental financing mechanisms, including commercial bank credit lines, domestic environmental funds, and IFI-supported environmental financing facilities. The section ends by discussing project preparation capacities, a basic requirement for accessing environmental financing.

3.1. *Role of financial markets*

Building a sound, market-oriented financial system is of fundamental importance in the transition from a command to a market economy. Financial institutions and markets play a central role in the

---

Box 6.6.   **Development finance**

OECD's Development Assistance Committee has adopted *Shaping the 21st Century*, a policy document which sets out a vision of development that fosters self-reliance, as developing countries and their peoples are ultimately responsible for their own development. Equally, the vast bulk of financing needed to meet development objectives must come from domestic resources mobilisation, complemented by external (private and official) resources. In ensuring adequate resources for development, partner country responsibilities include adhering to appropriate macroeconomic policies, creating a predictable climate favourable to enterprise development and the mobilisation of local savings for investment, and carrying out sound financial management, including efficient tax systems and productive public expenditure. Partner countries and donors together are responsible for creating conditions conducive to generating adequate resources for development.

The DAC development finance agenda emphasises the importance of using ODA to build institutions, governance and capacities in ways that address priority areas and catalyse the mobilisation of domestic and external private resources. Key elements on the agenda include:

– financial sectors and systems;

– public sector fiscal management;

– external debt; and

– enterprise development.

Targeted interventions need to be guided by partner countries' assessments of their own priorities and capacities. Each donor should also assess its own comparative advantages *vis-à-vis* those of other bilateral donors and the multilateral institutions active in this area, to ensure a strong value-added approach.

In areas or activities where private finance is or should be available, donors need to move away from direct financial support and switch towards assistance to meet the preconditions for private investment. Elsewhere they need to search for high-leverage uses of ODA where limited interventions effectively leverage the needed finance from other sources.

Source: OECD, 1999*a*.

allocation of resources in all market economies through ranking projects by risk and return, monitoring the uses to which borrowed funds are put, and sanctioning managers who fail to maximise shareholder value. In doing so, they help to establish hard budgetary constraints for enterprises. The efficiency with which financial markets and institutions carry out these tasks is a crucial determinant of a country's economic performance.

At the beginning of the transition period, virtually all countries in the region experienced high rates of inflation and negative real interest rates, *i.e.* bank lending rates lower than inflation rates (Table 6.2), which undermined incentives for financial institutions to provide loans for investments. During periods of high and volatile inflation, lenders have often been unwilling to make loans for more than a few months. Short periods of negative interest rates were usually followed by periods of soaring positive interest rates, which have effectively undermined willingness to borrow to finance investments. Advanced transition countries in Central and Eastern Europe were generally effective in implementing sound fiscal policies in ways that eventually reduced budget deficits without disturbing the development of the financial markets. Through comprehensive stabilisation programmes, inflation rates have been dramatically reduced and lending rates have fallen, often to 10-20%. The banking sector has been steadily expanding its portfolio of credits to investments undertaken by enterprises and municipalities.

Table 6.2.   **Nominal interest and inflation rates in selected CEEC/NIS**

	Lending rates (%)[a]		Change in consumer prices (%)[b]	
	1991	1997	1991	1997
CEE countries				
Bulgaria	83.9	6.7	333.5	1 082.3
Poland	40.0	25.8	70.3	14.9
NIS				
Kyrgyz Republic	..	50.1	85.0	25.5
Ukraine	77.0	49.0	91.0	15.9

..   Not available.
a)   CEEC: For loans less than or equal to one year in duration. NIS: Weighted averages over all maturities.
b)   Change from previous year. Annual average.
Sources: EBRD, OECD.

In most NIS countries, fiscal policy failures such as excessive, complicated and erratic taxation have led to insufficient tax revenues, chronic public deficits, and low liquidity in the enterprise and banking sectors. Capital shortages have been further aggravated by barriers to foreign capital and direct investments. Many NIS governments (particularly in Russia) have attempted to finance budget deficits by issuing speculative securities. This has provided banks and institutional investors with a lucrative alternative to lending to the "real" economy. Government has therefore "crowded out" bank credit for the enterprise and municipal sectors. These factors have underpinned the collapse of overall investment. According to one estimate, 1997 levels in Russia were about one-fifth of those at the start of the transition. As a result, Russia's old, often highly polluting capital stock has continued to age (Table 6.3).

The risk of investments in the real economy has been additionally inflated by the low level of protection given to private sector creditors. This has occurred in countries where underdeveloped legal and institutional systems have prevented creditors from acquiring collateral or initiating a change of management in the event of default. These economic policy failures have often been exacerbated by the lack of rule of law, institutionalised corruption, and underdeveloped democracy and civil society. Policy failures which have contributed to macroeconomic and fiscal imbalances have also led to the development of microeconomic incentive structures for enterprises that rewarded "rent-seeking" rather that "efficiency-seeking" behaviour.

International markets have judged the NIS to be high-risk countries, limiting their access to foreign capital and raising the cost of government borrowing. This further undermines government spending on environment. Increased nominal interest rates and related discount rates applied by governments usually inhibit financing for most public sector environmental investments, which are typically characterised by relatively low internal financial rates of return. Other features of distorted credit markets in the NIS include: preferences for short-term exposures, high nominal lending rates, large spreads between deposit and lending rates, and a low percentage of bank loans to enterprises. Nominal lending rates of around 40% in the NIS are still too high to be attractive to borrowers.

Table 6.3.   **Average age of industrial plants in the Russian Federation, 1990 to 1995**

	1990	1991	1992	1993	1994	1995
Average age of plant and equipment in industry	10.8	11.3	12.0	12.7	13.4	14.1

Source: OECD Economic Surveys: Russian Federation (1997).

3.2. *Private financial institutions*

CEEC/NIS *commercial banks*

Stabilisation policies have been reasonably effective in slowing inflation and restoring economic growth in some countries. However, in most cases domestic capital markets have responded slowly to enterprises' need for investment capital. Lending to the private sector remains low despite reduced demand for national budget deficit financing. In addition to macroeconomic instability and high inflation, this reflects inefficiencies in transition banking. Spreads between deposit and lending rates are also higher than in market economies, and loan terms often stipulate a payback period that is too short for long-term investments. Since restructuring and modernisation investments often result in reduced pollution, the development of effective financial institutions and markets providing improved access to capital should ultimately benefit the environment.

In EU countries, bank lending to enterprises represents about half of GDP. However, in most CEE countries it increased only slowly between 1994 and 1997, from just below to just above 25% of GDP. Lending to enterprises only reached 15% of GDP in the Baltic States in 1997; in the NIS it has fallen below 10%. Greater bank lending should help enterprises increase their level of investment (EBRD, 1998).

There are some promising initiatives to strengthen the role of banks in environmental financing, including co-operation with environmental funds, IFIs and donors. UNEP has worked with commercial banks world-wide to develop a Statement by Financial Institutions on the Environment and Sustainable Development. Over 100 banks – including a few in CEE countries – have signed the Statement, pledging to incorporate environmental concerns into their operations.

The case of the Polish Bank Ochrony Srodowiska SA (Environmental Protection Bank) is unique. It was established at the beginning of the 1990s as a major equity investment of Poland's public sector National Fund for Environmental Protection and Water Management. "Own capital" has been raised several times by attracting strategic private sector investors. Since 1997, the Bank has been listed on the Warsaw stock exchange. It is believed to be the first publicly-traded bank in the world specialising in providing funds for environmental protection. In 1997, the Bank granted more than 27 000 credits and loans worth Euro 363 million. Loans for specific environmental investments dominate the credit structure with a 66% share. The credit structure consists of credits granted to business entities (54%), public sector entities – mainly municipalities (26%), and individuals.

International commercial banks

International commercial banks provided almost US$8 billion in net capital to the region in 1997. Private export financing made up a large share of these loans, along with loans to governments. There have been a few large loans to CEEC/NIS enterprises. In 1997, international banks provided Gazprom of Russia with a US$3 billion loan. Although Western European and especially North American banks have paid increasing attention to environmental issues in their domestic loans, there is little information on the relationship between their international lending and environmental issues (Gentry). International commercial banks have sometimes co-operated with IFIs in financing packages, in which case the IFIs have focused on the environmental aspects of the loans.

International portfolio investments have increased during the transition. According to one estimate, they reached US$3.4 billion in 1997 (however, estimates of portfolio investment levels are uncertain and can differ greatly). In some of the CEEC/NIS, a large portion of international portfolio investments has been in government securities, including national as well as local government bond issues. Overall, portfolio investments have been very volatile and have moved quickly among countries and instruments to seek the best yields (EBRD, 1998). They rarely appear to have influenced enterprise environmental performance.

Other private financing arrangements

A few schemes use innovative mechanisms that overcome obstacles to financing environmental and related investments, such as the reluctance of many industrial enterprises to bear the related costs and risks. One example is energy service companies (ESCOs). ESCOs offer energy services with performance guarantees that generally provide customers with feasible means of reducing energy consumption costs. Two common ESCO approaches are *guaranteed savings* and *shared savings*. With *guaranteed savings*, the end user finances projects' initial investment cost through a third party. In turn, the ESCO guarantees that energy savings will at least cover the debt service. The ESCO receives a share of the net savings after debt servicing and operations and maintenance costs. If the savings fall short of the customer's financial obligations as stated in the performance contract, the ESCO assumes the shortfall. In this respect, the ESCO assumes all the risks associated with the project's performance and the third party assumes the end user's credit risk. With the *shared savings* approach, the ESCO finances the project's initial investment costs, usually by borrowing from a third party. It is compensated by a higher share of the project savings. The EBRD has supported ESCOs in Hungary and Slovakia.

There is also an increasing market in advanced transition countries for environmental leasing arrangements, whereby private firms provide equipment needed for environmental services. Typically, leasing involves vehicles or equipment used in solid waste collection, transport and disposal. Such arrangements enable municipalities to spread costs over a longer period, overcome collateral shortage problems, and shift the burden of raising capital to the leasing company.

An example of an established and successful leasing company focusing on environmental technology is the Polish Towarzystwo Inwestycyjno-Leasingowe Ekoleasing SA (Ekoleasing Investment and Leasing Company, a joint stock company), established in 1993. Currently the share capital is almost US$1 million, distributed between the Environmental Protection Bank (30%), private strategic investor Elektrim SA (30%), the public sector National Fund for Environmental Protection and Water Management (33.3%), and the Regional Fund for Environmental Protection and Water Management of Katowice (3.3%). The remainder is distributed among private individuals. More than 40% of the US$9 million in contracts concluded in 1998 was for leasing of environmental equipment.

3.3. IFI *mechanisms to support private financing*

IFIs and donors have established credit lines for environmental investments in co-operation with financial intermediaries in the region. With the local partner sharing the credit risk, these credit lines can reduce the costs of preparing projects and conducting financial appraisals of borrowers, and facilitate IFI support for smaller loans than would be available directly from the IFI. This co-operation often contributes to strengthening of the local financial intermediary, particularly its capacity to appraise environmental projects and non-environmental projects with environmental components, and to demonstrating the financial attractiveness of win-win environmental investments.

IFIs have co-operated with commercial banks in CEE countries to establish eight energy efficiency funds (EEFs) that provide loans for energy efficiency investments in the industrial and municipal sectors. The average fund size is about US$7 million, with capital provided by EC PHARE Programme, the World Bank, and the EBRD. Generally, EEFs provide 70-80% of costs for energy efficiency projects up to $400 000 in value. The commercial bank, which serves as the fund manager, underwrites the commercial risk of lending but is compensated by a negotiated margin of 5-8%. The EEF mechanism not only supports energy savings and reduced pollution, but also makes commercial banks aware of a potential market niche.

In addition to those which are specifically for environmental projects, IFIs have arranged a number of loans to large enterprises in the region to finance investments in increased production capacities. They have also helped foreign investors take equity stakes in some enterprises. In many of these cases, IFIs have conducted environmental audits of their potential clients and specified environmental actions for them to take. IFI loans for enterprise restructuring have often included components for environmental investments. Some IFIs have also provided financing to small and medium enterprises via intermediaries such as national banks. In a few cases, the IFIs have set environmental conditions and have provided the intermediaries with training in evaluating environmental risks in considering loan applications.

3.4. *Domestic environmental funds*

Environmental funds are institutions capitalised with working capital, usually revenues from environmental charges, to support environmental activities. In the CEEC/NIS, government funds have supported a wide range of environmental activities, mainly by providing grants and soft loans and sometimes by taking equity positions. Activities include investments in environmental improvements, research, education, and related expenditures such as the purchase of monitoring equipment and the outfitting of laboratories. A summary of major funds in the region, including revenues and expenditure, is provided in Annex VIII.

There is no exact equivalent to the CEEC/NIS environmental funds in other OECD countries (some institutions, such as French water agencies, have similar characteristics). From a public finance perspective, "earmarking" taxes, as do environmental funds, can result in inefficient use of public resources over the long term. Finance and environment ministries have debated these issues from the beginning of the transition period. A 1994 OECD Conference in St. Petersburg that brought together environmental and finance experts from OECD countries and the CEEC/NIS concluded that, due to the legacy of environmental problems arising from past practices of the state, and the imperfections of financial markets and institutions in transition countries, environmental funds could be useful *transition* instruments, provided they were well-managed. The *St. Petersburg Guidelines on Environmental Funds in the Transition to a Market Economy* that emerged from this conference (Box 6.7) provide guidance on how environmental funds should be established and managed. Not only have these guidelines helped with the design of new environmental funds in the region, but they have also served as an effective instrument for reviewing the operations of existing funds and designing technical assistance programmes.

Box 6.7. **Main conclusions of the St. Petersburg Guidelines on Environmental Funds**

The main conclusions of the St. Petersburg Guidelines include the following:
- To avoid or minimize the long-term economic inefficiencies inherent in earmarking of funds, expenditure should be targeted to meet environmental priorities and promote projects with large environmental benefits relative to their costs.
- Environmental funds should play a catalytic role in financing, ideally offering no more support for projects than is necessary, adapt to changing economic conditions, and support, not compete with, emerging capital markets.
- Environmental funds should be used in conjunction with, and reinforce, other environmental policy instruments, such as compliance schedules, environmental auditing programmes and voluntary agreements.
- Environmental funds should develop an overall financing strategy, follow clear and explicit operating procedures for evaluating and selecting projects, adopt effective monitoring and evaluation practices, and make effective use of internal and external expertise to enhance administrative efficiency.
- For investment projects, funds should have well-designed programme and project cycles to ensure cost-effective use of resources.
- Environmental funds should leverage increased private sector resources and capital market financing for environmental investments.
- In designing and evaluating fund revenue mechanisms, environmental authorities should try to ensure environmental effectiveness, economic and administrative efficiency, equity and acceptability. Systems should provide a stable base of revenues, be simple in structure, and be easy to monitor and enforce.
- Environmental funds should ensure transparency and should be accountable to government, parliaments, and the public for their actions.

Source: OECD, 1995*a*.

Nearly all countries in the region have at least one national environmental fund, and a few (Poland, Lithuania, Latvia, Bulgaria, Russia and Ukraine) have two or more. There are also a number of regional and local funds. These funds share a common goal – assisting in the co-financing of environmental activities. However, they differ in their size, organisational structure, procedures for selecting projects, sources of revenue, and methods of disbursement. Environmental funds generally fall into two groups: those capitalised by domestic revenues generated principally from environmental fees and fines or product charges; and those established and capitalised by donor grants or IFI loans. The first group includes most national, regional and local funds. The latter group includes:

- debt-for-environment swaps (Switzerland agreed to a swap with Bulgaria at the time of the Sofia Conference, and Poland had previously concluded swaps with several donors);
- Environmental Investment Funds in Lithuania and Latvia capitalised by PHARE grants.

Major trends in regard to the role of environmental funds in the region include:

- In many CEE countries, environmental funds have provided an important share of financing for environmental investments: up to 40% in Poland, and 20% in Hungary, Lithuania and Slovenia.
- Many CEE funds have expanded their revenue base, due to government restructuring of environmental charge rates and improved collection efficiency, introducing new revenue sources (*e.g.* charges on natural resource use or purchase of products such as packaging or fuels) and shifting a portion of their disbursements to soft loans, thereby generating revenue from repayment of loans.
- There has been some progress in implementing the *St. Petersburg Guidelines*, notably among the funds receiving financial support from donors and IFIs. Among funds relying on domestic revenues, six regional (*"voivode"*) funds in Poland have strengthened project cycle procedures in line with the Guidelines.
- With the exception of the Polish EcoFund (Box 6.8), CEE funds receiving external support are revolving funds offering only soft loans (with generally smaller subsidy components than the soft loans provided by other CEE funds).
- In the NIS, the institutional base and legal foundations for environmental funds are much weaker than in CEE countries. In Russia, the expenditure of the Federal Environmental Fund in 1996 was about US$14 million. The fees and fines which generate the Fund's revenues are much lower than in the CEEC. For example, the charge for one tonne of SO_2 is over 40 times lower in Russia than in Poland (Table 5.2).
- The collapse of other sources of financing for environmental management and non-environmental activities at the local and regional levels has placed additional pressure on NIS funds, shifting disbursements from environmental investments to support for public environmental institutions. Failure to recirculate revenues to enterprises paying pollution charges, and the diversion of revenues for non-environmental purposes, has undermined the government's collection efforts.
- In Russia and Kazakhstan, environmental funds are being consolidated into government budgets, increasing the risk that their resources will be allocated for non-environmental purposes.

In most CEEC/NIS, government environmental funds have provided only a small share of their financing support to manufacturing enterprises. Most funds have focused on infrastructure projects, such as municipally owned waste water treatment plants, or on the power sector. NIS funds have had few resources, and consequently have had a limited role in financing investments. Where they have assisted enterprises, most funds have financed pollution control rather than "win-win" investment projects such as implementation of cleaner production programmes or less polluting production methods (Chapter 7).

3.5. *Other environmental financing facilities*

The National Pollution Abatement Facility (NPAF) in Russia is an example of an IFI/donor-financed national facility. It is financed by a US$55 million loan from the World Bank, augmented by US$13 million in grants from Switzerland. The NPAF provides loans for 70% of project costs on terms that are attractive

143|

Box 6.8.   **The Polish Ecofund**

The Polish Ecofund was established in 1992, following Poland's debt relief agreement with the "Paris Club" of western creditor nations. Only two environmental funds in the CEEC/NIS region have been established through such "debt-for-environment" swaps, and possibilities for replicating this mechanism are limited. However, there are important lessons to be learned from the operations of the Ecofund which are relevant to all environmental funds, irrespective of how they are capitalised.

The Ecofund is obliged by its statute to provide grant support for projects in Poland addressing transboundary air pollution by sulphur and nitrogen oxides, pollution and eutrophication of the Baltic Sea, global climate change gases, biological diversity, and waste management and the reclamation of contaminated soil. The Ecofund's budget is relatively small in the context of overall environmental financing in Poland. Its disposable resources in 1995 represented about 2.3% of Poland's environmental investments for that year. Annual disbursements now run at about US$30 million. Nonetheless, the Ecofund has become an important financing mechanism. It provides "value added" by:

- financing environmental priorities insufficiently supported by other institutions (nature protection, transfer of innovative environmental technologies, geographic regions of special interest, and competitions for specific types of projects);
- providing a powerful leveraging effect through "gap-filling" financing for projects that are co-financed by other sources;
- creating domestic environmental financing capacity, improving project preparation skills, and instilling financial discipline among applicants; and
- promoting the development of an environmental goods and services industry in Poland and encouraging foreign investment in this industry.

The Ecofund employs rigorous project cycle management procedures. These procedures incorporate clearly defined environmental priorities and project eligibility requirements; guidelines for maintaining strictly professional relations with applicants; transparent appraisal criteria emphasising environmental benefits and cost-effectiveness; and careful monitoring of projects to ensure proper use of the Ecofund's resources and achievement of environmental effects.

The Ecofund's close attention to high benefit-cost ratios has avoided the inefficiencies sometimes associated with earmarked programmes. Several other factors are crucial to the Ecofund's effectiveness: political independence; stable, predictable long-term revenues; strong leadership and highly qualified staff; objective, accountable and transparent decision-making; and competitive tendering procedures.

Source: OECD and EC (1998).

---

compared to those offered by Russian commercial banks The NPAF supports investments yielding positive net economic benefits and other investments in pollution control (if the enterprise can demonstrate adequate financial resources to repay the loan). The World Bank loan has been secured by a sovereign guarantee, and the Ministry of Finance (MoF) on-lends on behalf of the NPAF. While this approach has advantages (applicant confidence in the lender, transparent procedures and MoF monitoring), the effective cost of loans is increased since MoF requires applicants to secure bank guarantees or to deposit loan payments in escrow accounts six months in advance. Administrative delays have also impeded disbursements.

A second stage of the NPAF was planned using a more region-oriented approach, with loans on-lent through financial intermediaries in Russia acceptable to MoF (commercial banks, regional environmental funds or other institutions) and with repayment guarantees provided by regional governments. However, this initiative was postponed indefinitely in the wake of the financial crisis.

An example of an IFI/donor-financed multi-country facility is the Cleaner Production Revolving Facility established by the Nordic Environmental Finance Corporation (NEFCO). The NEFCO Facility will initially be capitalised with US$2.23 million for projects in north-west Russia (US$1.49 million) and

Lithuania (US$743 000). The Facility is designed to provide financing for up to 90% of project costs (in exceptional cases, up to 100%) for investments between US$50 000 and US$200 000, with short payback periods of up to three years. Priority will be given to customers who have participated in programmes provided in Lithuania and Russia through the Cleaner Production Centres. NEFCO plans to co-operate with the Russian NPAF and Lithuanian Environmental Investment Fund to support larger projects. The Facility's operating expenses will be covered by an up-front loan processing fee (NEFCO).

3.6. *Project preparation*

Effective project preparation, which is essential for access to financing mechanisms, serves as the crucial link between the demand and supply sides. While technical capacity is strong, there is often a lack of skills in the region for financial analysis and related activities. Countries need to strengthen capacity to prepare project descriptions, conduct feasibility analyses, evaluate investment alternatives, and propose cost recovery plans, particularly as different sources of funds require different forms of information. Donors can play an important role in assisting countries to develop these capacities (Box 6.9).

Box 6.9. **EAPS: support for project preparation**

The Environmental Action Programme Support (EAPS) Project, funded by USAID, has operated since 1995 in several CEE countries, including Bulgaria, the Czech Republic, Lithuania, Poland and Slovakia. One of its goals has been to assist in strengthening the capacity of local governments and municipalities to package their environmental projects.

EAPS Poland has implemented two types of activities. Project packaging activities provided technical assistance to project proponents (primarily municipalities) for the preparation of environmental investment projects. These activities were designed to increase proponents' capacities to attract financing for their projects and improve the projects' prospects for implementation. Capacity to plan, finance and manage infrastructure projects was stressed through selection of projects with a high potential for replication. Institutional strengthening activities included developing management tools for local financing institutions, providing training for municipalities in applying for funds, and disseminating information about the availability of concessional financing through an environmental financing sourcebook.

An integral part of project identification and screening was the creation of local project ownership by establishing steering committees and engaging local experts. EAPS enhanced the capacity of local consultants by using them for most activities, with selective use of foreign consultants only to contribute know-how that was unavailable in Poland. EAPS staff worked closely with project proponents and involved them in each major decision throughout project development. The project screening phase was used to build informal and formal ties with representatives of the municipality in order to secure their commitment to, and participation in, the development of the project. An additional condition of EAPS assistance was a positive response from local financial institutions (such as environmental funds) to the possibility of co-financing the project investment phase.

EAPS Poland prepared 80 investment packages. Thirty-seven applications had been approved by environmental funds as of early 1998, and most of the others were approved thereafter.

Source: Chemonics International.

---

4. Municipal Environmental Financing

Municipal environmental services are essential to protect the environment and human health. In many countries, investments in this sector represent the largest component of public environmental financing. Under central planning, the provision of services such as drinking water, sewage collection and treatment, and municipal waste collection and management was the responsibility of ministries or state committees, which had few incentives to operate efficiently. These services were provided to users, in particular households, at no or low cost and often without metering of actual consumption levels, limiting incentives for conservation and efficient use.

In the transition period, responsibility for providing and maintaining most of these services has been decentralised to local authorities. These authorities inherited a variety of administrative problems, such as a backlog of unfinished projects, infrastructure in varying states of disrepair, and, in most of the CEEC/NIS, a cut-off of financial support for these services from central government budgets.[8] Corresponding environmental problems have included:

- inadequate access to safe drinking water in some NIS, particularly Caucasus and Central Asian republics;
- high levels of drinking water consumption, as well as water losses from ageing pipe networks;
- often, severe water pollution created by waste water discharges from outdated and inefficient sewerage systems and treatment plants; and
- inadequate solid and hazardous waste management, often involving disposal in unlined landfills where leaching contaminants can pollute soil, groundwater and surface waters, as well as inefficient incinerators that create heavy air pollution.

Financing to improve these services has been a major challenge during the transition. This section focuses in particular on financing issues related to drinking water supply and waste water treatment. It should be noted that, in most OECD countries, central governments have provided substantial subsidies for municipal investments. The US federal government provided about US$52 billion in grants to municipalities between 1972 and 1989 for the construction of waste water treatment facilities. However, such subsidies encourage investments in end-of-pipe technologies at the expense of pollution prevention, lead to oversizing of treatment systems, and discourage efficient water use and pollution reduction since user fees paid by households and industry only cover a portion of capital costs. Many OECD countries have moved away from subsidies in this area. In any case, most CEEC/NIS governments have been subject to severe budgetary constraints, making it difficult to subsidise this type of investments.

Ideally, revenue from user fees would provide the bulk of financing for municipal environmental infrastructure. As infrastructure investments involve high initial costs, these must usually be financed by loans, bond issues or other sources. Revenues from user charges can then pay for both operations and maintenance (O&M) costs, annualised capital costs, and debt servicing (these would preferably be spread over a relatively long period, such as 15 or 20 years). During the transition, municipalities have faced two difficult obstacles in putting such mechanisms into practice. The first is obtaining financing for investment. When domestic financial markets are poorly developed and there is macroeconomic instability, domestic financing would involve high interest rates if it were available at all. Many municipalities have looked to IFIs for loan financing, but IFIs usually require national governments to provide sovereign guarantees for loan repayment. Most CEEC/NIS national governments have limited such guarantees to only a few municipal environmental projects. Second, the higher fees necessary to cover debt repayments would be difficult for many users (especially households) to pay, in particular during a period of economic crisis.

4.1. *Financing waste water treatment in CEE countries*

In most advanced transition countries, user fees for drinking water supply, waste water treatment and waste management services have been raised to levels that enable service providers to recover most or all O&M costs, reducing their reliance on central government transfers (in a few cities, fees have been raised to a level that would cover capital costs). In many CEE countries, local governments have been given some authority to raise revenues through local taxes, which could also be used to pay O&M costs.

Water companies in a number of cities have installed meters for most users, shifted to consumption-based billing, and increased water tariffs. Consequently, consumers have reduced water consumption (Box 6.10) and waste water flow. This, in turn, has resulted in lower utility operating costs and less need for new investments, making it possible to shift resources to badly needed rehabilitation and efficiency improvements.

Box 6.10. **Demand management and water consumption in Poland**

Introduction of metering and consumption-based billing has often resulted in significant reductions in billed water consumption in advanced reform countries such as Poland.

- In some neighbourhoods of Bydgoszcs, metering led to a 30% reduction in water consumption over three years.
- In Gdansk, the city government and SAUR International, a private company, formed a joint enterprise in 1992 to manage and operate the city's water and sewage network. From 1992 to 1995, the company introduced individual metering and raised tariffs. Total water consumption subsequently fell 33%.

**Metering and annual water consumption
in Gdansk's Morena district**

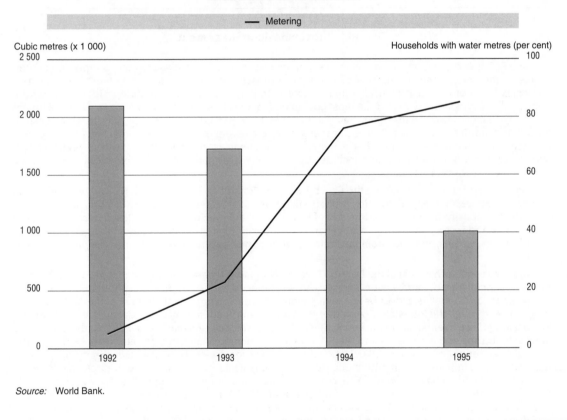

Source: World Bank.

Nonetheless, there is a strong need for new investment. A 1998 World Bank study evaluated municipal waste water treatment in 362 towns in five CEE countries (Somlyody and Shanahan). It found that although the current state of water supply and sewerage collection was adequate, the level of waste water treatment was poor. Less than half the waste water received secondary biological treatment, and biological treatment plants were often overloaded, leading to inadequate treatment for biological oxygen demand (BOD). Since a substantial amount of the waste water was discharged without treatment, removal   147|

of influent BOD was no more than 25% for the entire region. Sludge was inadequately treated and was often contaminated by metals from industrial wastes. Ageing sewerage, the prevalence of combined sewerage systems, and inadequate stormwater management were also serious problems.

The study urged countries to tackle these problems cost-effectively, in order to use available resources to obtain the greatest possible environmental improvements. For example, waste water treatment facilities can be constructed and upgraded in a multi-stage fashion, with consideration of the cost-effectiveness of each upgrade. Moreover, while some waste water treatment plants were overloaded, others were not fully utilised owing to a lack of sewers, interceptors or pumping stations. There were also more than 1 000 partially constructed treatment plants in the five countries, the largest number of which were in Poland. The report urged countries to plan investments and other actions at the river basin level, allowing the most cost-effective choice of treatment alternatives. The EAP had made a similar recommendation, but as yet this approach has only been partially implemented (Box 6.11).

Box 6.11. **River basin management**

The EAP urged countries in the region to set up *river basin authorities* to manage water supply and related issues at the water basin level. This eco-system approach can identify and implement cost-effective strategies for improving and managing inland waters. In particular, river basin authorities can work with municipalities and industry to find the most cost-effective ways to upgrade existing waste water treatment plants and invest in new ones. River basin authorities have played an important role in a few Western European countries. France has six agencies that receive the revenues from waste water charges, using them to finance treatment plants and other activities. These agencies are guided by basin committees and supervisory boards whose members include representatives of national ministries, local governments, industrial enterprises and farmers.

A few CEE countries – including the Czech Republic, Poland and Romania – have created river basin authorities. However, these authorities lack adequate financial resources, decision-making authority and institutional capacity. In Poland, the Ministry of Environmental Protection, Natural Resources, and Forestry proposed to redirect a part of waste water charge revenues from regional environmental funds to the river basin authorities, but opposition from the regional funds as well as local and regional governments blocked this transfer.

In a few cases, such as that of the Danube River Environment Programme, international co-operation on the protection of transboundary rivers and seas has encouraged the development of multilateral river basin management. In Central Asia, river basin management has been an important element of the Aral Sea Basin Programme, through the Interstate Committee for Water Co-ordination (ICWC), which covers the whole Aral Sea basin, and two river basin organisations (BVOs: *Basseino-Vodokhozyaistvennye organizatsii*) for the main rivers flowing to the sea, the Amu Darya and the Syr Darya. The ministers in charge of water management in the Central Asian republics sit on the ICWC. National and international water basin management bodies, including BVOs, are to implement committee decisions. Most financial resources are expected to come from the International Fund for Saving the Aral Sea, created by the five Central Asian republics. They include contributions from these countries (0.3% of the national budgets of Kazakhstan, Turkmenistan and Uzbekistan, and 0.1% of those of the Kyrgyz Republic and Tajikistan) and international assistance from the GEF (about US$20 million), the European Commission (more than US$2 million), UNDP, the Netherlands, Sweden, Switzerland, USAID and other bilateral donors (Demydenko, 1999).

In the CEE countries seeking accession, current EU legislation will require extensive new investments in municipal services, in particular drinking water supply and waste water treatment. The costs could greatly depend on how the relevant directives are interpreted and the length of time allowed for compliance. The World Bank has estimated that the total cost of upgrading Poland's waste water infrastructure (both urban and rural) to meet the requirements of EU legislation could range from US$9 billion to US$13 billion, depending on these factors. The necessary investments in drinking water supply systems would cost a further US$3 to 8 billion (World Bank, 1999). A separate study, commissioned by the EC, estimated that Poland would have to invest Euro 6.4 billion (about US$6.6 billion) through 2010 in its urban waste water infrastructure alone (Agriconsulting). Given such estimates, the challenge for Poland and other countries will be to develop carefully planned strategies, supported by efficient financing mechanisms, to ensure investments are as cost-effective as possible. River basin management approaches could play an important role in these efforts.

4.2. NIS *municipal issues*

In the NIS, municipally owned water companies usually provide piped drinking water as well as waste water treatment services. However, large industrial enterprises in a number of municipalities provide drinking water, sewerage, and waste water treatment for inhabitants. Commonly, municipal water companies can set rates for industrial users. Local, regional or even national governments set them for households. These rates are usually low. Industrial users often do not pay their charges, or pay in non-monetary means (Box 6.12). As a result, both households (which usually are not metered and pay a flat rate) and industrial users tend to consume excess amounts of water, and water companies lack the resources to adequately maintain or refurbish drinking water distribution and sewerage systems. Many NIS cities have therefore seen a serious deterioration of their water infrastructure.

Inadequate access to safe drinking water presents a major health threat across the NIS. It is especially severe in the Central Asian republics, where drinking water infrastructure remains underdeveloped, particularly in rural areas. However, the water companies' lack of resources for proper operation, maintenance and repair has created health risks in cities across the NIS. Without new financing, there could be a significant increase in water-borne disease in the coming years (Annex II).

Policy and institutional reforms are urgently needed to stop the rapid deterioration of water infrastructure, promote efficient use of water, and generate revenues for needed investments. The institutional capabilities to manage these services and place them on a firmer financial basis also need to be strengthened. As household incomes are low in many NIS, subsidies and external financing must also play a role. They could be applied to catalyse improvements in municipal environmental services. Ideally, financial support should be targeted to the neediest households. It is most efficient if decoupled from the pricing of services. Subsidies are most useful as financing for capital investments or public partnerships. They should not be applied in a way that discourages energy and water conservation or public-private partnerships.

4.3. *Municipal financing mechanisms*

New and creative approaches will be needed to finance municipal services in the CEE countries and NIS. Some approaches, such as issuing municipal bonds, are already being tried in advanced transition countries (Box 6.13). Others, such as public-private partnerships, have been little used in the region so far.

The private sector could play a greater role in financing and managing municipal services. Although public-private partnerships have been rare in the CEEC/NIS (the Gdansk water company described in Box 6.10 is one of the few examples), they have been used increasingly in other parts of the world. These partnerships can take many different forms, including: Build-Operate-Transfer (BOT) schemes; contracting private sector firms to commercialise existing services or to manage their renovation or expansion; privatising parts or all of a municipal service; and providing private concessions to operate a service while maintaining municipal ownership of assets. They can benefit from the private sector's focus on quality of service and incentives to discover the most cost-effective practices, as well as tapping capital resources that the private sector may be able to provide or raise. Undertaking public-private partnerships can be difficult. They require innovations in government practice, as well as individual champions in government, NGOs and business to promote and support them. Such partnerships also need effective government institutions to ensure that public interests are served and to provide a stable, long-term framework for private sector partners. These conditions are rare in the NIS and other countries where state governance remains weak.

149

Box 6.12. Municipal water services in Nizhniy Novgorod

In the city of Nizhniy Novgorod in Russia, the municipal water company (*Vodokanal*) supplies the approximately 1.4 million inhabitants with drinking water and provides sewerage and waste water treatment services. The company relies on water supply and waste water treatment charges for its main revenue (grants from the city and other governments have diminished dramatically during the current economic crisis). Industrial enterprises pay the highest rates and provide about 60% of total revenues. In effect, they subsidise municipal services (governments, schools, etc.) and households. The *Vodokanal* sets rates for other enterprises and municipal services (although the government must approve them) and has steadily increased these rates in line with inflation. The city government sets household rates for water use and waste water treatment, usually once a year. These have remained significantly lower. The figure shows the evolution of the *Vodokanal's* costs, industrial tariffs and debts between 1993 and 1996. Costs are currently increasing faster than inflation, and unpaid charges, which represent a major revenue problem for the company, are growing.

**Nizhniy Novgorod's water company:
trends in operating costs, tariff rates and unpaid charges**
Index values, 1993 = 100

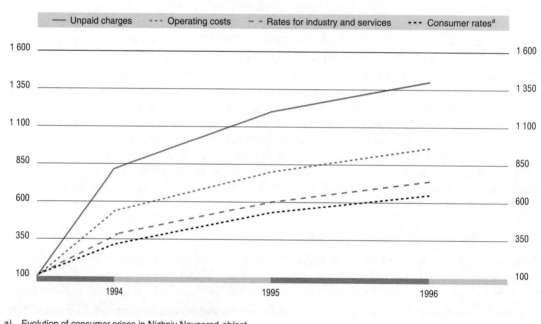

a) Evolution of consumer prices in Nizhniy Novgorod *oblast*.
Source: OECD, 1998*b*.

When partnerships are formed to provide a municipal service that has been lacking, there are three major roles to be assumed: provider, user and regulator of the service. Different parties, including government, business and NGOs, can undertake any of these roles in a particular case. However, it is important that these roles' allocation and definitions are clear (particularly to avoid conflicts of interest), and that there is adequate dialogue to ensure that the needs of different parties are met. Transparent and informal communication among stakeholders early in the process, prior to formal negotiations, can contribute to a good outcome.

Box 6.13. **Municipal bonds**

As capital markets have developed in advanced reform countries, municipal governments have been able to obtain financing through bond issues. By the end of 1996, 18 municipalities in the Czech Republic had issued municipal bonds, and institutions and procedures necessary to sustain a competitive municipal credit market were in place. In fact, there was vigorous competition between use of loans and bonds to support municipal investments.

In Poland, such institutions were also in place by 1996, and the use of municipal bonds for infrastructure and environmental financing has grown steadily. The town of Miescisko started to plan construction of a waste water treatment plant and sewerage network in the late 1980s, but encountered a variety of financial and technical difficulties. In 1996, authorities renewed efforts to undertake the construction project and raised PLZ 1 million (about US$371 000), half the project's total cost, through the issue of municipal bonds. (The remaining project costs were financed by national and regional agricultural agencies, as well as by sewerage connection fees charged to local residents.) The bond issue allowed this relatively small municipality to contract long-term debt at a lower price than that typically offered by banks for capital investment projects in Poland. The money raised constituted the municipality's share of project financing and played a role in securing co-financing from other sources.

Source: Bazaniak.

As there are many different forms of public-private partnerships, choosing among them depends on a number of factors, including the degree of control desired by government; the government's capacity to provide the desired services; the capacity of private parties to provide the services; legal frameworks for public investment and regulatory oversight; and the availability of financial resources from public or private sources (Gentry and Fernandez).

NOTES

1. Negative externalities are effects associated with either production or consumption of a good or service that generate costs to some third party other than the producer or consumer of that good or service.

2. Public and community pressures can also motivate enterprises (Chapter 4 and 5).

3. OECD defines pollution abatement and control (PAC) activities as "purposeful activities aimed directly at the prevention, reduction and elimination of pollution or nuisances arising as a residual of production processes or the consumption of goods and services. This definition specifically excludes expenditure on natural resource management and activities such as the protection of endangered species (fauna and flora), the establishment of natural parks and green belts and activities to exploit natural resources (such as the supply of drinking water)" (OECD, 1998d). This definition has been used in collecting comparable data from the six case study countries, as national definitions of environmental expenditures vary. OECD regularly collects data on Member countries using this definition.

4. Questions have been raised about the accuracy of Russian statistics (Golub, 1996). For example, the widespread use of barter and other non-monetary means of exchange is an important concern in considering these and other investments.

5. Based on the abater principle. Environmental fund spending is excluded. Source: OECD.

6. Golub (1996) notes that the Russian pollution charge offset system, which waives facilities' environmental charge payments when they are used for environmental investments, may account for nearly three-fourths of total payments due to funds. This suggests that the role of revenues earmarked for environmental funds is larger than that of the funds.

7. An approximate external financing share was derived from an estimate of annual investment assistance per capita divided by expenditures per capita.

8. In many countries, district heating systems have also been handed over to municipalities. While not strictly an environmental service, they share many characteristics, including low tariff rates under central planning together with old and inefficient equipment. In many CEE countries, district heating plants burned domestic coal. Their high emissions contributed to poor local air quality.

REFERENCES

Adeishvili, M. and D. Waughray (1999),
The Use of Economic Instruments for the Environment in Georgia, Presentation for EAP Task Force Workshop on Economic Instruments, Moscow.

Agriconsulting (1998),
Costing and Financial Analysis of Approximation in Environment, prepared for PHARE-DISAE-project POL-101, Brussels.

Bazaniak, W. (1998),
Non-Public Issue of Municipal Bonds in the Miescisko Commune as a Pioneering Source of Financing a Waste-Water Treatment Plant and Sewerage Project in Poland, in Innovative Financing for Environmental Investments: Looking Toward the Future, US Agency for International Development (USAID).

Chemonics International (1998),
Environmental Action Programme Supports Project: Final Report, prepared for US Agency for International Development (USAID).

Declaration by the Ministers of Environment of the Region of the United Nations Economic Commission for Europe (Sofia Declaration) (1995),
Sofia, 25 October.

Demydenko, A. (1999),
Personal Communication to EAP Task Force concerning Aral Sea Basin Capacity Development Project, 9 June.

EDC and Environment Policy Europe (1997),
Compliance Costing for Approximation of EU Environmental Legislation in the CEEC, Brussels.

European Bank for Reconstruction and Development (EBRD) (1997),
Transition Report 1997, London.

European Bank for Reconstruction and Development (EBRD) (1998),
Transition Report 1998, London.

European Bank for Reconstruction and Development (EBRD) (1998),
[http://www.ebrd.org].

European Bank for Reconstruction and Development (EBRD) (1999),
Municipal and Environmental Infrastructure, London.

European Commission (EC) (1998),
Meeting the Challenge of Enlargement with the Candidate Countries in Central and Eastern Europe, Communication from the Commission to the Council, the European Parliament, the Economic and Social Committee, the Committee of the Regions and the Candidate Countries in Central and Eastern Europe on Accession Strategies for Environment, Brussels, June.

European Commission (EC) DG1A (1999),
Guidelines for PHARE Programme Implementation in Candidate Countries for the Period 2000-2006 in Application of Article 8 of Regulation 3906/89 (Draft), Brussels.

Gentry, B.S. (1998),
Foreign Direct Investment and the Environment: Boon or Bane?, prepared for OECD Conference, The Hague.

Gentry, B.S. and L. Fernandez (1997),
Evolving Public-Private Partnerships: General Themes and Examples from the Urban Water Sector, Workshop on Environmental Policy: Globalisation and the Environment: New Challenges for the Public and Private Sectors, OECD, Paris.

Golub, A.,
Environmental Financing in the Russian Federation, prepared for OECD Workshop, Nizhniy Novgorod, Russia, 1996.

Ministry of Environment of the Czech Republic (1999),
Comments on the Draft EAP+5 Report, Ministry of Environment letter, 23 April.

Nordic Environmental Finance Corporation (NEFCO) (1997),
NEFCO Revolving Facility for Cleaner Production Investments, unpublished, Oslo.

OECD (1990),
   Financial Assistance Systems for Pollution Prevention and Control in OECD Countries, Environment Monographs No. 33, Paris.

OECD (1995),
   The St. Petersburg Guidelines on Environmental Funds in the Transition to a Market Economy, Paris.

OECD (1998a),
   Environmental Financing in CEE/NIS: Conclusions and Recommendations, Paris.

OECD (1998b),
   Environmental Financing in the Russian Federation, Paris.

OECD (1998c),
   Pollution Abatement and Control Expenditure in Central and Eastern Europe, Paris.

OECD (1998d),
   Pollution Abatement and Control Expenditure in OECD Countries, Paris.

OECD (1999a),
   Development Co-operation: Efforts and Policies of the Members of the Development Assistance Committee – 1998 Report, Paris.

OECD (1999b),
   Aid and Other Resource Flows to the Central and Eastern European Countries and the New Independent States of the Former Soviet Union (1990-1996), Paris.

OECD (1999c),
   Trade and Investment and Development: The Challenges of Policy Coherence in a Global Economy, Paris (forthcoming).

OECD and European Commission (EC) PHARE programme (1998),
   Swapping Debt for the Environment – the Polish Ecofund, Paris.

OECD and Project Preparation Committee (1995),
   Integrated Report on Environmental Financing, prepared for the Third Ministerial Conference "Environment for Europe, Sofia.

Peszko, G. and T. Zylicz (1998),
   Environmental Financing in European Economies in Transition, in *Environmental and Resource Economics* 11(3-4), 521-538.

Project Preparation Committee (PPC) (1998),
   PPC *Report to the "Environment for Europe" Conference* Aarhus, Denmark, EBRD, London, June.

Somlyody, L. and P. Shanahan (1998),
   Municipal Waste Water Treatment in Central and Eastern Europe, World Bank, Washington, DC.

United Nations Conference on Trade and Development (UNCTAD) (1997),
   Environmental Management Standards, Particularly the ISO 14 000 Series: Trade and Investment Impacts on Developing Countries, August.

World Bank (1998),
   Transition Toward a Healthier Environment: Environmental Issues and Challenges in the Newly Independent States, Washington, DC.

World Bank (1999),
   Poland: Complying with EU Environmental Legislation, Washington, DC.

Zylicz, T. (1998),
   Public Institutions and Mechanisms Offering Concessional Financing for Municipal Environmental Projects in Poland, prepared for the Municipal Development Agency, Warsaw.

Chapter 7

ENVIRONMENTAL MANAGEMENT IN ENTERPRISES

1. Introduction

Under central planning, CEEC/NIS industry generated high pollution levels. Countries in the region had a high concentration of heavy industries such as iron and steel. Most industrial enterprises used outdated, highly polluting production methods. Enterprise management often paid little attention to economic efficiency, and in many enterprises plant maintenance was neglected. Both of these factors exacerbated pollution levels, as well as risks to worker health and safety.

The EAP argued that government policies could play a major role in encouraging reductions of enterprise pollution. Economic reforms to establish competitive markets would prompt industrial restructuring, set the stage for new investments, and provide incentives for greater production efficiencies. Together with effective environmental policies and instruments, these reforms would create incentives and sanctions that would encourage enterprises to improve their environmental performance.

The EAP also underlined that enterprises themselves had a major role to play. For example, CEEC/NIS enterprises could undertake many low-cost investments and actions to simultaneously improve their economic and environmental efficiencies. Many enterprises could start to make such "win-win" gains simply through much-needed improvements in plant maintenance. Further reductions could be achieved through pollution prevention, waste minimisation and other low-cost *cleaner production* opportunities. More generally, the EAP noted that better enterprise management would play a crucial role in reducing environmental pressures, as efforts to improve production efficiencies would often, by cutting waste, also reduce pollution and other environmental pressures. In the long run, enterprises could become even more effective in reducing pollution if they became partners in environmental protection with government and NGOs.

This chapter looks first at the progress of policy reform. It then considers the roles of foreign direct investment and of government cleaner production programmes in improving enterprise environmental management. The last section examines evidence of trends in enterprise environmental performance. It concentrates on one highly polluting industry, iron and steel. Throughout, the chapter refers to three closely related environmental management approaches: *cleaner production, environmental management systems* and *eco-efficiency* (Box 7.1).

The chapter focuses on manufacturing enterprises, which have been one of the main sources of pollution in the region. The EAP identified several industries whose pollution created serious threats to human health (Box 7.2). In many countries, particularly many of the NIS, natural resource exploitation – for example, mining activities and oil and gas extraction – has also created extensive pollution and damage to the landscape (UN/ECE 1998). This topic is not covered in depth, but such activities remain one of the most important areas in which environmental protection and sustainable development policies are needed. Many new CEEC/NIS enterprises have been created in the service sector. While they usually have less environmental impact than manufacturing enterprises, they can contribute to more recent environmental problems such as increasing motor vehicle traffic and greater use of packaging materials and other items that contribute to municipal waste.

> ## Box 7.1. Environmental management in enterprises: three approaches
>
> **Cleaner production (CP)**
>
> Cleaner production is the continuous application of an integrated, preventive environmental strategy to processes, products and services to increase eco-efficiency and reduce risks to humans and the environment. This leads to improved environmental performance, cost savings, and risk reduction. For production processes, cleaner production includes conserving raw materials and energy, eliminating use of toxic materials, and reducing the quantity and toxicity of all emissions and wastes before they leave the process. Typical CP activities are process-oriented. They include pollution prevention, source reduction, waste minimisation and energy conservation. Implementing CP at industrial enterprises usually involves several steps: investigating the root causes of pollution, identifying CP opportunities, undertaking feasibility studies, implementing feasible measures, and measuring results.
>
> **Environmental management systems (EMS)**
>
> Environmental management systems within enterprises aim to ensure the consistent and systematic control of company procedures and operations that can have a significant impact on the environment, in order to achieve economic and environmental benefits and sustainable use of natural resources. Enterprise management can use these systems to keep aware of enterprise environmental impacts and to improve environmental performance. Environmental management systems do not necessarily use cleaner production methodologies. International standards such as the ISO's 14 000 series and the EU's EMAS (Eco-Management and Auditing Scheme) provide model frameworks for the development and assessment of enterprise environmental management systems and environmental performance. These frameworks call for: the development and disclosure of enterprise environmental policies and principles; a review (sometimes an in-depth *environmental audit*) of enterprise activities to develop an objective understanding of all environmental aspects and impacts; specification of enterprise environmental objectives and targets, together with a plan to achieve them; audits of the system to ensure effectiveness and compliance; and periodic management reviews to ensure that the system continues to be suitable and effective for the organisation and its goals. One important difference is that EMAS calls for improvements in enterprise environmental performance and for public disclosure of results, while ISO 14 001 refers only to continuous improvements in environmental management systems.
>
> **Eco-efficiency**
>
> Eco-efficiency refers to the efficiency with which environmental resources are used to meet human needs. It was defined by the World Business Council for Sustainable Development (WBCSD) as a combination of ecological and economic efficiency: "Eco-efficiency is reached by the delivery of competitively-priced goods and services that satisfy human needs and bring quality of life, while progressively reducing ecological impacts and resource intensity throughout the life cycle, to a level at least in line with the earth's estimated carrying capacity" (OECD, 1998e). Proponents of eco-efficiency emphasise reducing environmental impacts throughout the life cycle of products as well as processes. Three steps are involved in implementing eco-efficiency: first, developing specific goals and targets, together with indicators to measure them; second, implementing innovations in technology, management and approaches to reach these goals; and third, monitoring progress via the indicators and modifying the strategy as necessary.
>
> *Sources:* DeSimone and Popoff; OECD (1998b, 1998e); UNEP; World Bank.

2. Economic Reform, Industrial Restructuring and Corporate Governance

Three main forces have encouraged industrial enterprises to seek greater efficiencies and, on a national level, have changed industrial structures. The creation of competitive market, the development of government institutions and laws to support them, and the development of effective corporate governance (EBRD, 1998).

Box 7.2. **Highly polluting CEEC/NIS industries identified by the EAP**

Industry	Priority environmental problems
Non-ferrous metallurgy	Air emissions of particulates, heavy metals and sulphur dioxide (SO_2).
Ferrous metallurgy (iron and steel)	Air emissions of particulates and heavy metals.
Pulp and paper	Waste water discharges containing chlorinated and halogenated organic compounds and other chemicals.
Chemicals and petrochemicals	Air emissions of volatile organic compounds (VOCs) and hydrocarbons; waste water discharges containing saline waters, chlorinated organic compounds, hydrocarbons and other pollutants.

2.1. Developing competitive markets

Most CEEC/NIS have made strong progress in opening their economies to international trade (Annex V presents indicators of this and related market reforms). Competition from *imports* has required CEEC/NIS enterprises to restructure. A study of several hundred Russian manufacturing enterprises found that those subject to the greatest competition from imports were most likely to increase labour productivity and change their product mix. Domestic competition appears not to have had a similar impact (EBRD, 1997). In response to the 1998 economic and financial crisis, however, the Russian government re-established some currency controls and took other measures to restrict imports.

Many CEEC/NIS have re-oriented their *exports* towards Western Europe and other markets outside the former COMECON countries. For many CEE countries, chemicals and intermediate manufacturing products have continued to represent an important share of their exports, suggesting that at least some of the highly polluting heavy industries identified by the EAP will remain important elements of their industrial structures. In Russia, fuels and other raw materials have accounted for about half of exports. As in other NIS, natural resource extraction will likely remain a central pillar of the economy (EBRD, 1998). This sector can have extensive environmental consequences. Russian authorities have yet to address some of the key problems associated with oil production, such as widespread pollution in fragile environments in Siberia (Zamparutti and Kozeltsev).

Most CEE countries and several NIS (including Kazakhstan, the Kyrgyz Republic and Russia) have privatised an important share of their large industrial enterprises. Due to privatisation and the creation of new enterprises, the private sector accounts for at least half of GDP in all CEE countries and in about half of the NIS (EBRD, 1998). In CEE countries, privatised enterprises have become more efficient. A study of 6 000 enterprises across six CEE countries found that their total productivity increased an average of 5% per year after privatisation (EBRD, 1997). However, some forms of privatisation have created corporate governance structures that hinder enterprise reform: for example, leaving enterprise control in the hands of previous managers with limited opportunities for shareholders, creditors and other stakeholders to influence corporate behaviour. In Russia, in particular, the lack of institutions and laws to support new markets has compounded this problem.

2.2. Laws and institutions to support markets

Markets need a strong legal infrastructure to support them, as well as government institutions to implement these laws and support nascent markets. Some governments, particularly in the NIS, have been slow to establish new laws and institutions, including those needed to support competitive markets.

One area of vital importance is the development of "hard budget constraints" for enterprises, including the threat of bankruptcy for those that are not viable. Most CEE countries have developed bankruptcy laws, but many have been slow to apply these and other mechanisms to restructure heavy industry. In some countries, including Poland, large enterprises in heavy industries such as iron and steel, coal mining and chemicals often remain state-owned. These large enterprises continue to be unprofitable. This slow pace of restructuring has delayed the closure of old plants as well as investment in new, less polluting production methods.

Many CEE governments have also established other basic elements of state governance that support market economies: security of property ownership; a reliable and impartial judiciary; predictable laws and government policies; overall stability of the political system; and restraints on levels of corruption (EBRD, 1997). These elements have helped foster the creation of new private enterprises, which in turn has helped renew economic growth. In Poland, new enterprises accounted for almost two-thirds of the growth in industrial production between 1992 and 1995. Environmental implications have been mixed. While many firms are engaged in light manufacturing, contributing to the shift away from heavy industry, governments have faced a challenge in enforcing environmental requirements at these new small enterprises.

In the NIS, despite formal goals to establish competitive markets, government policies and actions have instead produced a "barter economy" in which enterprises carry on a majority of their business through non-monetary transactions. The barter economy has helped sustain unprofitable enterprises which, by 1998, outnumbered profitable ones in Russia. Governments have fueled this barter economy through indirect subsidies to enterprises, often by allowing them to accumulate large tax arrears and large arrears in their energy and municipal service payments. In addition, Russia and most other NIS have been slow to establish basic laws and institutions to support markets in areas such as bankruptcy provisions and competition policy. Many enterprises have therefore continued to operate at only a fraction of their capacity, and essentially no large industrial enterprises in Russia (or any other NIS) has entered bankruptcy. This situation has delayed restructuring, along with its related social costs (Box 7.3).

Box 7.3.   **The social effects of industrial restructuring**

In many CEE cities and regions, industrial restructuring has led to widespread unemployment. In the NIS, few enterprises have closed or laid off employees amidst the collapse of economic output. Instead, they have paid wages late, in kind or not at all. Industrial restructuring could have serious social effects in those NIS cities dominated by a single industry or plant. For example, in Mariopol, Ukraine, and Magnitogorsk, Russia, huge steel mills have been the main employers. Under central planning, large enterprises often managed social services such as schools and health clinics and other services such as waste water treatment. In most CEE countries these have been transferred to local governments, but in the NIS local governments often lack the resources to undertake these services, which then remain under enterprise control.

In this economic context, industrial enterprises have had few incentives to improve their production efficiencies. Viable enterprises have had little credit or other resources to make new investments. The age and maintenance of capital equipment has continued to worsen, exacerbating pollution levels. Government tolerance of arrears in energy payments and municipal service charges, including those for waste water treatment and solid waste disposal, have in particular blunted any incentives to improve energy efficiency or minimise waste generation. Although pollution levels in NIS industry have fallen, pollution per unit of production has often increased.

In the NIS, inadequate state institutions and governance have often presented further obstacles to enterprise development. Corruption, in particular, has been a severe problem in many countries. Business surveys have rated the NIS as among the world's most corrupt regions (EBRD, 1997). Corruption – together with economic and political instability – has discouraged both foreign direct investment and domestic investment. It has played a role in capital flight in many countries (EBRD, 1998).

2.3. *Corporate governance*

Good corporate governance is necessary for enterprises to act as effective agents in national and international markets – particularly to maximise profits and use their resources efficiently. With growing globalisation, OECD countries and others are increasingly recognising the importance of fostering good corporate governance in national and multinational enterprises (Box 7.4). Effective corporate governance is a prerequisite for environmental management. In OECD countries, many medium and large enterprises that have focused on improving long-term competitiveness have incorporated environmental goals into their management. These enterprises have found that quality management and related approaches to strengthening productivity and competitiveness can also strengthen their environmental management and performance.

Box 7.4. The OECD principles of corporate governance

In 1999, the OECD Council approved a set of Principles of Corporate Governance. These non-binding principles are intended to serve as a benchmark for governments, and to provide guidance to stock markets, investors and other parties that may elaborate codes of conduct. The preamble to the OECD principles explains that:

Corporate governance involves a set of relationships between a company's management, its board, its shareholders and other stakeholders. Corporate governance also provides the structure through which the objectives of the company are set, and the means of attaining those objectives and monitoring performance are determined. Good corporate governance should provide proper incentives for the board and management to pursue objectives that are in the interests of the company and shareholders and should facilitate effective monitoring, thereby encouraging firms to use resources more efficiently.

In many ways, corporate governance is similar to state governance. Good corporate governance requires mechanisms to ensure proper accountability and transparency of decision-making. For example, to ensure transparency the enterprise should disclose timely and accurate information on its financial situation, performance, ownership and governance. Outside audits and international accounting rules help reinforce transparency. Good corporate governance should also involve adequate consultation with key stakeholders, including workers and others.

There have been several models for corporate governance in OECD countries. In the US and the UK, active capital markets play a strong role in rewarding good corporate governance. In Germany, banks and other stakeholders play a much greater role and are often represented on the supervisory boards of large industrial enterprises.

Sources: Brom; OECD (1999*c*).

In the CEEC/NIS, creating enterprise management structures that provide effective corporate governance has been a key challenge of the transition. Privatisation methods have produced different corporate governance structures across the region. In many slower reform countries, including many NIS, privatisation has not created effective corporate governance. Rather, it has given enterprise "insiders" – in particular, managers appointed under central planning – strong powers in the newly private enterprises without adequate oversight from shareholders or other stakeholders. A recent study in Russia showed that such "insiders" had gained controlling shares in the majority of enterprises privatised. The study indicated that many of the managers running Russia's large enterprises still look for government assistance and direction to cope with their difficulties (Brattle). Moreover, "insider" control has slowed enterprise restructuring (EBRD, 1998). Many managers have resisted efforts to be more accountable to employees, shareholders, financial institutions or other stakeholders. In these enterprises, often little attention has been paid to improving production methods or planning for long-term viability. In Russia, in particular, the privatisation process also sparked long fights between stakeholders over control of key enterprises, further delaying any attention to their long-term viability (Box 7.11). In these circumstances, it is unlikely that managers and others will pay great attention to environmental requirements.

Some CEEC/NIS governments have sold controlling shares of large enterprises to strategic foreign investors. These enterprises have shown the greatest improvements in productivity. Where domestic banks and investment funds have acquired controlling stakes in newly privatised enterprises, they have not pushed strongly for restructuring. Few have much expertise in this area. Many banks and investment firms in the region themselves have poor corporate governance structures (EBRD, 1998).

2.4. The Role of Environmental Policy

Government environmental policies and instruments are of crucial importance in creating incentives and sanctions that stimulate enterprises to improve environmental performance. A clear, transparent and predictable environmental policy framework can also steer industrial restructuring in a more environmentally favourable direction. Many CEE countries have strengthened their environmental policy instruments, as well as their enforcement mechanisms, during the transition. Progress has been slow in most NIS, where there have been few such incentives or sanctions.

Public and community pressures can also play an essential role. In some OECD countries, these pressures – together with effective enforcement of policy instruments – have led enterprises to accept basic environmental goals and incorporate them into their overall corporate objectives (Box 7.5). By encouraging enterprises and municipalities to invest in environmental protection, effective environmental policy requirements can also promote a strong environmental goods and services industry (Annex IX).

Box 7.5. **The evolution of environmental management in the Netherlands**

In the Netherlands, strong public and community support for environmental protection – as well as financial institutions that pay close attention to the environmental compliance and performance of their clients – have helped ensure enterprise commitment to effective environmental management. The interaction between environmental enforcement and enterprise environmental management has passed through four phases:

- In the first phase, there is low awareness of the environment within the enterprise, whose compliance with environmental regulations is inadequate. Government therefore has to ensure detailed requirements, as well as strong systems of monitoring and sanctions to ensure compliance.

- In the second phase, the enterprise accepts compliance with environmental regulations, but it is still regarded as something of a business burden. This allows government to be slightly more flexible in setting permitting and other requirements.

- In the third phase, environmental compliance has become a regular part of enterprise actions. Environmental awareness is well-embedded, and the enterprise has a well-developed environmental management system.

- In the fourth phase, the enterprise has included environmental performance as an integral corporate objective that it pursues through continuing product and process improvements. Environmental compliance is ensured through certification of the enterprise's environmental management system. In this case, government can greatly reduce monitoring and enforcement activities, as the enterprise is largely self-regulating.

Source: OECD, 1997*a*.

3. Foreign Direct Investment (FDI)

When foreign investors take large stakes – including majority shareholdings – in CEEC/NIS enterprises, they also assume a direct management role. Some foreign enterprises have instead opened subsidiaries in the region. Both types of foreign direct investment usually involve long-term commitments. This section looks first at the amount of FDI going to the region and then at its impacts on the environment. (The interaction between FDI and the environment is a new area for research, and further investigation of its impact in CEEC/NIS is needed.)

Flows of foreign direct investment to the region increased steadily to 1997, when they reached US$17 billion. FDI fell to an estimated US$15 billion in 1998, amidst the financial and economic crisis in the NIS. A small number of CEEC/NIS have received the great majority of these inflows: the Czech Republic, Hungary and Poland in Central and Eastern Europe; Russia and Kazakhstan in the NIS, followed by Azerbaijan and Turkmenistan (EBRD, 1998). On a per capita basis, FDI flows to Hungary and Poland have exceeded those to many developing countries and those to Russia have been quite low (Table 7.1).

Table 7.1. **Foreign direct investment to the main CEEC/NIS recipient countries compared to selected developing countries**

	Total inflows		Inflows per capita	
	1997 (US$ million)	Cumulative, 1989-98 (US$ million)	1997 (US$)	Cumulative, 1989-98 (US$)
CEEC/NIS[a]				
Czech Republic	1 280	8 470	124	820
Hungary	2 100	16 900	207	1 670
Poland	3 040	12 470	79	320
Kazakhstan	1 320	5 730	84	360
Russia	3 750	9 200	25	60
Total – five top recipients	11 490	52 750	51	230
Total – all CEEC/NIS	17 100	74 470	43	190
Selected developing countries[b]				
Argentina	..	23 790	..	870
Brazil	..	23 270	..	270
Singapore	..	43 360	..	17 310
Thailand	..	14 150	..	290

.. Not available
a)   *Source*: EBRD, 1998. 1998 data, included in cumulative inflows column, are projections.
b)   *Source*: OECD, 1998c. Cumulative inflows refer to 1990-96 only.

The relationship between foreign investment and environmental protection is complex. Depending on the situation, FDI can have positive, negative or neutral effects on the environment. Some observers have expressed concerns that foreign investment can put new pressures on a country's environment and that host governments, in order to attract foreign investors, will be reluctant to develop or enforce effective environmental standards (Zarsky). This appears not to have occurred in the CEEC/NIS region, where there has been a strong correlation between national progress in economic reform and inflows of FDI – excluding foreign investment for natural resources extraction (EBRD, 1998). In turn, countries advanced in economic reforms have established strong environmental institutions and policies. Plans for political and economic integration with the EU have encouraged this pattern. Proximity to the EU and the prospect of accession have spurred economic and environmental policy reforms in many CEE countries, as well as stimulating FDI. Since many investors in the CEEC/NIS region appear to have established

161

manufacturing plants to gain access to the region's markets rather than to set up "export platforms" (the latter are more common in low-income developing countries), environmental compliance costs should not be a major factor in decisions to invest in CEEC/NIS.

Existing environmental problems at CEEC/NIS industrial sites and uncertainty about the future implementation of environmental policies may have discouraged some foreign investors. A number of CEE governments have put in place policies to address these investor concerns (Box 7.6).

Box 7.6. **Environmental impediments to foreign investment**

Early in the transition, a number of foreign investors raised concerns about environmental problems, in particular past environmental damage such as soil contamination, at companies being privatised in CEE countries. Based on experiences in the west, foreign investors were worried about the possibility of future liability to pay for the clean-up of contamination caused before their purchase. In a 1992 World Bank/OECD questionnaire, executives of the 1 000 largest multinational corporations in Western Europe and North America ranked these liability issues as a key impediment to investment in Poland, Hungary or Czechoslovakia, particularly when they considered investing in plants at heavily polluted sites. While these concerns may not have changed overall direct investment flows to the region, they may have delayed investments and prompted some investors to build new "greenfield" plants rather than refurbish existing enterprises, which could have further reduced overall environmental pressures. A number of international fora drew attention to this issue, including a 1992 conference organised by the World Bank, OECD and the EBRD. Western business leaders expressed their concerns, as did a few bilateral donors. The Gore-Chernomyrdin Commission of the US and Russia addressed this issue.

Consequently, privatisation and environmental officials worked together in a number of CEE countries to address potential liability problems. At first they approached these problems on an *ad hoc* basis. However, this led to some costly incidents where investors asked CEE governments to pay for expensive clean-ups at plants they had purchased. Since 1992, several CEE governments have put in place institutions, policies and an array of tools to address past environmental damage issues, including: regulations to help define liability; environmental audits to estimate past environmental damage at enterprises undergoing privatisation; risk assessment and management to identify cost-effective clean-up actions; and financing mechanisms for clean-up. In the Czech Republic, 5% of the proceeds from the country's second "wave" of privatisation was set aside for environmental clean-up; all enterprises in this privatisation programme were eligible to undertake audits and to apply for clean-up funding. In Estonia, 5% of privatisation proceeds has also been earmarked for clean-up projects. Some government bodies, such as Poland's inter-ministerial unit, have developed extensive experience negotiating with foreign investors on environmental issues.

The NIS have not addressed environmental issues in privatisation. One reason is that many privatisation programmes in the NIS (including Russia's) have not pursued sales to foreign investors. In a few NIS, such as Belarus, privatisation has hardly started. Most foreign investors appear to have judged environmental issues to be of little importance compared to the political and economic risks in these countries. Nonetheless, privatisation and environment officials in a few countries have discussed the question. In Ukraine, the Administration of the President held a workshop on the issue in late 1997. Subsequently, the environment ministry and the privatisation fund established a joint working group to consider policy options.

Source: Goldenman.

3.1. FDI *in the manufacturing sector*

In many CEEC/NIS, a large share of FDI (often between 40 and 60%) has gone to manufacturing industry (EBRD, 1998), where good environmental performance may provide commercial advantages (Gentry) by:

– improving productivity through more efficient use of energy, raw materials and other inputs;

– maintaining a "social license" to operate – environmental NGOs, shareholders, customers, and the media in both home and host countries may closely monitor the environmental performance of large enterprises;

– ensuring access to finance – as noted, IFIs and international banks have paid increasing attention to environmental issues;

– ensuring access to OECD country export markets, where firms and consumers may consider environmental issues in their purchasing choices.

As a result, foreign investors may introduce new financing, technology, and management methods to help tackle environmental problems in the CEEC/NIS manufacturing sector.

Financing. The financial resources of new investors can help modernise existing plants in the region, paying for integrated investments (those with both economic and environmental benefits) and pollution control equipment. Large western corporations in particular have access to financing from international commercial banks and financial institutions. Their projects in the region have often had an important environmental investment or clean-up component. In 1993, Siemens of Germany purchased two electronics manufacturing enterprises in Poland and a plant in Hungary. Siemens invested in clean-up of past environmental damage at these sites and in reducing ongoing environmental pressures, such as solid waste generation and air pollution. Governments can encourage this in the privatisation process by explicitly including environment as an element for consideration in evaluating investor bids, as Poland did in its "capital" privatisation scheme.

Technology. New technologies introduced by foreign investors can include more efficient, less polluting production methods. In Poland, Pilkington Glass of the UK (with financing from the EBRD and other sources) has planned a new state-of-the-art glass factory on the site of an existing glass plant, which will be shut down when the new one is completed. The new facility, costing about ECU 100 million (about US$115 million), will use advanced furnace and other equipment to produce sheet glass, significantly reducing pollution and other environmental pressures (EBRD, 1998b).

Management. Many large corporations have set up environmental management systems, often following international frameworks such as the ISO 14 000 series or EMAS. These corporations may bring their high environmental standards (reflecting strong environmental enforcement in their home country) to their foreign investments, in part because they have found it more efficient to operate under a single set of management practices world-wide (Esty and Gentry). For example, Tetra Pak, the Swedish packaging company, has built plants in several CEEC/NIS, including Ukraine, where it invested in 1989. Tetra Pak requires all of its plants world-wide to adopt environmental management systems; it aims to have all plants certified under ISO 14 001 by the year 2000. Corporations have found that actions by their international subsidiaries may be closely scrutinised by public groups in their home countries.

In some cases, even minority foreign shareholders have encouraged better environmental management. When HolderBank of Switzerland invested in Hungary's Hejocsaba Cement Works, it encouraged the company to obtain ISO 14 001 certification for its environmental management system (it was already certified for ISO 9 000, total quality management). Hejocsaba was the first Hungarian company to be certified under ISO 14 001, and it now requires its suppliers and sub-contractors to meet basic environmental standards.

Products. Foreign investors have also brought new products to the region. Some corporations have introduced more environmentally friendly products, such as low-energy light bulbs. Many, however, have promoted new consumer goods that have created new environmental pressures. Automobile manufacturing has been a major area for foreign investment. Western investors have also bought or set up many food processing plants in the region. This has made new consumer goods available, but has increased the use of associated packaging, contributing to greater waste generation at least among higher-income households. NGOs and others have criticised companies such as Tetra Pak for introducing packaging that is difficult to recycle into the region.

Not all foreign investors have a commitment to high environmental standards, or the financing, technologies and management systems to achieve them. Some investors – in particular those interested in taking advantage of low production costs – may seek high returns and short-term payback on investments in the region and thus look for ways to reduce their environmental compliance costs. In addition, some small and medium enterprises investing in the region may lack the financial, technological and management resources to make environmental improvements (OECD, 1998c).

3.2. FDI *in the natural resources sector*

In the NIS in particular, a significant portion of foreign investment has gone into industries, including forestry and oil and gas production, that extract natural resources for export. By their nature, these investments can have extensive environmental effects. Many of the most important controversies over FDI in different regions of the world have focused on the natural resources sector (Zarsky).

Several NIS have experienced large inflows of foreign investment in natural resources extraction, in particular that of oil and gas. In Russia and other NIS, domestic oil production under central planning created extensive environmental damage (Zamparutti and Kozeltsev). Foreign investment could help reduce existing environmental problems, such as frequent leaks from ageing pipelines. In Azerbaijan and the Central Asian republics, however, foreign investors have been increasing the level of oil and gas production, which could exacerbate environmental risks.

Foreign investment in logging also has major environmental implications. On the one hand, it could help improve the inefficient forestry practices used under central planning, particularly in Russia, potentially reducing the forest area needed for logging. At the same time, there have been cases of foreign companies using unsustainable techniques to log Russia's extensive old-growth forests with their high levels of biodiversity. Finnish companies working in the Republic of Karelia, Russia, have pledged not to log old-growth forests and have introduced more efficient forestry management techniques in other forest areas. Pressure from Russian and international NGOs helped to encourage these actions (Chapter 4).

The influence of foreign investors on the sustainable management of natural resources should be closely monitored, particularly in the NIS, many of which have weak environmental institutions and policy frameworks. Public information on FDI operations (and domestic investor activities) and their environmental impacts can encourage investors to undertake appropriate environmental protection measures and can help disseminate information on good industry practices.

3.3. *Foreign investment prospects*

As CEE countries move towards EU accession, they are expected to receive even greater inflows of foreign investment. In the manufacturing sector, in particular, new foreign investors should try to meet EU environmental requirements.

In Russia and other NIS, renewed economic and political difficulties have created additional uncertainties for potential foreign investors. Some NIS politicians have suspected foreign investors of compromising national interests. In these risky circumstances, foreign investors may be interested only in projects with high potential returns and their attention to environmental issues may be low. In Central Asia and the Caucasus, foreign investment in resource extraction is likely to continue and grow. This will create continuing environmental pressures, as well as providing opportunities for strengthening capacities to address these problems.

Studies of FDI have shown that, in general, foreign investors have not been discouraged by strong environmental requirements, but rather by uncertain policies whose implementation can be subjective (for example, differing according to whether investors are foreign and domestic) or unpredictable (Gentry). Effective domestic policies are needed to ensure that foreign and domestic investors alike meet adequate environmental standards. For example, environmental impact assessment procedures can help reduce adverse impacts of new investments, but EIAs only look at individual projects. Attention must also be paid to the cumulative impacts of investment in a sector. Strategic environmental impact assessment provides one method for doing this (Chapter 5).

One potential role of foreign as well as domestic investors is to help finance, build and operate urban infrastructure such as waste water treatment plants. Private-public partnerships in this area have so far been rare in the CEEC/NIS, but national and local governments should look further at these opportunities.

4. Promoting Cleaner Production and EMS

The EAP emphasised that CEEC/NIS enterprises could reduce their pollution levels and other environmental impacts through better management, better plant maintenance, and low-cost measures such as waste minimisation. This section describes programmes that have encouraged enterprises in the region to take such steps through cleaner production (CP) and environmental management systems (EMS).

4.1. *Cleaner production and EMS programmes*

During the transition, several donors and CEEC/NIS governments have undertaken programmes to promote enterprise adoption of cleaner production and EMS. *Bilateral donors and international organisations* have provided the initial impetus for cleaner production approaches in the region (Box 7.7). Although most international CP programmes have operated in CEE countries, a few have recently undertaken projects in the NIS.

Box 7.7. **Major international programmes to disseminate cleaner production**

The *Norwegian Society of Chartered Engineers*, with the support of the Norwegian government, has trained local CP experts in the Czech Republic, Lithuania, Poland, Russia and Slovakia. This programme trains local trainers, who then train CP advisors, who subsequently carry out cleaner production audits at local companies. The Norwegian government, often working with the UNIDO/UNEP programme, has helped establish and initially funded CP Centres in the Czech Republic, Poland, Slovakia and Russia. Between 200 and 800 CP experts have been trained, and between 100 and 500 companies audited, in each participating country.

A global UNIDO/UNEP *programme* has helped establish and finance CP Centres in the Czech Republic, Slovakia and Hungary. It is participating in the establishment of new CP centres in Slovenia and Croatia.

The US-based *World Environment Centre* (WEC) has helped establish CP Centres in Bulgaria, the Czech Republic, Estonia, Hungary, Latvia, Lithuania, Poland, Romania and Slovakia. It has financed and carried out demonstration projects at industrial enterprises in a dozen CEEC/NIS. These demonstration projects also involve training for enterprise staff and for national experts. WEC has translated several CP resource documents, including its own *Waste Minimisation Manual*, into local languages.

Source: EAP Task Force, 1998*a*.

After demonstrating CP approaches through pilot programmes, many donors have reduced their support for CP activities in CEE countries. In some cases, *national governments and industry associations* have supported the CP Centres set up by international programmes. Domestic sources have taken over financing of Poland's six CP Centres. In other countries, CP Centres have been in danger of closing due to lack of long-term financial support.

Although many CEE environmental policies have referred to CP goals, few environmental authorities have integrated their CP programmes with other environmental activities or policy instruments. Often, there appears to be no clear "slot" for CP activities within broader pollution management activities. EU accession may encourage this integration in candidate countries. The EU's EMAS and integrated permitting directives, for example, promote environmental management in enterprises.

Several *international business associations* have promoted CP and EMS in the region. The International Network for Environmental Management (INEM), based in Germany, has opened chapters in the Czech Republic, Estonia, Hungary, Latvia, Lithuania, Poland, Slovenia and Slovakia. INEM has worked in particular with small and medium enterprises. Its CEE chapters have disseminated information on environmental management methods and established twinning arrangements between CEE and Western European companies. The European Chemical Industry Council (CEFIC), based in Brussels, has promoted the industry's environmental management guidelines, "Responsible Care", through its member associations in the Czech Republic, Hungary, Poland, Slovakia and Slovenia (Macek). Trade pressures may also encourage some CEEC/NIS firms to adopt environmental management systems (Box 7.8).

Box 7.8. Environmental management and market access

A growing number of firms in Western Europe and other regions have adopted environmental management systems, such as EMAS and the ISO 14 000 series. By mid-1997, over 1 000 German enterprises had EMAS certification and about 400 had ISO 14 001 certification. Many of the firms adopting environmental management systems require their suppliers to do the same. This is one reason CEEC/NIS enterprises' interest in these systems is growing, as certification may be important to become or continue as suppliers to large Western European companies. However, some observers have warned that enterprises adopting EMS for these reasons may focus attention on meeting formal requirements rather than actually improving environmental performance.

Sources: OECD, 1998e; UNCTAP.

Enterprises have often had difficulty obtaining financing for CP actions. Environmental funds in the region have often favoured "end-of-pipe" pollution control investments. IFIs have rarely supported CP investments, which have usually been too small for their minimum loans. Recently, however, the Nordic Environment Finance Corporation (NEFCO) set up a pilot Revolving Facility of about US$2 million to lend for CP and other "win-win" projects that cost between about US$50 000 and US$200 000. NEFCO will initially operate in Lithuania and north-western Russia, with the assistance of local institutions that will review project proposals.

4.2. Achievements

Dissemination of environmental management approaches has proceeded slowly in the region. By mid-1998, seven countries had achieved a "basic capacity level" (BCL) for cleaner production (Table 7.2).[1] Five other countries were close to achieving the basic capacity level. However, this progress fell short of the goal expressed by environment ministers at Sofia in 1995: that all CEEC/NIS would achieve the basic capacity level by 1998.

Almost 1 000 CP demonstration projects have been carried out in the region since the early 1990s, 600 of them in Poland. These projects have demonstrated that CP methods can reduce both production costs and pollution. Many low-cost CP measures have reduced enterprise pollution levels by 20-40% (EAP Task Force, 1995). Only a few enterprises have adopted EMS. As of mid-1997, seven enterprises in the Czech Republic were certified under ISO 14 001, as well as two each in Hungary, Poland and Slovenia. (Box 7.9 presents three examples of enterprise CP programmes. Two of these enterprises also developed environmental management systems, for which they have received ISO 14 001 certification.)

Despite some success, CP programmes have probably only had an important impact, in terms of reducing environmental pressures, in one or two countries. Many enterprises in the region are either unaware of CP and its potential rewards, or the attention of their managers remains focused on coping with uncertain market conditions.

Table 7.2. **Basic capacity level for cleaner production**

As of mid-1998

	Number of trained persons	Number of demonstration projects	Number of CP centres	Number of universities with courses on CP
Countries achieving BCL				
Czech Republic	196	68	2	3
Estonia	40	22	1	1
Hungary	100	50	2	3
Lithuania	80	18	1	1
Poland	1 800	600	6	5
Russia	400	150	2	1
Slovakia	163	79	2	3
Countries close to achieving BCL				
Bulgaria	30	23	1	n.a.
Latvia	20	18	1	–
Romania	80	32	1	–
Slovenia	26	3	Planned	Planned
Ukraine	30	16	1	–

Source: EAP Task Force, 1998a.

Box 7.9. **Cleaner production programmes in CEEC/NIS**

Znovín Znojmo s.r.o., a small winery, was one of the first participants in the Czech CP programme. The company implemented a CP and EMS programme in 1996, and by 1997 it had reduced water consumption by 30% and BOD discharges by 69%, despite a concurrent increase in production. An investment of approximately US$4 000 to re-utilise part of the winery's organic waste water saved the municipal waste water treatment plant about US$65 000 in construction costs and saved the winery about US$2 000 in annual operating costs. Znovín became the first enterprise in the Czech Republic to integrate its CP and EMS programmes and receive ISO 14 001 certification (this work was supported in part by an Austrian assistance programme). It is the first winery in the world with ISO 14 001 certification. The company showed that CP and EMS are mutually supportive and can be integrated to improve enterprise economic and environmental performance.

DauER, a manufacturer of industrial grade hand tools in Latvia, participated in the World Environment Center's CP programme in that country and undertook a waste minimisation initiative. Production operations include ferrous metal casting, mechanical treatment, plastic moulding, electroplating and painting. In 1994, DauER's electroplating operation used large quantities of steam supplied from the municipal boiler house. By installing a well-insulated electric boiler next to the electroplating baths at a cost of US$2 500, the company eliminated energy losses along the municipal steam supply lines and saved about US$57 000 in energy costs. The electroplating operations also consumed large amounts of freshwater. By adopting several operational changes, and investing US$9 000 in process control instrumentation, the company reduced water usage (and discharge) by 21 000 m^3/year, resulting in annual savings of US$10 500.

Stirol produces ammonia-based fertilisers and other chemical products in the town of Gorlovka, Ukraine. Through a WEC demonstration project, it made several production process improvements that reduced losses of ammonia and ammonium nitrate, lowered water pollution and saved energy. In addition to technical advice, WEC provided production monitoring equipment costing about US$10 000. These improvements save the company an estimated US$400 000 per year.

Source: Macek.

The introduction of CP and EMS has been particularly slow in the NIS. Economic policy frameworks that discourage improvements in productivity, together with weak environmental policies, have given enterprises little to gain from implementing these approaches. Technical assistance programmes have found that many enterprise managers have strong technical skills, including an understanding of CP concepts and opportunities, but that their enterprises have rarely applied CP methods. Moreover, government officials and enterprise managers in the NIS have focused attention on the need for investments in new pollution abatement equipment and less polluting production technologies, even when these cannot be financed, but have overlooked opportunities for low-cost CP actions as a first step. This reflects the traditional practice under central planning of increasing output by increasing production, rather than though productivity improvements.

4.3. Strengthening implementation of CP and EMS

As many CEEC/NIS enterprises remain unaware of CP and EMS opportunities, as well as their potential economic rewards, information programmes can help disseminate these approaches, in particular among small and medium enterprises. Most government programmes to promote CP and EMS have remained separate from environmental policy instruments and enterprise development initiatives. Greater integration could disseminate CP and EMS concepts more widely. In the long term, integrating of these topics into university curricula – particularly at engineering and business schools – will build awareness. Trade unions have as yet rarely been involved in CP programmes. Strengthening their role can help disseminate and implement CP more widely in industry (Box 7.10).

Box 7.10. **Strengthening worker and union participation in cleaner production**

Employees and trade unions in the CEE countries and NIS can play an important role in developing and implementing cleaner production. Employees and unions in the region have lacked information about CP and EMS benefits, including better employee health and safety. Other obstacles to a greater union role in CP and EMS programmes have included lack of union human and financial resources, inter-union rivalries, and low government and enterprise recognition of the contributions that unions could make in this field. There has also been a lack of employee awareness of CP and EMS opportunities, often related to distrust of management, fear of unemployment and poor communication within enterprises. Only in a few cases have CEEC/NIS unions played an important role in CP or EMS activities. Some of these have concerned highly polluting industries such as chemicals and ferrous and non-ferrous metallurgy.

Steps to increase the role of employees and unions include:
- establishing clear union/employee environmental rights, similar to those for occupational health and safety;
- increasing collective bargaining, and including environmental issues in bargaining discussions;
- involving unions in environmental audits;
- integrating environmental and workplace health and safety issues;
- improving co-operation between employers and trade unions;
- strengthening institutional arrangements, including tripartite discussions between government, employers and unions;
- developing CP and EMS manuals and educational materials for unions and employees;
- providing greater information on international and national CP and EMS discussions to unions;
- involving unions in CP programmes at the international, national and enterprise levels.

Source: EAP Task Force, 1997.

---

5.   Trends in Industry Environmental Performance

This section looks at several trends in enterprise environmental performance. Trends in the iron and steel industry are highlighted.

In most CEEC/NIS economies, the weight of industry in GDP has fallen as industrial production has declined and services, stunted under central planning, have grown rapidly. Nonetheless, in 1995 industry continued to play a larger role overall in the region's GDP than it did in that of Western European countries (Figure 7.1).

Figure 7.1. **Industry as a share of GDP in selected countries**[1]

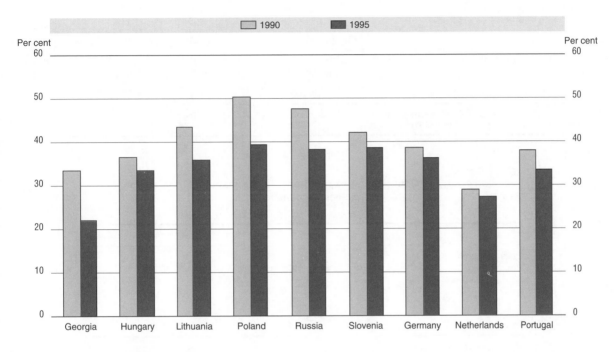

1. For Germany, data refer to western Germany only.
Sources: World Bank and OECD data.

5.1. *Overall trends*

Industrial environmental performance has progressed most strongly in the advanced reform CEE countries. In Poland, total production in the manufacturing sector has increased beyond its 1990 levels while indicators of environmental pressure have fallen (Table 7.3). Various factors have contributed to this result. Polish enterprises have made strong progress in implementing CP programmes; restructuring and modernisation have been underway in key heavy industries such as iron and steel; and enterprise investments in pollution abatement and control (PAC) have been high – over 1% of sector output in 1995 (Table 7.4). Investments in new, less-polluting production technologies have been added to PAC investments, which usually involve "end-of-pipe" equipment. A recent study of nine industrial enterprises in different industrial branches showed that nearly all had made both types of investments (Sleszynski). Affordable financing from capital markets, as well as Poland's large environmental fund system, has enabled Polish firms to undertake such investments.

Similar trends can be seen in other CEE countries. In the Czech Republic, the manufacturing sector's air pollution emissions and waste water discharges fell more rapidly than total production (OECD, 1999a). Sector spending on pollution abatement equalled levels in Western European countries such as Germany (the Czech power sector's separate pollution abatement expenditures have been even higher). In Bulgaria, total SO_x emissions from manufacturing have fallen even as production rose in key sectors such as non-ferrous metals, a major source of these emissions.

169

Table 7.3. **Output and environmental pressures in Poland's manufacturing sector**

	Units	1990	1996	Change (%)
Output	Index 1990 = 100	100	149	+49
Environmental pressures				
Air emissions				
SO_x from power generation	1 000 tonnes	500	406	−18.8
SO_x from industrial processes	1 000 tonnes	270	200	−25.9
NO_x from power generation	1 000 tonnes	130	128	−1.5
NO_x from industrial processes	1 000 tonnes	200	118	−41.0
Water abstraction[a]	Million m³	9 549	8 573	−10.2
Waste water generation[a]	Million m³	1 801	1 162	−35.5
of which: treated	Million m³	1 381	1 058	−23.4
Solid waste generation[a]	Million tonnes	144	125	−13.5

a)   Includes mining and quarrying, gas, electricity and water and construction as well as manufacturing.
Sources: OECD, Central Statistical Office of Poland.

Table 7.4.   **PAC investment expenditures in the manufacturing sector, selected countries**

Share of sector output, **1995**

	%
Czech Republic[a]	0.6
Hungary[b]	0.3
Lithuania[a]	0.2
Poland	1.2
Germany	0.5
Portugal (est.)	0.4

a)   Includes mining and quarrying.
b)   1994 data.
Source: OECD, national data.

In many NIS, however, industrial restructuring and modernisation have essentially not started, and these trends have not emerged. In Russia, investment has not renewed ageing capital stock: the average age of manufacturing capital increased from just under 11 years in 1990 to over 14 years in 1995 (OECD, 1995). Only a small share of enterprises have adopted CP methods or invested in pollution control equipment. As a result, the manufacturing sector's waste water discharges to rivers and SO_x emissions to the atmosphere have fallen *less* than its output; air emissions of particulates have fallen in step with the decline in output (Figure 7.2). Moreover, the number of industrial accidents releasing pollution has increased over the transition.

Some highly polluting enterprises in the NIS have essentially taken no steps over the transition period to address their environmental problems. Norilsk Nickel in Russia provides an example (Box 7.11). Environmental authorities have had few effective sanctions to wield against the company, which has strong political power in the regions where it operates. The strong role of "insiders" in the corporate governance structure – together with ongoing uncertainties regarding the company's ownership – have delayed restructuring and new investment that could reduce pollution levels.

5.2. *Industrial restructuring and modernisation: a case study of the iron and steel industry*[2]

The process of restructuring and modernising large industrial enterprises can be long and costly. Iron and steel, a key industry in the centrally planned CEEC/NIS economies, was characterised by ageing mills

Figure 7.2. **Trends in manufacturing sector output and pollution levels in Russia, 1991 to 1997**

Index value 1991 = 100

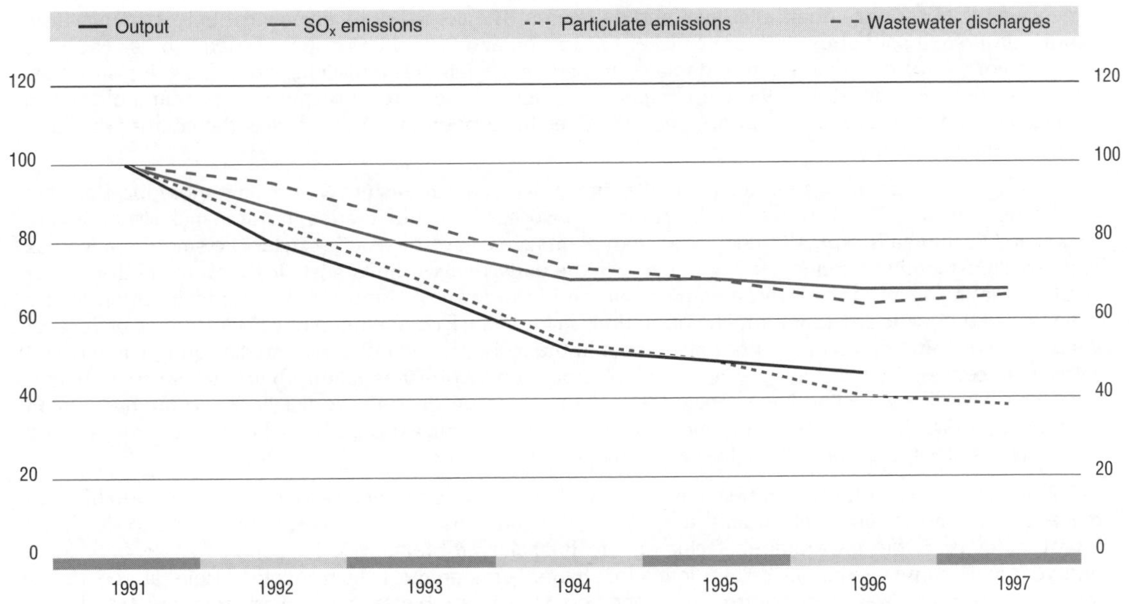

Source: OECD, national data.

using inefficient production practices and old, highly polluting technologies such as open hearth furnaces. In contrast, steel producers in OECD countries have steadily improved the efficiency of their production methods and 40% of OECD steel production is now based on recycled scrap metal rather than iron ore, reducing environmental impacts throughout the production cycle (OECD, 1999*b*).

Demand for steel in the CEE countries and NIS has fallen over the transition, but steel-makers have had success in finding new markets, including in OECD countries. However, in a highly competitive sector with significant global over-capacity, their exports threaten steel production in other countries and have prompted claims of unfair competition. Less stringent environmental requirements in the CEEC/NIS are sometimes cited as a factor.

In some CEE countries, such as Poland and the Czech Republic, the iron and steel industry has made progress in modernising plants, reducing excess capacity, and addressing environmental problems. Foreign investors, international commercial banks and IFIs have played a limited role in financing this process. Restructuring and modernisation have been slower in the NIS.

The iron and steel industry in Central and Eastern Europe

Poland and the Czech Republic have privatised a number of major iron and steel producers. So far, foreign investment has been relatively limited (although one investor, Lucchini of Italy, purchased a small mill in Warsaw). Restructuring has closed or replaced old facilities. For example, the Nova Hut mill in Ostrova, Czech Republic, is replacing three open hearth furnaces with a single electric arc furnace. The Vitkovice mill, also in Ostrava, is shutting down its three blast furnaces, in part due to severe environmental problems. In Poland, open hearth furnaces accounted for only 10% of total crude steel capacity in 1995, compared to 29% in 1990. As a result of restructuring and modernisation (as well as some pollution control investments), the Polish iron and steel industry has significantly reduced its emissions of key air pollutants since 1992, even though production has increased (Table 7.5).

Box 7.11. **Environmental issues at Norilsk Nickel**

The Russian company Norilsk Nickel mines and produces about one-fifth of the world's nickel and a large share of its copper, cobalt, platinum and palladium. The company receives most of its earnings from exports. In 1996, it sold about 60% of its nickel production and 70% of its copper abroad. Norilsk Nickel is also a major source of environmental damage, in particular high SO_2 emissions from its ageing smelters. Since privatisation started in 1994, the company has been the centre of disputes over shareholder and management control. During this period, no initiatives have been taken to address the company's major environmental problems.

Norilsk Nickel has a huge mine and smelter in Norilsk in north-eastern Siberia, a remote location that can be reached only by air or water. The company also has two subsidiaries in Murmansk *oblast*: Severo Nickel and Pechenga Nickel. All these mines and plants are above the Arctic Circle. The smelter in Norilsk emitted almost 2 million tonnes of SO_2 per year in the early 1990s – the largest single source in the former USSR – creating severe health-threatening pollution in the town of Norilsk and acid precipitation over a wide area of the Arctic environment. The operations in Murmansk *oblast* emit over 200 000 tonnes of SO_2 per year. Acid precipitation damages not only forests in the *oblast* but also those in neighbouring Finland and Norway. Recent emissions data are not available, but production has fallen about 30% since 1991 and emissions have likely declined as a result. Despite the fall in production, Norilsk Nickel's earnings remain high (about US$3.3 billion in 1996), of which a large share came from exports. According to press reports, the company has repatriated little of its foreign earnings.

Privatisation of Norilsk Nickel began in 1994, leading to a long-running dispute over its ownership and management. The government initially sold 49% of the company's shares to employees and to domestic investors. In 1995, the government, facing severe financial problems, used its shares as security for a one-year loan from Oneximbank. This "loans-for-shares" programme (which involved several of Russia's largest enterprises) was very controversial and led to a court battle and a Parliamentary Resolution disputing control of Norilsk Nickel. In addition, a range of parties including Oneximbank, the company's management, workers, and local, regional and federal administrations wrangled over several key issues. These included: management control of the company; financing for social costs such as worker housing; payment of wage arrears to workers; and payment of tax arrears.

In early 1997, Norilsk Nickel owed about 1.4 trillion roubles (almost US$300 million) in unpaid taxes and a similar amount in unpaid wages. The government did not repay the loan to Oneximbank. In August 1997, Oneximbank held an auction for the shares but allowed only one serious bidder, one of its subsidiaries. The auction led to a new round of court cases, but by 1998 it appeared that Oneximbank had won effective legal control of the company. In late 1997, Oneximbank announced plans to restructure the company and proposed to spend about US$1 billion to modernise its ageing capital equipment, which would contribute to reducing emissions and other environmental pressures. However, Oneximbank suffered heavy losses in Russia's August 1998 financial crisis. As of early 1999, it appeared that no investments had been made at Norilsk Nickel.

Throughout, foreign leverage for environmental improvements has been limited. Negotiations between Finland and Norway and the Russian government to cut emissions from Norilsk's Murmansk plants, underway since the late 1980s, have not resulted in agreement or action, in part because the Russian counterparts have not offered to share the costs. The company's environmental problems do not appear to affect its international sales or its position in world markets. By early 1998, several international banks and investment firms had purchased 20% of Norilsk's capital, but this appears to have had little effect on the company's environmental performance.

Sources: Kotov and Nikitina; Renaissance Capital Group; Samsonova-Massey.

In other CEE countries, restructuring has proceeded more slowly. Steel enterprises have had difficulty raising financing for major new investments. In Romania, for example, a recent study estimated that modernising the country's steel industry would require up to US$2.8 billion (UN/ECE, 1997).

Table 7.5. **Air pollution emissions from Poland's steel industry,**[a] **1992 and 1996**

	1992	1996	(%) change
Total emissions (thousand tonnes)			
SO_x	30.4	18.9	−38
Particulates	38.4	18.0	−53
Steel production (million tonnes)[b]	7.5	8.5	+13

a) Basic iron and steel, ISIC 3271.
b) Estimates.
Source: Central Statistical Office of Poland.

The iron and steel industry in the NIS

In the late 1980s, the Soviet Union was the world's leading steel producer. Since then, steel production in the NIS has fallen about 50%. It fell from about 120 million tonnes in 1992 to under 80 million tonnes in 1994, although it has remained relatively constant since. Demand for steel within the NIS has plummeted. There are widespread non-payment problems. In Russia, which accounts for about two-thirds of NIS steel production, barter may have accounted for up to 80% of domestic sales in 1997. The region's steel mills have turned to exports to keep production from collapsing. Russia's mills exported over 60% of their production in 1996.

Russia's iron and steel industry has ageing production equipment. However, enterprises have moved slowly to close old capacity or lay off unneeded workers. The industry therefore has high production costs but lacks internal resources for new investments (Kaiser).

Iron and steel mills have created severe environmental problems. In Russia in 1995, they generated eight times the air emissions of particulates per tonne of steel as the international average (Table 7.6). The industry generated 50% of all industrial waste from the manufacturing sector. Much of this waste contained metals that can be recovered. Across the NIS, although the decline in production has reduced the use of inefficient and highly polluting open hearth furnaces, in 1995 they produced 35% of Russia's steel and 50 per cent of Ukraine's.

Table 7.6. **Air pollution emissions intensities for Russia's iron and steel industry**
Kg/tonne of steel produced

	Russia, 1995	**Intl. average**
Particulates	8.6	1.1
Sulphur dioxide (SO_2)	5.5	2.2
Carbon monoxide (CO)	3.2	2.3

Source: *Ecology and Environment.*

A few NIS mills have started to modernise their production methods and address some of their environmental problems, often under the influence of external investors or financing. In Kazakhstan, LNM (a steel-maker based in London) purchased the huge Ispat-Karmet plant, the country's largest manufacturing enterprise. In 1998, the EBRD and the IFC participated in a US$800 million financing package to modernise the plant, refurbishing two blast furnaces and closing a third, along with the mill's open hearth furnace. Most of Russia's mills have been privatised, and foreign companies have taken shares in a few of these. Glencor of Switzerland, for example, has purchased 60% of the shares in the large Chelyabinsk Integrated Iron and Steel Works. A number of Russian and foreign investors have taken minority holdings in NIKOM of Nizhniy Tagil.

These and other large Russian steel-makers have negotiated with IFIs and international commercial banks for loans. In early 1998, the EBRD and commercial banks participated in a US$105 million loan to MMK, a huge steel-maker in Magnitogorsk, Russia. Conditions for the loan included the preparation of an environmental programme to address major problems at the plant, including high air emissions of particulates, SO_2, and NO_x (EBRD, 1999). As a result of these and other investments, all of Russia's open hearth furnaces are expected to close by 2005. Strong global competition – including the need to ensure access to western markets – may be a factor in encouraging these and other efforts to address the industry's environmental problems. In contrast, Norilsk Nickel, which has not addressed its severe problems, accounts for a large share of total production world-wide and may face fewer market pressures and market access concerns.

The industry's difficult economic situation is likely to continue. Ongoing economic problems in the NIS will probably restrict domestic demand as well as access to domestic financing. Further export growth will be difficult, due to ongoing global overcapacity. Restructuring and modernisation will likely continue to be a long and difficult process. In 1998, OECD's Steel Committee proposed that Member governments and steel-makers increase co-operation and information exchange with their counterparts in Russia and Ukraine. It suggested that environmental issues be a major issue for dialogue (Box 7.12).

Box 7.12.   **An international initiative for Russian and Ukrainian steel-makers**

In late 1998, the OECD Steel Committee recommended that OECD Member governments and steel companies increase their co-operation with governments and steel mills in Russia and Ukraine, to promote industrial restructuring and environmental clean-up in the sector as well as the development of sound business and marketing methods. The Committee had several specific suggestions, including:

– Steel companies in OECD countries could offer to host, at their mills, managers of Russian and Ukrainian steel mills for visits and training programmes;

– Information exchange programmes could discuss possible worker retraining and safety-net programmes for unemployed steel workers;

– Information exchange programmes could discuss approaches to environmental clean-up of obsolete steel mills and related employment and job training opportunities;

– Technical co-operation could be considered towards full closure, dismantling, and environmental clean-up of retired capacity; and

– Recommendations could be made to international agencies for additional targeted programmes.

Source: OECD, 1998a.

---

6.   Strengthening Environmental Management in Enterprises

At the 1998 Aarhus "Environment for Europe" Conference, environment ministers endorsed a Policy Statement on Environmental Management in Enterprises, under which they undertook "to catalyse, facilitate and strongly support the implementation of effective environmental management in enterprises in CEEC/NIS [and] to give increased priority to environmental management in enterprises within bilateral co-operation" (Box 7.13). Through this statement, ministers intended to extend government and business attention beyond CP and EMS approaches to a broader policy framework. The statement called for greater partnership among governments, business and industry, financial institutions, environmental NGOs and other stakeholders in promoting environmental management. In parallel, the European Round Table of Industrialists, which brings together 44 chairmen of major Western European corporations, presented a paper underlining that "good environmental practice is also good business practice" for their investments in CEEC/NIS (ERT).

Box 7.13. **The Aarhus Policy Statement on Environmental Management in Enterprises**

At Aarhus, environment ministers endorsed a *Policy Statement on Environmental Management in Enterprises*, prepared within the EAP Task Force. The statement uses "environmental management" to refer to CP and EMS approaches as well as to the broader concept of *eco-efficiency*.

- The statement calls on governments in the region to make *policy commitments* to catalyse and facilitate environmental management in enterprises, through economic reforms and environmental policy measures.

    • In particular, governments should provide *information, education and training* to help overcome barriers – within and outside enterprises – to the adoption of better environmental management practices.

    • For this, governments need to establish *institutional arrangements* involving all relevant ministries. The statement also calls on business and industry, trade unions, environmental NGOs and other stakeholders to work with governments.

    • CEEC/NIS governments, bilateral donors and IFIs should work together in establishing *appropriate financing mechanisms* for investments that strengthen the environmental management and performance of enterprises.

The statement invited the EAP Task Force to facilitate this process and to report on progress to the next "Environment for Europe" Conference.

Source: EAP Task Force, 1998*b*.

These statements provide common principles for bilateral donors, IFIs and foreign investors to use in supporting better environmental management in CEEC/NIS enterprises. However, governments and enterprises in the region must take the central roles in this effort. To lay the groundwork, many CEEC/NIS governments need to continue their efforts to establish and support competitive markets and encourage better corporate governance. Many governments can also improve the design and enforcement of their environmental policy instruments.

As the region's enterprise sector accepts environmental management approaches, it can become a partner in environmental policy. In a few CEE countries, elements of the enterprise sector have started to take on this role. Several business associations have worked with government to implement CP and EMS programmes; other groups have participated in environmental policy discussions (Box 7.14). In most of the NIS, few business associations have formed and environmental protection has not been a focus of enterprise attention.

In advanced reform countries, government and business and industry associations could work together to introduce new policy instruments that encourage better environmental management in enterprises, such as PRTRs (Chapter 5), as well as *eco-labels*, which inform consumers about their product choices. In addition, governments and enterprise associations could encourage enterprises to introduce *environmental accounting*, a tool increasingly used by enterprises in OECD countries, and to adopt *extended producer responsibility*, under which enterprises address environmental impacts of the materials and services they purchase and the use and disposal of the products they sell.

The process of EU accession will likely increase policy and enterprise attention to environmental management in candidate countries. Economic integration is also likely to increase market pressures to adopt EMS, as well as public attention in current EU countries to the environmental performance of CEE enterprises. Candidate countries should consider early adoption of the EU directive on the Eco-Management and Audit Scheme (EMAS) to encourage environmental management, as well as the directive on Integrated Pollution Permitting and Compliance, which incorporates a PRTR mechanism. The EU's extensive array of assistance programmes for CEE enterprises could provide opportunities to disseminate CP and EMS information. The Euro-Info Centres, which provide advice, information and assistance to SMEs in candidate countries regarding EU policies, opportunities and issues, could be a valuable network for encouraging environmental management.

175

Box 7.14.   **The development of enterprise-government co-operation and dialogue in CEE countries**

In a number of CEE countries, industrial enterprises have formed associations to represent them and to facilitate a dialogue with government on policy issues. A few of these associations have focused specifically on environmental policy, particularly cleaner production and EMS.

– The Czech Environmental Management Centre (CEMC) is an important link between enterprises and environmental authorities. The CEMC is an industrial association whose board members include representatives of the Ministries of Environment and Industry. It disseminates information about environmental management systems, conducts round table discussions about the effects of new environmental laws on enterprises, and conveys the opinions of industry to environmental policymakers. Other business associations have also worked closely with government. For example, a representative of the Association of Chemical Industries sits on committees responsible for drafting environmental regulations.

– The Slovak Association of Industrial Ecology (ASPEK), whose members include over 100 enterprises, disseminates information on environmental issues and policies to its members and provides the government with business's perspective on new and proposed environmental legislation. For example, in 1997 the Slovakian Ministry of Environment asked ASPEK to comment on its draft waste management law. ASPEK has also worked with the Slovak Cleaner Production Centre to prepare an EMS Training Kit for enterprise managers.

– In Hungary, the Chemical Industry Association regularly comments on proposed environmental policy. In Bulgaria, the national association of industry co-finances a Cleaner Production Centre.

– The World Business Council for Sustainable Development (WBCSD), whose members include many large multinational corporations, has established several national associations in CEE countries, including Croatia and the Czech Republic. The national associations bring together domestic enterprises and foreign investors to discuss and promote sustainable development issues.

– The European Round Table of Industrialists (ERT) and the Regional Environmental Centre (REC) jointly organised an Industry-Government Dialogue on EU enlargement in Szentendre, Hungary, in March 1999. Government and industry representatives examined the opportunities for and obstacles to improved environmental performance by enterprises. This is the first in a series of dialogues planned within the framework of the Aarhus Business and Environment Initiative. A report on progress will be prepared for the 2002 "Environment for Europe" Ministerial Conference in Kiev.

Sources: Macek; REC/ERT.

In the NIS, both governments and assistance programmes could take a greater role in disseminating CP ideas, in particular to those enterprises most interested in restructuring and modernisation, possibly through business development programmes. A number of donor programmes have already tried this approach. For example, US AID, working with the International Executive Service Corps, has sponsored US executives who advise CEEC/NIS enterprises on a variety of issues, including environmental management. Nordic governments, in co-operation with WBCSD, have sponsored a management training project, *Norlett*, for Russian managers, with an important environmental management component.

NOTES

1. The EAP Task Force defined "basic capacity level" to include: an active core of CP experts and trainers; a set of CP case studies, demonstration projects and model business plans; a functioning CP Centre; training materials in the local language; university courses that include CP as a topic; and monitoring and quality assurance.

2. This section is based on several sources, in particular Ecology and Environment, Kaiser/ICF, OECD (1997b), OECD (1998a) and UN/ECE (1997).

REFERENCES

Brattle, B. (1997),
   Restructuring Russian Enterprises: Lessons Learned from Russian Experience Since 1994, presented at the US AID Conference on Enterprise Restructuring in Russia, Moscow, March, [http://www.bcc.ru].

Brom, K. (1998),
   Issues of post-privatisation corporate governance, in A Regional Approach to Industrial Restructuring in the Tomsk Region, Russian Federation, OECD, Paris.

DeSimone, L. and F. Popoff (1997),
   Ecoefficiency: the Business Link to Sustainable Development, MIT Press, Cambridge.

EAP Task Force (1995),
   Best Practices Guide for Cleaner Production Programmes in Central and Eastern Europe, OECD, Paris.

EAP Task Force (1997),
   Strengthening the Role of Workers and Their Trade Unions in Promoting Cleaner Production in Central and Eastern Europe", presented at the eight meeting of the EAP Task Force, Paris, 19-21 November.

EAP Task Force (1998*a*),
   Progress in Achieving Basic Capacity Level for Cleaner Production in Central and Eastern European Countries/New Independent States, OECD, Paris, February.

EAP Task Force (1998*b*),
   Policy Statement on Environmental Management in Enterprises in CEEC/NIS, OECD, Paris.

Ecology and Environment, Inc. (1998),
   Executive Summary: Sectoral Environmental Action Plan – Russian Ferrous Metals Sector, prepared for the Centre for the Preparation and Implementation of International Projects (CPPI), Moscow.

Esty, D.C. and B.S. Gentry (1998),
   Foreign Investment, Globalisation and Environment in Globalisation and Environment: Preliminary Perspectives, OECD, Paris.

European Bank for Reconstruction and Development (EBRD) (1997),
   Transition Report 1997, London.

European Bank for Reconstruction and Development (EBRD) (1998),
   Transition Report 1998, London.

European Bank for Reconstruction and Development (EBRD) (1999),
   [http://www.ebrd.com/].

European Round Table of Industrialists (ERT) (1998),
   Company Investment in Central and Eastern Europe – Good Environmental Practice is also Good Business Practice, presented to the "Environment for Europe" Conference, Aarhus, Denmark, June.

Gaddy, C. and B. W. Ickes (1998),
   Why are Russian Enterprises not Restructuring, in Transition (Vol. 9, No. 4), World Bank, Washington, DC, August.

Gentry, B. (1999),
   Foreign Direct Investment and the Environment: Boon or Bane?, presented at the OECD Conference on Foreign Direct Investment and the Environment, The Hague, Netherlands, 28-29 January.

Goldenman, G. (1997),
   Privatisation and Environmental Liability in CEEC and the NIS: Reviewing Progress since the 1992 Warsaw Conference, OECD, Paris, November.

Golub, A. (1998),
   Environmental Financing in the Russian Federation, in OECD Environmental Financing in the Russian Federation, Paris.

Kaiser/ICF (1998),
   Russian Iron and Steel Industry: Current Trends and the Potential for GHG Emissions Reduction (draft), prepared for US EPA.

Kotov, V. and E. Nikitina (1996),
   Russia Wrestles with an Old Polluter, Environment Vol. 38, No. 9, November.

Macek, K.J. (1998),
    Environmental Management within Enterprises of Transitioning Economies, background paper for OECD, January.

OECD (1995),
    Economic Survey: Russia, Paris.

OECD (1997a),
    Reforming Environmental Regulation in OECD Countries, Paris.

OECD (1997b),
    The Steel Market in 1996 and the Outlook for 1997 and 1998, OECD, Paris.

OECD (1998a),
    Co-operation between OECD and Russia and Ukraine in the Steel Sector, press release, 21 December.

OECD (1998b),
    Eco-efficiency, Paris.

OECD (1998c),
    Foreign Direct Investment and the Environment: An Overview of the Literature, [http://www.oecd.org], March.

OECD (1998d),
    Recent Trends in Foreign Direct Investment, [http://www.oecd.org].

OECD (1998e),
    Review of the Development of International Environmental Management Systems: ISO 14 000 Standards Series, April.

OECD (1999a),
    Environmental Performance Reviews: Czech Republic, Paris (forthcoming).

OECD (1999b),
    Environmental Requirements for Industrial Permitting. Vol. I: Approaches and Instruments, Paris.

OECD (1999c),
    Principles for Corporate Governance, [http://www.oecd.org], Paris.

Regional Environmental Center for Central and Eastern Europe (REC) and The European Round Table of Industrialists (ERT) (1999),
    Industry – Government Dialogue on EU Accession: Business Opportunities for Best Environmental Practices, report on Seminar, 17-19 March.

Renaissance Capital Group (1997),
    Norilsk Nickel – Hidden Depths, Company Profile, Moscow, October.

Samsonova-Massey, E. (1998),
    Norilsk Nickel Case Study, prepared for the EAP Task Force, February.

Sleszynski, J. (1998),
    Pollution Abatement and Control Expenditures in Poland, (unpublished).

Stigson, B. (1998), *Sustainability in an Era of Globalisation: The Business Response*, in *Globalisation and the Environment: Perspectives from OECD and Dynamic Non-Member Economies*, OECD, Paris.

United Nations Conference on Trade and Development (UNCTAD) (1997),
    Environmental Management Standards, Particularly the ISO 14 000 Series: Trade and Investment Impacts on Developing Countries, August.

United National Economic Commission for Europe (UN/ECE) (1996),
    Statistical Survey of Recent Trends in Foreign Investment in East European Countries: Note by the Secretariat, December.

United National Economic Commission for Europe (UN/ECE) (1997),
    The Steel Market in 1996 and Prospects for 1997, Geneva.

United National Economic Commission for Europe (UN/ECE) (1998),
    Environmental Performance Review: Ukraine (draft), Geneva.

United Nations Environment Programme (UNEP) (1996),
    Sustainable Production and Consumption: Cleaner Production (brochure), UNEP Industry and Environment, Paris.

World Bank (1997),
    Pollution Prevention and Abatement Handbook: Toward Cleaner Production, unpublished Annual Meetings edition, September.

Zamparutti, A. and M. Kozeltsev (1998),
    Environmental Issues in Tomsk Oblast, in *A Regional Approach to Industrial Restructuring in the Tomsk Region, Russian Federation*, OECD, Paris.

Zarsky, L. (1999),
    Havens, Halos and Spaghetti: Untangling the Evidence about Foreign Direct Investment and the Environment, Foreign Direct Investment and the Environment, forthcoming.

Chapter 8

PROTECTING BIODIVERSITY

1. Introduction

The CEE countries and the NIS have a remarkable wealth of biodiversity and landscapes. Their natural habitats range from arctic to desert. They have huge river systems as well as several enclosed or nearly enclosed seas. Some ecosystems are of global importance. Russia's boreal and sub-boreal forests in Siberia and the Far East account for 22% of the world's forested area and 54% of its coniferous forests. Several mountain ecosystems are particularly rich in biodiversity, including those in the Caucasus and the West Tien Shan mountains of Kazakhstan, the Kyrgyz Republic and Uzbekistan (World Bank, 1998b). Natural habitats in the NIS contain a number of rare and endangered species, including the Amur tiger and Amur leopard, found only in the forests of Russia's Far East. The Bialowieza Forest in Poland and Belarus is Europe's largest remaining old-growth forest. Central and Eastern Europe also contains important landscapes that bring together traditional agricultural systems and cultural sites with forests, wetlands and other natural habitats rich in species. Both CEE countries and the NIS have populations of species that have largely disappeared from Western Europe, such as the brown bear.

Under central planning, many remote habitats – particularly in the former Soviet Union – were little touched by human activities and remained in a natural or near-natural state. However, biodiversity and landscape values were degraded in many areas. While almost half of Russia's immense land area has remained essentially untouched, economic activities have substantially altered 20% of the country's arid and semi-arid lands, 33% of its deciduous and mixed forests, 40% of its steppes, and large parts of other major ecosystems.

In the former Soviet Union and other countries with central planning, pollution together with large water engineering projects reduced biodiversity in key river basins such as the Volga and the Vistula as well as regional seas, including the Aral, Black and Caspian Seas. Threats to biodiversity also harmed commercial fishing. The most dramatic case has been the Aral Sea, whose two main tributaries were diverted for massive agricultural irrigation in the 1950s. By the 1990s, it had lost 70% of its volume. This disaster has largely destroyed the sea's ecology. A fishing industry that once employed 60 000 people has disappeared. Salt and other particles from the 3 million hectares of former seabed now blows over inhabited and agricultural areas, threatening human health as well as agricultural production (World Bank, 1998b).

Industrial air pollution has also harmed biodiversity. In Russia, it has killed an estimated 1 million hectares of forest and damaged even more. Air pollution from Norilsk Nickel's smelters has killed about 350 000 hectares of forest, particularly in Siberia (World Bank, 1998b). Large areas of forest in the CEE countries have also been damaged by air pollution, in particular acid deposition (although some of this has originated in other countries, including those in Western Europe).

The EAP recommended that, in setting priorities, national policies should incorporate two criteria that refer to natural resources and biodiversity:

- reducing productivity losses caused by damage or destruction of physical capital and natural resources; and
- halting threats of irreversible damage to biodiversity, particularly in wetlands, grasslands, coastal and marine ecosystems, forests and mountain habitats.

This chapter provides an overview of the interaction between economic changes during the transition and the region's biodiversity, as well as its natural and semi-natural landscapes (Box 8.1). This interaction is of vital importance, as the majority of biodiversity has been and will continue to be found outside protected areas such as natural parks. The chapter examines CEEC/NIS policies and actions to protect biodiversity and identifies key challenges. It also looks at international assistance to support these national actions.

Box 8.1. Key terms for biodiversity and landscape protection

Biodiversity or biological diversity means the variability among living organisms from all sources including, *inter alia*, terrestrial, marine and other aquatic ecosystems and the ecological complexes of which they are part. This includes diversity within species, between species and of ecosystems. Biological diversity can be described in terms of three levels: the variety and frequency of different ecosystems (ecosystems diversity), of different species (specifies diversity), and of genes and/or genomes (genetic diversity).

Landscape diversity is the formal expression of the numerous relations existing in a given period between the individual or a society and a topographically defined territory, the appearance of which is the result of the action, over time, of natural and human factors and a combination of both.

Conservation means a series of measures required for maintaining or restoring the natural habitats and the populations of species of wild fauna and flora.

Ecosystem management: Good ecosystem management will maintain the integrity of ecosystem functioning to avoid rapid undesirable ecological or environmental change. It will aim to maintain and, where possible, enhance biodiversity and environmental services such as water quality and food chain support. The ecosystem approach provides a wider basis for management, as the size of the management unit covered can be adjusted for different temporal and spatial scales, according to the nature of the problem and to the scales on which the ecosystem processes are operating.

Source: Glowka, based on the Convention on Biological Diversity.

---

2. The Economic Transition and Biodiversity Protection

The types of economic activity that have the greatest impacts on biodiversity and landscapes include: agriculture, forestry, urbanisation, fisheries, mining, water use, transport and tourism (EEA). This section focuses on those of agriculture and forestry.

2.1. Agriculture

Agriculture has close and complex links with the natural environment, especially biodiversity. Some types of farming activities can help preserve traditional landscapes, habitats and biodiversity. Under central planning, agricultural policies paid little attention to environmental issues and farming systems created a number of environmental problems. In the former Soviet Union, large areas of low-quality land were converted to farmland in often ineffective efforts to boost production. Intensive farming used large quantities of agricultural chemicals, harming local biodiversity and, through runoff, marine and other ecosystems. The development of collective farms disrupted traditional landscapes, which were often rich in biodiversity. Despite these and other practices, the huge agricultural lands of the region still have high levels of biodiversity. In several CEE countries, small-scale farming continued in many areas, preserving wildlife, traditional landscapes and rural economies. In Poland, small private farms remained the largest agricultural sector throughout the communist period. In a number of CEE countries and NIS, low-intensity grazing in mountain and other remote areas has maintained grassland ecosystems rich in biodiversity.

Structural changes in the transition

Agricultural reforms have affected biodiversity. During the transition, the CEEC/NIS dramatically reduced high farming subsidies, including those for agricultural chemicals. In the Czech Republic, total subsidy equivalents fell from over 60% of agricultural output in the mid-1980s to only 10% by 1986 (OECD, 1998*a*). Largely as a result, use of fertilisers and pesticides fell by over 50%. In the mid-1990s, fertiliser use in the Czech Republic, Hungary and Poland fell to levels slightly below those in Western European OECD countries; pesticide use was significantly lower (Figure 8.1). These and other changes in agricultural activities, have favoured biodiversity in rural areas. There has been a marked increase in the population of grassland birds in the Czech Republic (OECD, 1999*a*). In Hungary, the sharp drop in the use of agricultural chemicals is related to an improvement in river quality. Nitrate concentrations in the Tisza river fell by 50% in the early 1990s (OECD, 1998*a*).

Figure 8.1. **Fertiliser and pesticide use in selected CEE countries and OECD Europe**

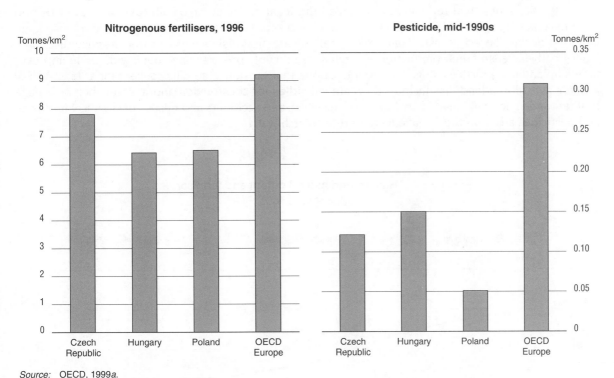

Source: OECD, 1999*a*.

In Russia, the decline in farm subsidies – from about 90% of final sales prices in 1990 to under 30% in 1996 – has reduced the use of mineral fertilisers from an average 90 kg/ha in 1990 to under 20 kg/ha in 1996. As a result, pesticide residues in soil have decreased significantly (OECD, 1998*b*; Pisniatchevsky). In recent years, however, the Russian government has increased its direct subsidies to farms, including those for fertiliser purchases, which reached about US$600 million in 1997 (Schmidhuber).[1]

Many CEE countries have reformed their agricultural structures. Most have divided large state-owned farms into small private holdings. The environmental effects are complex and not yet clear. In Hungary, the government split up large state-owned farms in the early 1990s, creating over half a million private farms, most of which have been under five hectares. In the short term, many of these small farms have adopted less intensive farming practices. A number of small "biological" farms have also been

183

established. However, since privatisation began there has been some consolidation and an increasing number of owners have rented their land to enterprises that farm large areas. These changes may have contributed to the 40% increase, between 1992 and 1996, in fertiliser use in Hungary, although this is still below the levels of the 1980s (Toth).

In a few countries, incoherent agricultural reform has created economic problems. In Bulgaria, delays in developing land registries have derailed land privatisation (OECD, 1996). Owing to the uncertainties of land tenure, newly private farmers have left many fields fallow. Since 1992, the number of sheep and cattle has fallen over 50% (Damary). This collapse in farming is not sustainable and needs to be reversed for long-term growth. In Baltic countries, too, the slow pace of land privatisation has disrupted agriculture, although not as drastically as in Bulgaria. Changes in land use, including the abandonment of some agricultural land, will affect biodiversity and change landscapes. The net results, however, depend on the new forms of land use. Without policies to support them, small farms and low-intensity grazing could disappear, particularly in CEE countries whose economies are increasingly integrated into the European Union. This could reduce biodiversity and alter traditional landscapes in many rural areas (Garcia Cidad and Hopkins).

In Russia, agricultural reforms have changed the legal status of large collective farms, but by and large have not changed their management or farming practices (OECD, 1998b). Output from these large farms has declined precipitously (Figure 8.2). Small private plots, using only a fraction of agricultural land, have greatly increased their production. Overall, there do not appear to have been wide-scale improvements in land use practices; in fact, there are reports that erosion, a serious concern for at least half of Russia's agricultural land, has increased.[2] State subsidies for construction and maintenance of storage facilities and agricultural machinery have also declined, and accidents and misuse of chemical fertilisers and pesticides are reported to have increased (Pisniatchevsky).

Figure 8.2. **Russia: agricultural output and fertiliser use**
Index 1990 = 100[a]

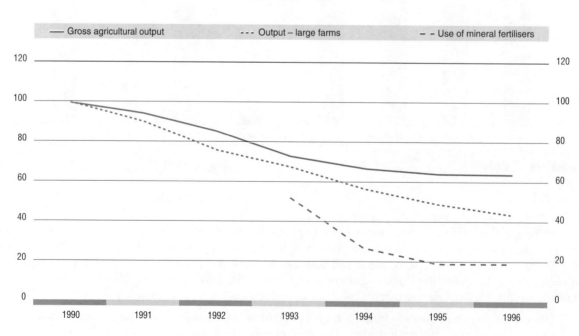

a) For all values including fertiliser use.
Source: OECD.

Integrating biodiversity and agriculture

A few CEE governments have started programmes to encourage environmentally beneficial agriculture (Box 8.2). Several have also established agricultural extension services to provide training and information to farmers, including on methods to protect the environment. Such initiatives have been less common in the NIS. In Russia, a few federal environmental programmes have aimed to reduce the environmental impacts of farming, but these have had funding problems. A recent initiative for Moscow's water basin was intended to promote alternative tillage methods and pesticide application schedules to reduce runoff. Bilateral donors have provided some initial financing for this initiative, but domestic funds have remained blocked (Pisniatchevsky).

Box 8.2.   **Integrating agriculture and environment policies in CEE countries**

In several CEE countries, environment and agriculture ministries have worked together on joint actions to integrate policy actions. In Hungary, they have developed a joint action programme to protect agricultural land and preserve biodiversity. The two ministries will work together to monitor soil quality, remediate closed mining sites, and encourage traditional and extensive farming methods (those using few agricultural chemicals), particularly in and near protected areas.

In the Czech Republic, the Ministries of Agriculture and Environment have established a joint Landscape Care programme to support activities such as erosion prevention and maintain landscape diversity. The programme has had a budget of about CZK 150 million (US$5 million) per year. Separately, the Ministry of Agriculture has provided about CZK 1.5 billion a year (US$50 million) in environmental subsidies for agriculture.

Lithuania allocated almost US$1 million in both 1996 and 1997 to encourage less intensive agriculture in the country's northern Karst region. The government also introduced restrictions on agriculture in environmentally sensitive areas. Governments in a number of countries have established regulations for agricultural chemicals. In Estonia, the Environment Ministry introduced regulations that limit the amounts of fertilisers that can be used per hectare.

Sources: OECD, 1997; 1999a.

In Central and Eastern Europe, economic integration with the EU and future accession will bring further changes to agriculture and to rural landscapes. In many EU countries, mechanised agriculture, supported by large production subsidies, occurs on huge fields where traditional landscape features such as hedgerows and small woods have been removed. This has reduced natural habitats and biodiversity. As small farms in mountainous and remote rural areas have disappeared, EU countries have seen a fragmentation of these traditional landscapes (Wascher). The reform of the EU's Common Agriculture Policy, and the CAP's eventual application in new Member States, are now under discussion. Candidate countries need to consider how EU accession will affect their agricultural sector and, in turn, how it will influence biodiversity and landscapes. Under the EU's biodiversity policies, Member States must develop national agriculture and biodiversity action plans. Accession countries should consider preparing similar plans as part of their accession strategies.

2.2. *Forestry*

Forests in the region yield valuable timber and non-timber products. As habitats, they have high biodiversity. Under central planning, many CEEC/NIS forests were untouched by timber cutting, especially in Siberia and Russia's Far East. In other areas, however, poor timber and replanting practices wasted timber and degraded forest land (WRI).

185

Over the transition, forestry practices have varied widely across the region. A few CEE countries have privatised forests, but they have also tried to develop more sustainable forest management approaches (Box 8.3). In the Baltic countries, timber cutting has increased over the transition as these countries have gained access to Western markets. In Estonia and Latvia, new private owners in particular have increased cutting. At the same time, the volume of forest stands in the three Baltic states has continued to (BEF).

Box 8.3. Privatisation and forest management in CEE countries

In several CEE countries, some forest land has been privatised. In Hungary, privatisation of agricultural land has also allocated 700 000 hectares of forest (about 8% of national territory) to 180 000 private owners. There are reports that new owners have lacked experience in forest management, often cutting the most valuable timber for immediate profits rather than undertaking long-term management. In this process, natural values such as biodiversity may have been harmed. Some CEE countries have privatised even larger portions of their forest land. The Czech Republic has privatised about 22% and Lithuania has considered privatising up to half of its forests.

A few CEE countries have worked to introduce more sustainable forms of forestry management. In Hungary, government policy has promoted afforestation that has increased total forested area from 18 to 19% of the national territory between 1990 and 1996. Although afforestation may not necessarily improve biodiversity, the Ministries of Environment and Agriculture have also set a goal of increasing the area of natural and semi-natural forests to 12% of national territory (compared to 9% in 1996). In the Czech Republic, the 1995 Forest Act established a new management approach, emphasising non-timber functions such as nature protection, water conservation and recreation. Under this legislation, owners of forests larger than 500 hectares must formulate 10-year management plans and owners of smaller plots must follow simplified forestry guidelines.

Sources: OECD, 1999a; Toth; UN/ECE, 1998a.

Forest management policies in many NIS have been in disarray. In Russia, whose forests cover almost half of the national territory, timber cutting has fallen by about two-thirds over the transition as energy, transport and other costs have risen dramatically. Timber production in Tomsk *oblast* in western Siberia fell from over 7 million cubic metres per year in the 1980s to about 2.5 million in 1995 (Korhonen and Rantapuu). In some areas, however, timber cutting has increased. In Russia's Far East, relatively close to Asian export markets, clear cutting of old-growth forests has threatened biodiversity (Matloff; WRI). Forestry throughout Russia continues to be unsustainable. There is cutting in some protected areas, and little attention is given to forest restoration and regeneration or to biodiversity protection. In a number of regions, there has been an increase in illegal logging.

In Ukraine, deforestation, in particular through conversion to agricultural land, has reduced the once extensive forests to about 15% of national territory since the beginning of the century. Although recent afforestation efforts are increasing the amount of forest land, and current forest policies have emphasised the importance of protecting biodiversity and other values, logging has increased in recent years as timber imports have declined. There is a danger that, if new policies are not implemented, it could increase further when economic growth returns (UN/ECE, 1999). In Moldova, whose forests cover less than 10% of national territory, and in other countries there has been a significant level of illegal cutting by individuals collecting fuelwood as energy prices have risen (UN/ECE, 1998b).

In many NIS, government bodies in charge of timber cutting have often retained responsibility for forestry policy, a joint role which was common under central planning. This has slowed consideration of non-timber values, including biodiversity, in forestry management. In Moldova, a government-owned agency, Moldsilva, has held both functions. A few CEE countries have also continued this joint role, including Bulgaria.

2.3. Tourism and other pressures

Many CEE countries have started infrastructure projects, in particular for highways, that have created new pressures on biodiversity, threatening to fragment habitats and disrupt migration patterns. Individual projects in some countries have undergone environmental impact assessments, but overall infrastructure development programmes, whose cumulative impacts exceed those of their individual projects, have not had such reviews. In some urban areas, tight land-use restrictions under central planning have been relaxed without land-use policies to replace them. A number of cities, including Warsaw, have experienced growing urban sprawl as private developers have built new office buildings, shopping centres and housing developments on agricultural land, threatening both biodiversity and landscape values (OECD, 1995).

In a number of CEE coastal zones and mountain areas, increasing tourism has encroached on natural habitats and traditional landscapes. In Bulgaria, large-scale seaside tourism was restricted under central planning to small areas of the Black Sea coast. New developments can threaten pristine areas along the coastline, in particular as land-use management has weakened. New skiing centres have threatened CEE mountain areas. However, well-managed tourism can provide revenues for biodiversity protection. In Poland and other countries, revenue is obtained from, for example, national park entrance fees. Many countries have sought to develop ecological and rural tourism, but in practice such goals have often conflicted with pressures to develop mass tourism, which promises higher short-term revenues. Nonetheless, several CEE countries, such as Slovenia, have linked their natural and landscape wealth with national tourism development and international tourism marketing (Hall).

Mining activities have also had a significant impact on landscapes and natural habitats. Under central planning in a number of CEEC/NIS, including Bulgaria, the Czech Republic and Hungary, open pit mining for coal, uranium and other minerals scarred the landscape. A number of CEE countries have taken initial steps to close unproductive mines and repair landscapes. For example, Hungary has established a fund to manage tailings at former coal mines (IEA). In Ukraine, coal and metal ore mining has been a basis for industrial activity, but has disfigured the landscape with slag heaps and polluted rivers with acid mine waters. Inefficient mining and processing methods have aggravated these problems. In contrast to CEE countries, there has been little reform of this sector in, for example, Ukraine (UN/ECE, 1999).

In Russia, oil extraction has contaminated vast areas of often fragile sub-arctic land in Siberia (Wernstadt). International assistance and financing, including a World Bank loan, have helped address some problems, for example, replacing old, leaking pipelines. Oil production has also polluted the Caspian Sea, in particular along the coast of Azerbaijan (World Bank, 1998b). Oil production is set to increase dramatically in other NIS, in particular the Central Asian and Caucasus republics, creating new risks for natural habitats.

Overfishing has been a concern in a number of regional seas. In the Caspian, it has contributed to a dramatic decline in valuable sturgeon stocks, whose caviar has provided important export revenues. Illegal hunting has also increased significantly in several CEEC/NIS. In Russia, it has threatened several endangered species including the Siberian tiger (WWF).

In many of the NIS in particular, natural resource use and extraction have played and will likely continue to play a central economic role. However, as a result of poor economic policies during the transition, revenues from natural resource sectors have rarely been used for domestic economic investment in these countries. Rather, they appear to have been used for domestic consumption or to have disappeared in capital flight. This indicates that, parallel to environmental considerations, more effective policies are needed if natural resource extraction is to sustain economic growth (Averchenkova).

3. Biodiversity and Landscape Protection Policies[3]

During the transition, many CEE countries and NIS have developed new biodiversity and landscape policies. International initiatives, including the global Convention on Biological Diversity (1992) and the Pan-European Biological and Landscape Diversity Strategy (1995), have stimulated national policies and international co-operation. This has been crucial for conservation efforts in many CEEC/NIS. While most national policies have referred to the importance of integration, in many countries the expansion of protected areas has been the most prominent achievement so far.

3.1. National biodiversity and landscape policies

International agreements and initiatives have accelerated the development of national policies in many areas. Almost all countries in the region have ratified the 1992 Convention on Biological Diversity, which sets out key policy actions for contracting parties to take. These include: developing national biodiversity strategies and programmes; planning protected area networks; and integrating the conservation and sustainable use of biodiversity into economic and sectoral policies. Many countries in the region have ratified other multilateral agreements on nature conservation and biodiversity protection, such as the Bern Convention on the Conservation of European Wildlife and Natural Habitats, which aims to conserve endangered species and habitats, and the Ramsar Convention on the Protection of Wetlands of International Importance.

At the 1995 Sofia "Environment for Europe" Conference, ministers approved the Pan-European Biological and Landscape Diversity Strategy (PEBLDS). The Strategy aims to provide a framework for European co-operation on biodiversity and landscape protection, including implementation of the Convention on Biological Diversity and other key conventions (Box 8.4).

Box 8.4.   The Pan-European Biological and Landscape Diversity

The Strategy has six major objectives:

– conserving, enhancing and restoring key ecosystems, habitats, species and landscape features across Europe, through the creation of a Pan-European Ecological Network;

– managing and using Europe's biological and landscape diversity sustainably;

– integrating biological and landscape diversity conservation and sustainable use across policy sectors;

– improving information on and awareness of biological and landscape issues, and increased public participation in actions to conserve and enhance such diversity;

– improving scientific and public understanding of the state of Europe's biological and landscape diversity and the processes that render them sustainable; and

– raising adequate financial resources to implement the Strategy.

The Strategy is implemented through international actions organised in four five-year plans. The first plan, through 2000, has focused on 12 "action themes" corresponding to specific ecosystems. In 1999, the international Council guiding implementation of the Strategy decided that the next phase, from 2001 to 2006, will focus on integration of biodiversity into social and economic sectors.

Sources: Drucker; McCloskey.

When they endorsed the Strategy, ministers at Sofia also called on countries in the region to help implement the CBD and PEBLDS by developing "national strategies, plans and programmes" for biodiversity protection by the end of 1998. Nearly all CEE countries and most NIS have met this goal. The Global Environment Facility played a key role, supporting the development of national strategies in 19 countries, with support from UNEP, UNDP and the World Bank (Delbaere).

3.2. *Networks of protected areas*

Before the transition, governments in the region created a number of national parks and nature reserves. In many countries, however, these protected areas covered a smaller share of national territory than their counterparts in OECD countries. The first national park in Russia was only created in 1983. During the transition, restrictions on personal movement and territorial development have been lifted. Designated areas have become more important for the protection of biodiversity and landscapes.

During the transition, many countries in the region have increased their networks of protected areas. In the first years of transition (from 1989 to 1993), Poland created five new national parks. Russia has designated over 30 new *zapovedniks* (nature reserves) since 1990, bringing the total to almost 100. By 1996, a few CEE countries had protected over 10% of their national territories, including both strictly protected areas (IUCN categories I and II) and those with less stringent protection (IUCN categories III to VI). In comparison, most NIS – which on average have far larger land areas than CEE countries – had protected a smaller share of their territories, although much larger land areas (Table 8.1). A number of protected areas in both CEE countries and the NIS have been listed on international registries, such as UNESCO's Man and the Biosphere Reserves and the wetlands protected under the Ramsar Convention. Nonetheless, many important habitats in the CEEC/NIS remain unprotected. Countries in the region need to continue developing their networks of protected areas, and to work towards meeting the IUCN's goal of protecting at least one example of each type of natural habitat within their frontiers.

Table 8.1. **Protected land area in CEEC/NIS, 1997**[a]

	Total land area (km^2)	Protected areas (% of total land area)		
		IUCN Types I and II	IUCN Types III-VI	Total
CEE countries				
Albania	27 400	1.2	2.3	3.5
Bosnia and Herzegovina	51 129	0.3	0.2	0.5
Bulgaria	110 550	2.6	1.8	4.4
Croatia	55 920	1.8	5.2	7.0
Czech Republic	77 280	1.0	15.1	16.1
Estonia	42 270	3.9	8.0	11.9
FYROM	25 430	4.2	2.8	7.0
Hungary	92 340	1.7	5.3	7.0
Latvia	62 050	0.8	12.1	12.9
Lithuania	64 800	2.6	7.2	9.8
Poland	304 420	0.5	8.9	9.4
Romania	230 340	4.4	0.3	4.7
Slovakia	48 080	14.7	60.8	75.5
Slovenia	20 120	4.1	1.8	5.9
NIS				
Armenia	28 200	7.1	0	7.1
Azerbaijan	86 600	2.2	3.3	5.5
Belarus	207 480	1.5	2.8	4.3
Georgia	69 700	2.8	0	2.8
Kazakhstan	2 670 730	0.4	2.2	2.6
Kyrgyz Republic	191 800	1.5	2.0	3.5
Moldova	32 970	0.6	0.9	1.5
Russia	16 888 500	2.2	0.8	3.0
Tajikistan	140 600	0.6	3.5	4.1
Turkmenistan	469 930	1.7	2.4	4.1
Ukraine	579 350	1.2	0.3	1.5
Uzbekistan	414 240	1.8	0	1.8

a) Based on IUCN categories: I – strict nature reserves and wilderness areas; II – national parks; III – natural monuments; IV – habitat/species management areas; V – protected landscape (or seascape); VI – managed resource protected area.
Source: WCMC.

A few countries have developed strong institutions to manage their protected areas. By the mid-1990s, Poland had 1 500 staff working in its national parks and 500 in its landscape parks (OECD, 1995). Many protected areas in the NIS have experienced severe resource problems. In Russia, budget cuts have severely curtailed the management of protected areas. External sources, including private organisations such as the World Wide Fund for Nature, have played an important role in supporting vital activities.

National policies and international initiatives have increasingly recognised the importance of estab-lishing ecological networks that link protected areas and strengthen the conservation of habitats, species and landscapes. Typically, such networks contain several basic elements: *core areas* to conserve eco-systems, habitats, species and landscapes of European importance; national and international *"corridors"* and *"stepping stones"* to connect the core areas, allowing species to migrate; *restoration areas*, to restore dam-aged elements; and *buffer zones* to protect the network from adverse external influences. Several CEEC/NIS have started to develop networks. At the international level, the development of a Pan-European Ecological Network has been one of the main areas of activity for PEBLDS. This network will encompass protected areas designated under international conventions and national networks of protected areas, including strictly protected areas and those where policies seek to integrate nature conservation objectives with economic development (Delbaere).

3.3. Domestic financing

In most CEEC/NIS, government budgets have provided the main source of domestic financing for nature, biodiversity and landscape protection. Environmental funds have provided only a small share of their resources for these sectors. One notable exception has been the Polish EcoFund, which includes biodiversity among its four funding priorities. Between 1992 and 1996, biodiversity accounted for about 35% of the EcoFund's projects and 12% of its disbursements (OECD and EC). As yet, private and market sources such as revenues from eco-tourism and sustainable use have only provided a small share of financing.

A few CEE governments have provided significant budget resources to fund protected areas and other biodiversity and landscape activities. The government of the Czech Republic allocated almost CZK 270 million (US$8 million) in 1997 for national parks and nature conservation (in 1998, budget funding dropped about 20%). The government budget also provided about CZK 250 million (US$7 million) a year for the River Restoration Programme, which has aimed to re-establish natural values and drainage regimes in agricultural areas (OECD, 1999a).

In many countries, financing for biodiversity protection has involved a combination of domestic sources (largely national budgets) and external sources. Domestic sources have typically funded recurring institutional costs, such as staff costs, while external sources have played a more catalytic role, supporting the development of strategies and plans, restoration of habitats, and other new projects. In Russia, the federal budget provided the largest source of financing for *zapovedniks* (natural reserves) in 1996, although both environmental funds and foreign sources provided important shares (Table 8.2). In a few countries, domestic budget financing has largely collapsed and foreign sources have provided the bulk of funding for biodiversity financing. They provided over 90% of such financing in Bulgaria in the mid-1990s (OECD, 1996).

Many CEEC/NIS have introduced charges for nature use activities, including park entrance fees, timber fees, and hunting and fishing permit fees. Only in a few cases – such as at Poland's Roztoczanski National Park, where they have provided over 50% of the park's budget – have charges provided signifi-cant revenues to finance protection activities (Table 8.3).

4. International Assistance and Finance[4]

International financing for biodiversity protection has been low compared to that for other environ-mental sectors. Donors and IFIs have reported that about 1% of their total environmental commitments went for biodiversity.

Table 8.2. **Sources of financing for natural reserves, Russia**

1996

Source	Share of total (%)
Federal government budget	68.6
Regional and local budgets	4.5
Environmental funds	9.9
Foreign assistance	10.7
Other sources	6.3

Source: Koc and Drucker.

Table 8.3. **Revenue sources for Roztoczanski National Park, Poland**

Revenue sources	US$ thousand	Share of total revenues (%)
State budget	360	29.6
Grant from National Environmental Fund	162	13.4
Grants from Zamosc and Lublin Regional Environmental Funds	37	3.1
Grant from Polish EcoFund	108	8.9
Timber sales, entrance fees and other revenues[a]	546	45.0
Total	1 213	100

a) Includes timber sales, sale of game animals and wild horses, seedlings, publications, entrance to the park and museum, revenues from transport services, agriculture and fisheries.
Source: Sleszynski.

The Global Environment Facility (GEF) has been the largest international source of biodiversity financing. Up to mid-1998, GEF provided over US$40 million in grants for biodiversity projects in the region. About three-quarters went to two countries: about US$26 million to Russia and US$6 million to Poland. GEF has supported the development of national biodiversity strategies and plans in many CEEC/NIS, in co-operation with UNDP and UNEP.

IFIs have provided few loans for biodiversity projects. Many such projects have been below minimum IFI loan amounts; they have rarely generated financial returns that could help to repay the loan. Many CEEC/NIS governments have given low priority to loan financing for biodiversity projects. While biodiversity has played only a minor role in the PPC's portfolio, a few PPC projects have included important biodiversity components. For example, the 1995 Klaipeda Environment Project supported the construction of waste water treatment facilities in Klaipeda, Lithuania, as well as the environmental management of Kursiu Lagoon and nearby coastal zones (the project was co-financed by the World Bank, four bilateral donors and the EC). A number of biodiversity projects have been in the PPC's "pipeline". The PPC held a workshop in 1997 at Lake Ohrid, between Albania and Macedonia; as a result, the GEF and a number of bilateral donors have planned a project to sustain biodiversity and improve waste water treatment at the lake.

A few bilateral donors have devoted an important share of their environmental assistance to biodiversity and landscape projects. Their projects have supported protected areas as well as biodiversity efforts in other rural areas (Box 8.5). In Ukraine, the US government has supported a small grants programme that provided up to US$5 000 each for biodiversity projects proposed by NGOs, students and scientists. Projects supported have included the expansion of the Carpathian National Park and the publication of a biodiversity protection newsletter (US AID). The European Commission has also been an important source of bilateral grants for biodiversity projects through its LIFE, PHARE, and TACIS programmes. The latter has supported projects to strengthen natural resources management in the water basin of Russia's Lake Baikal. EC support is expected to expand greatly, particularly in CEE candidate countries.

191

Box 8.5. **Swiss support for biodiversity and landscape protection in Bulgaria**

The Swiss government has supported a series of projects in Bulgaria to protect biodiversity and landscapes. Two of these have focused on Bulgaria's Central Balkan highlands, an area rich in biodiversity. The first helped prepare management programmes for the alpine meadows of the Central Balkans National Park. The second established an agricultural extension service for farmers in the region. The extension service will encourage small farmers to use sustainable methods. It will also provide advice and help that should allow farmers to raise their current low levels of productivity. The two projects are intended to help link farmers and environmental NGOs in efforts to protect biodiversity and landscapes.

Source: Damary.

Many donors and IFIs have supported international programmes for regional sea and transboundary rivers such as the Baltic Sea Joint Comprehensive Action Programme, in which protection of biodiversity and sustainable management of shared natural resources have been central goals. The Baltic Programme in particular has been a major focus of PPC efforts. Donors and IFIs have taken only initial steps to integrate biodiversity considerations into their support for non-environmental sectors, such as that for agriculture (the Swiss project in Bulgaria's Central Balkan highlands is a notable exception).

International NGOs and private foundations have also played a key role in supporting biodiversity efforts in the region. The World Wide Fund for Nature, based in Gland, Switzerland, has provided crucial support to expand and manage nature reserves in Russia, where domestic government funding for these areas has been cut drastically (WWF).

5. Integrating Biodiversity into Sectoral Policies

While many CEEC/NIS have made significant progress in expanding their networks of protected areas, the key challenge now is to strengthen the integration of biodiversity issues into sectoral policies and actions. Several international fora have underlined the importance of integration, including the Sofia Initiative on Biodiversity (Box 8.6) and PEBLDS. The 1998 Aarhus Conference endorsed a resolution, presented by the PEBLDS Council, that called on countries to increase their efforts to integrate the conservation of biodiversity and landscape diversity into sectoral policies. A World Bank review of CEEC and NIS biodiversity strategies, including both those completed and underway, has noted that, in particular, governments will need to make further efforts to integrate biodiversity and sectoral policies if they are to implement these strategies successfully (World Bank, 1998a).

Box 8.6. **The Sofia Initiative on Biodiversity**

The Sofia Initiative on Biodiversity involves 15 CEE countries, as well as international organisations and NGOs. At a workshop in April 1998, participants in the initiative identified four key areas for future work:

- transposition and implementation of EC nature conservation legislation, which includes a directive on conservation of wild birds and one on conservation of natural habitats;
- integration of biodiversity into agricultural policies;
- use of EC financing to support programmes with strong biodiversity objectives; and
- institution building within CEEC/NIS countries.

The OECD's *Handbook for the Implementation of Incentive Measures for the Conservation and the Sustainable Use of Biodiversity* underlines that successful approaches to biodiversity protection often entail a combination of economic and regulatory instruments. These instruments could include taxes, fees and subsidy removal to encourage environmentally favourable structural changes, together with access regulations to remove immediate pressures, for example in protected areas (OECD, 1999b). In the first step of this approach, policy-makers need to look at the underlying causes of biodiversity threats (Table 8.4).

Table 8.4. **Underlying causes of biodiversity threats and suggested policy responses**

Underlying cause	Policy response
Market failures, including unsustainable patterns of production or consumption	Address externalities through economic incentives and regulations; remove barriers to markets for biodiversity products
Information failures	Develop and disseminate information about biodiversity, its values and causes of itslosses
Policy failures, including subsidies for activities that threaten biodiversity	Remove reform-adverse subsidies, including below-cost pricing of natural resource concessions
Open access to natural resources	Establish and clearly define property and use rights, ensuring capture of natural resource rents and long-term planning of resource use and regeneration

Source: OECD, 1999b.

Biodiversity policies need to encourage "win-win" actions that can integrate rural development, agriculture and biodiversity goals (as a first step, many CEEC/NIS need to improve linkages between biodiversity strategies and overall national environmental policies). Poland's "Green Lungs" project provides one example of a "win-win" approach. It has encouraged environmentally friendly development, including eco-tourism, together with biodiversity and landscape protection in the country's north-eastern Mazurian Lakes region. IUCN, working with the EAP Task Force, developed guidelines for conservation planning in rural areas for the CEEC/NIS (Box 8.7). In order to convince sectoral ministries and interests of the importance of biodiversity, environmental authorities should also consider methodologies that estimate its value, along with that of valuable landscapes, in monetary terms.

The integration of biodiversity and sectoral policies is a key issue for EU accession. Two EU directives focus on biodiversity conservation: those on the conservation of wild birds and of natural habitats.[5] In particular, the latter calls on Member States to develop a common network of protected areas. The EU's 1998 Biodiversity Strategy, developed in response to commitments under the Convention on Biological Diversity, focuses on integrating biodiversity into sectoral policies, including those for agriculture, fisheries, forestry and transport (Delbaere).

While EU biodiversity policies have focused on improving integration, accession could significantly increase sectoral pressures on biodiversity. This is a concern in particular for agriculture. High EU subsidies have encouraged intensive cultivation methods in Member States. These have harmed biodiversity and altered traditional landscapes. The future of EU agricultural policies, which have started to refer to environmental considerations, and their application to accession countries remain important unresolved issues for negotiation. Infrastructure development is of basic concern in regard to biodiversity. As part of accession, the EU is financing the development of international transport networks, especially new highways linking candidate with current EU countries. These threaten to greatly increase infrastructure impacts on biodiversity, in particular fragmenting habitats, cutting migration paths, and augmenting indirect effects such as pollution.

Box 8.7. **Best practice for conservation planning in rural areas**

IUCN has prepared guidelines for donors, CEEC/NIS governments, NGOs and others undertaking projects to conserve biological and landscape diversity. These guidelines, presented to the 1995 Sofia Conference, include 10 key points for project planning and implementation:

- following a project planning process;
- establishing strong and stable institutional structures;
- using and developing the skills and knowledge base of the project participants, local communities, government bodies, and experts;
- involving key economic sectors and interest groups in policy development;
- conserving cultural values and artefacts;
- ensuring the participation of local communities, NGOs and the general public;
- promoting a strong legislative framework that supports conservation efforts and sustainable development;
- securing financing for all phases of the project;
- setting realistic schedules for key project tasks, in particular for fund-raising, and using time constructively.

Source: IUCN, 1995.

In the NIS, natural resource management remains a key issue for biodiversity protection. Effective management – of Russia's extensive forests, oil and gas extraction in the Caucasus and Central Asian republics, mining in several NIS, and a host of other activities based on natural resources use – will be of vital importance for maintaining biodiversity, as it will be for supporting economic development.

NOTES

1. Calculated using purchasing power parities.
2. This may be because Russian farms are using less organic fertiliser, and the organic content of soil appears to be decreasing. Many farms have given low priority to anti-erosion measures amidst the current changes and economic difficulties. Previous government programmes to combat erosion have been cut, while new ones lack financing.
3. This section draws on several sources, in particular Koc and Koc and Drucker.
4. This section is based closely on Koc and Drucker.
5. Directives 79/409/EEC and 92/43/EEC, respectively.

REFERENCES

Averchenkova, A. (1999),
Reforming Resource-rich Economies: The Transition Experience in Russia and Other Countries of the Former Soviet Union, presentation to the Reading University Workshop on Contemporary Environmental Policies and Issues in Eastern Europe and the Former Soviet Union, Reading, United Kingdom, July.

Baltic Environmental Forum (BEF) (1998),
Baltic State of the Environment Report, Riga.

Bulgarian-Swiss Biodiversity Conservation Programme (BSBCP) (1997),
Interaction Between Agriculture and Nature Conservation in Bulgaria, Bulgaria.

Damary, P. (1999),
How the Introduction of Sustainable Agricultural Methods Can Help the Maintenance of a Rich Bio-diversity in a Economically Poor Region such as the Central Balkans, unpublished note, the Research Institute for Organic Agriculture, Frick, Switzerland, February.

Delbaere, B.C.W. (1998), ed.,
Facts and Figures on Europe's Biodiversity, States and Trends, European Centre for Nature Conservation, Tilburg, Netherlands.

Drucker, G. (1999),
personal communication, European Centre for Nature Conservation, Tillburg, Netherlands, May.

European Commission (EC) (1998),
European Community Biodiversity Strategy: First Report on the Implementation of the Convention on Biological Diversity.

European Environment Agency (EEA) (1998),
Europe's Environment: The Second Assessment, Elsevier Science Ltd., Oxford.

Garcia Cidad, V. and L. Hopkins (1998),
General Overview of the Situation of Agriculture and Biodiversity in the Accession Countries, IUCN, Brussels, July.

Glowka, L., *et al.* (1994),
A *Guide to the Convention on Biological Diversity*, IUCN, Gland, Switzerland, and Cambridge, UK.

Government of Hungary (1997),
personal communication, Agricultural statistics yearbook, Gergeley, Toth.

Hall, D. (1999),
East-west Approaches to Rural Tourism and Sustainability, presentation to the Reading University Workshop on Contemporary Environmental Policies and Issues in Eastern Europe and the Former Soviet Union, Reading, UK, July.

IEA (1995),
Energy Policies of Hungary, 1995 Survey, OECD, Paris

IUCN (1995),
Best Practice for Conservation Planning in Rural Areas, Gland, Switzerland, and Cambridge, UK.

Koc, A. (1998),
Overview of Biodiversity in CEEC/NIS, background paper for the OECD, IUCN, European Regional Office, Tilburg, Netherlands, July.

Koc, A. and G. Drucker (1998),
External Financing for Biodiversity Protection in the CEEC/NIS Region, background paper for OECD, European Centre for Nature Conservation (ECNC), Tilburg, Netherlands, October.

Korhonen, T. and K. Rantapuu (1998),
Forest Sector Review and Investment Opportunities, in A *Regional Approach to Industrial Restructuring in the Tomsk Region*, OECD, Paris.

McCloskey, C. (1998),
PEBLDS Explained, IUCN, Tilburg, Netherlands.

Matloff, K. (1998),
   Facing Burning Forests, Russia Can't Afford a Bucket, Christian Science Monitor, 15 October.

OECD (1995),
   Environmental Performance Reviews:Poland, Paris.

OECD (1996),
   Environmental Performance Reviews: Bulgaria, Paris.

OECD (1997),
   Agricultural Policies in Transition Economies: Monitoring and Evaluation, Paris.

OECD (1998a),
   The Environmental Effects of Reforming Agricultural Policies, Paris.

OECD (1998b),
   Review of Agricultural Policies: Russia, Paris.

OECD (1999a),
   Environmental Performance Reviews: Czech Republic, (forthcoming), Paris.

OECD (1999b),
   Handbook for the Implementation of Incentive Measures for the Conservation and the Sustainable Use of Biodiversity, (forthcoming), Paris.

OECD and European Commission (EC) PHARE Programme (1998),
   Swapping Debt for the Environment: the Polish Ecofund, Paris.

Pisniatchevski, N. (1998),
   Agriculture and Environment in the Russian Federation, background paper for the OECD, April.

Schmidhuber, J. (1999),
   personal communication, Directorate for Agriculture and Fisheries, OECD, Paris, April.

Sleszynski, J. (1998),
   Pollution Abatement and Control Expenditures in Poland, background paper for OECD and the Danish Environmental Protection Agency.

Toth, G. (1998),
   Indicators of the Effects of Changed Agricultural Practices on Biodiversity in Hungary, unpublished background paper, April.

United Nations Economic Commission for Europe (UN/ECE, 1998a),
   Environmental Performance Review of Lithuania (draft), Geneva.

United Nations Economic Commission for Europe (UN/ECE, 1998b),
   Environmental Performance Review of Moldova, United Nations, Geneva.

United National Economic Commission for Europe (UN/ECE, 1999),
   Environmental Performance Review of Ukraine, United Nations, Geneva, 1999.

US Agency for International Development (US AID) (1998),
   Contributions to the Environmental Action Programme: Environmental Assistance to Central and Eastern Europe and the New Independent States, Program Descriptions, June.

Wascher, D.M. *et al.* (1997),
   European Landscapes – Classification, Evaluation, Conservation, draft monograph, European Centre for Nature Conservation (ECNC), Tilburg, Netherlands [http://www.ecnc.nl], January.

Wernstedt, K. (1996),
   Oil and Water Don't Mix: Risk on Tap in Western Siberia, Resources for the Future, Washington, DC, December.

World Bank (1998a),
   National Biodiversity Strategies and Action Plans. Preliminary Summary of Findings from Eastern Europe and Central Asia, Washington, DC.

World Bank (1998b),
   Transition Toward a Healthier Environment: Environmental Issues and Challenges in the Newly Independent States, World Bank, Washington, DC, June.

World Conservation Monitoring Centre (WCMC) (1998),
   1997 United Nations List of Protected Areas: Annex Summary of all protected areas recorded in the WCMC *Protected Areas Database* [http://www.wcmc.org.uk/protected_areas/data/un_annex.htm], Cambridge, UK, May, based on 1997 *United Nations List of Protected Areas*, IUCN, Gland, Switzerland.

World Resources Institute (WRI) (1996),
   World Resources Report 1996-97, Oxford University Press, Oxford.

Worldwide Fund for Nature (WWF) (1998),
   WWF *in Russia*, [http://www.panda.org/resources/ inthefield/wwfin_archives/russia.htm], February.

Chapter 9

INTERNATIONAL CO-OPERATION

1. Introduction

In many CEEC/NIS, international co-operation has been of crucial importance for environmental protection. This chapter first reviews the work of the EAP Task Force and the Project Preparation Committee, the two bodies set up to support implementation of the EAP. It then looks at other international initiatives, including multilateral environmental treaties, pan-European initiatives and regional sea programmes. Trends in official assistance and financing for CEEC/NIS are also examined.

2. International Co-operation to Implement the EAP

The 1993 Lucerne "Environment for Europe" Conference that endorsed the EAP created two international fora to assist in its implementation: the EAP *Task Force* and the *Project Preparation Committee* (Chapter 1).

2.1. The EAP Task Force

The EAP Task Force has provided a forum for all countries involved in implementing the EAP – OECD countries, central and eastern European countries and the NIS – together with IFIs and other international organisations. (A few NIS joined the Task Force only after its creation: Uzbekistan after the 1995 Sofia Conference, and Tajikistan and Turkmenistan after the 1998 Aarhus Conference.) Representatives of the private sector, NGOs and trade unions, as well as parliamentarians, have participated as partners in the Task Force's work. The Task Force is co-chaired by an EC official and a representative chosen by CEEC/NIS countries. They are supported by an eight-member Bureau that guides the secretariat's work between Task Force meetings (OECD hosts the Task Force secretariat).

The work of the EAP Task Force has followed three main themes:

– *supporting central and eastern European countries and the NIS in articulating their environmental priorities and exchanging experience with their implementation of the EAP.* Through exchange of experience, countries of the region have provided mutual support in EAP implementation – a process of "learning by doing".

– *building partnerships among CEEC/NIS, donors, international institutions, NGOs and the enterprise sector.* Many OECD countries have participated in the Task Force's work, sharing relevant experience with environmental management practices and establishing a dialogue on how technical co-operation programmes can be redesigned to better meet the needs of recipient countries. Equally, parliamentarians and independent partners – the enterprise sector, trade unions and environmental NGOs – have been directly engaged in Task Force activities.

– *identifying and disseminating best practices and encouraging co-ordination and exchange of experience among donors.*

Disseminating the EAP

The first task after the Lucerne Conference was to disseminate the EAP – both the document and its approach. The Regional Environmental Center for Central and Eastern Europe (REC) supported the Task Force by translating the EAP into 12 languages of the region and organising a series of national workshops in Central and Eastern Europe to present the translations. Many of these workshops served as kick-off meetings for the development of national environmental policy initiatives, such as NEAPs. The Task Force secretariat organised similar workshops in the NIS to disseminate the Russian translation of the EAP. These workshops were often influential, as implementation of the EAP depended on the participation, decisions and actions of many different national actors, including government agencies, industrial enterprises and NGOs. The EAP could be described as a "programme for national action programmes".

The workshops highlighted a problem: while the EAP had been endorsed by ministers throughout the region, in many cases its dissemination within CEEC and NIS governments (even within environment ministries) was proceeding slowly. Other obstacles impeded its implementation in the region. First, the EAP was intended as a framework for the transition to democracy and a market economy; in many countries, particularly some of the NIS, this transition has been slow and difficult, hindering environmental policy reforms. A second obstacle concerned the extent of high-level commitment. In some CEEC/NIS, ministerial endorsement at Lucerne did not lead to immediate efforts to implement the EAP's recommendations. Third, most of the EAP's analysis and examples focused on CEE countries and northern NIS such as Belarus, Russia and Ukraine. Dissemination, adoption and overall "ownership" of the EAP developed only slowly in other NIS. Fourth, few economic and sectoral ministries participated in the preparation of the EAP. Their support for the EAP's framework and, more generally, for integration of environmental policy into other sectors was weak. Although these factors slowed implementation, the previous chapters show that, by the 1998 Aarhus Conference, many CEEC/NIS had adopted important elements of the EAP framework.

The work of the Task Force

The meetings organised by the EAP Task Force helped build momentum for the EAP's implementation. In the five years between the 1993 Lucerne Conference and the 1998 Aarhus Conference, the Task Force held nine plenary meetings that brought together CEE countries and the NIS. These discussions were reinforced in joint meetings of the Task Force and the PPC.

The EAP Task Force (mainly through its secretariat) has undertaken a work programme to assist in the implementation of the EAP, focused on identifying best practices and on exchanging CEEC and NIS experience in three areas:

- implementation of environmental policies, including National Environmental Action Programmes;
- environmental financing; and
- cleaner production/environmental management in enterprises.

The bulk of the Task Force's work has been carried out in workshops and through networks of policy makers. In the period between the Lucerne and Aarhus Conferences, about 65 international workshops and meetings have been organised in 20 different CEE countries and NIS, involving about 3 000 experts. Through its work, the Task Force – together with governments in the region – has extended the ideas of the original EAP. For example, it has developed several "best practice" guides such as the *St. Petersburg Guidelines for Environmental Funds* and the *Best Practices Guide for Cleaner Production Programmes in Central and Eastern Europe*.

The 1995 Sofia Conference reviewed the Task Force's work and renewed its mandate, together with that of the PPC. By this time, environment ministers reported that "there are clear signs that policy reforms, institutional strengthening and environmental investments have been producing improvements in environmental conditions in CEE countries" and reaffirmed their endorsement of the EAP as a strategy for the region. The Sofia Conference also launched the "Sofia Initiatives", fora led by CEE countries under the EAP Task Force (Box 9.1). Between the Sofia and Aarhus Conferences, CEE countries and the NIS assumed a larger role in its discussions and work. The Task Force held about twice as many workshops and meetings in this period as it had before Sofia.

At the Aarhus Conference, environment ministers again discussed key issues related to the EAP's implementation: environmental challenges in the NIS; environmental financing and economic instruments; and business and environment. By the time of Aarhus, however, the European Union had invited

---

Box 9.1. The Sofia Initiatives

At the 1995 Sofia Conference, CEE governments launched a new set of activities in the framework of the EAP Task Force: the Sofia Initiatives. These activities, proposed by Bulgaria's Environment Minister, brought CEE governments together in four fora, each working on an environmental issue identified as a common priority for implementation of the EAP. CEE countries have taken the lead in setting the agendas, while donors have provided both technical and financial support – in fact, the Initiatives have represented an important step forward for CEE "ownership" in regard to international co-operation.

Two fora have worked on specific environmental problems: local air pollution management (led by Bulgaria) and biodiversity protection (led by Slovenia). They have linked EAP activities with work to implement multilateral agreements – in particular, the UN/ECE Convention on Long-Range Transboundary Air Pollution and the global Convention on Biodiversity. The other two fora have focused on strengthening economic instruments (led by the Czech Republic) and environmental impact assessments (led by Croatia). In each forum, governments have discussed common policy problems, shared experience with positive approaches, and considered upcoming challenges. The REC has acted as secretariat for the four groups.

---

10 CEE countries to work towards EU accession. In these countries, accession had become the main driving force for environmental policy (Annex III). At the same time, other CEE countries and most NIS faced ongoing difficulties in tackling their environmental problems. In their final declaration, the environment ministers called on the EAP Task Force and the PPC to re-focus their activities to assist these countries.

Since Aarhus, the EAP Task Force has continued to focus on its three core areas, which it will develop through inter-related but separate sub-programmes for CEE countries and NIS. The Regional Environmental Center for Central and Eastern Europe (REC) in Szentendre, Hungary, has taken the lead in organising activities for the CEE sub-programme, thereby strengthening ownership of the process by countries in the region. The full Task Force continues to meet regularly, bringing together OECD countries, CEE countries and NIS, and encouraging ongoing co-operation and exchange of experience.

2.2. The Project Preparation Committee (PPC)

In 1993, a number of observers, including the European Parliament and the parallel Lucerne NGO Conference, criticised the Lucerne Ministerial Conference for not promising new donor financial commitments (Parlement européen; Coordination pour l'Europe). The EAP – and the ministers gathered at Lucerne – accepted this political reality. The ministers created the Project Preparation Committee to overcome some of the obstacles hindering international assistance and financing. The PPC has improved co-ordination between donors and IFIs, and facilitated the preparation and implementation of environmental investment projects (Chapter 6). It has co-ordinated nearly all IFI-financed environmental investment projects in the region since the Lucerne Conference (Annex I describes trends in IFI financing).

Observers in the region have criticised the PPC for lack of CEEC/NIS participation (only the CEEC/NIS co-chair of the Task Force is invited to PPC meetings). The PPC has taken a number of initiatives to strengthen communication with governments and other actors in the region. In addition to its own meetings, the PPC has held regular joint meetings with the EAP Task Force. These have served both to inform the CEEC and NIS about its work and the project cycle within IFIs, and to share policy lessons from the implementation of investment projects. Recently, the PPC has also organised meetings in CEEC/NIS to help identify and develop projects in specific geographical areas. Meetings were held at Lake Ohrid, between FYR Macedonia and Albania in 1996; at St. Petersburg, focusing on Baltic issues, in 1997; at Tbilisi, focusing on Central Asia and the Caucasus, in June 1998; and at Dnepropetrovsk, Ukraine, focusing on opportunities in Ukraine and Moldova, in October 1998.

The Aarhus Conference called on the PPC to strengthen its efforts to identify and finance environmental projects in the NIS. The PPC plans to continue its meetings in the region and will appoint officers to help identify and structure projects in the NIS. At Aarhus, the PPC reported that it would explore

---

opportunities for private sector involvement in its activities and try to broaden its work beyond the water and air pollution sectors that had dominated its portfolio up to then. The PPC is also expected to play an important role in financing environmental projects related to EU accession in CEE candidate countries.

3. The EAP and Other International Environmental Initiatives

Implementation of the EAP has interacted with other multilateral environmental initiatives: global initiatives, such as *Agenda* 21; binding global and regional environmental agreements (treaties and conventions); other regional initiatives under the "Environment for Europe" process; and "sub-regional" partnerships to protect common resources.

Communication and co-ordination among these different initiatives have often been poor. The "Environment for Europe" Conferences have provided one of the few mechanisms for reviewing progress across different areas. In the end, however, countries in the region have been the main actors co-ordinating implementation of different international initiatives, at least where sufficient domestic interest to do so has existed.

Although this section focuses on environmental initiatives and agreements, other areas of international co-operation also have an important influence. For example, several CEEC/NIS have acceded to international economic organisations with an important environmental dimension. Accession to the EU will transform environmental policy in the countries concerned. The Czech Republic, Hungary and Poland have joined the OECD, whose Members have agreed on common policies in regard to many types of national environmental activities, as well as committing themselves to legally binding decisions concerning chemicals management, hazardous waste management and other areas. Many CEEC/NIS have joined the World Trade Organisation, which can settle disputes regarding some environmental aspects of international trade.

3.1. *The Environmental Action Programme and Agenda* 21

The Lucerne Conference that endorsed the EAP took place almost a year after the UN Conference on Environment and Development (UNCED) at Rio de Janeiro, which adopted *Agenda* 21 as a global programme for sustainable development combining environmental, economic and social goals. After Rio, many CEE countries and NIS started to develop long-term sustainable development strategies. Often, the committees and groups working on these strategies have had difficulty translating the complex nature of sustainable development into policy reforms and other practical measures. These strategies have also often lacked broad support within governments, as economic and sectoral ministries did not give them high priority.

The EAP represented a limited approach to these goals, focusing on short-term actions. After the Lucerne Conference, many countries in the region began developing NEAPs and other policy initiatives that implemented EAP recommendations. Consequently, some countries created two, often conflicting planning streams. Some proponents of the EAP suggested it was an alternative to *Agenda* 21, as the latter's broad focus and long-term perspective provided few hints for immediate action (Stritih). On the other hand, critics of the EAP, including the European Parliament, contended that the Action Programme did not give sufficient weight to sustainable development goals (Parlement européen).

Over the course of the transition, several national initiatives have brought together EAP and Agenda 21 processes: Kazakhstan's National Environmental Action Programme for Sustainable Development (Chapter 3) has been one of the most successful efforts. Moreover, by the time of the 1998 Aarhus Conference, after several years of implementation of both *Agenda* 21 and the EAP, the synergies between the two had become clearer. Both focus on linkages between the economy and the environment and emphasise the need to integrate economic and environmental policies. In particular, the EAP's framework incorporated the region's short-term economic goals – which emphasised the transition to market-based economies – into environmental policy. While the EAP did not address social goals directly, these formed an important part of its framework. The EAP recommended that the protection of human health be a key criterion for environmental action, and it encouraged governments to promote public participation in decision-making on environmental policy.

Officials in the region have increasingly recognised that the EAP and *Agenda* 21 complement each other: "Today ... most CEE policymakers regard *Agenda* 21 as a broad set of long-term goals and values while the EAP provides the tools for implementing them" (Stritih). Many processes, methods and capacities are common to the two activities. The two can and should be mutually supportive. Nonetheless, there are also differences in time-frame and scope, particularly regarding social issues.

3.2. *Multilateral environmental agreements*

Binding agreements, such as multilateral conventions and treaties, have been an important element of environmental co-operation in Europe. The CEEC/NIS countries have subscribed to many such agreements, which in turn have influenced their environmental policies and actions (Annex X). These have included global and regional (*i.e.* Europe-wide) agreements, many of which have been developed under the aegis of the UN/ECE, and sub-regional agreements, in particular those to protect enclosed seas and other common resources. Many agreements have focused on global or transboundary pollution and identify national actions or targets for pollution levels. For example, under several protocols to the Geneva Convention on Long-Range Transboundary Air Pollution, CEEC/NIS governments have agreed to targets to reduce national emissions of air pollutants. Other agreements have harmonised specific environmental policy mechanisms. The European governments that signed the Convention on public participation at Aarhus in 1998 agreed to common standards and provisions for public access to environmental information and public participation in environmental policy.

While the EAP encouraged the CEEC/NIS to integrate their international commitments into national policies, it expressed concern that international agendas could "drive" national environmental actions, leading the CEEC/NIS to take actions that would not be cost-effective and would not address their most serious problems. The EAP urged countries in the region to follow a "bottom-up" approach, starting with local and national priorities. It noted that many of these actions would also contribute to achieving international commitments. For example, actions to reduce local air pollution, together with the influence of economic restructuring, would reduce emissions of transboundary air pollutants regulated under the Geneva Convention, such as SO_2. Thus, the EAP suggested that countries tackle "low-stack" air emissions, such as those from household coal combustion in urban areas, before devoting a large share of domestic resources to reducing sulphur emissions from "high-stack" sources, such as large power plants, which can have greater transboundary effects but often do not contribute strongly to local air pollution. The EAP also encouraged CEEC/NIS governments to focus on policy measures and policy integration as strategies for pollution reduction rather than expensive pollution control investments (encouraged under some multilateral agreements). On the other hand, the EAP encouraged donor countries to provide assistance for pollution control actions that mainly have transboundary effects, such as reduction of sulphur emissions from "high-stack" sources.

Moreover, the EAP followed a different approach to goal-setting. It encouraged countries in the region to set realistic goals and use their available resources as effectively as possible. Many multilateral agreements establish ambitious goals for ratifying countries, but do not identify means to achieve them – which has slowed practical implementation. A recent REC/UNEP study noted that the CEEC/NIS have been slow to implement multilateral agreements, even though many countries in the region have a strong record in terms of formal steps of ratification and the development of corresponding national laws (REC).

The EAP's approach provides important lessons for the implementation of multilateral agreements. The CEEC/NIS have found that implementing multilateral agreements requires a mix of policy, institutional and financial actions. For example, to implement the Basel Convention on transboundary movements of hazardous waste, countries in the region have had to develop new institutions and procedures to regulate cross-border movements (REC). Economic reforms and changes have also had a major effect on compliance with international commitments, such as the Climate Change Convention's targets for greenhouse gas emissions. Reducing GHG emissions will require actions in the transport and other sectors. Overall, a number of CEEC/NIS have found that stronger national policies can play a major role in integrating actions to implement multilateral agreements with other national priorities.

More generally, adoption of binding agreements and implementation of non-binding initiatives such as the EAP have increasingly been recognised as complementary. For example, the latter are better able to introduce innovations in environmental policy, while many governments are more cautious about agreeing to the requirements of binding conventions (REC). However, binding multilateral conventions provide environmental authorities with a lever to move non-environmental ministries and other stakeholders into action towards environmental goals.

3.3. Pan-European environmental initiatives

The 1995 Sofia "Environment for Europe" Conference launched two long-term initiatives, the *Pan-European Biological and Landscape Diversity Strategy* (PEBLDS) and the *Environment Programme for Europe* (EPE). These initiatives cover both CEEC/NIS and Western European countries.

PEBLDS presented a framework and common goals for international activities and national actions to protect biodiversity and landscapes across Europe over 20 years (Chapter 8). Its objectives include strengthening European implementation of international conventions, such as the global Convention on Biological Diversity, and promoting common priorities for regional action. It emphasises integration of conservation efforts into the actions of key economic sectors, such as agriculture and transport.

The Environment Programme for Europe (EPE) represented the first initiative for common, long-term environmental priorities across the region. It aimed to promote implementation of *Agenda* 21 as well as integration of environmental and economic policies. The EPE covered a wide range of issues and contained 100 recommendations. To assist implementation, the UN/ECE has held workshops on issues such as economic instruments and local initiatives to support sustainable consumption. Several multilateral initiatives have focused on key issues identified in the EPE, including public participation (particularly the Aarhus Convention), energy conservation (supported in the declaration of the Aarhus Conference) and the phase-out of leaded gasoline. (The EAP also identified these as key environmental policy issues during the transition.)

At the 1998 Aarhus Conference, ministers emphasised that policy integration was a key challenge for improving environmental conditions in Europe. The EAP, PEBLDS and EPE all emphasise the importance of integration. Co-ordination between these different initiatives has so far been weak, which has not helped national environmental authorities pursue integration. Integration and co-ordination are also issues for initiatives under other fora, such as the Environment and Health Action Plan for Europe (Box 9.2). Overall, policy integration has remained difficult in both CEEC/NIS and Western European countries.

Box 9.2. The Environment and Health Action Plan for Europe

The 1994 Helsinki Conference on Environment and Health in Europe endorsed an Environment and Health Action Plan for Europe, to help prevent and control environmental hazards to human health. The Conference also created a European Environmental Health Committee, bringing together health and environment officials, to oversee implementation of the Plan, and particularly the development of National Environment and Health Action Plans (NEHAPs) in the CEEC/NIS (as well as in Western European countries). The World Heath Organisation's European Office has acted as secretariat for the Committee.

This initiative shares many common elements with the EAP, which proposes the protection of human health as a key criterion for identifying environmental priorities in the CEEC/NIS. The EAP Task Force secretariat and WHO/Europe have co-operated on selected activities, such as a 1997 workshop on the use of data and indicators for setting policy priorities. An increasing number of CEEC/NIS have formally linked their NEAP and NEHAP work: for example, Hungary's NEHAP was included in the NEAP approved by Parliament in 1997. Overall, however, the establishment of separate international processes, despite their common objectives, has not broken down institutional barriers between environmental and health authorities in CEEC/NIS. In June 1999, a follow-up Conference on Environment and Health in Europe in London focused on the implementation of NEHAPs and related initiatives (see http://www.who.dk/london99).

3.4. *Regional sea programmes and related initiatives*

Several international initiatives have brought together neighbouring countries for the protection of regional seas such as the Aral, Baltic and Black Seas, as well as other shared natural resources such as the Danube basin (Box 9.3). One international partnership, the Black Triangle Programme, has focused on reducing air pollution in bordering regions of the Czech Republic, Germany and Poland. These initiatives have developed common strategies and action programmes, and each has set up a secretariat to help co-ordinate implementation. In a number of cases, international conventions have established a legal basis and formal commitments for co-operation efforts. IFIs and other international bodies have played a catalysing role in the development and early implementation of many such initiatives.

Box 9.3. **Principal regional sea programmes and related initiatives in CEEC/NIS**

The Aral Sea

Strategy/action document: Aral Sea Basin Programme, adopted in 1994.

Participating countries and organisations: Kazakhstan, the Kyrgyz Republic, Tajikistan, Turkmenistan and Uzbekistan, with the support of the EC, GEF, UNDP, the World Bank, and the Netherlands and other donors.

The Baltic Sea

International convention: Helsinki Convention on the Protection of the Marine Environment of the Baltic Sea Area, 1992.

Strategy/action documents: Baltic Sea Joint Comprehensive Environmental Action Programme, adopted in 1992.

Agenda 21 for the Baltic Sea Region, 1998.

Participating countries and organisations: the 14 countries of the Baltic Sea basin, as well as the EC, EBRD, EIB, NIB, NEFCO, the World Bank, the International Baltic Sea Fishery Commission and NGOs.

The Black Sea

International convention: Bucharest Convention on the Protection of the Black Sea against Pollution, 1992.

Strategy/action documents: Black Sea Environmental Programme, 1994; Black Sea Strategic Action Plan, adopted in October 1996.

Participating countries and organisations: Bulgaria, Georgia, Romania, Russia, Turkey and Ukraine, with the support of the EC, GEF and other donors.

The Black Triangle

Strategy/action documents: Black Triangle Environment Programme, adopted 1991.

Participating countries and organisations: Czech Republic, Germany, Poland and the EC.

The Caspian Sea

Strategy/action document: Caspian Environment Programme, 1998.

Participating countries and organisations: Azerbaijan, Iran, Kazakhstan, Russia and Turkmenistan, as well as EC-TACIS, UNDP, UNEP and the World Bank.

The Danube Basin

International convention: 1994 Budapest Convention on Co-operation for the Protection and Sustainable Use of the Danube River.

Strategy/action documents: Strategic Action Plan for the Danube River Basin, adopted 1994.

Participating countries and organisations: Austria, Bulgaria, Croatia, Czech Republic, Germany, Hungary, Moldova, Romania, Slovakia, Slovenia, Ukraine, as well as the EC and international organisations.

These initiatives were developed separately from the EAP. Their goals usually focus on the protection of a common natural resource. The Baltic Sea Joint Comprehensive Action Programme (JCP), for example, was established "to assure the ecological restoration of the Baltic Sea". These programmes focus only indirectly on local issues in CEEC/NIS, which the EAP urged should receive attention first. Many regional programmes initially devoted attention to identifying investment projects: the Baltic Sea Programme proposed almost ECU 7 billion (US$8 billion) in investments to reduce pollution levels. However, the most successful regional partnerships have come to place a strong emphasis on policy reform and institutional strengthening. In the Baltic Sea region, a variety of bilateral and multilateral programmes have supported work in these areas, including, most recently, the preparation of an Agenda 21 for the region (Box 9.4). The Aral Sea Programme has identified institutional development as a key priority in its participating countries and has emphasised the importance of a "multi-sectoral" approach to encourage policy integration.

Box 9.4. Environmental co-operation in the Baltic Sea region

There is strong co-operation among the countries in the Baltic Sea region, based in part on their historical ties. The area includes both donor countries and CEEC/NIS, reinforcing co-operation to protect a shared natural resource. Donor countries on the Baltic Sea have recognised that the most cost-effective pollution reductions are often to be made in recipient countries. They have contributed both assistance and financing for environmental actions. By mid-1997, technical assistance activities were underway in 74 of the over 100 CEEC/NIS hot spots identified in the Baltic Sea Joint Comprehensive Action Programme (JCP). In many of these, investment projects had also started. Financing for Baltic projects has been a large share of the PPC's portfolio. By mid-1997, two hot spots, both in Estonia, had been removed from the JCP list.

Baltic Sea countries have co-operated in a variety of other multilateral and bilateral initiatives:

– Many Baltic initiatives have focused on institutional strengthening and policy development. For example, the three Baltic States have participated in the Baltic Environmental Forum (supported by Germany and the EC), whose work has included support for NEAPs and other national policies as well as development of common environmental indicators and a common state of the environment report for the three countries.

– Innovative financing approaches in the region have included the Nordic Environmental Finance Corporation (NEFCO) under the Nordic Investment Bank. NEFCO has provided equity financing for environmental projects and financed cleaner production projects (Chapters 6 and 7).

– In June 1998, environment ministers from the Baltic Sea region endorsed *Baltic 21*, a joint *Agenda 21* document developed with the participation of NGOs, business, and international organisations. *Baltic 21* focuses on agriculture, energy, fisheries, forestry, industry, tourism and transport.

Sources: Baltic 21 secretariat; Helsinki Commission; Stratmann.

Active CEEC/NIS participation in and "ownership" of these initiatives has been crucial for their implementation, as governments in the region have had to co-ordinate actions to implement these commitments (as well as those of other international initiatives) with their national policy priorities. This appears to have been most successful in the Baltic Sea region: the three Baltic States considered the JCP's objectives and priorities in developing their environmental strategies and NEAPs. Although these countries sometimes put domestic priorities first, their relatively strong national policies and institutions made them effective partners in the regional process. Domestic support has been important for implementing investment projects, as national resources have had to provide the largest share of financing despite the strong role of external assistance and financing. In some other regional initiatives, CEEC/NIS commitments have been less strong, project financing has been weaker, and overall implementation has been less effective (Stratmann).

These initiatives and the EAP institutions have co-operated mainly on project-related issues. The PPC played a role in developing financing for investment projects identified through these regional initiatives. In a few cases, the Task Force and PPC joint meetings have presented key policy lessons from innovative projects developed under regional sea programmes. More could probably be done to share the achievements and lessons of these regional initiatives across donors, the CEEC/NIS, and international organisations active in the region.

4. Evolution of International Assistance and Finance

For many CEEC/NIS, donor country and IFI programmes have played a critical role in supporting domestic environmental protection efforts. Annex I describes trends in the level of donor and IFI assistance and financing for the environment. This section considers the *effectiveness* of aid, as well as emerging assistance and financing priorities.

4.1. *Improving the effectiveness of international assistance and financing*

In the early years of transition, poor communication among donors, IFIs and recipient countries, together with the lack of a common strategy, often hindered the effectiveness of international assistance and financing. Over the course of the transition, many donors, IFIs and recipient countries have worked to improve the effectiveness of co-operation efforts. Many have used the EAP's framework, as well as that of regional sea programmes and other initiatives, to improve overall coherence and effectiveness. Communication among donors, IFIs and recipients has increased through several channels, including fora such as the EAP Task Force and the PPC, as well as the regular "Environment for Europe" Ministerial Conferences.

Since the endorsement of the EAP, many donors and IFIs have increased their attention to the interdependence of institutional strengthening, policy reform and investment support. This has been a crucial step. A recent World Bank review of world-wide aid underlined the importance of policy reform and institutional strengthening for all types of aid programmes (World Bank). In recent years, a number of bilateral donors have increased support for environmental institutions and policies in the CEEC/NIS. Experience over the transition has shown that this support has been most effective when donor programmes sought to establish long-term relationships with recipient countries, and when they responded to requests for assistance (Box 9.5).

CEEC/NIS environmental authorities have gained experience working with donors and IFIs. Many have set up offices to manage external assistance. Efforts to co-ordinate international assistance and financing have often contributed to improving effectiveness, focusing donor and IFI efforts on national priorities, and strengthening recipient "ownership".

Overall, both assistance and financing have been most effective when supporting domestic initiatives. The World Bank's study on global aid noted that the success of policy reform has depended first of all on domestic political and social factors. International co-operation is more effective in supporting ongoing domestic reforms than trying to impose reform (World Bank). In the CEEC/NIS, progress and commitment to reform – economic and democratic reforms as well as those to strengthen environmental institutions and policies – have played a strong role in facilitating support. In general, the countries in the region that have been most successful in implementing reform have also been the most effective in raising and using international assistance and financing. (Strategic donor interests, ethnic and cultural ties and concerns about transboundary issues have also been important factors in these countries' assistance and financing decisions). External support has sometimes helped maintain a place for environmental policy on domestic political agendas which it might not otherwise have had.

Despite progress, donors, IFIs and CEEC/NIS governments can still take important steps to improve the effectiveness of assistance and financing. Donor and IFI activities have frequently influenced recipient country priorities more than they supported them. This has imposed costs on recipient countries, which must often raise national resources to match external financing and must devote their often scarce institutional resources to help manage investment projects and technical assistance. Donor co-ordination and donor/recipient communication have in many cases remained insufficient. As a result, donor and IFI efforts have overlapped in some fields while other key issues in the region have not received adequate

205

Box 9.5.   Effective donor support for institutional strengthening and policy development

In the early stages of transition, many donors provided short-term consultants who used analytical methods to review CEEC/NIS environmental problems and gave policy advice. Often, this form of assistance did not have lasting effects. Some donors supported foreign experts who prepared national policy strategies for countries in the region. These reports were usually high in quality, but they often failed to generate national commitment.

Assistance has been more effective when it responded to recipient requests and facilitated a country-owned process. This occurred in Kazakhstan, where several donors responded to a Kazakh request and provided experts to assist the country's NEAP/SD office (Chapter 3). In Latvia, the Netherlands and the United Kingdom provided consultants who helped the Environment Ministry develop its 1995 Environmental Policy and its 1997 NEAP. The consultants helped Latvian officials plan the process and manage working groups that brought together key interest groups and government agencies. They did not (and were not asked to) assist on substantive issues.

A number of assistance programmes have provided effective long-term support for policy development. The US government, working with the Harvard Institute for International Development (HIID), placed environmental economics and finance advisors in seven CEE countries, as well as Russia and Central Asia. Most of these advisors worked directly in the Ministry of Environment. They stayed for two years or longer and organised national advisory committees, bringing together local experts from government, universities and NGOs to help direct and support their work. The EC PHARE Programme placed long-term advisors in Estonia, Hungary and Lithuania to assist Environment Ministries in policy development. Switzerland has worked with Bulgarian authorities over several years on efforts to strengthen biodiversity protection, both within and outside protected areas. Long-term advisors – and more generally, long-term relationships between bilateral donors and recipient countries – have been able to develop effective responses to CEEC/NIS requests and needs. Long-term programmes have been able to tap in-country experts. In many cases, this has reinforced national ownership of the process and helped strengthen the skills of national experts.

In a few cases, faced with weak environmental institutions, foreign programmes have created new structures for policy development, either within or parallel to existing authorities. While this approach has created effective temporary structures, it can weaken existing environmental institutions when not properly designed and managed. The most effective approach has usually been to build the capacity of domestic institutions, even though this has often been slow and difficult. Technical assistance efforts have generally needed high-level political support to ensure their long-term success. Such support has been difficult to obtain and maintain where there is rapid turnover of high-level officials and political leaders, a common problem in weak environmental authorities.

Sources: EAP Task Force, 1998*a*; 1998*b*.

---

attention. For example, few donors have supported policy integration efforts in the CEEC/NIS. Many donors and IFIs have not integrated their own programmes for assistance and financing in areas with potentially conflicting goals, such as transport and environment.

In strengthening their programmes in the CEEC/NIS, some donors could consider more closely the technical assistance guidelines of OECD's Development Assistance Committee (Box 9.6). However, one ongoing dilemma for donors and IFIs is how to assist countries where domestic political support for stronger environmental protection remains weak. This has been a difficult issue for bilateral donors and IFIs across all sectors and in all parts of the world. Without domestic support for reform, international aid programmes face considerable obstacles to achieving results. In a recent review of foreign aid, the World Bank identified several elements of an approach for such conditions (World Bank, 1998):

- find and support reformers;
- support knowledge creation, including innovative pilot projects and approaches as well as education and training;
- engage civil society, such as NGOs who support innovative reforms and actions; and
- work in a long-term perspective, encouraging reformers and others to develop a vision for change.

Box 9.6.   The DAC guidelines on technical assistance

In 1991, donor countries meeting in OECD's Development Assistance Committee (DAC), endorsed a set of *Principles for New Orientations in Technical Co-operation*. Key elements of these principles include:

- focusing on long-term capacity development;
- emphasising the central role of recipient countries in the planning, design and management of technical co-operation;
- co-ordinating support for sectoral objectives and policies, in particular through a programme rather than a project-by-project approach;
- encouraging recipient "ownership", including responsibility and control, of technical co-operation;
- emphasising the sustainability of institution-building, particularly in areas such as policy analysis;
- recognising private sector needs;
- encouraging greater use of local expertise and existing structures;
- defining objectives in terms of outcomes to be achieved rather than inputs to be provided;
- paying greater attention to costs and to cost-effectiveness.

Subsequent studies and guidelines built on this approach, including the DAC's *Orientations for Donor Assistance to Capacity Development in Environment*. These called for an integrative, cross-sectoral approach, focusing on the process rather than specific products. The *Orientations* recognised that, in the end, donors have only a limited role in the process of capacity development. Actors in the recipient countries are ultimately responsible for determining and implementing effective environmental policies. Donor co-ordination – led by the recipient country – can greatly strengthen the effectiveness of external support for capacity development.

Source: OECD, 1995.

4.2. *New priorities for environmental co-operation*

The process of EU accession will transform the nature of assistance and financing for the 10 CEE candidate countries. The level of assistance and financing should greatly increase: the EU has set up new financing mechanisms, and IFIs plan to support accession-driven projects. The accession process should greatly intensify co-operation among candidate countries, the European Commission, and EU Member States. Although this process will increase attention to environmental issues within candidate countries, it threatens to replace domestically determined environmental priorities with ones driven by accession requirements (Annex III).

The EC, bilateral donors, IFIs and others have pledged to increase their assistance and financing in many areas, including environment, to the Balkan countries.

New mechanisms outlined in the 1997 Kyoto Protocol to the Framework Convention on Climate Change could also provide significant international resources to CEEC/NIS, which could be used to finance projects and policies for reduction of greenhouse gas emissions (Annex IV).

The "Environment for Europe" process: re-focusing on the NIS

The NIS have encountered much greater difficulty in the transition to democratic societies and market-based economies than most CEE countries. Differences in income levels per capita between CEEC and NIS have grown wider as many CEE countries have returned to economic growth. Although many NIS have developed NEAPs and other policy initiatives incorporating the EAP's recommendations, implementation has become even more difficult since the 1998 economic and financial crisis.

207

In this context, the countries participating in the 1998 Aarhus Conference renewed their support for environmental progress in the NIS. In particular, ministers called on donors and IFIs to "re-focus" their efforts on the NIS, which could lead to increased and more effective assistance and financing. Ministers at Aarhus reaffirmed the importance of Europe-wide environmental co-operation to share experience among all countries and to ensure that a new "curtain" does not divide the region.

The Balkan war of 1999 recalls the divisions and strife which have marked much of Europe's history. It is to be hoped that co-operation on environmental issues will continue to contribute to the process of reconstruction and development in the countries concerned and throughout the CEEC/NIS region.

REFERENCES

Baltic 21 secretariat (1998),
   Baltic 21: Agenda 21 for the Baltic Seas Region, Press release, Stockholm, June.

Conclusions of the Conference "Environment for Europe" (1991),
   Dobris Castle, Czech and Slovak Federal Republic, 21-23 June.

Coordination pour l'Europe (1993),
   Luzern: Participation of Environmental Organizations, NGO Statement, mimeograph, Lucerne, Switzerland.

Declaration by the Ministers of Environment of the Region of the United National Economic Commission for Europe (UN/ ECE) (1993),
   Lucerne, Switzerland, 30 April.

Declaration by the Ministers of Environment of the Region of the United National Economic Commission for Europe (UN/ ECE) (1995),
   Sofia, 25 October.

EAP Task Force (1998a),
   Evaluation of Progress in Developing and Implementing National Environmental Action Programmes (NEAPs) *in* CEEC/NIS, OECD, Paris.

EAP Task Force (1998b),
   Supporting National Environmental Action Programmes in Central and Eastern Europe: Best Practices Guide for Donor Involvement – draft report, mimeograph, OECD, Paris.

Helsinki Commission (1997),
   The Baltic Sea Joint Comprehensive Action Programme: Fifth Activity Inventory, Espoo, Finland, August.

McCloskey, C. (1998),
   PEBLDS *explained*, IUCN, Tilburg, Netherlands.

OECD (1995),
   Donor Assistance to Capacity Development in Environment, Paris.

OECD (1999),
   Aid and Other Resource Flows to the Central and Eastern European Countries and the New Independent States of the Former Soviet Union (1990-1996), Paris, January.

Parlement Européen (1993),
   Résolution sur les résultats de la Conférence pan-européene des ministres de l'Environnement, (33-0846/98), Strasbourg.

Prillevitz, F.C. (1998),
   The Pan-European Biological and Landscape Diversity Strategy, in *Innovative Financing Opportunities for European Biodiversity: Towards Implementing the Pan-European Biological and Landscape Diversity Strategy*, GRF Drucker, editor, European Centre for Nature Conservation (ECNC), Tilburg, Netherlands.

Project Preparation Committee (PPC) (1998),
   PPC *Report to the Fourth Ministerial Conference "Environment for Europe" in Aarhus*, EBRD, London.

Regional Environmental Center for Central and Eastern Europe (REC) (1998),
   Report on the Status of Multilateral Environmental Agreements in the European Region, prepared on behalf of the United Nations Environment Programme, presented to the "Environment for Europe" Conference, Aarhus, Denmark, June.

Stratmann, G. (1997),
   Sectoral Coordination of International Assistance to Central and Eastern Europe 1990-1996: The Cases of Environment and Education, Working Paper S002, Universitat Leipzig, Institute of Political Science, Dept. of International Relations, June.

Stritih, J. (1997),
   Destination Rio or Aarhus, in *the* REC Bulletin, Szentendre, Hungary, summer.

United Nations Economic Commission for Europe (UN/ECE) Committee on Environmental Policy (1998),
   Progress Report on the Implementation of the Environmental Programme for Europe, submitted to the "Environment for Europe" Conference, Aarhus, Denmark, June.

World Bank (1998),
   Assessing Aid: What Works, What Doesn't, and Why, Oxford University Press, Oxford.

World Resources Institute (WRI) (1992),
   World Resources Report 1992-1993, Washington, DC.

209|

Annex I

INTERNATIONAL ASSISTANCE AND FINANCING

As part of the preparation for 1998 Aarhus Conference, the EAP Task Force secretariat surveyed donor countries and IFIs on their level of assistance and financing for the environment in CEEC/NIS. This section outlines the main results presented at Aarhus.[1]

Level of assistance and financing

Official *assistance* refers to grants and concessional or "soft" loans (as well as other types of concessional support) from governments and international organisations, including IFIs; official *financing* refers to loans, with interest rates close to those in international capital markets.[2] IFIs, which provide the main share of official financing for environmental projects in the region, usually ask recipient governments to provide sovereign guarantees that loans will be repaid. Thus, unlike assistance, official financing does not result in a net inflow of resources. (Official assistance and financing are distinguished from private financial flows, such as foreign direct investment, whose trends and environmental linkages are reviewed in Chapter 6).

Total official assistance – mainly grants – to CEEC/NIS across all fields fell to US$5.5 billion (ECU 4.9 billion) in 1997 from a peak of US$9.7 billion (ECU 7.4 billion) in 1995. The bulk of this assistance has come from donor country grants; the EC has been a major source, providing about US$1.5 billion (ECU 1.2 billion) per year. Over this period, official financing from IFIs has remained about US$7 billion per year (ECU 6 billion); the IMF has provided about one-half of these loans.[3] Assistance and financing for the environment has represented a significant portion – probably over 10% – of this total.[4]

Donor countries and the EC

Between 1994 and 1996, the level of environmental assistance and financing from both donor countries and the EC decreased from nearly ECU 500 million (US$600 million) to about ECU 400 million (US$450 million) (Table I.1). However, the 1994 and 1995 totals include large loans and export credits from Japan. In contrast, the bulk of donor commitments have been grants; it appears that these remained fairly constant – just below ECU 400 million. (Total OECD country assistance to developing and transition countries across all areas fell from an average of 0.30% of GDP in 1994 to 0.22% in 1997.) The European Commission was the largest single donor, in particular through its PHARE Programme for CEE countries (the EC's TACIS Programme for the NIS only started to support environmental projects in 1995). In 1996, total commitments from European Union donors – including the EC and EU countries – reached about two-thirds of donor contributions. Moreover, EU commitments rose steadily between 1994 and 1997. (Table I.1 does not include some forms of donor country assistance, such as the US government's debt-for-environment swap with Poland, which started in 1992. Not all donors provided information on their 1997 commitments.)

International financial institutions

IFI financing for environmental projects in the region varied considerably, from about ECU 500 million (US$600 million) to ECU 300 million (US$350 million). In particular, IFI financing for the NIS has fluctuated (most IFI financing has gone to large projects and thus can vary greatly from year to year) while IFI financing for environmental projects in CEE countries has decreased steadily (Figure 6.4). These trends refer specifically to environmental projects. EBRD reported that the environmental components of its non-environmental projects exceeded its total environmental loans (these components include, for example, pollution abatement and control investments at new plants financed by EBRD). In addition, EBRD and the World Bank financed several large projects for flood prevention and reconstruction after flood damage in CEE countries. These projects can have important environmental benefits, including reforestation activities (Table I.2). A large share of IFI environmental projects, as well as some energy efficiency projects, have gone through the PPC.

211

Table I.1. **Trends in donor commitments for environmental assistance and financing**

Million ECU

Bilateral donors	Type[a]	1994	1995	1996	1997[b]	Total
Japan[c]	G/L/O	131	93	9	1	**235**
Norway	G	6	11	11	9	**37**
Switzerland	..	19	17	28	10	**75**
United States	G	70	41	19	..	**131**
Austria	..	14	3	5	..	**23**
Denmark[d]	G	33	54	42	68	**197**
Finland	G	8	10	15	14	**46**
France	G/S	7	2	3	9	**21**
Germany	..	18	28	47	26	**120**
Netherlands	G	16	11	17	27	**71**
Sweden[e]	G	27	..	18	13	**59**
United Kingdom[f]	G	4	4	3	3	**14**
Eur. Commission						
PHARE[g]	G	139	142	134	166	**581**
TACIS	G	..	12	24	29	**65**
LIFE	G	2	1	1	1	**4**
Total		**494**	**431**	**375**	**377**	**1 677**

.. Not available.
a) G-grants; L-loans; O-export credits and other mechanisms; S-soft loans.
b) Some responses are not complete for 1997.
c) 1994: 123 mECU loans; 1995: 20.3 mECU export credits.
d) 1995 data include grant equivalent of soft loans. Data do not include the Danish environmental investment facility, created in 1995. Through 1996, the facility provided 3.7 mECU in equity and 6.6 mECU in loans.
e) Preliminary data for the Swedish EPA and Swedish International Development Agency only. Includes some energy projects. Due to change in fiscal year, part of 1995 data are included in 1996; not included in subsequent figures and tables.
f) Data include only technical assistance grants through the UK Environmental Know How Fund.
g) Preliminary estimates.
Source: OECD, based on IFI data.

Table I.2. **Trends in IFI commitments for environmental assistance and financing**

Million ECU

International financial institutions	Type[a]	1994	1995	1996	1997[b]	Total
Asian Development Bank[c]	G	0.0	0.4	0.0	1.1	**1.5**
EBRD	L/G					
Environmental projects		46	62.0	96.2	93.9	**298**
Environmental components of non-environmental projects[d]		..	157.1	200.6	218.7	**576**
Energy efficiency projects			64.1	71.0	90.0	**225**
EIB[e]	L	95	200	15	0	**310**
NEFCO	E/G/L	19	6	11	13	**49**
GEF	G	6	28	25	10	**69**
NIB	L	41		9	118	**169**
World Bank[f]	L					
Environmental projects		155	204	89	66	**514**
Projects with significant environmental benefits		..	..	288	717	**1 005**
Non-env. projects with environmental components[g]		851	740	99	223	**1 913**

.. Not available.
a) G-grants; L-loans; E-equity.
b) Some responses for 1997 are incomplete.
c) Technical assistance only.
d) Values for environmental components only, as calculated by EBRD. 1994 data not available.
e) In addition to the loans reported, EIB signed 555 mECU of projects with significant environmental benefits in 1997, including 425 mECU for flood damage reconstruction. Data on such projects in previous years are not available.
f) Loans to Turkmenistan not included.
g) Total value of loans, not just the environmental components.
Source: OECD, based on IFI data.

Recipient countries

Most assistance and financing, both in absolute terms and on a per capita basis, has gone to CEE countries: approximately half of total donor commitments, and an even greater share of total IFI loans, even though the latter decreased steadily over the period (Figure 6.4). These differences are striking on a per capita basis, where CEE countries as a group received almost eight times the level of assistance and financing as the NIS (Table I.3). Among recipient countries, Poland has received the greatest assistance and financing, over ECU 500 million (US$600 million) or about 17% of total commitments. Four other countries – the Czech Republic, Hungary, Romania and Russia – received over ECU 200 million (over US$240 million) in commitments; these four, together with Poland, received about half all of technical co-operation assistance and investment financing in the region. On a per capita basis, however, the three Baltic States ranked among the top four countries in the region in terms of assistance commitments.

Table I.3. **Donor commitments of environmental assistance and financing to CEEC and NIS, 1994 to 1997**

Million ECU

Partner country	Institutional and policy development	Investment preparation	Investments	Total[a]	Total per capita (ECU)
Albania	20.7	0.0	12.9	48.5	14.3
Bosnia and Herzegovina	0.3	0.9	32.2	33.5	9.3
Bulgaria	20.2	2.4	90.1	135.7	15.9
Croatia	0.9	1.2	88.8	90.9	20.2
Czech Republic	39.8	5.0	313.5	398.2	38.5
Estonia	7.5	7.1	70.7	129.3	86.8
Hungary	16.1	0.5	172.9	209.4	20.4
Latvia	9.5	7.0	96.5	124.4	48.8
Lithuania	15.7	10.7	86.9	139.0	37.1
Macedonia, FYR	1.3	0.0	5.4	10.3	4.8
Poland	34.6	18.1	259.8	524.8	13.6
Romania	12.4	25.1	172.5	253.4	11.1
Slovakia	9.6	2.2	20.1	33.7	6.2
Slovenia	19.1	0.1	14.2	37.9	19.6
Region-wide – CEE	12.0	15.8	23.0	105.8	
Total CEEC	219.7	96.0	1 459.5	**2 274.6**	19.1
Armenia	0.1	0.3	0.0	0.4	0.1
Azerbaijan	0.4	0.0	20.0	20.4	2.7
Belarus	3.1	3.2	1.0	7.3	0.7
Georgia	42.0	0.0	0.0	42.0	7.7
Kazakhstan	14.5	1.1	0.0	15.6	0.9
Kyrgyz Republic	3.0	0.0	0.0	3.0	0.7
Moldova	4.8	1.3	1.4	7.5	1.7
Russia	102.8	16.2	94.6	373.4	2.5
Ukraine	22.2	11.4	22.8	56.4	1.1
Uzbekistan	11.6	8.4	67.5	87.4	3.8
Region-wide – NIS	36.5	0.0	0.0	36.5	
Total NIS	240.0	41.9	207.4	**649.9**	2.4
Region CEE + NIS	11.4	2.2	0.0	13.5	
Total	471.2	139.8	1 666.9	**3 029.2**	7.7

a) Totals are larger than the sum of technical assistance and investments, as some donors did not classify commitments.
Source: OECD, based on donor and IFI data.

The impact of external assistance and financing has varied greatly across the region. For many countries, the total level of international flows has remained small compared to national expenditures on environmental investment. This has been true for two of the largest recipients, Poland and Russia, where international assistance and financing were less than 10% of domestic expenditures. In a number of cases, however, donors and IFIs have supported innovative projects with a catalytic role in terms of institutional strengthening, policy development and environmental investment. In contrast, external flows have financed half or more of the environmental investments in some lower-income countries; in Georgia, these have been practically the only source (Chapter 6).

NOTES

1. The results presented here only cover donors and international organisations that responded to the survey.

2. About the half CEEC/NIS are on the "DAC list" of developing countries. These include: in CEE, Albania,* Bosnia and Herzegovina,* Croatia, FYR Macedonia,* and Slovenia; and the NIS, Armenia,* Azerbaijan,* Georgia,* Kazakhstan, Kyrgyz Republic,* Moldova,* Tajikistan,* Turkmenistan and Uzbekistan. Those marked by an asterisk are lower-income countries eligible to receive concessional loans from the International Development Association, a wing of the World Bank. (Usually, concessional loans are defined as those with at least a 25% grant component.) In addition, a few donor countries have provided low-interest or "soft" loans.

3. ECU/dollar equivalents have been calculated on the basis of average yearly exchange rates, which have varied over the period considered (1993 to 1998).

4. The exact share of assistance and financing for environmental purposes cannot be determined, as data on total flows refer to actual disbursements while data on environmental assistance and financing refer to commitments, which are often disbursed in later years.

Annex II

COMPARING HEALTH IMPACTS OF AIR POLLUTION
AND DRINKING WATER PROBLEMS

These estimates of the health impacts of air pollution and drinking water problems are based on World Bank research. This annex presents an overview of the results of that research.[1]

1. Air Pollution

Significant reductions in air pollution have been achieved in many transition economies, especially with respect to particulates and sulphur dioxide (SO_2). There is evidence that reductions in total emissions have been translated into real improvements in levels of exposure, at least in the CEE countries.[2]

Drawing upon a sample of CEEC/NIS cities, and using dose-response relationships established through a number of studies and economic valuation techniques, the following analysis models the impacts and costs of changes in exposure to key air pollutants on mortality and morbidity in the exposed population. There are, of course, other non-health costs associated with air pollution that are not taken into account in this analysis. However, most studies that have attempted to quantify the full range of social costs of air pollution have concluded that the health costs of excess mortality and illness account for more than 80% of the total.

The following analysis concerns 57 CEE and NIS cities for which comparable data for 1990 and 1995 were available. It examines reductions in mortality and illness that would be achieved by reducing annual average levels of exposure to not more than 50 ug/m^3 of particulate matter 10 microns or less in aerodynamic diameter (PM_{10}). This represents a realistic target (it is in the middle of the range recommended in the pre-1997 WHO guidelines, and is similar to pre-1997 standards for the United States and the European Union). Generally speaking, the two largest components of overall health damage are premature mortality and excess cases of chronic bronchitis, primarily resulting from exposure to particulates.

With the 50 µg/m^3 target as a basis, it was possible to estimate excess mortality (the number of premature deaths) attributable to exposure to key air pollutants in the 57 sample cities (which have a combined population of 61 million). As Figure II.1 shows, the estimated number of excess deaths in the 57 cities was 32 000 in 1990 and increased to 40 000 in 1995. There was a large difference between CEE and NIS cities. In the CEE cities (with a combined population of 15 million) the number of estimated excess deaths fell sharply (from 5 700 in 1990 to 3 700 in 1995). By contrast, the NIS cities (with a combined population of 46 million) experienced an increase (from 26 000 in 1990 to 36 000 in 1995).

The factors underlying these differences are complex. They include changes in the levels of ambient concentrations, the size of populations exposed, and the overall health status of the population. For example, the average mortality rate for NIS countries has increased from 11 per 1 000 population in 1990 to 14 per 1 000 in 1995). Epidemiological evidence suggests that even with constant or improving levels of ambient air quality there will be higher numbers of excess deaths because of the deteriorating health of NIS populations.[3] Most of the increase in mortality, from other causes as well as from air pollution, is concentrated among males. (There has also been a small increase in the average mortality rate in CEE countries, from 11 to 12 per 1 000 population, but it was not sufficient to offset the gains from decreased exposure to particulates.)

Figure II.2 shows the number of excess new cases of chronic bronchitis, one of the most serious morbidity impacts associated with exposure to particulates. (These figures are not affected by the increase in mortality rates and thus reflect changes in average levels of exposure.) The total number of excess new cases was estimated as constant (at about 110 000 per year), but differences between the various country groups were significant: in the CEE countries, the estimated number of new cases fell by nearly one-half, while the NIS experienced a small increase.

Using economic valuation techniques,[4] it is possible to estimate the monetary cost of the damage to health caused by air pollution. The results of this analysis are shown in Figure II.3. For the 57 cities as a group, the estimated cost per year increased from US$5.3 billion in 1990 to US$6.5 billion in 1995. These costs represented nearly 5% of total urban income for these cities in 1995. As would be expected from the earlier results, the total estimated cost for the CEE cities fell from US$1.2 billion (29% of urban income) in 1990 to US$0.7 billion (1.6% of urban income) in 1995. For the NIS cities, the cost burden imposed by air pollution is much heavier and has increased by 40%, from US$4 billion (4.6% of urban income) in 1990 to US$5.7 billion (6.6% of urban income) in 1995.

Figure II.1. **Excess mortality due to air pollution, 1990 and 1995**

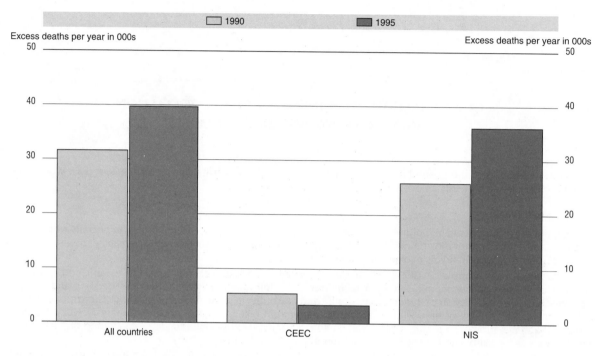

Source: World Bank estimates using data for 57 cities with comparable data for 1990 and 1995.

Figure II.2. **Excess new cases of chronic bronchitis due to air pollution, 1990 and 1995**

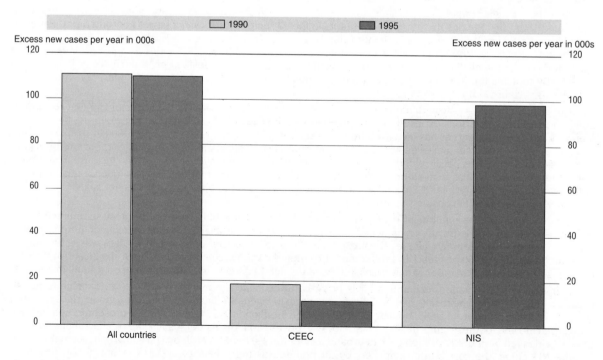

Source: World Bank estimates using data for 57 cities with comparable data for 1990 and 1995.

Figure II.3. **Total costs of air pollution, 1990 and 1995**

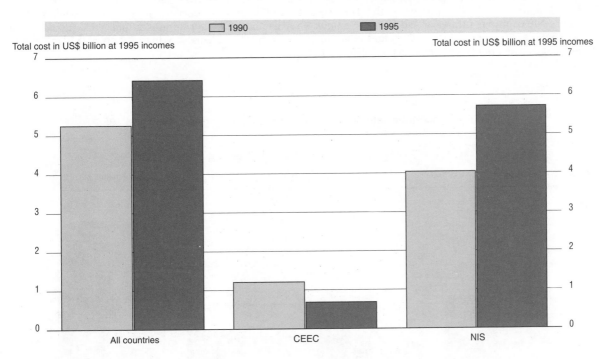

Source: World Bank estimates using data for 57 cities with comparable data for 1990 and 1995.

2. Water Pollution

The earlier analysis of trends in water quality and discharges of water pollutants in selected "hot spots" showed that both industrial discharges and agricultural runoff have declined as a consequence of changes in economic activity and in the use of production inputs. However, the effects of water pollution *per se* on the health of the population may be relatively small. Individuals or small communities may suffer severe problems as a result of exposure to high levels of nitrates, heavy metals and toxic chemicals in the water supply or through the food chain. But, in most countries, such problems do not represent a large threat to the health of the general population so long as people have access to piped supplies of drinking water. It is relatively easy to ensure that piped water supplies are protected from hazardous pollutants or are treated to remove microbiological and other contaminants.

The key questions are whether households have piped supplies of water in their dwellings, and whether water quality is compromised by lack of proper treatment at the treatment plant or by contamination resulting from deterioration of the distribution network. In most CEE countries and NIS, more than 90% of urban households have access to piped water supplies,[5] so the access problem largely concerns rural households.

The relative importance of access to adequate sanitation depends upon how households obtain their water and the effectiveness of the public health system. Rural or urban households that rely upon surface water or shallow wells for drinking water are most severely affected by cross-contamination due to poor or no sanitation. Even septic tanks may cause high levels of nitrates in water drawn from nearby wells if improperly built or maintained. More generally, poor management of sewage may result in people being exposed to a range of infectious diseases either via contamination of drinking water supplies, where distribution networks are in poor condition, or via recreational activities (such as boating and swimming) that bring them into contact with contaminated water. There have been notable instances of such problems in many NIS countries since 1990.

Exposure to contaminated water is an intermittent problem. The actual burden of ill-health that it causes depends greatly on the response of the public health system. Prompt and effective action to prevent exposure and transmission, and to treat those affected, can minimise the cost of such incidents. Most CEE countries and NIS had relatively effective mechanisms, based on networks of institutes of public health and epidemiology, for dealing with outbreaks of infectious diseases. The break-up of the former Soviet Union has caused particular problems in this sphere for some NIS countries, as so much of the expertise in this field was concentrated in Moscow.

217

A key indicator of the burden of illness resulting from water-related problems is the level of infant mortality.[6] As Figure II.4 shows, average infant mortality rates for all CEE countries and NIS declined slightly between 1990 and 1995, from 22 to 21 per 1 000 live births. The average for CEE countries declined from 18 to 16, while that for southern NIS countries (Armenia, Azerbaijan, Georgia, Kazakhstan, the Kyrgyz Republic, Tajikistan, Turkmenistan and Uzbekistan) fell from 32 to 31. Only for the group of northern NIS (Belarus, Moldova, Russia and Ukraine) was there an increase, from 16 to 17 deaths per 1 000 live births.

Figure II.4. **Infant mortality rates in various country groups, 1990 and 1995**

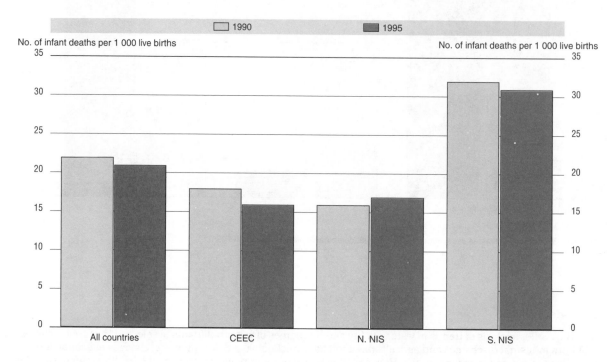

Source: World Bank estimates.

Thus there is no evidence of any clear increase in water-related health problems outside the northern NIS country group. Within that group, the deterioration occurred primarily in Moldova and Ukraine. The statistics for Moldova are difficult to interpret because of internal divisions, but the worsening in Ukraine's infant mortality rate, from 13 in 1990 to 15 in 1995, suggests a significant problem. Infant mortality rates have also worsened in Azerbaijan (from 23 to 25) and Tajikistan (from 40 to 42). In those countries, capacity to deal with public health problems has been seriously affected by war and the resulting movements of population. Infant mortality rates deteriorated in several other countries (*e.g.* Kazakhstan, Russia and Uzbekistan) immediately after the break-up of the former Soviet Union, but by 1995 they were no worse than in 1990 or had even improved.

Improved access to water and sanitation can have a significant impact on infant mortality rates, especially where the rates are relatively high. Because it is unrealistic, at least in the medium term, to expect that countries with large rural populations can reach 100% access to piped water supplies or sewer networks, it is necessary to set achievable targets. The targets used here are: *a*) at least 95% of the population with access to piped water supplies; and *b*) all urban households with access to sewer connections.[7]

Figure II.5 shows the reductions in infant mortality that would be expected given achievement of the water supply target alone, and the water and sanitation targets together. Ensuring that 95% of the population in the southern NIS has access to piped water supplies would reduce the average rate of infant mortality by over 20%, from 31 per 1 000 live births to 24 (this represents an estimated reduction of over 11 600 in the annual toll of infant mortality in this group of countries). The effect is much smaller in the CEE countries as a whole because the proportion of the

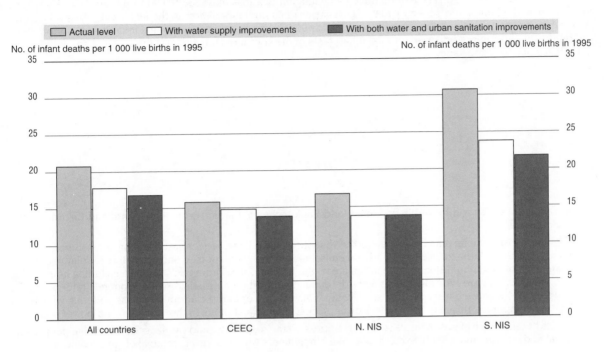

Figure II.5. **Improving water and sanitation:
estimated benefits, in terms of infant deaths avoided**

Source: World Bank estimates using expected values from cross-section regression analysis.

population which already has access to piped water exceeds 90% (the exception is Albania, which, with little more than 60% access to piped water, is very similar to the southern NIS). Just over 70% of the population in the northern NIS has access to piped water supplies, but reaching 95% coverage would only decrease the average infant mortality rate from 17 to 14 (reducing infant deaths by about 5 400 per year). The much smaller change reflects the current success of these countries in achieving relatively low levels of infant mortality through public health and other measures even though the water and sanitation infrastructure is in a poor state, especially in rural areas.

The additional effect on infant mortality of ensuring 100% access to sewer connections for urban populations is much smaller than the impact of access to piped water. Even in the southern NIS, where the existing average level of access to sewer connections is less than 35% and the urban population is 50% of the total, reaching both water supply and sanitation targets would bring average infant mortality down to 22 per 1 000 live births from the level of 24 for the water supply target alone.

In addition to increased infant mortality, children and adults are affected to a greater or lesser extent by diarrheal illnesses or other water-related parasitic and infectious diseases. Health analysts have developed the concept of a disability-adjusted life year (DALY) to calculate the overall burden caused by diseases and injuries of varying duration and severity (Murray and Lopez, 1996).[8] Based on the findings of an internationally established ratio of DALYs lost due to water-related mortality and illnesses, it is estimated that the southern and northern NIS lose 1.1 million and 0.45 million DALYs each year, respectively, as a result of limited access to piped water alone. The total number of DALYs lost each year as a result of water-related illnesses over the whole region would fall by 1.6 million if the target of 95% access to piped water was achieved. This figure would increase to 1.8 million per year if both the water and urban sanitation targets were met.

Estimates for individual countries, while subject to significant uncertainty, reinforce the importance of water problems, particularly in Central Asia. Among CEE countries, the highest water-associated health risks are found in Albania, with levels close to those seen in southern NIS. Among these NIS, the most severe water problems are found in Tajikistan, Turkmenistan and Uzbekistan (the estimated costs exceed 20 DALYs per 1 000 population per year).[9] These results suggest that, to achieve the highest returns in terms of improving human welfare, priority should be given to improving access to water and urban sanitation in these countries, particularly in rural areas, which suffer most from lack of access to adequate piped water supplies.

219|

Rural populations have the lowest levels of access to piped water and experience a greater incidence of mortality and sickness from water-related diseases. The rural population is about 35 million in the southern NIS and 60 million in the northern NIS. Thus the above estimates imply a loss of about 31 DALYs per year per 1 000 rural inhabitants in the former and about 7 DALYs per year per 1 000 rural inhabitants in the latter. The situation is much better than in East Asia, where the average loss is nearly 90 DALYs per year per 1 000 rural inhabitants. Nonetheless, the burden of water-related disease for rural inhabitants of the southern NIS implies a reduction of about two years in their average life expectancy.

NOTES

1. A complete version will be published in a World Bank technical paper, "Economic Reform and Environmental Performance".

2. The link is less obvious than it may seem. The reductions have been concentrated among large sources (power plants and heavy industrial activities) whose emissions are widely dispersed and account for a relatively minor share of ambient air pollution in large urban areas. But it is emissions from small sources, including households and vehicles, that are typically the primary determinants of urban air quality. While economic reform may be expected to influence emissions from small sources via fuel prices and the adoption of less polluting vehicles or heating equipment, this may be a much slower process than adjustments in the industrial and power sectors.

3. This is because such exposure increases overall stress on the respiratory and cardiac systems, so that people who are already sick are more likely to die as a result of their illness while others are more likely to become sick.

4. The analysis was based on World Bank estimates of the willingness to pay to reduce the risks of premature mortality, chronic bronchitis, and other illnesses or symptoms provoked by exposure to particulates and other pollutants.

5. The main exceptions are cities such as Baku and Dushanbe, where water supply infrastructure has been overwhelmed by large influxes of people displaced by or fleeing from war.

6. Reported rates of infant mortality show substantial differences. In particular, UN estimates of infant mortality for the Central Asian countries are much higher than those used here. For consistency over time, the figures used in this analysis are World Bank estimates, which correspond in most cases to national estimates.

7. Access to urban sanitation has been shown to have a significant impact on infant mortality, whereas the influence of rural sanitation is slight or zero.

8. See Chapter 2 for a description of DALYs.

9. Considering that these estimates refer to both urban and rural populations, rural water problems in these countries could come close to those measured in East Asia, where the average loss is nearly 90 DALYs per year for rural inhabitants.

Annex III

THE CHALLENGE OF EU ACCESSION

From the outset of the transition, most CEE countries identified membership in the European Union – and integration into EU markets – as being among their central political and economic goals. In 1993, the members of the European Union agreed in principle to the accession of 10 CEE countries once certain criteria had been met, including the establishment of democracy and market economies, the development of national capacities to undertake the responsibilities of membership, and the EU's capacity to absorb new members (Mayhew).

The criteria for the candidate countries can be divided into political and economic requirements and the adoption of the EU's *"acquis"* of common legislation. The political criteria were stated at the EU's 1993 Copenhagen summit, which began the accession process: "membership requires that the candidate country has achieved stability of institutions guaranteeing democracy, the rule of law, human rights, and the respect for and protection of minorities." The Copenhagen summit also defined economic requirements, in particular the existence of a market economy and the capacity to withstand competitive pressure and market forces within the EU. The other obligations include adherence to the EU's aims of political, economic and monetary union; adoption of the *"acquis"*; and development of administrative and judicial capacities to apply the *"acquis"* (EC, 1998c).

In early 1998, EU members designated five CEE countries – the Czech Republic, Estonia, Hungary, Poland and Slovenia – to be in the first tier for accession, together with Cyprus. The EU started formal negotiations with these countries. It designated five other countries – Bulgaria, Latvia, Lithuania, Romania and Slovakia – for the second tier; for these countries, negotiations are to start at a later stage. All ten, however, have begun the process of "approximation" with EU requirements, including adoption of the EU's environmental legislation

1. Adopting the EU's Environmental Legislation

By the time of the June 1998 Aarhus "Environment for Europe" Conference, "approximation" with the EU's legislation had become the driving force for environmental policy in the 10 CEE candidate countries, and it will probably remain so for the next decade or two. All 10 accession countries must adopt the EU's environmental legislation, a three-step process: the *transposition* (full incorporation) of the EU's directives into national legislation – a difficult task in itself, as the EU has over 300 EU environmental directives and regulations covering a wide range of issues (Box III.1); the *implementation* of this legislation; and its *enforcement* (EC, 1998a). Candidate countries will need to strengthen their institutions, improve policy implementation, and increase their environmental spending to undertake these tasks. Full implementation and enforcement could take more than a decade or two.

Many CEE environmental authorities have already faced difficulties starting the "transposition" of EU environmental legislation, which extends to thousands of pages. One obstacle has been a lack of environmental lawyers. Environmental authorities will also need to strengthen enforcement capacities: a number of directives, such as the recent one on Integration Pollution Prevention and Control (IPPC), will require inspectorates to develop and put in place new enforcement approaches. Local and regional governments, which will have to play a major role in implementing directives on waste water treatment and other issues, will also need to strengthen their environmental capacities (EC, 1998a).

Approximation will create pressures on countries to significantly change their approaches to environmental policy. For example, EU legislation at present makes little use of economic instruments, although the EU's Fifth Environmental Action Programme has called for greater application of these and other "flexible" mechanisms. There is a danger that candidate countries may abandon their extensive use of pollution charges, rather than adapting them to EU legislation and improving their effectiveness (Chapter 5).

A number of EU directives will entail high investment costs. For example, an estimate by the World Bank indicated that Poland will have to spend at least US$22 billion (ECU 19 billion) to meet the EU's requirements for urban waste water treatment on the Odra River alone (Eliste and Söderström). A survey of earlier studies on the costs of approximation suggested that total costs (including discounted operations and maintenance costs) could reach about ECU 120 billion (US$140 billion) – over ECU 1 000 (US$1 100) per person. In contrast, annual spending on environmental investment was about ECU 50 (US$55) per person in Poland and Slovenia. The EC has reoriented its PHARE Programme to support the accession process and has also created new financial facilities to help assist and

221

Box III.1.   Key areas of EU environmental legislation

The EU's environmental legislation includes over 200 directives in nine key areas:

- *cross-cutting issues*, such as environmental impact assessment procedures and environmental information requirements;
- *air quality;*
- *waste management;*
- *water quality;*
- *nature and biodiversity protection;*
- *industrial pollution control and risk management;*
- *chemicals and genetically modified organisms;*
- *noise;*
- *nuclear safety.*

---

finance environmental infrastructure projects related to accession. The European Investment Bank, an EU institution, will provide financing to support accession projects. Nonetheless, the EC has emphasised that the candidate countries themselves will have to provide the bulk of financial resources needed to meet accession requirements (Chapter 6).

2.   Pollution Management: the Challenge of EU Approximation

A number of EU environmental directives use "command-and-control" approaches such as uniform emissions standards and technology-based approaches. The EAP warned that these approaches should be introduced gradually, with sufficient lead times for existing plants to reach compliance, so that plants could invest more cost-effectively in new, less polluting production methods rather than installing expensive end-of-pipe controls.

Early in the transition, several CEE countries introduced uniform air pollution emissions standards for power plants and several other categories of large polluters, based on the uniform standards in the EU's 1988 Directive on Air Pollution from Large Combustion Plants (88/609/EEC). The Czech Republic took the most stringent approach, going beyond EU obligations to require that all *existing* power plants meet strict new standards by the end of 1998 (the original EU Directive only required stringent standards for new plants). Many Czech power plants are fueled with highly polluting brown coal and lignite. Although a few have shut down, many have met the new standards by installing expensive pollution control equipment. While this has drastically reduced Czech air pollution emissions, the cost of compliance has been high: in 1995 alone, over 0.6% of GDP was spent on desulphurisation equipment for coal and lignite-fired power plants (OECD,1999). In the process of EU accession, CEE countries will need to further revise their approach to emissions requirements, in particular regarding the introduction of technology standards (Chapter 5).

Other EU environmental directives specify "command-and-control" mechanisms for pollution. For example, the directive on urban waste water sets standards for waste water discharges. In addition, the 1997 Directive on Integrated Pollution Prevention and Control calls for best available technology standards in industrial permits. Many OECD countries use technology standards, while CEE countries have not had any experience with them. Governments have suffered from various limitations – including poor institutional capacity, accountability and transparency – in their negotiations with polluters. Environmental inspectorates will need to develop appropriate guidelines, as well as staff capacities, to implement technology standards.

At present, EU legislation makes little use of economic instruments. However, in its Fifth Environmental Action Programme (for 1992 to 2000) and other policy documents the EU has called for greater flexibility in environmental management, including greater use of economic instruments. The European Commission has recommended that economic instruments and other mechanisms supplement the "command-and-control" approach of current EU directives (OECD, 1997). In a few EU countries, these have already played an important role: France, Germany and the Netherlands have used charges on waste water; Sweden has used a charge on NO_x emissions; Sweden and Norway have set charges on the sulphur content of combustion fuels. Thus, EU statements as well as the practice of some of its Member States suggest that CEE candidate countries can adapt their current economic instruments, including their pollution charge systems, to EU legislation. Economic instruments could help candidate countries reduce the high costs of meeting the requirements of EU environmental directives. Adapting current mechanisms to these directives will require careful analysis and preparation, however. In addition, candidate countries will probably need to improve the effectiveness of their current instruments.

3. Developing National Strategies

The EU has requested each accession country to develop a "National Programme for the Adoption of the Acquis", setting forth its strategy for approximation across all areas, including environment. Although these strategies must have the same end point – the full adoption of EU legislation – choices regarding the approach and sequence of legislative and institutional actions and investments could have a major impact on domestic costs and benefits in the environment sector in particular (Anderson and Peszko). This is the case in areas such as waste water treatment investments, where it is likely that countries will have to programme their efforts over at least a decade and likely longer. For example, the World Bank study of Poland's Odra River indicated that a flexible interpretation of EU legislation could reduce costs by as much as 40%, while ensuring that water quality fully met EU requirements (Eliste and Söderström). CEE experience in implementing the EAP, including the development of NEAPs, would provide a basis for developing cost-effective environmental accession strategies (even though EU accession presents a far different challenge than EAP implementation – Box III.2).

Box III.2. The EAP recommendations and EU legislation

For the 10 candidate countries, EU approximation will present a very different task from that of implementing the EAP. Most obviously, these countries must adopt the EU's extensive body of environmental legislation while the EAP presented only a set of broad recommendations for the development of national policies and laws. Thus approximation will present a much more difficult task, but one with less opportunity to address specific national priorities and conditions. The European Commission will play a strong central role in the accession process. The EAP process has had an informal character as well as a multilateral rather than a centralised one.

Some EAP environmental policy recommendations diverge from EU practice, in part because the EAP was based on best practices in different countries and regions, while the extensive body of EU legislation has evolved over many years of compromise among EU countries and interest groups. For example, few EU environmental directives promote cost-effectiveness or risk analysis approaches. Nonetheless, the EU's environmental policy approach is under continual development, fuelled in part by regular policy programmes. Its Fifth Environmental Action Programme (for 1992 to 2000) encouraged the use of more flexible policy approaches. This Programme, entitled "Towards Sustainability", also placed strong emphasis on the integration of environmental considerations into sectoral policies. The EU's 1998 Cardiff summit stressed the importance of better integration of environmental and sectoral policies. For CEE countries, integration can be an important means of reducing the costs of compliance with EU requirements.

---

4. Initial Progress of Candidate Countries

In late 1998, the EC published its first progress report, evaluating the first year of candidate country approximation efforts. The EC concluded that the performance of the 10 candidate countries was "mixed" in regard to environmental accession. In its summary of country progress, the report stated that:

- "Hungary's rhythm of approximation has slowed but attention has been focused on necessary preparation of implementation and enforcement structures."

- "Estonia, Latvia and Lithuania have made important progress in transposition but without a commensurate effort as concerns the preparation and strengthening of related implementation structures and investment."

- "The Czech Republic and Slovenia have developed detailed approximation programmes and strategies but have not yet put them into practice."

- "Romania, Poland and Slovakia have made little progress in the environmental field."

(EC, 1998c).

The EC also presented detailed country-by-country assessments. Its report on Bulgaria illustrates the types of problems found in accession countries:

"Further efforts are needed to develop framework legislation, specifically in the water and waste sector. There are ambitious plans for transposition, and their implementation will suffer from the serious lack of staff within the Ministry of Enviornment and Waters. Full implementation will require a more realistic time frame than foreseen by Bulgaria" (EC, 1998b).

223

Overall, the EC's first progress report indicates that most CEE candidate countries need to substantially increase their efforts in order to satisfy the environmental requirements associated with accession.

5. The Accession Process and Policy Integration

The accession process raises a number of questions concerning the integration of environmental policies with economic and sectoral ones. While the EC has emphasised that candidate countries will need to increase cross-ministerial co-operation in several areas, such as chemicals management, accession could bring new environmental pressures. For example, the accession process is likely to accelerate the integration of CEE and EU economies, increasing trade between them. While this trend would bring economic benefits, it would also increase freight traffic on CEE roads unless the EU and candidate countries worked together to identify transport alternatives, such as improving rail freight service.

Candidate countries have an opportunity to address links between environmental and sectoral policies as they develop and revise their National Programmes, identifying "win-win" opportunities as well as trade-offs that need to be made. Analysis of this sort, possibly as part of EC assistance and financing programmes, could help promote the implementation of more coherent and effective accession strategies.

REFERENCES

Anderson, G. and G. Peszko (1997),
Methodological and Empirical Issues, background paper for the EC/OECD Workshop on Assessing the Costs of CEE Approximation with EU Environment Directives, Paris, April.

Eliste, P. and S. Söderström (1998),
Europe and Central Asia Region, in Environment Matters at the World Bank, World Bank.

Environment Policy Europe (EPE) and EDC Ltd. (1997),
Compliance Costing for Approximation of EU Environmental Legislation in the CEEC, final report to DG XI, May. European Commission (EC) (1997), Guide to the Approximation of European Union Environmental Legislation, August.

European Commission (EC) (1998a),
Accession Strategies for Environment: Meeting the Challenge of Enlargement with the Candidate Countries in Central and Eastern Europe, Communication from the Commission.

European Commission (EC) (1998b),
Regular Report from the Commission on Bulgaria's Progress Towards Accession, [http://europa.eu.int/comm/dg1a/enlarge/].

European Commission (EC) (1998c),
Reports on Progress Towards Accession by Each of the Candidate Countries: Composite Paper, [http://europa.eu.int/comm/dg1a/enlarge/].

Mayhew, A. (1998),
Preparation of EU and CEEC Institutions for the Accession Negotiations, in Preparing Public Administrations for the European Administrative Space, SIGMA Papers No. 23, OECD, Paris.

OECD (1997),
Reforming Environmental Regulation in OECD countries, Paris.

OECD (1999),
Environmental Performance Reviews: Czech Republic, Paris.

Annex IV

CLIMATE CHANGE COMMITMENTS AND THE KYOTO PROTOCOL MECHANISMS

In December 1997, the Parties to the UN Framework Convention on Climate Change (FCCC) met in Kyoto, Japan, and negotiated a new protocol to the treaty, under which 13 CEEC/NIS as well as most OECD countries set national commitments for greenhouse gas reductions (nearly all such countries are listed on Annex 1 to the Convention).[1] The Protocol outlined three "Kyoto mechanisms" that would allow countries to co-operate in sharing the costs of emissions reduction. These mechanisms could become an important source of financing for environmental projects in the region.

The 13 CEEC/NIS have made commitments to limit their greenhouse gas (GHG) emissions in the period 2008 through 2012, in comparison with their base year. In addition, nearly all OECD countries have made commitments to reduce their GHG emissions.

In the 13 CEEC/NIS, emissions of carbon dioxide (CO_2) and other greenhouse gases have fallen dramatically since 1990, mainly because of the decline in economic activity (Table IV.1).[2] Although the region's emissions levels will likely be higher in the period 2008 to 2012 (the period during which countries must meet their Kyoto commitments) than in the late 1990s, they should remain below 1990 levels. In contrast, many OECD countries have increased their CO_2 emissions since 1990 and some may have difficulty meeting their commitments without the use of the Kyoto mechanisms, if current trends continue (Figure IV.1).

These 13 CEEC/NIS should be able to participate in two of the flexibility mechanisms in agreements with OECD countries in Western Europe and elsewhere: *Joint Implementation* and *Emissions Trading*. They and other CEEC/NIS should also be able to participate in the *Clean Development Mechanism* (see Box 6.5 in Chapter 6).

Table IV.1. **Kyoto Protocol commitments by CEEC/NIS Annex 1 countries**[a]

| Country[b] | Base year | | Reduction commitments for 2008-12 | | 1995[c] | |
	Year[d]	Total emissions reported (Gg CO_2 equiv.)	Per cent	Target level (Gg CO_2 equiv.)	% below base year	Total emissions reported (Gg CO_2 equiv.)
Central and Eastern Europe						
Bulgaria	1988	136 093	−8	125 206	−36	87 100
Czech Republic	1990	192 130	−8	176 760	−21	151 783
Estonia	1990	40 719	−8	37 461	−44	22 803
Hungary	1985-87	101 634	−6	95 536	−24	77 242
Latvia	1990	35 669	−8	32 815	−46	19 261
Lithuania	1990	51 548	−8	47 424	..	..
Poland	1988	564 286	−6	530 429	−22	440 143
Romania	1989	..	−8	..	..	..
Slovakia	1990	72 496	−8	66 696	−21	57 272
NIS						
Russia	1990	2 998 767	0	2 998 767	−30	2 099 137
Ukraine	1990	905 878	0	905 878	..	..

.. Not available.
a) Total anthropogenic emissions of the main GHG (CO_2, CH_4 and N_2O), excluding land-use change and forestry, 1990-1995 (gigagrams of CO_2 equivalent and percentage).
b) Croatia and Slovenia not included.
c) Or most recent year available.
d) The Kyoto Protocol allowed some transition countries to declare a base year, or set of years, other than 1990.
Source: UNFCCC.

Figure IV.1.   **IEA projections of CO$_2$ emissions to 2020**

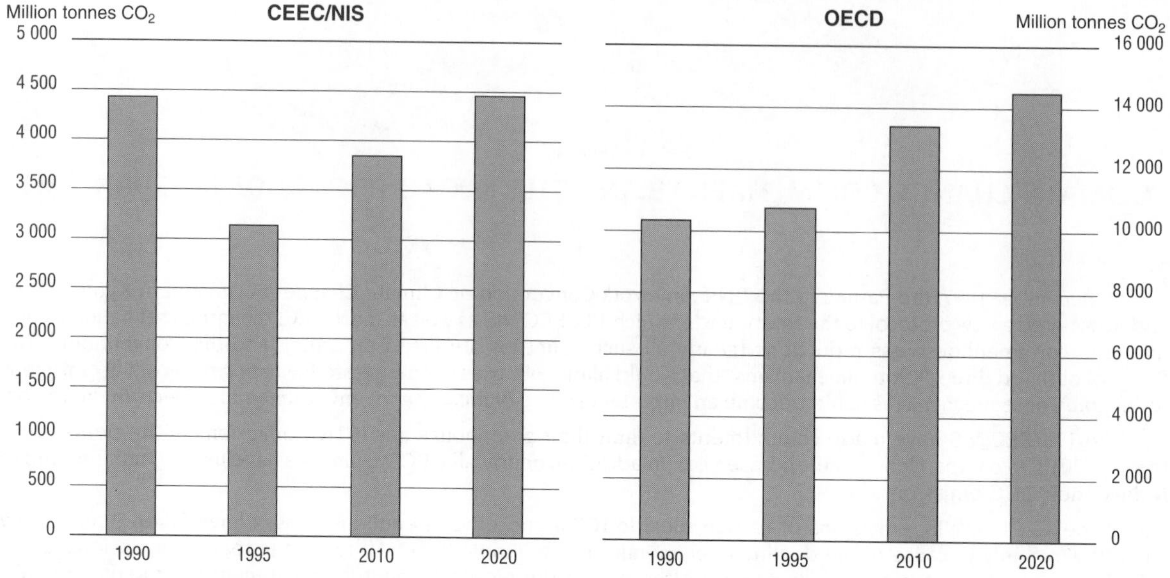

OECD data exclude Mexico, Korea, and Poland.
CEEC/NIS data exclude Czech Republic and Hungary.
Projections are based on national and international policies and trends in 1998.
Source: IEA-OECD *World Energy Outlook*, 1998.

A few CEEC/NIS have participated in a pilot phase for joint implementation. By late 1998, donor countries had sponsored almost 100 "activities implemented jointly" (AIJ) in the region. Two-thirds of these AIJ projects took place in the three Baltic States, many of them sponsored by the Swedish government.

In order to take advantage of the Kyoto mechanisms, CEEC/NIS need effective "national systems" for monitoring, reporting and verifying their GHG emissions. In several countries, estimates of national GHG emissions have had wide margins of uncertainty. To overcome these and other problems, their "national systems" will require strengthening. In addition, countries will need to develop adequate institutional structures to identify, prepare and co-ordinate JI projects and other agreements. Already in the pilot AIJ phase, a few CEEC/NIS, including Bulgaria, Poland and Russia, have set up national offices for this purpose (Petkova and Baumer).

Under the Climate Change Convention, all Annex 1 countries are committed to develop climate change policies. Those CEEC/NIS that take strong measures to mitigate their greenhouse gas emissions will be able to participate most actively in the Kyoto mechanisms. Here the Kyoto Protocol can provide an important incentive for the integration of environmental and sectoral policies. In particular, energy and transport are among the main sources of GHG emissions in most CEEC/NIS. Climate change policies – as well as full participation in the flexibility mechanisms – will require close co-ordination with policy initiatives in these sectors. In addition, many CEEC/NIS have extensive forests that sequester carbon; sustainable forestry policies can help maintain these carbon "sinks".

A few CEEC/NIS may have trouble meeting their emissions targets, making it difficult for them to participate as "sellers" in the Kyoto mechanisms. For example, Slovakia's 1998 national communication on climate change estimated that, without new policies, the country's base year emissions of CO$_2$ would be exceeded by 2010 (Petkova and Baumert). Thus some CEE countries enjoying rapid economic growth may need to develop strong domestic measures to mitigate their GHG emissions.

NOTES

1. These countries are also listed in "Annex B" to the Kyoto Protocol.
2. For most countries adhering to the Kyoto Protocol, 1990 is the base year; some CEEC, however, chose earlier years to correct for sharp declines in economic activity and GHG emissions at the start of the transition. In addition, the Kyoto Protocol refers to six greenhouse gases. This annex focuses on the most important one, CO_2.

REFERENCES

Petkova, E. and K. Baumert (1998),
   Capacity for Climate? Countries in Transition After Kyoto, WRI-REC Partnership, Washington, D.C., November.

Secretariat of the Framework Convention on Climate Change (UNFCC) [http://www.unfccc.de],
   Bonn.

Annex V

INDICATORS OF CEEC/NIS PROGRESS IN ECONOMIC REFORM

	Private sector, as % of GDP[a] mid-1997	Privatisation of large enterprises[b]	Enterprise governance and restructuring[b]	Price liberalisation[b]	Trade and foreign exchange system[b]
	CEE countries				
Albania	75	2	2	3	4
Bulgaria	50	3	2+	3	4
Croatia	55	3	3–	3	4
Czech Republic	75	4	3	3	4+
Estonia	70	4	3	3	4
Hungary	80	4	3+	3+	4+
Latvia	60	3	3–	3	4
Lithuania	70	3	3–	3	4
Macedonia, FYR	55	3	2	3	4
Poland	65	3+	3	3+	4+
Romania	60	3–	2	3	4
Slovakia	75	4	3–	3	4+
Slovenia	55	3+	3–	3	4+
	NIS				
Armenia	60	3	2	3	4
Azerbaijan	45	2	2	3	3
Belarus	20	1	1	2	1
Georgia	60	3+	2	3	4
Kazakhstan	55	3	2	3	4
Kyrgyz Republic	60	3	2	3	4
Moldova	45	3	2	3	4
Russia	70	3+	2	3–	2+
Tajikistan	30	2	2–	3	3–
Turkmenistan	25	2–	2–	2	1
Ukraine	55	2+	2	3	3–
Uzbekistan	45	3–	2	2	2+

a) EBRD estimates.
b) Classifications based on EBRD analysis. Overall, 1 = little progress; 4 = extensive reforms.

Classification system

Large-scale privatisation: 1. Little private ownership; 2. Comprehensive scheme almost ready for implementation; 3. > 25% of large-scale enterprise assets in private hands or in the process of being privatised, but possibly with major unresolved issues regarding corporate governance; 4. > 50% of state-owned enterprise and farm assets in private ownership and significant progress on corporate governance of these enterprises; 4+. Standards and performance typical of advanced industrial economies: > 75% of enterprise assets in private ownership with effective corporate governance.

Governance and restructuring: 1. Soft budget constraints; few other reforms to promote corporate governance; 2. Moderately tight credit and subsidy policy, but weak enforcement of bankruptcy legislation and little action taken to strengthen competition and corporate governance; 3. Significant sustained action to harden budget constraints and to promote corporate governance effectively; 4. Substantial improvement in corporate governance; significant new investment at enterprise level; 4+. Standards and performance typical of advanced industrial economies; effective cirporate control exercised through domestic financial institutions and markets, fostering market-driven restructuring.

Price liberalisation: 1.Most prices formally controlled by the government; 2. Price controls for several important product categories; state procurement at non-market prices remains substantial; 3. Substantial progress on price liberalisation; state procurement at non-market prices largely phased out; 4. Comprehensive price liberalisation; utility pricing approaches economic costs; 4+. Standards and performance typical of advanced industrial economies.

Trade and foreign exchange system: 1. Widespread import and/or export controls or very limited access to foreign exchange; 2. Some liberalisation of import and/or export controls; foreign exchange regime not fully transparent (possibly with multiple exchange rates); 3. Removal of almost all quantative and administrative import and export restrictions; almost full current account convertability; 4. Removal of all quantative and administrative import and export restrictions (apart from agriculture), all significant export tariffs, and direct government involvement in exports and imports; full current account convertability; 4+. Removal of most tariff barriers; membership in WTO.

Source: EBRD.

Annex VI

ENVIRONMENTAL POLICY INITIATIVES IN CEEC/NIS

		Policy	Approval
		CEEC	
Albania	1994	NEAP	G
Bulgaria	1992	Environmental Strategy Study	G
	1994	Environmental Strategy Study Update	M
Croatia		Env. Protection Strategy (under development)	
Czech Republic	1990	"Rainbow" Programme	Pl
	1995	State Environmental Policy	G
Estonia	1997	National Environmental Strategy	Pl
	1998	National Environmental Action Programme	G
Hungary	1997	Hungarian Environmental Protection Programme (HEPP)	Pl
	1998	Nat. Env. Action Programme for HEPP	G
Latvia	1995	National Environmental Policy Plan	G
	1997	National Environmental Action Plan	M
Lithuania	1996	Environmental Strategy	Pl
	1996	Environmental Action Programme	G
Macedonia, FYR	1997	National Environmental Action Programme	G
Poland	1991	National Environmental Policy	Pl
	1994	NEP Implementation Programme to the year 2000	Pl
Romania	1995	Environmental Protection Strategy	G
	1995	National Environmental Action Programme	G
Slovakia	1993	Strategies, Principles, Priorities of National Environmental Policy	Pl
	1996	National Environmental Action Programme	G
Slovenia	1995	National Environmental Action Programme	M
		NIS	
Armenia	1998	National Environmental Action Programme	Pr
			G
Azerbaijan	1998	National Environmental Action Plan	G
Belarus	1996	National Programme for Rational Use of Natural Resources and Environmental Protection for 1996-2000	G
Georgia		National Environmental Action Plan (under development)	
Kazakhstan	1998	National Environmental Action Plan for Sustainable Development	G
Kyrgyz Republic	1996	National Environmental Action Plan	G
Moldova	1995	National Environmental Action Plan for 1996-1998	G
Russia	1994	Actions Plans of the Government 1994-1995 and 1996-1997	G
	1998	National Environmental Action Plan 1999-2001	G
Ukraine	1998	Main Directions of the State Policy for the Protection of the Environment, Use of Natural Resources and Environmental Safety	Pl
Uzbekistan		National Environmental Action Plan (under development)	

Pl: Parliamentary approval.
Pr: Presidential approval.
G: Government approval.
M: Environment ministry approval.

OECD 1999

Annex VII
OVERVIEW OF SELECTED ECONOMIC INSTRUMENTS USED IN CENTRAL AND EASTERN EUROPE

	BUL	CRO	CZE	EST	HUN	LAT	LIT	POL	ROM	SR	SLO
Air emissions											
Air: emission charge	•	•	•	•	•	•	•	•	•	•	•
Air emission non-compliance fee		•	•	•	•	•	•	•	•	•	
CO$_2$ tax											
Water pollution											
Water effluent charge	•	•	•	•	•	•	•	•	•	•	•
Water poll. non-compliance fee	•	•	•	•	•	•	•	•	•	•	•
Sewage charges		•	•	•	•	•	•	•	•	•	•
Waste											
Municipal waste user charges	•	•	•	•	•	•	•	•	•	•	•
Waste disposal charges	•	•	•	•	•	•	•	•	•	•	•
Waste non-compliance fees			•	•		•	•	•		•	
Deposit refund on beverage containers		•	•	•	•	•	•	•		•	•
Levies related to the management of nuclear waste										•	
Waste related product charges											
Packaging material				•	•	•		•			
Batteries/accumulators					•	•					
Refrigerators and refrigerants					•						
Lubricants					•	•					
Tires					•	•				•	
Substances/products damaging ozone layer (CFCs)			•								
Transport											
Tax differentiation un-/leaded gasoline	•	•			•	•		•	•	•	•
Product charge on transport fuels					•			•	•	•	•
Increased import duty for used cars or without catalyzer	•	•	•	•	•		•				
Road tolls/pricing			•		•					•	
Noise/air pollution tax on air travel											
Nature protection and biodiversity											
Nature protection non-compliance fees	•	•	•	•	•	•	•	•		•	•
Natural resources and mining											
Natural resource or mining tax/charge[a]	•	•	•	•	•	•	•	•		•	•
Water extraction charges			•	•	•	•	•	•	•	•	
Other											
Income tax/VAT allowances for environ. Technology	•	•	•	•	•	•	•	•	•	•	
Duty/tax allowance on import of environ. Technology	•		•	•	•				•		
Environmental funds[b]											
At national level	•	•	•	•	•	•	•	•		•	•
At regional level	•			•		•		•			
At municipal level								•			
Debt-for-environment swap fund								•			

Abbreviations: BUL – Bulgaria; CRO – Croatia; CZE – Czech Republic; EST – Estonia; HUN – Hungary; LAT – Latvia; LIT – Lithuania; POL – Poland; ROM – Romania; SR – Slovakia; SLO – Slovenia.
• Instrument in force.
a) Only those natural resource or mining taxes/charges are reported which were introduced partly for environmental reasons or if part of the revenue is earmarked for environmental expenditure.
b) Environmental funds are described further in Annex VIII.
Source: REC.

Annex VIII

OVERVIEW OF SELECTED ENVIRONMENTAL FUNDS IN CEE COUNTRIES AND THE NIS

Table VIII.1. **Key characteristics of selected environmental funds in CEE countries**

Revenues and expenditures in mln USD[a]

	Bulgaria: National Environmental Protection Fund	Bulgaria: National Trust EcoFund	Czech Republic: State Environmental Fund	Estonia: Central Environmental Fund	Hungary: Central Environmental Protection Fund
Operational in current form since	1993	1996	1992	1990	1993
Total income/expenditure[b]	Income/expenditure 1993 3.60 2.18 1994 4.42 3.42 1995 5.94 6.25 1996 6.14 8.48 1997 9.49 4.38	Income/expenditure – – – – – – 5.53 – 5.24 0.39	Income/expenditure 94.94 98.41 155.93 123.11 186.87 183.84 197.21 169.55 167.15 103.97	Income/expenditure n.a. n.a. 0.93 1.08 1.78 1.83 6.78 5.41 7.69 8.78	Income/expenditure 29.90 17.19 61.13 25.61 55.32 26.30 93.22 53.85 80.99 84.56
Major revenue sources in 1997 (with % of total revenues)	– Liquid fuel charge (78.4%) – Privatization (13.8%) – Administrative fees (3.7%) – Environmental fines (2.5%) – Loan repayments with interest (1.6%)	– Debt swap with Switzerland (80.6%) – Profits from financial operations (15.9%) – World Bank grant (3.4%)	– Air/water/waste/land use charges and fines (51.5%) – Privatization (28.3%) – Loan repayments with interest (14.8%) – Profits from financial operations (6.1%)	– Environmental charges and fines (46.2%) – Privatization (27.4%) – Mineral extraction charges (17.8%) – Packaging excise tax (3.4%) – Loan repayments with interest (2.3%) – Other (2.9%)	– Fuel charge (46.9%) – Other product charges (30.8%) – Privatization (6.6%) – Environmental fines (4.7%) – Mining annuity (1.5%) – PHARE grant (4.1%) – Loan repayments with interest (5.1%) – Other (0.3%)
Major fields of expenditure in 1997 (with % of total annual environmental expenditures)	– Air (9.3%) – Water (43.7%) – Waste (16.8%) – Monitoring (20.5%) – Soil protection (8.3%) – Others (1.4%)	– Air (49.7%) – Water (49.9%) – Nature protection (0.5%)	– Air (36.5%) – Water (57.4%) – Waste (1.8%) – Nature/soil/landscape protection (4.2%)	– Air (1.9%) – Water (33.3%) – Waste (10.1%) – Building programme (19.3%) – "Supervision" (11.9%) – Other (23.5%)	– Air (21.6%) – Water (15.4%) – Waste (13.9%) – "Public purposes" (22.1%) – "Government decisions" (10.4%) – Other (16.6%)
Primary disbursement mechanisms in 1997 (with % of total disbursements for environmental projects)	– Grants (76.8%) – Interest free loans (7.7%) – Equity investments (15.6%)	– Grants (85.2%) – Interest free loans (14.8%)	– Grants (55.4%) – Soft and interest free loans (43.9%) – Interest subsidies (0.6%)	– Grants (89.6%) – Interest free loans (7.6%) – Soft loans (2.8%)	– Grants (~ 75%) – Interest free loans (~ 22%) – Soft loans (~ 3%)

n.a. Indicates that the information was either not available or not provided by the fund.
a) Nominal values based on average annual exchange rates.
b) Income data exclude start of year balances; expenditure data exclude overhead and administration costs and other non-environmental expenditure of the funds; expenditures may exceed revenues for a given year because of income carried over from previous years.
Source: OECD, based on national data.

Table VIII.1. **Key characteristics of selected environmental funds in CEE countries** *(cont.)*

Revenues and expenditures in mln USD[a]

	Poland: National Fund for Environmental Protection and Water Management	Poland: EcoFund	Poland: Cracow Provincial Fund for Environmental Protection and Water Management[b]	Slovakia: State Environmental Fund	Slovenia: Environmental Development Fund
Operational in current form since	1989	1992	1993	1991	1994
Total income/expenditure[c]	Income/expenditure	Income/expenditure	Income/expenditure	Income/expenditure	Income/expenditure
1993	266.70 / 204.94	8.85 / 4.62	2.03 / 1.00	31.89 / 34.94	– / –
1994	338.06 / 278.89	10.16 / 14.32	12.13 / 5.7	30.51 / 31.38	– / 2.02
1995	481.58 / 428.44	29.64 / 20.48	19.13 / 6.51	35.59 / 34.35	10.41 / 0.60
1996	432.60 / 510.12	31.30 / 21.64	17.16 / 19.05	40.19 / 40.62	15.11 / 10.52
1997	418.61 / 389.67	33.58 / 36.52	14.84 / 17.03	30.99 / 28.94	20.43 / 17.81
Major revenue sources in 1997 (with % of total revenues)	– Environmental charges (53.6%) – Environmental fines (1.3%) – International loans and grants (3.6%) – Loan repayments with interest (35.7%) – Profits from financial operations (5.8%)	– Debt swaps with US, Switzerland, France and Sweden (83.8%) – Profits from financial operations (14.9%) – Grant from Norwegian Government (1.3%)	– Environmental charges (57.5%) – Environmental fines (3.2%) – Loan repayments with interest (24.4%) – Profits from financial operations (14.9%)	– State budget allocation (23.1%) – Air/water/waste charges (73.3%) – Air/water/waste fines (2.1%) – Profits from financial operations (0.9%)	– Privatization (40.4%) – World Bank loan (26.8%) – Loan repayments with interest (23.1%)[d] – Interest (8.2%) – Land use fines (0.8%)
Major fields of expenditure in 1997 (with % of total annual environmental expenditures)	– Air (33.2%) – Water (39.0%) – Mining related (9.0%) – Soil protection (8.9%) – Nature protection (3.4%) – Emergencies (1.8%) – Education (1.6%) – Monitoring (0.8%) – Other (2.5%)	– Air (56.0%) – Water (41.3%) – Nature prot. (2.7%)	– Air (56.9%) – Water (25.4%) – Waste (0.6%) – Emergencies (6.8%) – Monitoring (4.0%) – Soil protection (1.7%) – Noise protection (1.5%) – Other (3.1%)	– Air (26.9%) – Water (55.0%) – Waste (9.5%) – Nature protection (2.3%) – Education (1.3%) – Research (1.1%) – Other (3.9%)	– Air (73.5%) – Water (21.7%) – Waste (4.8%)
Primary disbursement mechanisms in 1997 (with % of total disbursements for environmental projects)	– Soft loans (61.2%) – Grants (30.9%) – Interest subsidies (2.5%) – Equity investments (5.1%)	– Grants (100%)	– Grants (25.4%) – Soft loans (74.6%)	– Grants (100%)	– Soft loans (100%)

a) Nominal values based on average annual exchange rates.
b) Poland has a number of provincial environmental funds; the Cracow Fund is one of the largest of these and is presented for illustrative purposes.
c) Income data exclude start of year balances; expenditure data exclude overhead and administration costs and other non-environmental expenditure of the funds; expenditures may exceed revenues for a given year because of income carried over from previous years.
d) The fund also administers 277 loans extended by the Slovenian MoE before the fund was established, the value of which amounted to US$ 14.8 million as of 31.12.1997.
Sources: OECD, based on national data.

Table VIII.2. **Key characteristics of selected environmental funds in the NIS**

Revenues and expenditures in mln USD[a]

	Belarus:[b] Republican Environmental Fund	Kazakhstan: National Environmental Protection Fund	Kyrgyz Republic: Republican Environmental Fund	Moldova: National Environmental Fund	Russia: Federal Environmental Fund
Operational in current form since[c]					
Total income/expenditure[c]	Income/expenditure	Income/expenditure	Income/expenditure	Income/expenditure	Income/expenditure
1993	1.87 1.56	3.09 2.77	0.08 0.08	0.02 0.02	3.66 2.70
1994	0.44 0.39	4.03 2.87	0.17 0.16	0.02 0.02	9.50 7.54
1995	3.35 2.9	1.79 1.68	0.35 0.35	0.04 0.04	10.41 8.92
1996	6.80 6.4	3.45 3.12	0.44 0.44	0.05 0.05	14.23 13.15
1997	5.12 4.82	9.73 3.46	0.49 0.46	0.04 0.04	18.48 17.31
Major revenue sources in 1997 (with % of fund's total revenues)	– Air/water charges (88.2%) – Waste charges (3.3%) – Bank interest (3.0%)	– Air pollution charges (46.1%) – Waste water charges (21.6%) – Waste charges (13.1%) – Air pollution fines (14.6%) – Waste water fines (2.0%) – Waste fines (2.7%)	– Air pollution charges (58.0%) – Waste charges (15.6%) – Other charges (14.9%) – Air pollution fines (1.8%) – Water charges (9.7%)	– Pollution charges and fines transferred from the local environmental funds (100%)	– Pollution charges and fines transferred from the regional environmental funds (65.7%) – Loan repayments with interest (5.4%) – Transfers from Far East and Northwest Marine Funds (26.5%)
Major fields of expenditure in 1997 (with % of total environmental expenditures)	– Construction/repair of environmental facilities (71.0%) – Soil (10.1%) – Nature protection (3.7%) – Environmental Authorities (3.4%) – Research (1.8%) – Purchase of instruments and equipment (7.4%)	– Construction/repair of environmental facilities (24.6%) – Research (8.0%) – Nature protection (23.9%) – Program/project development (4.2%) – Education (2.4%) – Protected areas (6.5%) – Environmental authorities (12.3%) – Other (17.6%)	– Regional programmes (40.2%) – Protected areas (6.5%) – Env. authorities (45.7%) – Education (1.1%) – Monitoring (6.4%)	– Nature protection (15.8%) – Education (66.4%) – Monitoring (17.8%)	– Air (5.3%) – Water (13.6%) – Waste (20.4%) – Soil/land (2.1%) – Nature (34.2%) – Education (3.9%) – Monitoring (15.3%) – Research (1.4%) – Other (3.0%)
Primary disbursement mechanisms in 1997 (with % of total disbursements for environmental projects)	– Grants (100%)	– Grants (100%)	– Grants (including barter transactions) (92.8%) – Interest free loans (7.2%)	– Grants (100%)	– Grants (52.6%) – Equity investments (37.3%) – Interest free loans (8.2%) – Soft loans (1.9%)

a) Nominal values based on average annual exchange rates.
b) The survey response from Belarus provided data on revenues and expenditures for the country's *entire environmental fund system*, which also includes local and regional funds. The figures presented here for the Republican Environmental Fund were calculated by the author as a proportion (10%) of total income and expenditures of the entire fund system, and thus must be considered as merely indicative. (Revenues are initially collected by the local authorities, who are required by law to transfer 10% of most revenue types to the Republican Fund.)
c) Expenditures may exceed revenues for a given year because of income carried over from previous years.

Source: OECD. based on national data.

Table VIII.2. **Key characteristics of selected environmental funds in the NIS** *(cont.)*

Revenues and expenditures in mln USD[a]

	Russia: National Pollution Abatement Facility	Russia: Novgorod Regional Environmental Fund	Ukraine: Republican Environmental Fund	Uzbekistan:[b] Republican Environmental Fund
Operational in current form since	1995	1990	1992	1993
Total income/expenditure[c]	Income/expenditure	Income/expenditure[d]	Income/expenditure	Income/expenditure
1993	– –	0.23 0.20	1.65 0.33	0.00 0.00
1994	– –	0.81 0.47	0.85 0.85	0.03 0.25
1995	59.00 0.13	0.54 0.66	0.26 0.08	0.10 0.10
1996	8.00 0.78	0.71 0.58	1.37 1.48	0.14 0.11
1997	0.09 1.58	0.63 0.67	1.94 1.94	0.08 0.09
Major revenue sources in 1997 (with % of total revenues)	– Loan repayments with interest (100%)	– Air pollution charges (17.3%) – Water pollution charges (48.5%) – Waste disposal charges (29.7%) – Fines for violating hunting and fishing rules (1.6%)	– Pollution charges (94.9%) – Other charges (1.8%) – Pollution fines (1.1%) – Other (2.2%)	– Transfers from the local environmental funds (100%)
Major fields of expenditure in 1997 (with % of total environmental expenditures)	– Air (100%)	– Construction of environmental protection facilities (57.9%) – Research (3.2%) – Monitoring (2.8%) – Nature protection (1.8%) – Education (3.1%) – Environmental authorities (31.0%) – Other (0.3%)	– Nature protection (14.2%) – Reduction of environmental health impacts (32.5%) – Equipment for environmental organisations (25.0%) – Research (4.7%) – International co-operation (4.2%) – Cleanup of accidents (3.3%) – Other (11%)	– Nature protection (8.4%) – Other (91.6%)
Primary disbursement mechanisms in 1997 (with % of total disbursements for environmental projects)	– Soft loans (100%)	– Grants	– Grants (100%)	– Grants (100%)

a) Nominal values based on average annual exchange rates.
b) The survey response from Uzbekistan provided data on revenues and expenditures for the country's *entire environmental fund system*, which also includes local and regional funds. The figures presented here for the Republican Environmental Fund were calculated by the author as proportions (25%) of total income and expenditures of the entire funds system, and thus must be considered as merely indicative. (All revenues are initially collected by the regional funds, which are required by law to transfer 25% of most revenue types to the Republican Fund.)
c) Expenditures may exceed revenues for a given year because of income carried over from previous years.
d) Expenditure figures include pollution charges "offset" in return for agreement by the polluter to use the money for investments in pollution reduction measures (36% of total environmental expenditures in 1997).

Source: OECD, based on national data.

Annex IX

GROWTH OF THE DOMESTIC ENVIRONMENTAL GOODS AND SERVICES INDUSTRY IN THE CEEC/NIS

Stronger environmental policies in many CEEC/NIS have increased environmental investments, which in turn have encouraged the development of the region's environmental goods and services industry. According to one estimate, total environmental spending in the region reached almost US$4 billion in 1995; of this total, companies based in the region provided about US$600 million. A recent estimate suggests that the value of this industry had reached US$15 billion by 1998. The domestic industry in CEEC/NIS is growing rapidly, often with the support of foreign direct and portfolio investment.

Under central planning, most CEEC/NIS had a small number of state-owned enterprises that supplied pollution control equipment and constructed waste water treatment plants and other facilities. During the transition, however, this sector saw great expansion. By 1995, a survey found that most environmental companies in the Czech Republic, Poland and Slovakia were recently created small and medium-sized enterprises. Technical education has remained strong in the region, and many new businesses – both manufacturing enterprises and environmental consultancies – have been spinoffs from universities and research institutes. Domestic companies often can offer low-cost solutions, in particular for small and medium-sized enterprises that may not be able to afford imported equipment. A 1995 survey reported that 40% of the enterprises in this field exported at least some equipment. (Under 10% of companies, however, reported that exports accounted for more than half of their sales.) Most of these exports are probably within the CEEC/NIS region.

In a few CEE countries, recently formed business associations have supported this sector. These have included the Czech Environmental Management Centre and ASPEK, the Slovakian Association of Industrial Ecology. In a few other countries, industry-wide associations have the environmental goods and services industry. For example, the Lithuanian Confederation of Industrialists has a special section devoted to it.

This sector is expected to continue growing strongly, particularly in CEE countries seeking accession to the EU, as harmonisation with EU environmental legislation will require increased environmental investments (Annex III). In addition, as they develop, CEE firms should be able to compete more strongly for contracts with companies from outside the region. In December 1997, EBRD, the Swiss government, and several Western European financial companies set up a "green equity fund", initially capitalised with ECU 22 million (US$25 million), to invest in small and medium-sized enterprises producing pollution control and other environmental equipment, as well as environmental consultancies.

237|

Annex X
PARTICIPATION OF SELECTED CEEC/NIS IN MULTILATERAL ENVIRONMENTAL AGREEMENTS (AS OF EARLY 1999)

Selected global agreements

Year	Place	Title	In force*	ALB	BUL	CRO	CZE	EST	HUN	LAT	LIT	MAC	POL	ROM	SLO	SLV	BLR	MOL	RF	UKR
				CEEC													**NIS**			
1989	Basel	Conv. – Control of transb. movements of hazardous wastes and their disposal	05.05.1992		R	R	R	R	R	R		R	R	R	R	R	R		R	
1982	Montego Bay	Conv. – Law of the sea	16.11.1994		R	R	R		S	R	R	R	S	R	R	R	S		S	S
1971	Ramsar	Conv. – Wetlands of international importance especially as waterfowl habitat	21.12.1975		R	R	R		R		R		R	R	R	R		R	R	
1973	Washington	Conv. – Internat. trade in endangered species of wild fauna and flora (CITES)	01.07.1975		R		R	R	R				R	R	R	R	R		R	
1979	Bonn	Conv. – Conservation of migratory species of wild animals	01.11.1983			R		R	R				R		R					
1992	Rio de Janeiro	Conv. – Biological diversity	29.12.1993	R	R	R	R	R	R	R	R	R	R	R	R	R	R	R	R	R
1985	Vienna	Conv. – Protection of the ozone layer	22.09.1988		R	R	R	R	R	R	R	R	R	R	R	R	R	R	R	R
1987	Montreal	Protocol (substances that deplete the ozone layer)	01.01.1989		R	R	R	R	R	R	R	R	R	R	R	R	R	R	R	R
1990	London	Amendment to protocol	10.08.1992			R	R		R		R		R	R	R	R	R		R	
1992	Copenhagen	Amendment to protocol	14.06.1994		R	R	R	R	R	R	R	R	R	R	R	R		R		
1992	New York	Framework convention on climate change	21.03.1994	R	R	R	R	R	R	R	R	R	R	R	R	R	S	R	R	S
1997	Kyoto	Protocol			S	S	S	S	S	S	S	S	S	S	S	S	S	R	S	S

S Signed
R Ratified.
* Data of entry into force.
Source: IUCN; OECD

239

Selected regional agreements

	Place	Title	In force*	ALB	BUL	CRO	CZE	EST	HUN	LAT	LIT	MAC	POL	ROM	SLO	SLV	BLR	MOL	RF	UKR
				CEEC													NIS			
1991	Espoo	Conv. – Environmental impact assessment in a transboundary context	10.09.1997	R	R	R	S		R				R	S	S		S	R	S	S
1991	Salzburg	Conv. – Protection of Alps	06.03.1995													R					
1992	Helsinki	Conv. – Transboundary effects of industrial accidents	Pending	R	R			S	R	S	S		S					R		R	
1993	Lugano	Conv. – Civil liability for damage resulting from activities dangerous to the env.	Pending																		
1994	Lisbon	Treaty – Energy Charter	Pending	S		S	S	S	S	S	S		S	S	S	S	S	S	S	S	S
1994	Lisbon	Protocol (energy efficiency and related environmental aspects)			S	S	S	S	S	S	S		S	S	S	S	S	S	S	S
1974	Helsinki	Conv. – Protection of the marine environment of the Baltic Sea area	03.05.1980					R		R	R		R						R	
1992	Helsinki	Conv. – Protection of the marine env. of the Baltic Sea area (amendment)	Pending					R		R	S		S						S	
1992	Bucharest	Conv. – Protection of the Black Sea against pollution	15.01.1994	R									R	R					R	R
1992	Bucharest	Protocol (combatting pollution by oil and other harmful subst. in emgy sitns.)	..	R									R	R					R	R
1992	Bucharest	Protocol (prot. Black Sea marine env. against pollution from land based sources)		R									R	R					R	R
1998	Aarhus	Conv. – Access to env. info. and public participation in env. decision-making		S	S	S	S	S		S	S		S	S	S	S	S			S
1960	Geneva	Conv. – Protection of workers against ionising radiations	17.06.1962		R	R		R	R	R			R		R				R	R
1963	Vienna	Conv. – Civil liability for nuclear damage	12.11.1977		R	R		R	R		R		R	R	S	R		R		R
1979	Bern	Conv. – Conservation of European wildlife and natural habitats	01.06.1982	S	R	R	R	R	R	R	R	R	R	R	R	R	R		R	R
1979	Geneva	Conv. – Long-range transboundary air pollution	16.03.1983		R	R	R	R	R	R	R	R	R	R	S	R	R	R	R	R
1984	Geneva	Protocol (financing of EMEP)	28.01.1988		R	R	R	R	R	R	R	R	R	R	R	R	R	R	R	R
1985	Helsinki	Protocol (reduction of SOx emissions or their transb. fluxes by at least 30%)	02.09.1987		R	R	R	R	R	R			R		R	R	R	R	R	S
1988	Sofia	Protocol (control of emissions of NOx or their transboundary fluxes)	14.02.1991		R	R	R		R				S		S	R	R	R	R	S
1991	Geneva	Protocol (control of emissions of VOCs or their transboundary fluxes)	29.09.1997		R	R	R		R							R	R			S
1994	Oslo	Protocol (sulphur emission ceilings and percentage emission reduction)	05.08.1998		S	S	R		S	S	S		S	S	R	R			S	S
1998	Aarhus	Protocol (heavy metals)		S	S	S				S	S		S	S	S	S		S		S
1998	Aarhus	Protocol (persistent organic pollutants)			S	S	S			S	S		S	S	S	S		S		S
1996		Agreem. – Exchange of immissions data in the Black Triangle					S						S							
1992	Helsinki	Conv. – Protection and use of transboundary water courses and internat. lakes	06.10.1996	R	S	R	R	R	R	R	S		R	S	R	S		R	R	
1994	Sofia	Conv. – Co-operation for the protection and sust. use of the Danube river	Pending		S	S		S	S				S	S	S	S		S		S

S Signed.
R Ratified.
* Data of entry into force.
Source: IUCN, OECD.

Annex XI

NUCLEAR SAFETY

The safety of nuclear power plants and the management of the radioactive wastes they produce, as well as military nuclear wastes, are major concerns in CEEC/NIS.[1]

1. CEEC/NIS Nuclear Power Plants

The nuclear power plants built in CEEC/NIS, in particular those using the earliest reactor designs, lack key safety features. The RBMK reactors, an early version of which caused the Chernobyl accident, present perhaps the greatest safety problems: for example, early versions of these reactors lack containment vessels to limit potential releases in the event of an accident (EBRD, 1996). Power plants built with RBMK reactors include: Ignalina in Lithuania; Kursk, St. Petersburg and Smolensk in Russia; and Chernobyl in Ukraine (Angelo). The early Soviet pressurised-water reactors (the VVER 440/230 reactors) also present high risks. Power plants using this type of reactor include Kozloduy in Bulgaria, Metsamor in Armenia, Novovoronezhskiy in Russia and Bohunice in Slovakia. Although more recent Soviet pressurised-water reactors have enhanced safety features, in general they present greater risks than reactors built in OECD countries.[2]

Under central planning, safety was not a priority for national policies or for power plant operations. Countries in the region lacked framework legislation for nuclear operations and safety. Moreover, safety was not a priority in training for or operation of nuclear power plants (EBRD, 1996; NEA).

1.1. National policies and institutions to manage nuclear power

Over the transition, all CEEC/NIS with nuclear power plants have adopted framework legislation to establish basic obligations and rights related to nuclear energy and have established nuclear regulatory agencies to oversee civilian nuclear activities. These agencies are responsible for licensing the construction, operation and decommissioning of nuclear power plants and the production, transport and storage of nuclear materials (such as fuel) and radioactive wastes (NEA).[3] Most of these countries have made strong progress in terms of adopting nuclear safety treaties (see Table XI.1). Most countries have also worked to improve the technical safety features and training at their nuclear power plants, often with strong support from bilateral and multilateral assistance programmes.

1.2. International assistance to improve safety

Several bilateral donors provided assistance to improve nuclear safety in CEEC/NIS from the start of the transition. At their July 1992 summit, the G7 countries proposed a multilateral initiative to address this issue, focusing on technical improvement projects at the highest-risk reactors to improve their safety. An international working group, the G-24 Nuclear Safety Co-ordination mechanism (NUSAC), has met regularly to co-ordinate this initiative.[4] Bilateral donors and IFIs have provided over ECU 1.8 billion (about US$2 billion) in grants for nuclear safety projects in CEEC/NIS. The European Commission has provided by far the largest share: almost ECU 800 million (close to US$1 billion) in grants from 1991 to 1997 (G-24). In parallel, the EC and 14 OECD countries have financed a Nuclear Safety Account, located within EBRD, that provides grants for nuclear safety projects in the region. Through the end of 1998, these donors had provided US$260 million to the Account (EBRD, 1999).

1.3. Addressing the effects of the Chernobyl accident

Radioactive fallout from the 1986 Chernobyl accident affected large areas of Europe and parts of the Middle East (EBRD, 1996). Particularly hard hit were parts of Belarus, Russia and Ukraine close to Chernobyl. Both Belarus and Ukraine established "exclusion zones", close to the plant, from which inhabitants were evacuated after the accident. In Belarus alone, over 130 000 people were evacuated from the most contaminated areas or left voluntarily. In Ukraine, about 15 000 people work within the exclusion zone, many at the plant itself. Management of Chernobyl-related effects, including compensation to those evacuated from the exclusion zones and others affected, has been a major cost for these two countries: in 1995, Belarus spent almost 8% of its national budget (equivalent to almost 3% of its GDP) on responses to the Chernobyl accident – about 60% of these funds went to support living conditions and infrastructure projects in areas affected by radioactive fallout (OECD, 1997; UN/ECE, 1999).

241

Table XI.1. **CEEC/NIS adoption of international convention on nuclear safety, early 1999**

	1963 Convention on Civil Liablity for Nuclear Damage	1988 Joint Protocol to the Vienna and Paris Conventions on Civil Liablity	1997 Protocol to Amend the 1963 Convention on Civil Liablity	1994 Convention on Nuclear Safety	1997 Convention on Radioactive waste and Spent Fuel Mgmt.	1997 Convention on Supplementary Compensation for Nuclear Damage
Armenia	Yes	Signed	No	Yes	No	No
Belarus	Yes	No	Signed	Yes	No	No
Bulgaria	Yes	Yes	No	Yes	Signed	No
Croatia	Yes	Yes	No	Yes	Signed	No
Czech Rep.	Yes	Yes	Signed	Yes	Signed	Signed
Estonia	Yes	Yes	No	No	No	No
Hungary	Yes	Yes	Signed	Yes	Yes	No
Kazakhstan	No	No	No	Signed	Signed	No
Latvia	Yes	Yes	No	Yes	No	No
Lithuania	Yes	Yes	Signed	Yes	Signed	Signed
Poland	Yes	Yes	Signed	Yes	Signed	No
Romania	Yes	Yes	Yes	Yes	Signed	Yes
Russia	Signed	No	No	Yes	Signed	No
Slovakia	Yes	Yes	No	Yes	Yes	No
Slovenia	Yes	Yes	No	Yes	Yes	No
Ukraine	Yes	No	Signed	Yes	Signed	Signed

Notes: Only for CEEC/NIS with nuclear power plants.
"Yes" indicates that the country has either ratified, acceded to or succeeded to the instrument.
"Signed" indicates that the country has signed the instrument but has not yet ratified it, and therefore the instrument is not legally binding on that country.
Source: NEA.

A large number of problems remain from the Chernobyl accident. In particular, there is a risk of further, potentially serious radioactive releases from the fuel remaining inside the former reactor. This is compounded by structural problems of the "sarcophagus", a structure that was hastily built after the accident to cover the reactor. A UN/ECE survey reported that the sarcophagus "represents a permanent risk for people and the environment at least in the 30-km [exclusion] zone" (UN/ECE, 1999). In addition, the accident created large amounts of radioactive waste. Some is stored at Chernobyl in unlined trenches, where it is a potential threat to groundwater; some contaminated equipment is stored in the open air.

In 1997, bilateral donors and Ukraine reached agreement on a project to address the serious risks presented by the sarcophagus. The G-7, the European Commission and Ukraine created a Chernobyl Shelter Fund, hosted by EBRD. This Fund will finance the Chernobyl Shelter Implementation Project. The project, estimated to take 10 years and cost US$760 million (EBRD, 1998), is meant to resolve the serious structural and environmental problems of the sarcophagus. Through the end of 1998, the EC and over 20 countries had provided ECU 335 million (over US$350 million) for the Fund.

The full closure of the Chernobyl plant remains unresolved. The 1986 accident destroyed one of the plant's four RBMK reactors. Of the three remaining at the plant, one reactor was shut down in 1991 after a major fire; although it was repaired, it has not been restarted. Another reactor was closed in 1996. The third unit remains in operation. G-7 and Ukraine have been negotiating financing for new electric power generating capacity. Ukraine is seeking the completion of two new nuclear reactors at other power plants, to compensate for the loss of capacity from the closure of Chernobyl. The need for new power generating capacity in Ukraine has been questioned, as demand for electric power has declined by 50% since 1991 and opportunities for energy efficiency remain abundant (UN/ECE, 1999). It is also not clear whether the new reactors would be the most appropriate and cost-effective approach for developing new generating capacity in the country.

1.4. *Achievements and issues remaining*

In a number of countries, national efforts together with international assistance have improved the safety of nuclear power plants. In Lithuania, for example, equipment and training – largely supported by the Swedish government and the EBRD Nuclear Safety Account – have helped to improve safety conditions at the Ignalina Power Plant and supported the development of government institutions to regulate nuclear safety (UN/ECE, 1998). Nonetheless, critics maintain that this plant's RBMK reactors continue to present excessive risks (EU Enlargement Watch). Although Lithuania had announced that one reactor at Ignalina would be closed in 2005 and the other in 2010, it has since suspended this decision (UN/ECE, 1998).

Nuclear safety concerns have grown in a few countries, particularly in the NIS. In Ukraine, for example, many industrial and household consumers have not paid their electricity bills; as a result, operating companies have lacked resources for spare parts and equipment, limiting the effectiveness of their safety improvement programmes. Companies have often paid wages late, reducing incentives for power plant operators to pay close attention to proper procedures, including those for safety. The number of human errors recorded has increased since 1995 (UN/ECE, 1999).

As yet, despite questions about their long-term safety and calls for the closure of at least the highest risk reactors, no CEEC/NIS nuclear power plants have been closed and no closure dates have been fixed. This remains a difficult issue for international co-operation. Moreover, it is an important issue for EU accession. A recent panel of high-level advisors to the European Commission reported that it did not "foresee major difficulties for Applicant Countries in reaching, at the time of Accession, a level of nuclear safety comparable to that of current EU Member States." The panel did, however, refer to the "early closure" of several reactors: units 1 and 2 of the Kozloduy Power Plant in Bulgaria; unit 1 of Ignalina in Lithuania; and unit 1 of Bohunice in Slovakia (EC). However, specific plans have yet to be fixed. Although the EC has mentioned nuclear reactor safety as an important issue in accession, the EU does not set standards in this area, which is left for Member government regulation. There are no specific requirements for candidate countries to meet (EU Enlargement Watch). Closing nuclear power plants will raise new issues, including the costs of decommissioning and storage of eventual wastes. A few CEEC/NIS, including Lithuania, have started to build funds for these tasks (UN/ECE, 1998).

2. Managing Radioactive Wastes

The management and storage of radioactive wastes, including high-level wastes such as spent reactor fuel, has been an important concern in many CEEC/NIS. Before the transition, most countries in the region sent their highly radioactive spent reactor fuel to Russia for reprocessing. Over the transition, however, Russia first suspended reprocessing of fuels from third countries and then announced high charges to accept spent fuel. (In 1995, Russia announced plans to build a reprocessing plant specifically to reprocess fuel from other countries; however, construction has been delayed.) Most CEEC/NIS nuclear power plants currently store their spent fuel on site. The storage of low and medium-level radioactive waste has also been an important issue in many countries of the region.

Radioactive waste management is also a major problem in Russia. Its nuclear power plants store over 6 000 tonnes of spent fuel; a storage facility holds another 1 000 tonnes. Military and research facilities have accumulated large amounts of radioactive waste. Industrial accidents and poor waste management have severely contaminated several areas, including at least two military reprocessing plants. Although the federal government adopted a programme to address radioactive waste management in 1995, federal budgets have provided only a tiny fraction of proposed funding levels. Consequently, radioactive waste storage facilities have had scarce funding, and many are reaching the limit of their storage capacities, both quantitatively and qualitatively. (OECD, 1999)

3. Military Issues

Military operations, including nuclear weapons production, created a great number of radioactive waste problems and nuclear safety issues. International concern has focused in particular on radioactive contamination of marine and coastal areas. The Soviet Navy dumped containers of solid nuclear waste, as well as nuclear reactors (some containing spent fuel) and ships containing radioactive waste and reactors, in parts of the Barents and Kara Seas and off the east coast of Novaya Zemlaya. The Soviet Navy also released liquid radioactive wastes into these seas (indeed, in the last reported incident, the Russian Navy did so in 1993). Moreover, the Russian Navy, which has inherited the nuclear-powered, nuclear missile submarines of the Soviet Navy, lacks adequate storage for radioactive materials and wastes, in particular for its decommissioned submarines left in harbours on the Kola Peninsula and along the White Sea (OECD, 1999). The 1996 Declaration on Arctic Military Environmental Co-operation between Norway, Russia and the United States has provided a framework to address some of these issues (Sawhill). Norway and the US have helped Russia upgrade a radioactive waste processing plant in Murmansk. Japan has provided support for temporary waste storage near Vladivostock (OECD, 1999). Although Russia and other NIS have publicly released a great amount of information on radioactive contamination created by the Soviet military, monitoring data and other information are often not available on important issues. Problems such as radioactive waste management at formerly "closed" research and military nuclear production facilities remain. For example, environmental officials in the Tomsk region of western Siberia have not had access to data on radioactive waste management in Seversk, a formerly closed nuclear production site 13 kilometres from the city of Tomsk (Zamparutti and Kozeltsev).

NOTES

1. In most OECD countries and CEEC/NIS, independent government agencies oversee nuclear safety issues, which are thus managed apart from other environmental questions. International co-operation on nuclear safety in the region has also been organised separately. The EAP did not cover these issues.

2. Two CEE power plants use western-designed reactors: Cernovoda in Romania and Krsko, located in Slovenia and owned jointly by Croatia and Slovenia (EU Enlargement Watch).

3. The Nuclear Energy Agency, located at OECD, together with bilateral donors' multilateral programmes, has supported the development of nuclear regulatory laws and institutions in the region.

4. The EC has hosted NUSAC's secretariat. In July 1997, NUSAC changed its institutional structure, strengthening CEEC/NIS participation by bringing these countries into a single forum with 24 OECD countries (the G-24), and also re-oriented its priorities to give greater attention to policy issues (G-24).

REFERENCES

Angelo, P. (1996),
   Ex-USSR Nuclear Technology and the World: Commercial Soviet Reactors,
   [http://www.ida.net/users/pbmck/xsovnuc/exs_top.htm].

European Bank for Reconstruction and Development (EBRD) (1996),
   The Nuclear Safety Account, London, December.

European Bank for Reconstruction and Development (EBRD) (1998),
   Chernobyl Shelter Implementation Project, Environments in Transition, Autumn, London.

European Bank for Reconstruction and Development (EBRD) (1999),
   Nuclear safety, [http://www.ebrd.com/english/opera/nucsafe/spnsa01.htm], London.

European Commission (EC) (undated),
   Panel of High-level Advisors on Nuclear Safety in Central and Eastern Europe and the New Independent States: A Strategic View for the Future of the European Union's PHARE and TACIS Programmes, [http://www.europa.eu.int/comm/dg1a/nss/a.htm], Brussels.

EU Enlargement Watch *et al.* (1998),
   Real Ways to Reduce Nuclear Risk in Eastern Europe, London, October.

Nuclear Energy Agency (NEA) (1999),
   Update on nuclear law in Central and Eastern Europe, NEA Update issue No. 1, Paris.

G-24 Nuclear Safety Co-ordination Secretariat (NUSAC),
   G-24 Nuclear Safety Co-ordination, [http:// europe.eu.int/comm/dg11/g24], European Commission, Brussels.

OECD (1997),
   Environmental Performance Reviews: Belarus, Paris.

OECD (1999),
   Environmental Performance Reviews: Russia, Paris (forthcoming).

Sawhill, S. (1999),
   Arctic Military Environmental Co-operation, presentation to the Reading University Workshop on Contemporary Environmental Issues in Eastern Europe and the Former Soviet Union, Reading, UK, July.

United Nations Economic Commission for Europe (UN/ECE) (1998),
   Environmental Performance Review of Lithuania (draft), Geneva, July.

United Nations Economic Commission for Europe (UN/ECE) (1999),
   Environmental Performance Review of Ukraine (draft interim report), Geneva.

Zamparutti, A. and M. Kozeltsev (1998), *Environmental Issues in Tomsk Oblast*, in *A Regional Approach to Industrial Restructuring in the Tomsk Region, Russian Federation*, OECD, Paris.

OECD PUBLICATIONS, 2, rue André-Pascal, 75775 PARIS CEDEX 16
PRINTED IN FRANCE
(14 1999 08 1 P) ISBN 92-64-17110-X – No. 50857 1999